Free Enterprise in the United States

EUGENE D. WYLLIE
Associate Professor
Department of Business Education
Indiana University

ROMAN F. WARMKE
Professor and Chairman
Department of Economic Education
Ohio University

Published by

H36   **SOUTH-WESTERN PUBLISHING CO.**

CINCINNATI   WEST CHICAGO, ILL.   DALLAS   PELHAM MANOR, N.Y.   PALO ALTO, CALIF.

ISBN: 0-538-08360-3

Library of Congress Catalog Card Number: 79-63450

2 3 4 5 6 7 8 9 K 8 7 6 5 4 3 2 1

Printed in the United States of America

Preface

The free enterprise system in the United States is a fundamental part of our daily lives. It reflects our national ideals and it influences our levels of living. A basic understanding of how our free enterprise economic system functions is essential to our development as producers (workers), consumers (users), and citizens (voters). This book will acquaint you with the fundamentals of free enterprise in the United States and explain how this system affects your life.

The economic system in the United States is not a pure system of free enterprise; nevertheless, its origin and development is steeped in a system of free markets, private capital, and individual freedom to make choices in utilizing limited resources to satisfy unlimited wants. Thus, the economic system in the United States can correctly be identified as the free enterprise system since its dominant features are more adherent to the market mechanism than to the traditional or command mechanisms. For all intents and purposes, the following terms are synonymous when identifying the economic system in the United States: free enterprise, private enterprise, American enterprise, and market economy.

Free Enterprise in the United States was prepared in response to a mandate from a large number of states that schools provide youth with the opportunity to acquire knowledge and understanding of the economic system in the United States and its impact on the American way of life. In preparing the content for *Free Enterprise in the United States*, the authors reviewed a number of state curriculum guides to assure the acceptability and completeness of the content of this course in free enterprise.

Free Enterprise in the United States is an adaptation of *Consumer Economic Problems, Ninth Edition*, an established textbook combining the study of economics with consumer applications.

The primary focus of *Free Enterprise in the United States* is to demonstrate (1) how our economic system operates, (2) the unique qualities of the free enterprise system, and (3) how the individual operates within the system of free enterprise as a producer-worker, as a consumer-user, and as a citizen-voter.

Free Enterprise in the United States is organized into seven parts, the first five parts being devoted primarily to the operation and the unique qualities of the free enterprise system and the last two parts to the function of the individual within the free enterprise system. Each chapter is divided into sections (as are the end-of-chapter questions, problems, and projects), which enables the teacher who so desires to stress all or selected parts of a chapter with ease.

The variety of subject matter and problem material in this textbook enables the teacher to appeal to students of a wide range of abilities. There is sufficient material for a full year of work; however, the flexibility of the organization makes it possible to select subject matter content and problems for a one-semester course.

The Authors

Contents

PART 1 | ECONOMICS AND FREE ENTERPRISE

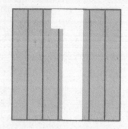

The Economic Setting

PURPOSE OF THE CHAPTER

We constantly try to satisfy our wants and needs as individuals and as a society. We set goals and make choices in order to reach these goals. Economics is basically the study of how we make these decisions.

After studying this chapter, you will be able to:

1. Define the nature of economics.
2. Describe the real cost of satisfying economic wants.
3. Identify some of the problems of society.
4. Identify some of our most important national economic goals.

A. WHAT ECONOMICS IS ALL ABOUT

Economics is a study of the process by which people make and spend their incomes. It examines how they satisfy their wants and needs for economic goods and services. More specifically, economics is the study of a process that involves choice making as people try to get the most satisfaction possible when they buy goods and services. The process is sometimes called *economizing*. The place where the choice-making process takes place is called the *economy*. Therefore, you can speak of the economy of the United States, the economy of Russia, the economy of Canada, or the economy of any other specific area.

If you are like most people, you are not able to buy all the goods and services you would like. Therefore, you must make choices: you must economize. Most individuals and *all* nations must economize. If a person or a nation is not able to have all the goods and services wanted, we say that economic *scarcity* exists.

Economic processes at any given time include everything that is being done as people attempt to satisfy their wants and needs. The process includes (1) production of goods and services, (2) distribution of goods and services, and (3) consumption of goods and services. What people seek through the economic process is the satisfaction of human wants and needs.

In order to produce goods, certain resources are needed. The main resources you will study in economics include land, labor, capital (tools and machinery), and management. The monetary returns for these resources are rent, wages, interest, and profits. You will learn much more about these resources — sometimes called *factors of production* — as you study economics.

Economic Goods and Services

An *economic good* is any material object useful to people in satisfying wants or needs and scarce enough so that people are willing to pay for it. Almost everything you own is an economic good. A material object must be useful and it must have monetary value in order to qualify. By scarce, we mean that it is not free. Your ball-point pen meets the requirements of an economic good.

A person may be able to perform a personal service, such as mowing a lawn, or a health service, such as your doctor provides. These services satisfy a want or need and have monetary value. They are classified as *economic services* rather than economic goods because they are not objects or something that you own.

Economic goods are classified as consumer goods and capital goods according to their use. A *consumer* is any person, business firm, or governmental unit that chooses goods and services, spends money for them, and uses these goods and services primarily to satisfy its own wants. *Consumer goods* and *services* are those used or consumed by the final user. They include such items as clothing, food, shelter, medicine, furniture, and carpets. *Capital goods*, or *producer goods* as they are sometimes called, are those used by manufacturers, farmers, transportation companies, and others who produce consumer goods or who produce goods for other producers. Farms, buildings, machinery, equipment, and raw materials are examples of capital goods.

Why People Work

Most of us work and earn money so that we can buy the goods and services we want and need. We want many things — necessary items, such as food, clothing, and shelter; desirable things, such

Courtesy Deere & Co. Moline, Il.

Wheat (a capital good) is used in the production of bread (a consumer good).

Brownberry Ovens Division
Peavey Company – Minneapolis

as education and the professional services of doctors and lawyers; and personal convenience services, such as dry cleaning, beauty and barber services, and the repair of automobiles and home appliances. All of these are economic goods and services.

A person may have enough income and wealth through inheritance or other sources so that he or she works solely for enjoyment and satisfaction. Most of us, however, need the income we get from our work to buy goods and services. Naturally, we do want our work to be enjoyable and to provide satisfaction as well as income. Although some people might be wealthy enough so that it is unnecessary for them to work, the same is not true for a total society. A society must have producers if it is to supply goods and services needed by the people. What might be true for an individual is often not true for a total society. We shall see this situation often in our study of economics.

Economic Wants

Our wants are of two types — intangible and tangible. The *intangible wants* include the desires for love and affection of our family, respect and admiration of our friends and acquaintances, recognition of our achievements, and freedom from worry and anxiety and other things that take away the joy of living. *Tangible wants* include our desires for physical necessities, such as clothes, food, and shelter. We also want other tangible things, such as athletic and sporting goods, stereo sets, sports cars, books, and magazines. Any goods that can be valued in terms of money, whether they are tangible or intangible, represent the *economic wants* of people. Usually, these wants tend to be tangible rather than intangible goods.

Clothing, record players, sports equipment, furniture, and food are the types of tangible or economic wants that we must earn money to obtain.

Sometimes we classify wants as *primary* or *secondary*. *Primary* or *essential wants* are those that must be satisfied for a person to live, such as food, clothing, shelter, and medicine. *Secondary* or *nonessential wants* are those that may be satisfied for pleasure or comfort, such as cosmetics, special foods, stylish clothes, or even an automobile. Of course, most of us would consider many goods classified as nonessential to be very important.

Your wants and the wants of most people usually change over time. The changes might be the result of getting older, increased education, increased income, a change in where you live, or many other factors. There are many sides to even your most basic needs and wants. For example, if you are hungry, there are many kinds and types of food that you could eat. You might even be influenced in your choice of what to eat by the way the food is packaged and prepared for use, such as being frozen, canned, or dried.

Money Is Needed to Satisfy Economic Wants

Economics is concerned only with those goods and services that have a monetary value (price) attached to them in some way.

If you are like most people, you probably have a desire for intangible wants such as love, respect, recognition, and freedom to do many things you would like. All of these intangible wants are important, but they are not part of economics because there is no money value placed on them. In your study of economics, you will be concerned only with those things for which you pay money.

Most people obtain money by working. This income is then used to buy goods and services to satisfy their wants. Sometimes people do not spend all the money they earn but save some to buy things they need at a later date. Some people use their savings to make more money by investing it in capital goods such as machines, tools, and buildings. Investment of savings in capital goods not only increases the investor's income but also makes it possible for business firms to produce larger amounts of goods. We raise our level of living in an economy when we continue to produce more goods and services for each person.

To Buy or Not To Buy

Part of the problem of satisfying our wants for economic goods and services is the price that must be paid and our ability to buy. The price may be too high for people to be willing and able to pay. The want is still there, but people must make choices as to how they will spend the limited resources they have for their many wants. If the price is reduced by efficient production or other means, people may then choose to buy.

Opportunity Cost

Many times you must make a decision between two things you want very much. For example, you might want to go to a particular movie or you might like to go bowling. You have only enough money available at the time to do one or the other. You must decide which way you are going to spend your money. The value of what you give up by making your decision is referred to in economics as the *opportunity cost* or the *real cost* of the thing you choose. In this case, the opportunity cost of going bowling is giving up going to the movie, and the opportunity cost of going to the movie is giving up going bowling. People generally cannot satisfy all of their wants. Therefore, each of us must make those choices that give us the most satisfaction.

In a practical sense, economics involves (1) determining what goods and services will give us the greatest satisfaction and pleasure and (2) deciding how to obtain, to choose, and to use these goods and services to the greatest advantage. The individual consumer and producer and the collective producers and consumers, as expressed through government, must all weigh the opportunity or real costs of their decisions.

One person might serve in three different economic roles at the same time: (1) as a consumer, (2) as a worker, and (3) as a citizen. As consumers we are concerned with obtaining and using the economic goods and services that will satisfy our wants. As workers we strive to earn an income that will provide us with an opportunity to satisfy these wants. As citizens we have a vital stake in the economic decisions that are made for the nation as a whole.

Scarcity and Supply

Sometimes you might think there is an oversupply or surplus of goods because certain items are not sold. Even if these goods are not sold, however, some people would like to buy them if they could. Therefore, these goods are scarce to the people who would like to have them.

For example, in the mid-1970s the economy of the United States was in a recession. People were faced with a lower real income and could not buy as many goods and services as they had been able to buy before. For instance, people simply did not have the money to buy the supply of automobiles that was available. Many automobile companies stopped production for a period of time. The manufacturers reasoned that it would be less expensive

---

A SUMMARY OF THE NATURE OF ECONOMICS

1. In a broad sense economics is a study of the process by which we earn and spend our incomes.

2. Most goods and services are economic rather than free.

3. The real cost of a good or service is the opportunity to use the same income to buy other goods and services.

4. Most individuals do not have sufficient income or wealth to provide all of the goods and services they would like.

5. The only way that a society can increase its level of living is to produce more goods and services per person.

6. There are unfilled wants even when there appears to be a surplus.

7. An individual can serve in three distinct economic roles — as a consumer, as a worker, and as a citizen.

for them to stop car production for a while than to continue production and lower the prices. If they had lowered the prices of the automobiles, they might have been able to sell more. However, from their point of view, it was better to keep prices high and to produce fewer cars. Even though there seemed to be a surplus of automobiles in the showrooms, many people who would have liked a new car would not buy at the price asked, even when cash rebates were offered. They needed to choose between buying a car, paying increased living expenses, providing an education for a child, or getting something else important to the family. Automobiles were scarce to people who would have liked to have them.

B. PROBLEMS OF SOCIETY AND ECONOMIC GOALS

The United States has the highest level of living in the world. A recent study[1] confirms this fact. The study analyzes the income and prices in major cities, then calculates how long employees must work to earn enough to buy certain consumer goods and services.

Employees covered in the study are a good cross section of workers, including teachers, bus drivers, auto mechanics, bank tellers, and secretaries. When foreign incomes are converted into U.S. dollars at the foreign exchange rates, the study finds that "the top salaries are paid in the United States."

As for what income will buy, the coverage includes a basic food basket of 37 items; men's and women's clothing; services such as haircuts, dry cleaning, laundry, telephone, and movie tickets; rent for a three-room unfurnished apartment; and appliances that include a range, refrigerator, and television. The information contained in the table shown on page 9 compares 15 foreign cities with a U.S. composite based on New York, Chicago, and San Francisco. From the table, note that U.S. workers overall earn enough to buy food, clothing, services, and appliances in less time than do similar workers in foreign cities. Only in the cost of rent is the U.S. about average.

This does not mean, however, that we do not have problems. In recent years, for example, we have become more and more concerned about the quality of the air we breathe and the water we drink. We are also concerned about providing enough food for all people, decent housing (especially for the aged), and proper health

[1]This study, titled "Prices and Earnings Around the Globe," was conducted by the Union Bank of Switzerland and covers the period from May to November of 1973.

WORKING TIME NEEDED TO PURCHASE GOODS & SERVICES*
U.S.A. (New York, Chicago & San Francisco) = 100

Food Basket		Men's Clothing		Women's Clothing		Services		Monthly Rent		Household Appliances	
Sao Paulo	300	Buenos Aires	250	Sao Paulo	316	Sao Paulo	229	Hong Kong	396	Buenos Aires	481
Hong Kong	282	Sao Paulo	229	Buenos Aires	303	Buenos Aires	171	Tokyo	247	Mexico	377
Mexico	236	Hong Kong	171	Mexico	245	Mexico	171	Buenos Aires	217	Sao Paulo	293
Tokyo	227	Tokyo	171	Vienna	177	Dusseldorf	157	Sao Paulo	209	Tokyo	269
Vienna	218	Mexico	153	Hong Kong	172	Vienna	157	Mexico	167	Vienna	247
Madrid	209	Paris	150	Paris	164	Stockholm	157	Paris	141	Madrid	240
Rome	200	Rome	147	Dusseldorf	126	Hong Kong	143	Vienna	114	Sydney	221
Stockholm	200	Madrid	138	Rome	124	Tokyo	143	Rome	105	Hong Kong	211
Dusseldorf	191	London	135	Stockholm	119	Paris	129	U.S.A.	100	London	173
Paris	173	Stockholm	135	Zurich	119	London	129	London	99	Paris	156
London	173	Dusseldorf	132	Madrid	118	Sydney	114	Dusseldorf	97	Zurich	139
Zurich	155	Vienna	121	Sydney	118	Madrid	114	Sydney	97	Dusseldorf	130
Buenos Aires	145	Sydney	118	London	106	Zurich	100	Madrid	95	Stockholm	129
Sydney	118	Montreal	118	U.S.A.	100	Montreal	100	Zurich	80	Montreal	125
Montreal	100	Zurich	100	Montreal	97	Rome	100	Stockholm	55	Rome	110
U.S.A.	100	U.S.A.	100	Tokyo	83	U.S.A.	100	Montreal	51	U.S.A.	100

Source: James M. Dawson, "United States Still Has the Highest Living Standards," (Cleveland, Ohio: National City Bank, July 19, 1974).

*(Average for teachers, bus drivers, auto mechanics, bank tellers, and secretaries)

care. Many people are also concerned about what has been happening to our environment through business activities that pollute our air and water or waste valuable resources. For example, land that is strip mined to obtain coal and not returned to a productive state loses a resource for the future. As citizens we have become more and more concerned about these social problems, and government is responding to the demand for action. Businesses are also cooperating more and more so that we can improve the quality of living in the United States.

Some Problems of Society

The United States of America has only 6% of the world's population but receives one third of the world's total income. In contrast, the poorest half of the world receives only 8% of the total world income. This does not mean that we can be satisfied with our level of living. We must constantly try to improve the quality of life in the United States as well as share a concern for people of other nations. Some of the problems that we have experienced in the United States in recent years are discussed briefly here. There are problems that could be added — especially if we look at the less-developed countries. However, our discussion of some of the problems gives a sample of areas that need special attention.

Consumer Protection. As our economy becomes more complicated, the need for consumer protection increases. Consumer protection can be viewed in several ways. First, the consumer needs to become more informed. Second, responsible business people need to plan together to eliminate or at least reduce misleading advertising, gyps, and other types of consumer "rip-offs." Third, the government needs to pass legislation that protects consumer interests. In the 1970s all three of these approaches were used.

An awareness of the need for consumer protection has existed for a long time. However, organized effort and concern on the part of consumers became widespread in the late 1960s through the 1970s. The present concern for consumer protection is different from the approaches used in the past. The consumer education movement of the 1980s is more comprehensive; it is more sophisticated; it is more relevant; it is more responsible; and it is more future oriented. The concern for consumer protection in the 1980s starts with the premise that personal economic decision making must be examined in the context of the total society. Just being a good buyer is not sufficient. Even when the consumer activities of borrowing, saving, and investing are added, the concern for consumer protection is still incomplete. A consumer of today must understand the consumer roles of earning or receiving an income and performing as a citizen-voter as well. Therefore, to understand the consumer it is necessary to study personal economic decision making in the context of market interactions, the market mechanism, and the role of government in protecting the consumer. All of these topics are discussed in some detail in this book.

Poverty. Even in a country as wealthy as the United States, some people have a very low level of living. They are not able to have a reasonable diet, proper education, or adequate housing. People who live in poverty add little to the economic development of a nation. Therefore, attempting to eliminate poverty is not only humane but also makes good economic sense.

Unemployment and Underemployment. Closely related to poverty is the problem of unemployment. When people are not working, they obviously are not producing goods and services. When this situation exists, fewer goods and services are produced and the level of living for the entire society goes down. Therefore, as a nation we like to have a situation where all those persons who are able and want to work can find employment.

Sometimes a person might be employed but working at a job that does not take advantage of his or her skills and training. Such a condition is called either *underemployment* or *disguised unemployment*. Underemployment also lowers the level of living of a nation.

Inflation. Inflation exists when there is a rising level of prices for goods and services without a corresponding increase in output. Under such a condition, the purchasing power of the dollar declines. A person on a fixed income has a shrinking real income, since fewer goods and services can be bought with the same amount of money.

Pollution. People no longer accept the idea of simply increasing the quantity of goods and services available. They are now concerned about the quality of life as well as the quantity. If economic growth simply means polluting the air you breathe and the water you drink, you might well question whether such growth is good for society. The cost of controlling pollution can be placed on:

1. The producers.
2. The consumers.
3. The general public through actions by the government.
4. A combination of any or all of these groups.

Controlling Big Business and Big Labor. As a country becomes more developed, big business and big labor also come into existence. When either businesses or labor organizations become too big, they are sometimes able to control prices simply because of their size. They have enough economic power to charge high prices or to obtain inflationary wage contracts that would be impossible if they were smaller or less powerful. Therefore, the government controls and restricts certain actions of both big labor and big business.

Controlling Crime. A society pays for the cost of crime several times:

1. In crime prevention programs.
2. By maintaining penal and correctional institutions.
3. By loss of income from persons who are confined.
4. For rehabilitation programs when an individual has been returned to society after a period of confinement.

Crime, therefore, reduces the level of living in a society through loss of income and production.

Maintaining National Security. In many ways the cost of maintaining national security is quite similar to the cost of controlling crime. Money spent on a bomb does, of course, create jobs and generate income. Expenses of this type, however, do not increase the productive capacities of a country. For example, the building of an irrigation dam would do a lot more for the future economic development of a nation than having the same amount of money spent on producing a bomb. More than that, the bomb might actually destroy resources rather than develop them.

Discrimination. Almost every society has some form of discrimination based on race, religion, sex, age, or some other characteristic. Such forms of discrimination are an economic waste. People who are discriminated against generally do not have the opportunity to produce as many goods and services as others. Consequently, society does not have the advantage of the full potential of the contribution these people could make.

Taxation. In recent years there has been much concern about inequities in the taxation plan of the United States. Taxation practices have changed over the years and, in the opinion of some people, certain taxation practices tend to be unfair. Obviously, taxation is necessary if we are to pay for goods and services that we consume together or that cannot be provided individually. We need to pay for our parks, schools, highways, national security, and many other public services; but we want our taxing practices to be as fair as possible. Also, government taxing and spending is used to smooth out the ups and downs of business activities. Much more will be said later in the book about taxation problems and procedures.

PROBLEMS OF SOCIETY

Some problems of society include:

1. Consumer protection — by consumers, by business, and by government.

2. Poverty — people not having enough money to meet their minimum essential needs.

3. Unemployment and underemployment — people not having the opportunity to work to their full potential.

4. Inflation — a rising level of prices for goods and services without a corresponding increase in output.

5. Pollution — damaging our environment.

6. Controlling big business and big labor — preventing businesses and labor organizations from getting so large that they can control prices without concern for what is best for society.

7. Controlling crime — the cost includes prevention programs, correctional practices, income foregone by persons confined, and rehabilitation costs.

8. Maintaining national security — using resources for national security that could be used in a more productive way if the need for national defense were not present.

9. Discrimination — people not given the opportunity to make the greatest use of their potential because of race, religion, sex, age, or some other characteristic.

10. Taxation — the problem of collecting in an equitable manner the money needed to pay for public goods and services.

National Economic Goals

In some economies the productive resources are owned and directed by government. They are owned by the group (all citizens combined) and not by individuals. The leaders set the goals for everyone. Thousands of decisions must be made by the leaders, and these decisions may be right or wrong. Great power is in the hands of a few who decide how resources will be used to fulfill wants and how each will share in production.

In our free enterprise economy, millions of people decide their own goals. Individuals are free to use their labor, savings, and other resources to set their personal goals and to produce to fulfill their own wants. Through elected officials or representatives, decisions are made as to the goals that will be directed by the government. National goals are political decisions, but the choices are made through democratic political processes.

In our society we must set our goals and make our choices based on careful reasoning. Whether as individuals or as a group, we cannot have everything we want. We cannot have all our personal pleasures, leisure, security, plenty of food and clothing, good highways, good police protection, and government controls without making choices. We must decide how much freedom we want and how much freedom we are willing to lose if decisions are made for us by our government.

How much of our limited income are we willing to give up for a government service? Should we give money to help foreign countries or should we spend it on our own schools? Should we spend billions of dollars to send someone to the moon or should we spend more for health and welfare? Should we spend billions of dollars for guns and missiles? These are some of the many basic questions each of us must face as consumers and citizens.

We have established through the years certain national economic goals on which most people agree. People do not agree as to the relative importance of each goal, but they do tend to agree as a nation that we should strive for (1) economic freedom, (2) economic efficiency, (3) economic growth, (4) economic stability, (5) economic justice, and (6) economic security.

Economic Freedom. *Economic freedom* refers to an individual's freedom to make economic choices.

When people are free to make choices, they must decide what they want and set their goals. As we said before, the real or opportunity cost of any choice is what people must give up to gain what they want. You might, for example, have to decide whether to spend money for a vacation or for more education; to buy shoes or a suit if you cannot buy both; to make a down payment on a house or to buy a new car; or to save or spend. If you are to make wise decisions, you must think carefully about the value of each choice.

Since economic freedom is basically a personal matter, we shall discuss it in more detail in later chapters where we analyze personal economic goals.

Economic Efficiency. *Economic efficiency* refers to making the best use of limited resources. Most goods and services have many uses. Land, for example, can be used to produce corn or wheat or to pasture beef cattle. The individual farmer attempts to determine what use of the land would net the greatest return. More than that, the farmer will need to determine the right amount of lime and fertilizer to use, the crop rotation schedule, and other conservation practices necessary for the greatest net profit over a period of time. The combination of resources that brings about the best or optimal level of production is considered to be the most efficient economic mix.

Economic efficiency can be viewed from the point of view of the individual consumer, the producer, the government, or the total economy. The pursuit of economic efficiency by the different persons or groups might, however, result in a conflict. For example, farmers might find an economic mix that will improve their efficiency to the point that a farm surplus will be created for the total economy. Similarly, some producers might, through a vigorous marketing campaign, increase their share of the market at the expense of other producers. For the ones who gain through this procedure, an efficient economic mix has been found. However, the cost of the marketing campaign might be inefficient for the total economy. Conflicts in goals occur often. In this case we have seen conflicts that arise within the pursuit of a particular goal, namely, economic efficiency.

Economic Growth. *Economic growth* refers to an ever-higher level of living. Most people expect to be better off than their parents; and for the most part, this is a reasonable goal. As we have increased our technology, our capital supply (tools and better equipment), and our education, we have been able to produce more and more goods and services per person. In general, we accept the notion that we will continue to improve our level of living through economic growth.

Economic Stability. *Economic stability* refers to smoothing out the ups and downs of business activities. It means the desire for a high level of employment without inflation or deflation. During inflation the dollar loses much of its value. This is very hard on persons whose incomes are relatively fixed — for example, retired persons living on insurance or social security payments. Deflation is equally undesirable in that it brings about mass unemployment, human misery, and a waste of economic resources. Americans want neither inflation nor deflation; we want economic stability.

Economic Justice. *Economic justice* refers to the distribution of wealth. *Wealth* is the total money value of the things we own at a given time. We should keep in mind that wealth is made up of tangible goods that have money value because they are relatively scarce, useful, and desirable. On the other hand, *income*, which is usually measured in money, is the reward for an individual's share in producing those goods, in rendering services, and in lending funds and the use of tangible property to others.

Thus, income results from the production of economic goods and the performance of economic services for the satisfaction of wants. You may think of income as your share of new wealth that you helped to create through your labor. You may think of income as the reward for performing economic services. Other examples of income are: interest on savings; rent received for land, machinery, or other tangible property; or transfer payments such as social security and government pensions. A *transfer payment* is income received by individuals from government, business, or other individuals for which no goods or services were currently exchanged or rendered.

Most of us as individuals want more wealth — we want to own more land, buildings, stocks in corporations, and personal possessions such as automobiles and good clothes. Income enables us to get these things. Income, however, is our share for having produced. Therefore, how do we become more wealthy? In general, we become more wealthy by working, producing, and investing successfully. Generally, the more you produce, the greater your income and the greater your potential for wealth.

Our wealth consists of things we own.

Economic Security. *Economic security* refers to the desire to have every person maintain a certain minimum level of living. Examples of programs designed to create economic security include: (1) care for the aged (such as Medicare and social security), the unavoidably unemployed (such as unemployment insurance and government training programs), and the dislocated worker; (2) aid for depressed areas (such as urban redevelopment); and (3) some form of farm program (such as price supports). These programs will be treated in more detail in later chapters. Not all persons agree on the types of economic security that should be provided in the United States, but nearly everyone supports some form of economic security.

SOME IMPORTANT ECONOMIC GOALS

1. Economic freedom — an individual's freedom to make economic choices.

2. Economic efficiency — making the most efficient use of limited resources.

3. Economic growth — a desire for an ever-high level of living.

4. Economic stability — smoothing out the ups and downs of business activities.

5. Economic justice — a fair distribution of the nation's wealth.

6. Economic security — the desire to have every person maintain a certain minimum level of living.

Use of Public Policy

The illustration on page 18 shows how public policy results from the interaction between the problems of society and its economic goals.

Sometimes it is difficult to attack the problems of society directly. Therefore, public policy is aimed at a particular economic goal that is in a sense a subdivision of a larger problem of society. For example, minimum wage legislation is really an attempt in many cases to eliminate discrimination. The economic goal of justice is closely related to the discrimination problem of society. Another example is a public policy attempt to reduce poverty, which would at the same time improve economic growth.

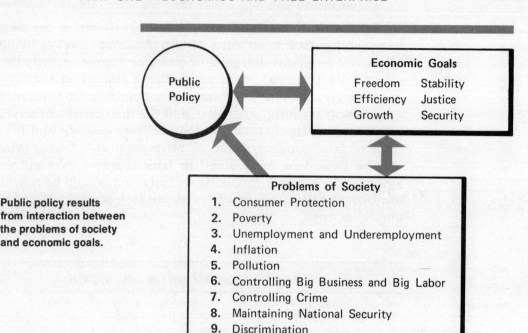

Public policy results from interaction between the problems of society and economic goals.

Public Policy

Economic Goals

Freedom   Stability
Efficiency Justice
Growth   Security

Problems of Society

1. Consumer Protection
2. Poverty
3. Unemployment and Underemployment
4. Inflation
5. Pollution
6. Controlling Big Business and Big Labor
7. Controlling Crime
8. Maintaining National Security
9. Discrimination
10. Taxation

REVIEW QUESTIONS

Section A
1. What is economics?
2. Why is income necessary?
3. What are tangible wants? What are intangible wants?
4. What is the difference between a primary or essential want and a secondary or nonessential want?
5. Why must we usually make choices in what we buy?
6. What do we mean by opportunity or real cost?
7. What are the three different economic roles that an individual person might serve at the same time?

Section B
8. What are some of our society's economic problems?
9. What are our major national economic goals?
10. What is the difference between income and wealth?
11. How does economic policy result from the interaction between the problems of society and its economic goals?

DISCUSSION QUESTIONS

Section A
1. How might a machine be either a capital good or a consumer good?
2. How might one item not be an economic good in one case because it is free but would be an economic good in a different situation?

3. How might one item be a primary or essential want for one person but a secondary or nonessential want for another?
4. Name and explain something that is not an economic good. Why is it not an economic good?
5. How and why do our wants sometimes change and increase?
6. If an automobile manufacturer is unable to sell the cars that have been produced, does this mean that there is no scarcity and no unfulfilled wants? Explain.

Section B
7. Give some examples of consumer ''rip-offs.'' How could consumers be protected against such actions?
8. How does the poor use or waste of natural resources lower a nation's level of living?
9. Why is discrimination based on race, religion, sex, age, or other characteristics an economic waste?

APPLICATION PROBLEMS

Section A
1. The opportunity cost of buying and eating an ice cream cone might be the candy bar you decided not to buy. Sometimes the opportunity involves merely a substitution of time. For example, you could not watch a television program and play tennis at the same time. (Assume that there is no direct monetary cost to you for either watching television or playing tennis.) Choosing either time or actual goods and services, give examples of what the opportunity cost might be for each of the following:
   (a) Going to a movie.
   (b) Buying a camera.
   (c) Mowing a lawn for pay.
   (d) Sleeping late on a Saturday or Sunday morning.
   In each case, compare the benefits of the action taken with the possible opportunity cost involved.

Section B
2. Six national economic goals were presented in this chapter. Rate these goals according to your feelings about their importance, explaining why you rated the goals as you did. Compare your list and your reasoning with that of other members of the class. Your teacher may call on you to participate in a panel discussion or debate in order to defend your ranking of goals in relation to the lists prepared by other class members.
3. Prepare a list of wants of individuals and families that are satisfied through public or government action at the local, state, and federal levels. When the list is complete, indicate which services are provided cooperatively by two or more levels of government. Why or why not are they provided cooperatively? Could some of these services be eliminated or provided by private enterprise? Why or why not?
4. Draw a circle to represent the six economic goals discussed in this chapter. Divide this circle into six pieces. Let each piece represent the relative importance that you feel Americans attach to each of the particular goals. Draw a second circle and complete the same procedure, but use another country. Compare your drawings with those of other members in the class. Complete the procedure a third time, but this time let the pieces represent the relative size you think would reflect an *ideal*

economy. Your teacher may call on you to participate in a panel discussion or a debate in order to defend your ranking of goals in relation to the rankings prepared by other class members.

COMMUNITY PROJECTS

Section A

1. Prepare a paper explaining briefly why most individuals and all nations must economize.

Section B

2. Prepare a paper explaining the effects on the individual and the economy when a person selects a job that will not make the most of his or her abilities.

3. Recycling, or the reuse of certain products, is often in the news. Prepare a paper on how recycling affects the use of natural resources and, therefore, our level of living. Perhaps there is a recycling center in your community. In your paper, you might wish to examine the effect the recycling center has on your local economy, or what effect might be had if there was one.

4. Industrialized countries tend to have similar problems of society. Choose another industrialized nation such as Japan, Great Britain, or Sweden and compare our problems with theirs. Your school or city librarian and your teacher will help you find the right reference materials to give you information about other countries' problems. Where possible, contrast the ways the problems are handled in the country you have chosen with the ways similar problems are handled in the United States.

5. Consumer legislation is constantly changing. Either as an individual assignment or as part of a group project, prepare a brief report on the current status of consumer protection legislation pending in Congress. Newspapers and magazines are a source of information on pending consumer legislation. Your school or city librarian can help you find reference materials. National legislation can be checked directly through the *Congressional Record* if it is available in your city or county library. If the *Congressional Record* is not available, your congressional representative can provide you with a summary statement of current legislation. (If you write to a member of Congress, submit your letter to your teacher for approval before mailing it.)

Economics in Action

PURPOSE OF THE CHAPTER

In Chapter 1 you learned that economics is basically a study of the process by which we make choices — individually and collectively — to satisfy our wants and needs. In this chapter we shall look at this process in more detail.

After studying this chapter, you will be able to:

1. Describe the major types of economic systems.
2. Explain what is meant by resource allocation and why it is important.
3. State how you can understand an economy by examining its flow of goods and services and its flow of money.
4. Explain what is meant by the coordination of an economic system.

A. HOW ECONOMIC SYSTEMS ARE ORGANIZED

There are three types of economic systems: (1) the traditional economy, (2) the command or directed economy, and (3) the free enterprise or market economy.

Traditional Economy

A traditional economy is one that is not industrialized. In a *traditional economy*, economic life is determined by such things as habit, custom, and religious traditions. The statement "what was good enough for my parents is good enough for me" would describe a traditional economy. Under this system people are content with their lives and do not want to change.

Command or Directed Economy

Under a *command* or *directed economy*, the basic economic decisions are made by a central authority that consists of either a person or a group. The central authority decides, for example, how much of the production shall be devoted to consumer goods and services. It also decides how much shall be devoted to the production of tools and machinery used to produce additional goods. Under this system the individual consumer has little influence over the nature of goods and services produced. It is a system in which people have no voice in economic decision making.

In a communist country (such as Russia, Red China, or North Korea) the command economy is at its severest. The central government owns almost all the capital goods and natural resources, controls all the industries, and does most of the economic planning. In a socialist country (such as Great Britain and some other European countries) the command economy is much in evidence, since the government owns and controls many of the capital goods and natural resources and does much of the economic planning.

Free Enterprise or Market Economy

Free enterprise simply means that each person is "free" to go into whatever business he or she chooses. People are "free" to choose whatever area of employment they wish. In a *free enterprise* or *market economy* the consumers vote in the marketplace (through buying or not buying) to determine the nature and the prices of goods and services produced. Private individuals and groups (businesses) rather than government own and control most of the capital goods (such as factories, tools, and machinery) and the natural resources (such as farm land, timber, and mineral deposits), not the government. The government does some economic planning, such as deciding how large a defense force the country will have or what highways and dams will be built. But the people, as buyers, and private businesses, as buyers and producers, make most of the economic decisions. Most of our discussion in this textbook is devoted to the free enterprise or market economy.

Mixed Economies

There are probably no pure economic systems. In the United States the free enterprise economy has elements of a command or directed system. For example, during wartime the government imposes rationing and decides what will be produced — tanks and bombs rather than private automobiles and stereos. In the United States the government owns some capital goods (power and chemical production) and natural resources (state and national forests;

oil fields; city, state, and national parks). If a system is largely a free enterprise or market system, it is so labeled. The same is true with the other systems. The main characteristic of a system is considered when applying the label of traditional, command or directed, and free enterprise or market economy. All of these systems tend to be mixed.

B. EXAMINING ECONOMIC SYSTEMS

No matter what type of economy you examine, economics can be divided into three parts:

1. How limited resources are shared or distributed (allocated) among the members of the society.
2. How the flow of goods and services and the flow of money function.
3. How the individual and group decisions influence (coordinate) the type of economic system.

These three areas of economics are called (1) resource allocation, (2) flows, and (3) coordination.

Resource Allocation

Since human wants are greater than resources available to fulfill them, goods and services must be distributed or allocated. The process whereby this allocation takes place and the choice making that people do in an attempt to get the most satisfaction when they buy goods and services is called *economizing*. Every economy must determine (1) what goods and services to produce and (2) how to distribute these goods and services among the people.

These two broad decisions can be subdivided further into four problems of resource allocation faced by all economies:

1. WHAT should be produced?
2. HOW should the goods and services be produced?
3. HOW MUCH should be produced?
4. HOW should production be shared?

The study of economics thus involves an analysis of WHAT, HOW, and HOW MUCH. The answers to these questions are to be found through a study of the circular flow of goods, services, and money in our production system. Another question related to HOW MUCH should be produced is the question of HOW FAST the economy should grow. The question of economic growth (more goods and services) will be studied in later chapters where we will examine how government policies affect economic growth.

Circular Flow of Goods and Services and Flow of Money

All people are consumers. Even the smallest child has certain needs and wants that must be satisfied. But some consumers are too young, too old, or too feeble to be producers. Consequently, the production of others must provide for the needs and wants of those who are not producers. Businesses bid for the productive services (such as labor) of consumers who, in turn, produce goods and services that are returned to the households of the consumers. In return for productive services such as labor, businesses provide consumers with income in the form of salaries or wages. The consumers, in turn, spend their income (money) for goods and services produced, providing the businesses with income from these expenditures by consumers. Thus, we have a circular flow of goods and services and a circular flow of money.

The circular flow of goods and services and the flow of money are illustrated below.

Circular Flow of Income

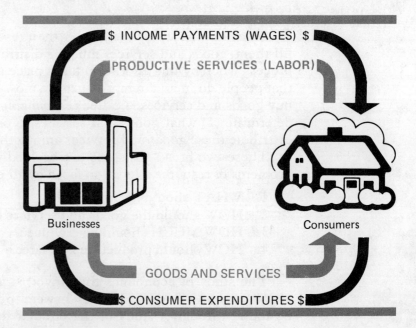

$ INCOME PAYMENTS (WAGES) $

PRODUCTIVE SERVICES (LABOR)

Businesses

Consumers

GOODS AND SERVICES

$ CONSUMER EXPENDITURES $

The productive services provided by consumers to businesses include the use of land, labor, capital (tools and equipment), and management. These productive services — land, labor, capital, and management — are called the *factors of production*. In return for the use of these factors of production, businesses make income payments in the form of rent, wages, interest, and profit (including dividends).

In the illustration the label "businesses" is used to represent all types of employment, including self-employment and employment by the government. As we examine economics in more detail, we shall study the effects of government spending and taxing, consumers' savings, operations of financial institutions such as banks, and foreign trade. Our purpose at this point is to introduce the basic parts of any economy.

To illustrate how useful the circular flow diagram is in analyzing the nature of the economy, we shall examine several of the resource allocation problems related to a market economy.

What to Produce. In our society owners of property (such as factories, farms, or materials) are free to produce what they want for themselves or to produce what others want and are willing to buy. Few of us could produce all the goods and services we need. Therefore, we use our resources to produce for others those items that will make it possible for us to obtain most of what we want. In other words, each of us produces those items that we find are most profitable to us.

In the illustration on page 24, the individual, who has free choice, directs business by his or her demand (through purchases) as to what to produce. The individual furnishes labor, land, money, and other resources with which the business firm produces (through management) the goods and services needed to satisfy consumer demand. These goods and services are delivered in needed quantities to consumers who pay for them and furnish income for the firm. The various individuals are paid for their contributions according to competitive values.

Businesses use resources to produce goods. Consumers also have resources that they lend to or invest in businesses to produce goods. Businesses hire workers to whom they pay wages. These workers are the consumers who buy the goods.

How to Produce. The profit motive is the incentive for the owner or manager of a business to satisfy most efficiently the wants of consumers. Management must always be aware of competition. In our society the owners of property (resources) are free to determine how they can most efficiently use available resources. This function is part of management.

Producers may use some of their own property, hire labor, borrow money, buy materials, rent or buy land, and buy or lease equipment to produce in the most efficient manner. In this process of production, the producers pay out income to workers, landowners, and suppliers of other materials and services. These paid-out incomes become part of the circular flow of money, making it possible for consumers to buy goods.

All factors entering into production must be put together by management. It is management's responsibility to enable the producer to sell the best product at the lowest price and still make the highest profit possible. Management's choice of materials may determine cost and quality. Management must decide how to use labor and machines to reduce cost, speed production, and improve quality. Management must also satisfy the customer as to design, color, and other characteristics because of competition with other producers.

How Much to Produce. The amount of goods and services produced is determined by how much consumers are willing to buy at the offering price. If people do not like the good or the service, or if the price is too high, they will not buy it and the producer will quit making it. If producers make good products that are well-liked and that can be sold at a profit, they will probably expand their business and make more goods. If a competitor offers a new product that is lower in price or that consumers like better, the first producer will have difficulty selling its good or service.

In a free enterprise economy, consumers influence what will be produced by the way they spend their income. Of course, businesses try to influence the demand of consumers through advertising and other selling activities; but the final decision is made by the consumers. They decide whether or not to buy and in what quantities and at what price. Because of the competitive nature of business, if consumers cannot obtain what they want from one producer, there is usually another producer from whom to buy.

How Production Is Shared. In a free enterprise economy, the market places different values on goods and services. Prices reflect these values, determined competitively by the people who buy the goods and services. How much we share in production is determined by the relative scarcity of what we offer and the productivity of our resources.

A worker who is well educated and well trained usually earns more than one who is not. Efficient workers produce more goods than inefficient workers and are generally paid higher wages because they are more productive. Highly skilled managers usually receive more pay than those with less ability. Goods and services of high quality usually sell for higher prices than those of low quality. In other words, in a competitive market we are paid for our resources, whether labor or materials, according to how they satisfy wants.

Summary of Flows in a Free Enterprise Economy. The illustration that follows summarizes how the basic economic questions are determined in a free enterprise economy.

The Free Enterprise or Market Economy (The Circular Flow)

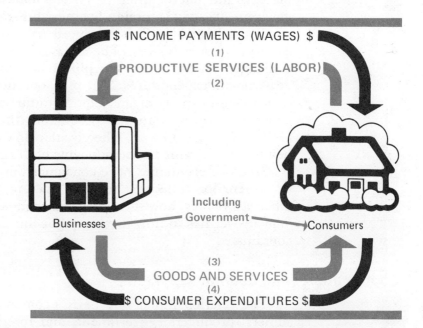

$ INCOME PAYMENTS (WAGES) $
(1)
PRODUCTIVE SERVICES (LABOR)
(2)

Including Government

Businesses ← → Consumers

(3)
GOODS AND SERVICES
(4)
$ CONSUMER EXPENDITURES $

EXPLANATION OF THE ABOVE ILLUSTRATION

1. How production is shared — payment for resources (both labor and materials) according to how they satisfy consumer wants.

2. How to produce — the use of productive services (land, labor, capital, and management) in a production process to satisfy wants.

3. How much to produce — amount of goods and services produced as determined by consumer spending.

4. What to produce — the demand for goods and services as expressed by consumer spending.

All economies have an active, forceful, or dynamic flow of goods and services and a flow of money. In addition, all economies have some form of collective decision making that we call government. Finally, all economies have some relationship to other countries — as in foreign trade. In the illustration shown on page 27, we have included the production and consumption activities of government within the boxes labeled "Consumers" and "Businesses." Foreign trade can be included in the same manner. Later we shall discuss the activities of our government and its relationship to other countries in more detail.

At this point let us note that all production in our society takes place within one of three parts: (1) domestic business firms, (2) government, and (3) foreign business firms. The total dollar value of all goods and services produced in a year is called the *gross national product* (GNP). The gross national product consists of consumer expenditures (C), plus business investment (I), plus government expenditures (G), plus our net foreign exports (F). (Net foreign exports means exports minus imports.) We generally express the gross national product in the following equation: GNP = C + I + G + F. The circular flow diagram on page 27 is helpful in analyzing the components of the gross national product.

Since all economies have consumers, producers, a governmental system for collective decision making, and a relationship to other economies, how then does one economy differ from another? The answer lies in how these components are brought together or coordinated.

Coordination of an Economic System

The relationship of the basic economic components — consumers, producers, government, and foreign trade — vary from economy to economy. We have noted that there are basically three types of economic systems — the traditional economy, the command or directed economy, and the free enterprise or market economy.

Under a traditional economy, tradition, custom, and habit determine the circular flow of goods and services and the flow of money. Under a strictly free enterprise or market economy, the circular flows are determined by consumers bidding for goods and services, while businesses compete with each other to furnish these goods and services in trying to earn a profit. Under a command or directed economy, a central authority — the government — makes the decisions regarding the circular flow. We have indicated, however, that all economies are mixed and that even in a market-oriented economy, the government often influences both production and prices. The outline below illustrates how the government influences resource allocation in a free enterprise economy.

HOW GOVERNMENT INFLUENCES RESOURCE ALLOCATIONS IN A FREE ENTERPRISE ECONOMY
(a few examples)

1. What to produce —
    Collects taxes to provide goods and services such as parks and schools.
    Places special taxes on luxuries.
    Pays farmers more than market price.
    Pays a subsidy (part of cost) to build ships and planes.
    Sets a high price for uranium ore.
    Makes production of narcotics illegal except as controlled.

2. How to produce —
    Regulates rates and competition of public utilities and transportation.
    Controls working conditions, such as safety regulations.
    Controls public education.
    Regulates use of resources, such as oil, gas, and water.

3. How much to produce —
    Pays subsidies to certain types of businesses, such as airlines.
    Regulates rates and competition of public utilities and transportation.
    Gives special tax inducements to business for expansion.
    Controls interest rates.
    Lowers taxes to increase spending.

4. How production is shared —
    Legislates hours of work, overtime, minimum wages.
    Taxes profits and income.
    Controls employment practices.
    Controls monopolies, such as public utilities and transportation.
    Regulates use of certain resources, such as land, oil, gas, and water.
    Operates businesses in competition with private businesses.

SOME ECONOMIC PRINCIPLES THAT EVERYONE SHOULD KNOW

1. Since our wants are greater than the resources available to satisfy them, people must economize.

2. The content of economics can be divided into (a) resource allocation, (b) flows, and (c) coordination.

3. Every economy must provide answers to the questions that determine (a) what goods and services shall be produced, (b) how goods and services shall be produced, (c) how much should be produced, (d) how production will be shared, and (e) how fast the economy should grow.

4. Improved education, advances in technology, and capital (tools and machinery) increase production.

5. The factors of production include land, labor, capital, and management. Business firms use the factors of production, for which they provide income payments in the form of rent, wages, interest, and profits.

6. There are basically three types of economic systems: traditional, command or directed, and free enterprise or market.

7. All economies have a dynamic flow of goods and services and a corresponding flow of money.

8. The gross national product is the dollar value of all goods and services produced in an economy in a given period, usually a year. Stated as a formula, GNP = C + I + G + F.

9. In a free enterprise economy most economic decisions are made in the marketplace and are sometimes changed through collective decision making by the government.

REVIEW QUESTIONS

Section A

1. What is a traditional economy? Give an example.
2. What is a command or directed economy? Give an example.
3. What is a free enterprise or market economy? Give an example.
4. What is meant by a mixed economy?

Section B

5. Into what three content areas can economics be divided? Explain each area.
6. What four problems are faced by all economies?
7. What is meant by the circular flow of goods and services and the circular flow of money?
8. What is the gross national product (GNP) and of what does it consist?
9. What is meant by the coordination of an economic system?

DISCUSSION QUESTIONS

Section A
1. What is meant by the statement "the consumer is king"?
2. What is the role of profit in the free enterprise system?
3. How does the priority of goals differ under each of the following economies: a traditional economy, a command or directed economy, a free enterprise or market economy?

Section B
4. The number of traditional economies in the world has been decreasing. Why is this so? Give examples of countries that formerly had a traditional economy and that today have either a free enterprise or market economy or a command or directed economy.
5. When a country's economy changes from traditional to either a free enterprise or market economy or a command or directed economy, what influences the kind of system selected? Give examples.

APPLICATION PROBLEMS

Section A
1. Give as many examples of traditional economies as you can. You can use examples of economies that existed in the past or that exist today. Since most traditional economies are moving toward a command or directed economy or a free enterprise or market economy, indicate for each example the direction in which you feel the economy is moving.
2. Since a free enterprise economy tends to have much less governmental intervention than a command or directed economy, use the line presented below to give examples of different economies and where they might fit on the line ranging from a total market or free enterprise economy to a total command or directed economy, This exercise should indicate clearly to you that every economy is really a mixture of free enterprise and command or directed, but that some economies tend to have more of one component than the other.

Total Free Enterprise or Market Economy	Total Command or Directed Economy

Section B
3. Using the flow diagram presented in this chapter, trace the effect of each of the following conditions on the total economy:
   (a) A reduction in spending for the space program.
   (b) Increased spending by government and private business to reduce water and air pollution.
   (c) A drastic decrease in the number of cigarette smokers.
4. Using the flow diagram presented in this chapter, illustrate what is meant by the statement: "Business buys in the factors market and sells in the products market."

COMMUNITY PROJECTS

Section A
1. Prepare a map of the world that identifies the countries that existed fifty years ago, using different colors for a traditional economy, a command or

directed economy, and a free enterprise or market economy. Color each country so as to identify the type of economy that existed in that country fifty years ago. Prepare another map of the world at present, coloring in the countries to identify those with a traditional, a command or directed, and a free enterprise or market economy today. Compare the two maps and indicate the major changes that have taken place in the types of economies. Your teacher may ask for either a written or an oral report.

Section B

2. Prepare a paper in which you explore this nation's scarcity of natural resources over a half century ago and the roles of Theodore Roosevelt and Gifford Pinchot in leading America into a program of conservation. You might want to give a few examples showing how effective this program has been.

3. Scarcity of our raw materials and natural resources is still very much a problem. It is a problem being attacked not only by our federal government but also by our state and local governments. Prepare a paper that points out and describes conservation measures (projects) which have been started recently in your state (or within a 100 mile radius of your home) and discuss (a) what such projects are designed to conserve or preserve, (b) what effects such projects will have on your life in the state or area, and (c) what led to such projects.

4. In this chapter you have seen examples of how the federal government regulates the free enterprise system. There are equally as many examples of local (community, village, city) government influence. Identify as many instances as possible where the local government in your city regulates the free enterprise system and give the reasons for such regulations. Could you classify any of the examples as being unfair in the system?

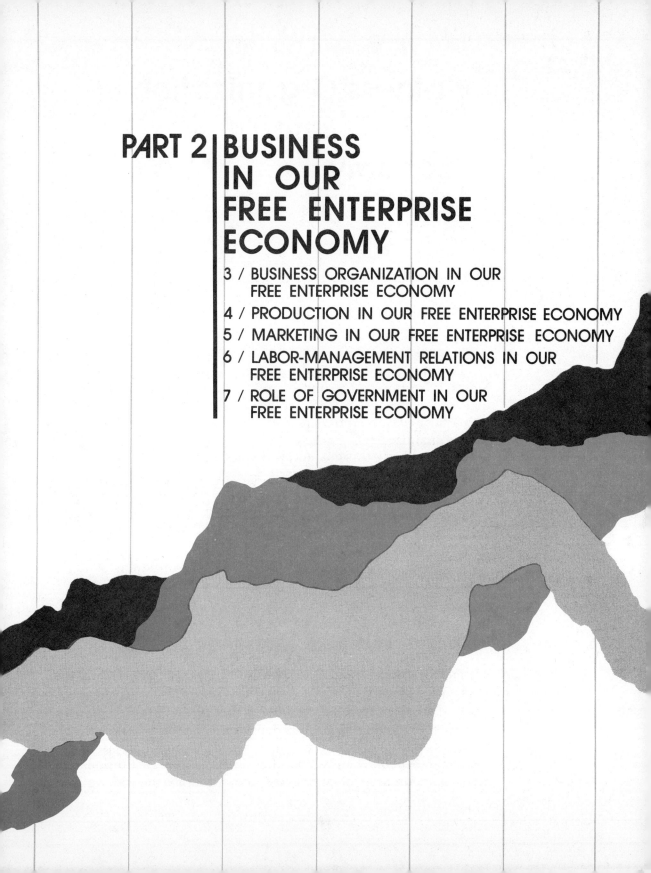

PART 2 | BUSINESS IN OUR FREE ENTERPRISE ECONOMY

Business Organization in our Free Enterprise Economy

PURPOSE OF THE CHAPTER

To understand the free enterprise economy in the United States, it is important to understand its characteristics and the role that business plays in it. Since every citizen has a right to enter into a business enterprise, it is also important to know how business is organized.

After studying this chapter, you will be able to:

1. Identify the major characteristics of the free enterprise system in the United States.
2. Define business.
3. State the objectives of business.
4. Identify the different types of business.
5. Describe the legal forms of business organizations.
6. Tell what functions are performed by business.

A. CHARACTERISTICS OF OUR FREE ENTERPRISE ECONOMY

The characteristics of an economy or any social arrangement can be better understood by examining its institutions. In economics we define an *institution* as a social arrangement that influences how we think and behave. This definition is probably broader than the one you have been using. Under this definition institutions are more than schools, banks, churches, and the like. Institutions are more than buildings or companies; they structure the way we live.

Our institutions consist of customs, rules, and laws. *Social institutions* include marriage, the family, the school, and the church. *Economic institutions* include rules, customs, and laws pertaining to the ownership and use of property, the use of money, the role of competition, and the role of profits.

An understanding of institutions will help you analyze the coordination of an economic system. It provides insight into the resource allocation process, and it will help you to understand the nature of the flow of goods and services and the flow of money. In this part of the chapter we shall examine several of the more important institutions of our free enterprise economy. This will highlight the environment in which economic decisions are made.

Private Property

The sources of our personal income include wages for work we do, profits from business transactions, interest for money we loan, rent for use of buildings or land, or transfer payments such as social security. After local, state, and federal taxes are paid, our free enterprise economic system permits us to spend or to keep as much of our income as we wish. This privilege is based on the belief that people are entitled to keep the rewards from their labor or their business efforts.

The portion of your income that you keep, regardless of whether it is kept in money, invested in bonds, or held in the form of material assets, is known as *private property*. By saving some of their income, people and businesses buy land, buildings, and other things. This private property may then be used to earn more income. Thus, property rights are very important in our free enterprise economy.

Let us assume for a moment that the government owned all property. This would mean that the government would have to direct the production of all economic goods needed by us to live. There would be no profit, hence little incentive to improve a product. Government ownership of property, and therefore the means of production, would have us receive goods as the government chose to allocate them. The right to own property and to use it in making a profit provides us with an incentive to start and operate business enterprises.

Examples of *public property* include public buildings, public schools, and other facilities that can be provided by local, state, or federal governments but that would be impractical, if not impossible, to provide through private ownership.

Freedom of Choice

The 217 plus million people in the United States want, need, and demand many economic goods and services. Business provides most products and services for consumers. But how does business know what goods and services consumers want? How does business know how much of each good or service to provide? How can the demands for goods and services by more than 217 million people be satisfied at prices they are able and willing to pay?

These economic questions are answered in the United States through the free enterprise or market system, a system based on freedom of choice. Under a free enterprise system no person, bureau, or government agency makes arbitrary decisions to answer the questions for the country as a whole. How consumer needs shall be satisfied is decided by individual consumers, workers, and owner-managers collectively. They provide the answers to such questions as what needs for goods and services shall be satisfied, who shall produce specific goods, and who shall be employed in certain businesses. One might say that the markets are *self-regulated* and *self-controlled*. This means that decisions on the basic economic questions of how to satisfy consumers' economic needs stem from the operation of the free enterprise system. The main regulating or controlling factors are profits and competition, discussed below.

The use of the free enterprise system means that consumers have freedom of choice. Their choices influence what shall be produced, how much of each product is needed, and the price that will be paid for it. To producers and manufacturers, the free enterprise system means that they are free to engage in any lawful business from which they believe they can make a profit. The free enterprise system means that you may live where you wish, work where you wish if a job is available, ask whatever wage or salary you wish, and buy whatever goods and services you wish.

Profit Motivation

Although most people get enjoyment and satisfaction from their occupations or professions, very few work just because they like to work. Certainly, few people would work hard every day if there were not some incentive or some driving force that makes them want to work. People work because they get satisfaction from accomplishment; they desire to help others by making needed products or providing services; and last, but certainly not least, they work to earn an income. The income enables them to maintain their level of living, and the part that is left over may be invested in private property which may be used to produce a profit.

You learned earlier in this chapter that to own private property is a basic right under our free enterprise economy. The right to use private property in a manner that will result in a profit is an equally important right. We obtain private property either as a gift from someone else or by investing a part of our income. The part of our income that we save may be deposited in a bank or invested in real estate or other property from which we hope to receive an income. There is another way we can invest our savings. The risk of losing our investment is greater, but the chances of a larger return are possible. This opportunity is to invest our savings in a business enterprise that we plan to operate ourselves. It may be a privately owned and operated business like an appliance repair shop, a lunch counter, a poultry farm, or any other business that provides goods or services that consumers want and need. The income from such a business must first be applied to the costs of running the business; the portion left over is profit.

People would be considered unwise if they were to invest their savings in a business in which there was no chance to make a profit. Furthermore, businesses could not continue to operate long if their income was only great enough to meet costs. Corporations like General Motors, Xerox, Exxon, and United States Steel are no different in this respect than are business enterprises owned and operated by a single individual. They, too, must make a profit to remain in operation.

WHAT ENTITLES A BUSINESS OWNER TO EARN A PROFIT?

1. The risk of losing invested money.

2. Creative ideas that will raise the level of living of consumers.

3. Ability, skill, and experience that enable a business owner to manage and operate the business.

4. Time and work expended in managing and operating the business. (To manage and operate the business, some firms employ persons whose salaries are paid before profits are computed.)

5. Use of money invested.

Usually, the more efficient a business is, the greater its profits will be. Likewise, a business increases its own chances for greater profits by giving consumers better products, lower prices, and better services than they receive from competing business firms. Thus, business owners, in their efforts to make a greater profit by making their businesses more efficient, also benefit consumers.

Almost half of the profits of corporations are kept for use in the business — to pay expenses in years when business is not good, to build new buildings, and to buy machines, equipment, and materials. Thus, profits are used to expand the business, which creates more jobs for more people by stimulating economic growth.

Private businesses in the United States would not exist were it not for the profit motive. If businesses did not exist, consumer goods and services would not be produced and jobs created by those businesses would not exist. In such an event the free enterprise economy would cease to exist and would be replaced by a different form of economy.

Competition

Since a primary motive of business is to make as large a profit as possible, what prevents a business firm from demanding excessively high prices for its products and services? Why can't business set its prices as high as it wishes?

A business would have practically no limits on how high it could set its prices if it were the only business firm that could supply consumers with a particular essential good. But even a *monopolist* (the only supplier of a good or service) sets the price at a point that will generate the most net income. There is a limit to the price one would pay for the use of a telephone, for example, even if the industry were not regulated by the government.

When two or more firms offer the same or similar goods or services, they try to attract consumers by offering their products and services at prices that are either lower than or comparable to those of other firms serving the same consumers. Such businesses are said to be competitors. *Competition* is the effort of many firms or individuals acting independently to attract a customer. A firm may compete with its rivals in several ways. It may lower prices or give more favorable credit terms; it may improve its goods or services or create new ones that will better satisfy consumer needs; or it may change its goods and services to include features that competing goods do not have, making its goods and services more attractive to consumers.

The right to compete is one of our major economic institutions. Everyone is free to enter any trade or business and to compete with anyone else. Individuals may be restricted, however, by limited education and by lack of availability of risk capital (money). Workers are free to move from job to job. Businesses are free to compete for workers' services.

Several federal laws have been passed to assure competition. These laws prevent businesses from agreeing upon prices to be charged for a good and thus eliminating the effect of competition. An exception to the laws of competition is public utilities, such as water, electricity, and telephone service. Public utilities usually have exclusive rights to provide service to a community; hence, they are *monopolies* since there are no competing firms. But to assure reasonable rates, public commissions control utilities.

SOME IMPORTANT ECONOMIC INSTITUTIONS IN THE AMERICAN ECONOMY

1. Property is privately owned, with the exception of certain public facilities such as public schools, court houses, and parks.

2. A free enterprise system provides freedom of choice for individuals and businesses.

3. The right to profits provides the incentive to enter and operate businesses.

4. Competition acts as an automatic control on the quality, kind, and price of goods and services offered by a business firm.

B. CHARACTERISTICS OF BUSINESS

Since we complete business transactions almost daily, we need to know what business is and how it is organized. This section defines business and examines some important facts that relate to it.

What Business Is

Organizations that produce and make available the economic goods and services we want and need are known as *business organizations. Business* is any organized activity conducted by either a person or an organization that in any way helps to satisfy the wants and needs of people for economic goods and services.

Objective of Business. The objective of business is to fulfill the needs and wants of people for economic goods and services in a manner that is most pleasing and satisfactory to consumers and at a price that they consider reasonable. To do this, business must determine what the specific wants of people are and what types or kinds of goods and services will best satisfy those wants. Products, services, and prices offered by individual businesses vary. The successful business achieves its objective of satisfying consumer wants and at the same time makes a reasonable profit.

Classes of Business. Business firms may be grouped into four classes according to the kind of activity in which they engage. Each of these classes is highly important in producing the goods and services people need. The four classes, which are intended to represent broad categories of business, are listed below.

CLASSES OF BUSINESSES BY ACTIVITY AND APPROXIMATE NUMBER OF WORKERS

1. Basic production — including farming, mining, fishing, and forestry. Approximately 5 million workers.

2. Processing — including manufacturing, construction, processing foods, oil refining, publishing, and printing. Approximately 30 million workers.

3. Distribution — including wholesale and retail trades, advertising, transportation, and some forms of communication and other public utility service. Approximately 25 million workers.

4. Service — including finance, insurance, and real estate; professional services, such as medicine and law; personal services, such as beauty and barbershops; maintenance and repair; local, state, and federal government service; and amusement and sports. Approximately 30 million workers.

Legal Forms of Business Organizations

The four principal types of business organizations are: (1) sole proprietorship, (2) partnership, (3) corporation, and (4) cooperative. The legal form of organization under which a business is organized automatically determines: (a) the laws to which the business will be subject, (b) the liability of the owners for debts of the business, (c) the specific taxes to which the business will be subject, (d) the voice that each owner will have in management, and (e) the manner in which the business may be financed.

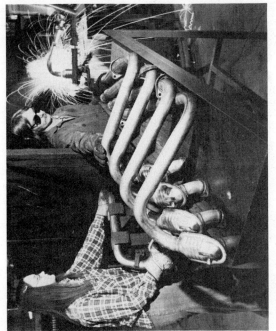

Arvin Industries, Inc.

© Rotkin, P.F.I. 1968

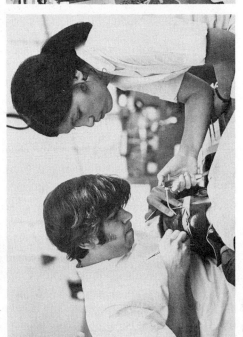

WORKLIFE Magazine

Representatives of the four classes of business are (clockwise from upper left): mining (basic production), manufacturing (processing), retail sales (distribution), and dentistry (service).

Sole Proprietorship. A *sole proprietorship* is a business that is owned by one person. It is sometimes called a single proprietorship, an individual proprietorship, or an individual enterprise.

CHARACTERISTICS OF A SOLE PROPRIETORSHIP

1. Owner provides the money for investment in the business either from savings or by borrowing.

2. Owner usually manages the business.

3. Owner makes policy decisions.

4. Owner usually works in the business.

5. Owner is responsible for acts of the business the same as an individual is responsible for what he or she does.

6. Owner is personally liable for all debts of the business.

7. Profit goes to the sole owner.

Partnership. A *partnership* is a business formed, owned, and managed by two or more persons.

CHARACTERISTICS OF A PARTNERSHIP

1. A partnership is based on a legal agreement or contract between partners.

2. A partnership operates under state laws to protect both the partners and persons with whom it does business.

3. Partners generally share equally in policymaking and management.

4. Decisions are made by the partners.

5. Partners are joint owners and share in profits according to agreement.

6. Each partner is responsible for the things done or promised by another partner in operating the business.

7. Each partner is legally liable for the total debt of the partnership regardless of his or her share in the investment.

8. A partnership is terminated automatically upon the death, retirement, or withdrawal of a partner.

9. Partnerships make it possible to combine the abilities and resources of the partners for better management and a larger business.

Disadvantages of the partnership form of organization are the unlimited liability of each partner for the total debts of the partnership and the uncertain life of the business due to the possibility of death, retirement, or withdrawal of a partner.

Corporation. A *corporation* is a business that has the legal right to act as one person but that may be owned by a number of people. The owners are called *stockholders*. A *charter* (basically a license) authorizing the formation and operation of a corporation is issued by the state in which the corporation is organized.

CHARACTERISTICS OF A CORPORATION

1. The authority for the creation and operation of a corporation rests with the states.

2. The corporation operates within the provisions of its charter.

3. Management rests with officers who are appointed by a board of directors, which is the legal managerial body of a corporation.

4. Ownership is represented by shares of stock that are held by stockholders.

5. Stockholders elect the board of directors and vote on policy matters.

6. Profits may be paid to stockholders as dividends, or they may be reinvested in the business for expansion.

7. A stockholder has no personal liability for the debts of a corporation, except in the case of certain financial institutions.

8. Ownership of shares of stock in a corporation may be transferred without obtaining permission and without affecting the existence or operation of the corporation.

9. The corporate form of business organization is economically significant in the United States. It has been largely responsible for mass production, which has made possible more goods for better living.

10. Profits distributed as dividends are taxed twice (usually called *double taxation*). The corporation pays taxes on its profits. It then distributes some of these profits to its stockholders in the form of dividends, and the stockholders pay taxes on all but a small part of the dividends received.

Among the major disadvantages of the corporate form of organization are the remoteness of management from ownership and the limitations placed on operations by laws of the states in which it does business.

A typical organization chart for a corporation showing the line of ownership and authority is illustrated below.

**Organization Chart
for a Corporation**

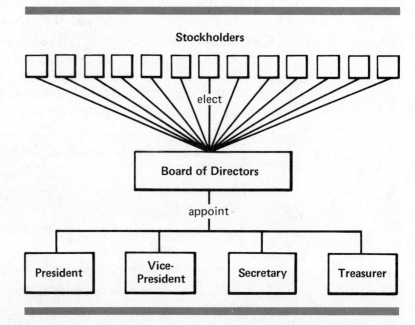

Stockholders

elect

Board of Directors

appoint

| President | Vice-President | Secretary | Treasurer |

Cooperative. A *cooperative* is a business that is owned by its members, who are also its customers. Individuals or businesses become members by depositing a sum of money or by purchasing

CHARACTERISTICS OF A COOPERATIVE

1. The cooperative organization ordinarily operates under the provisions of a charter authorized by the laws of a state or the federal government.

2. Management rests with an elected board of directors and officers. Each member has one vote regardless of the number of shares owned.

3. Capital is provided by sale of shares and by membership fees. Usually a fixed rate of return is set on shares purchased by members.

4. Cooperatives operate on the principle that goods and services will be priced at cost to members; hence, there is no profit. An accumulation of funds resulting from operations is returned to members as patronage dividends.

5. Members are not liable for the debts of a cooperative.

6. Death or withdrawal of a member does not affect the operations of a cooperative. Usually shares are not transferable.

shares. The purpose of a cooperative is to give members a financial advantage in buying the goods or services they want or in selling their products.

Although the cooperative form of business organization is widely used in agricultural purchasing and marketing, it is also common in such areas as personal credit, housing, health protection, insurance, telephone and electricity lines, and newspapers. For example, the Associated Press is a worldwide news-gathering agency that serves member news publishers. Thousands of individually owned grocery stores, jewelry stores, drugstores, and other businesses unite and jointly form cooperatives that serve as their own wholesale houses. The credit union, which is the most common type of cooperative, is a type of mutual savings association that pays interest on deposits and makes loans to members.

Number of Business Firms

The vast amount of business transacted daily requires the efforts of many firms. There are approximately 14 million businesses in operation in the United States. It should be noted, however, that the volume of business for many of these firms is relatively small. In fact, the top 200 businesses in size represent approximately 70% of the dollar volume of all business transactions.

The number of business firms in operation fluctuates according to general business conditions and the prosperity of the people. The table below shows the number of businesses in a recent year by industry and by form of organization.

NUMBER OF BUSINESS FIRMS IN OPERATION
(Numbers in Thousands)

Industry	Sole proprietorships	Partnerships	Corporations
Agriculture, forestry, and fisheries	3,367	123	56
Mining	56	16	14
Construction	892	61	191
Manufacturing	222	29	217
Transportation, communication, etc.	355	17	81
Wholesale and retail trade	2,193	193	615
Finance, insurance, and real estate	744	434	412
Services	3,034	199	436
Other	18	1	2
All industries	10,881	1,073	2,024

SOURCE: *Statistical Abstract of the United States*, 1978, p. 561.

FACTS EVERYONE SHOULD KNOW ABOUT BUSINESS

1. About 14 million businesses are in operation in the U.S. The typical business firm has a small volume and employs only a few workers. However, the bulk of business in the U.S. is conducted through large corporations. The top 200 largest corporations in the U.S. are responsible for 70% of all business conducted in this country.

2. The life of the typical business firm is relatively short; only one of five survives ten years. Competition eliminates the less efficient.

3. Hourly wage rates are usually dependent on knowledge, skill, experience, and productivity.

4. Approximately four out of every ten persons are in the civilian labor force. (This does not include military personnel.)

5. The primary legal forms of business organization are sole proprietorship, partnership, corporation, and cooperative. Each form has distinct characteristics that must be thoroughly understood before starting a business enterprise or investing in one.

C. FUNCTIONS OF BUSINESS

Many consumer wants can be fulfilled by materials that may be seen, weighed, or measured. Some wants can be satisfied only by the labor, skill, or knowledge of other people. Fulfilling wants for material things often involves several steps.

Business Makes Materials Useful

Business changes, processes, modifies, or organizes things that already exist, converting them in such a manner that they will be useful to consumers. Business makes materials useful to consumers by collecting raw materials, changing their form through manufacturing and other processes, moving or transporting them to where the consumer wants them, and having them available when the consumer wants them.

Let us use the making and selling of a wristwatch as an illustration of what business does to satisfy our wants. A mining company first extracts from the earth the metals, minerals, and precious stones of various kinds that are used in making a watch. These raw materials, however, have little usefulness to a consumer in satisfying the desire for a wristwatch until they have been through the manufacturer's various processes which change the form until finally a wristwatch is produced. Yet even a finished wristwatch will not satisfy the consumer's want for a watch if it is still in the stockroom of a watch manufacturer in Illinois or in Switzerland. It has to be transported to a place such as a hometown jewelry store where it can be examined. It also has to be available at the time the consumer wants it. Thus, business serves by making materials available in a form useful to consumers, at a place the consumer can use the product, and at the time the product is needed.

Business Performs Complex Tasks for Consumers

Satisfying the economic wants of people is a complex process. Some products go through many hands. For example, the milk you use in your cereal is the product of many steps. First, a farmer raises a calf and feeds and cares for it until it becomes a cow; the cow is then milked twice a day. The milk is cooled and sent by truck to a market. When the milk reaches a dairy processing plant, it is pasteurized and either bottled or put into a carton. It is then delivered either directly to your home or to a retail grocery where you purchase it. These steps are complex and no one of us as an individual consumer would perform all of them.

Business Raises the Level of Living

Imagine how different our lives would be if there were no business organizations to produce goods or provide services for the satisfaction of our economic wants. We would have to do everything ourselves as primitive people did. Our level of living would be at the low end of the scale. Business makes our high level of living possible by making goods and services available to us in useful form to meet our needs and satisfy our wants.

Business Develops New Products

In its continuous attempt to satisfy consumer needs in better ways, business improves many currently existing products and develops new ones. Inventions and improvements in production methods are constantly stimulated by the desire of business to serve consumers in a more satisfactory manner. Each year business spends great sums of money on research directed toward the discovery or invention of new and better products.

Almost everything we use has been either invented or improved through the efforts of business. It would be difficult to imagine how different life would be if all the economic goods and services that have been originated or improved by business were to be removed.

Business Creates Jobs

If all persons provided their own shelter and tools, made their own clothes, produced and prepared their own food, supplied their own medical care, and provided all the other goods and services they used, there would be no business. Hence, there would be no jobs.

Through the process of producing the economic goods and services to maintain our level of living, business creates jobs. The greater business activity is, the more jobs there are available. The income we receive from jobs enables us to pay for the goods and services we use.

The many different kinds of jobs created by business give an individual the opportunity to choose a job that one likes and for which one is best fitted. There would be no choice of occupations if business did not create jobs from which to choose.

Business Provides Tools and Equipment for Production

When a typist is employed, the personnel manager does not tell that person to bring a typewriter when reporting for work. Rather, the business firm provides the machine. Likewise, in manufacturing plants the business usually provides the tools and equipment necessary for production. Although the amount varies from one kind of firm to another, the average investment in plant and equipment per worker is about $42,000.

The greater output that tools and equipment make possible reduces the cost of production per unit, which should mean lower prices for the consumer. It is estimated that without the use of modern presses and other factory tools, it would cost $50,000 to make a car that now costs only $4,500 to make. This high cost would be prohibitive for most buyers. The lower cost per unit of production not only lowers the price of the product but also makes it possible to pay higher wages to workers producing the item than if their output per day were lower.

Business Assists in Paying the Cost of Government

The cost of government and the many services performed for special groups by government is paid through taxes of various kinds. It is estimated that 14% of the federal income is secured from corporation income taxes. The owners of sole proprietorship and partnership businesses also pay federal income taxes. All forms of business organizations pay local and state taxes.

Local, state, and federal taxes paid by business firms represent a great portion of the total income of those governmental units. Without the benefit of the taxes paid by business, either government services would have to be greatly reduced or the taxes paid by individuals greatly increased. In other words, businesses financially support the cost of local, state, and federal government to the extent that it would be impossible to continue government operations even at a greatly reduced level without that support. Although taxes paid by business are reflected in the cost of goods and services bought by consumers, the business taxes paid annually to government help to reduce the amount of taxes that must be paid by individuals.

Business Provides Organized Markets

Imagine how difficult it would be for each of us to obtain food, clothing, and other necessities directly from producers. Our marketing system performs that transfer service for us and, through advertising, acquaints us with products and services for sale. Perhaps you think the marketing system costs too much and is wasteful in some instances. It must be remembered, however, that the functions performed are essential. Since the field of marketing is competitive, only the most efficient firms can survive.

Our marketing system makes it possible for us to buy almost anything we want if we have the money to pay for it. This fortunate situation has been brought about by a complicated system that will be discussed in detail in Chapter 5.

FACTS EVERYONE SHOULD KNOW ABOUT BUSINESS FUNCTIONS

1. Business performs the many complex tasks that are necessary to make goods and services available to consumers in a form that is useful, at a place where they can be used, and at a time when they are needed.

2. Business raises our level of living by making more goods and services available, by developing new and better products, by creating jobs, and by providing tools and equipment for production.

3. The taxes paid by business represent a large part of the total income of local, state, and federal governments. Business taxes help to support a high level of government operations and to reduce taxes paid by individuals.

REVIEW QUESTIONS

Section A
1. In economics, what is meant by the word "institution"? Give examples of basic economic institutions in our free enterprise economy.
2. What is private property?
3. What determines how much profit a business can make under a free enterprise or market system?
4. What entitles a person or business to earn a profit?
5. What prevents one business from charging prices that are too high under a free enterprise or market system?

Section B
6. How does business serve the consumer while at the same time working in its own interest?
7. What are the four major classes of business as described in this chapter? Give examples.
8. How does the legal form of organization affect a business?
9. What are the main characteristics of a sole proprietorship?
10. What are the main characteristics of a partnership?
11. What are the main characteristics of a corporation?
12. What are the main characteristics of a cooperative?

Section C
13. What role does research play in the activities of a business?
14. Why is a business interested in developing new products?
15. How does business create jobs?
16. To what extent does business pay the cost of the federal government?
17. Why is our organized market system important to the consumer?

DISCUSSION QUESTIONS

Section A
1. If you lived under a government that owned all property, what are some of the freedoms that you would lose?
2. How do you think your local store determines what to sell and at what price?
3. How does profit determine whether a product will or will not be produced? Could there be cases where products that could satisfy wants and needs would not be produced? Explain.
4. What do we mean when we say that profits stimulate employment and economic growth?
5. What would happen to the consumer if there were no competition?

Section B
6. What, in your opinion, are the advantages and the disadvantages of a sole proprietorship?
7. If you are operating a sole proprietorship, what are possible advantages and disadvantages of changing to a partnership?
8. If you were trying to start a business and needed additional money, do you think it would be easier to get someone to invest in a partnership or in a corporation? Why?
9. Why are most large companies organized as corporations?
10. Since cooperatives formed by consumers and farmers are nonprofit organizations, they generally are not subject to the same taxes as other forms

of business. There is considerable argument about this. What is your opinion on the subject?

11. Who benefits from the use of modern equipment in production?
12. In the United States there are many products of high quality available in good supply and at more reasonable prices than in many other countries. Why is this true?

APPLICATION PROBLEMS

Section A
1. Prepare a chart or poster showing the aids and services government provides producers of economic goods and services.
2. Prepare a written report showing the historical record of governmental action to aid business by expanding markets or by preserving competition. Point out any instances where such action did not prove to be an aid to business.

Section B
3. In your school or city library examine a copy of *The World Almanac and Book of Facts* for the current year and find the following facts: (a) the trend in business failures (by types of business) in the United States for the past five years, (b) the trend of sales in retail stores (by types of business) for the two most recent years for which data are given, (c) the trend in profits as a percentage of sales before and after taxes for manufacturing corporations, (d) the trend of hourly earnings of employees in the manufacturing industries for the two most recent years for which data are given and (e) the total number of employees and total number of production workers in all manufacturing industries combined. What general conclusions can you draw from these facts?
4. Nancy Adams and Frank Perez entered into a partnership for the purpose of building and equipping a dry cleaning and laundering establishment. Adams invested $32,000 and Perez invested $24,000. They agreed that each should draw a small monthly salary for their labor and that they would divide annual profits or losses on the basis of the ratios of their investments when the business was started.
   (a) At the end of the first year, their profit was $12,000. They used $5,000 to purchase additional equipment and divided the remainder. What was each partner's share?
   (b) In the second year, another cleaning establishment was started only one block away. As a result, Adams and Perez suffered a loss of $3,500 for the year. What was each partner's share of that loss?

Section C
5. In your school or city library, examine a copy of the *Statistical Abstract of the United States* or the *Economic Report of the President*. From data obtained in either or both of these sources:
   (a) Prepare a pie chart (a circle divided into pie-like pieces) showing the name and the percentage of the various sources of tax income that the federal government receives.
   (b) Prepare a pie chart showing the name and the percentage of the various sources of tax income that state and local governments receive.
   (c) What general conclusions do you draw from these tax facts?

COMMUNITY PROJECTS

Section A

1. Question your local light and power company, water or gas company, telephone company, city transportation company, an insurance company, and a small loan company to find out how rates and fees are determined and who determines them. What conclusions can you draw?

2. In this chapter you have learned that there are several important economic institutions in the free enterprise economy of the United States. It is sometimes said that people generally do not know enough about our economic system and how it operates. Let us find out what people know and believe about our free enterprise economy. Ask the following people what the essential features and characteristics of the U.S. economy are: (a) five students who are not taking this course, (b) five teachers in your school, (c) five neighbors in the community who work in stores or factories, and (d) five persons who own or manage a business enterprise. Prepare a report in outline form, omitting the names of the persons you interviewed, in which you summarize what each of the four groups has said about our free enterprise economy.

Section B

3. Make a study of the business firms in your community, considering the following points for each; (a) how the business may be classified — basic production, processing, distribution, or service; (b) legal form of organization; (c) estimated number of employees; (d) number of years it has been in operation; (e) type of management, that is, by owners, employed managers, etc.; (f) nature of ownership — home owned, chain store, etc. If your town is small, include all business firms in the study; if your city is large, confine the study to the business firms in certain city blocks that are designated by your teacher. What general conclusions can be drawn about the characteristics of business in your community?

4. Assume that the students in your class decide to start a sandwich shop across the street from the school. A new building and new equipment will be needed. The students in the class will invest as much as they can, but investment from other sources also will be needed. Study thoroughly each of the four main legal forms of business organization for this enterprise. List all advantages and disadvantages of each of the four. Reach a conclusion as to the legal form of organization you believe to be best suited to this venture and state your reasons.

Section C

5. Select any business in your community with which you are familiar. It may be a business that offers a service, sells merchandise, or makes something people want.

   Make a complete study of the business you have selected, analyzing what the business does in light of the topics you have studied. Some of the topics will not apply to some types of business, but all topics should be considered in the analysis of what the selected business does. Write a report of the analysis you make covering the following items:

   (a) How does the business change the form or place of materials making them more useful to consumers?

   (b) What tasks does the business perform in connection with its products or services for consumers?

   (c) How does the product or service offered by the business contribute to raising the level of living?

(d) Has the business developed new products or services recently? What opportunities does it have to develop new products or services?

(e) How many jobs does the business provide?

(f) Through what means does the business strive for greater efficiency and for lower costs of production?

(g) To what extent does the business provide tools, equipment, and machinery that employees use? Can you estimate how much per employee is invested in tools and equipment?

(h) Estimate how much the business pays in local and state taxes and in federal income taxes.

(i) Summarize the effect the business has on consumers, on labor, and on the community.

Production in our Free Enterprise Economy

PURPOSE OF THE CHAPTER

Many resources are used in the production of goods and services to satisfy the wants and needs of people through our productive process. After studying this chapter, you will be able to:

1. List the factors of production.
2. Explain some of the basic economic elements of production.
3. Explain the unique characteristics of production in the United States.

A. ECONOMICS OF PRODUCTION

In this section we shall first review what is meant by the factors of production and then we shall examine certain economic elements of our production system.

Factors of Production

In thinking about economics, we have in the past considered the factors (resources) that contribute to production to consist of (1) labor, (2) land (natural resources), (3) capital, and (4) management (entrepreneurship). *Labor* means all forms of physical and mental effort. *Land* in its broad economic sense means land, minerals, water, oil, and all other *natural resources*. *Capital* means machines, tools, and buildings. *Management* (or entrepreneur) means the person who takes the risk of investing and borrowing money to put all factors to work in an attempt to earn a profit.

In modern practice one person may start a business and become an entrepreneur, but in a large corporation there are many investors who own the business and share the risk but take little or no part in the affairs of the business. They hire a manager to run the business for them. The manager becomes the agent of the investors and may also be one of the owners. We generally think of the manager as one who takes the place of or represents the entrepreneur. So investor (owner), manager (management), or entrepreneur may mean one and the same thing.

The mental and physical work performed by the manager of a business — either a hired manager or an owner — is a special form of labor. So the manager or entrepreneur may serve more than one economic function.

Some economists also consider government to be a factor of production because of the services it performs and the taxes it collects as its share of production.

All these factors of production are also called *resources*.

We can broaden our ideas about the factors or resources that contribute to production by saying that they consist of (1) labor, (2) land (natural resources), (3) capital, (4) management (entrepreneur), and (5) government.

Labor. Labor in its broadest sense includes all physical effort, mental effort, and use of technical skills. In the United States people generally have a great deal of freedom to choose the type of work they want to do, the geographic area in which they want to work, and the kind of business activity in which they want to be engaged. Under our political and economic system, a good deal of stress is placed on people's freedom to plan their own careers.

Land or Natural Resources. Natural resources are materials supplied by nature. Human beings did not create them, although people may have had to work to extract them from the earth or to put them in a usable form. Tangible economic goods, such as foods, fabrics, machines, and houses, all had their origin in the earth; hence they come from natural resources. Fabrics, for example, may be made either from natural fibers such as wool or cotton or from synthetic fibers such as dacron or rayon. But regardless of the type of fiber, the materials from which the fibers originated were natural resources. These resources comprise the basic elements for the production of tangible goods. One of our greatest economic problems is the conservation and wise use of natural resources.

Capital. In an economic sense, *capital* refers to any buildings, equipment, or other physical property (other than raw materials) used in a business. Goods used for productive purposes in a business are known as *capital goods*. One of the most important capital

A tree is a natural resource, a material supplied by nature then utilized by people.

Boise Cascade Corporation

goods is machinery. Machinery and other forms of equipment have not only contributed greatly to the prosperity of the United States by increasing our productivity, but have also made labor's work less burdensome. According to a *Twentieth Century Fund* report, human effort supplies less than 6% of the energy (power) used to produce all our economic goods, 94% being supplied by energy or power applied to machines. In other words, tools and machines make it possible to produce about 16 times as much goods as could be produced without them.

Management (Entrepreneurship). Management of a business involves: (1) developing ideas for the production of goods and services that people want, (2) planning and operating the business, (3) establishing policies, and (4) making decisions. Management is the key to successful business operation. Even if we had the most modern buildings and equipment and the most intelligent and industrious labor force, there could not be a successful business without good organization and management.

The same principles of management apply in a one-person business as in a large one, but management becomes more complicated in a large business. In all businesses, plans must be made, workers hired, raw materials obtained, and equipment purchased or built. The function of management is to put all these factors together.

Government. Under very simple and uncomplicated economic conditions, the main factors of production are probably limited to natural resources, labor, capital, and management. But where the number of business firms is large, where competition is great, and where the economic structure is very complex (such as in the United States), a fifth factor of production is present. This factor is government. Business depends on government for protection from unfair competition, development of standards, statistical information of aid to management, and establishment of favorable conditions for foreign trade. On the other hand, business is regulated and in some respects controlled by government. Government regulations pertain to markets and prices; labor, hours, wages, and employee-employer rights; financing; and similar aspects of business operations.

Some Economic Elements of Production

In addition to understanding the factors of production, you should also be familiar with the basic economic elements of our production system.

Performing Economic Services. Some producers create goods. Other producers perform services that satisfy wants directly and have no connection with the creation of goods. These people are producing economic services. Opera singers are producers because they satisfy a human want directly. Teachers, lawyers, physicians, and actors are also producers because they satisfy human wants directly. A stenographer who works for a doctor is performing an economic service that indirectly satisfies a human want.

Choices in the Use of Resources. If the resources we have as individuals and as a nation are used to satisfy one want, they cannot be used for another. The choice of using a resource to fill one want means losing the choice of using that same resource to fill another want. For example, if a factory uses labor and machines to make guns, it cannot use the same labor and machines to make refrigerators. If a nation uses its resources for an army and the manufacture of guns, it cannot use the same resources for education or for producing goods and services for consumer use.

The same principle applies to the individual. Very few people have enough income to satisfy all their wants. If a family buys a new refrigerator, it cannot use the same money to buy new clothes. If a family buys a new automobile, it cannot use the same money to pay for a vacation trip or to provide for the education of its children.

When either as a nation or as a society we fail to use all our productive resources — such as available labor, buildings, equipment, machines, and tools — we fail to produce as many goods as would be possible if all resources were used. We as a nation would have a higher level of living if all resources were productive.

Production Creates Value or Utility. Production involves creating value, which we call utility. *Utility* is the ability of goods and services to satisfy human wants. There are four basic types of utility: form, time, place, and possession.

PRODUCTION CREATES UTILITY

The four basic types of utility are:

1. Form utility — changing the structure or shape of products to better satisfy human wants.

2. Time utility — having goods and services available when they are needed.

3. Place utility — having goods and services available where they are needed.

4. Possession utility — having goods or services as the property of the consumer who needs or wants them.

Demand Determines Production. Human wants and needs are not the same as consumer demand. You may want or need something, but in the marketplace there is no *effective demand* unless you are willing and able (have the money) to buy. When wants become demand and the consumer buys and uses or consumes something, we have *consumption*.

Consumption of goods and services is the ultimate goal of all production. Consumption means buying and using or consuming. In our economic system, the consumer is the one who determines what goods and services to buy. Unless the consumer actually buys, there is no effective demand and, therefore, no need for the production of that good or service. Of course, consumers are influenced in their buying by what the producers produce; nevertheless, it is still the consumer who makes the final choice before consumption takes place.

**FACTS EVERYONE SHOULD KNOW ABOUT THE
ECONOMICS OF PRODUCTION**

---

1. Factors or resources of production are labor, land, capital, management (entrepreneurship), and government.

2. Capital is mainly equipment, buildings, machines, and other physical property used in production.

3. Teachers, lawyers, doctors, and others provide economic services.

4. We must choose how we use our resources.

5. Government sometimes determines how resources are used.

6. Production creates form, time, place, and possession utility.

7. There is no demand until there is a purchase.

8. Consumption is use.

B. CHARACTERISTICS OF U.S. PRODUCTION

Production includes many types of effort, such as farming, financing, transporting, storing, and selling. Efficiency determines how well a producer can compete with other producers and make a profit. Efficiency also determines how well a producer can increase production and reduce costs. When costs are reduced, people can buy more with the money they earn.

Production Efficiency

Efficiency is brought about in many ways. In manufacturing, efficiency is gained through good management, skill of workers, modern machines, mass production, and specialization.

American industry has increased its efficiency greatly through skilled managers and workers. Modern machines increase the amount and quality of goods that a worker can produce, usually with less effort.

Law of Diminishing Returns

The role of good management is to put together the right combination of each of the factors of production to get the best results (highest output at lowest cost). Increasing one factor of production while holding the other factors constant results in inefficient production when the law of diminishing returns starts operating. The *law of diminishing returns* is the point where adding additional amounts of one factor of production (land, labor, or capital) results in smaller returns per added factor.

Smaller returns may be looked at in two ways: (1) as less output per added factor of production and (2) as greater cost per unit of output, thus less profits. For example, if your factory has only 10 machines (capital), it would be inefficient to hire 15 machine operators. The additional 5 operators (labor) cannot add to production since there are no machines for them to operate. Therefore, you would have less output per operator since you must now divide total output by 15 instead of 10. Also, if your factory had 10 machines (capital) and 10 operators (labor), it would be inefficient to buy 5 more machines. The extra 5 machines without operators would not add to production (output). Thus, the cost of producing each unit of output would be higher since you would have added the cost of 5 idle machines.

Principle of Mass Production

The principle of *mass production* is that greater efficiency in business operation is attained by making one or a few products in large quantity rather than by making a smaller quantity of many products. For example, one business organization employing a thousand people may produce perhaps 100 fabricated metal products ranging from the chrome trim for automobiles to ironing boards. It divides its productive efforts among the 100 items. Another business organization also may produce fabricated metal products, but it limits its production to metal stepladders for household use, metal kitchen furniture, and metal ironing boards. It produces the three items in large quantities, and like the first business, employs a thousand people. Both businesses make stepladders, metal kitchen furniture, and metal ironing boards. In which business firm is the cost of production of each of these three items likely to be lower? The answer, of course, is easy; the business limiting its production to three items, but producing them in large quantities, probably will have a considerably lower unit cost. The firm limiting its production has employed mass production methods.

Mass production methods lower production costs per unit. The abundance of power and the use of machines have made mass production possible. Production costs are lowered by the use of power and tools. Science has helped improve manufacturing processes and products by developing new machinery and finding new uses for many raw materials that formerly were not used.

Principle of Specialization

One of the operational techniques developed by business is based on the principle of *specialization*. This principle means that greater efficiency results from assigning an employee to perform one particular task rather than to perform all tasks pertaining to an operation. For example, in the making of shoes, a worker could be assigned to the whole job of making a shoe, which would involve performing all the tasks that are required in its production. Or the worker could be assigned to one of the tasks in making a shoe, such as stitching or cementing the sole to the upper portion of the shoe. In the latter assignment, the worker's job is said to be specialized.

Specialization is sometimes referred to as *division of labor*. Specialization benefits both the worker and the consumer. In the past, when the worker performed every task necessary to make an article, production was low and consequently the costs of production were high. With specialization, production is high and workers can be paid greater wages; costs are low and thus consumers can buy more.

Specialization also permits the assignment of workers to the kind of work for which they are best fitted. Usually, we enjoy doing the things we can do well. Furthermore, the quality of peoples' work is better if they are well qualified for the job than if they are not so well fitted to it.

Advantages of Specialization. Some of the advantages of specialization are:

1. It increases production and therefore the amount of wealth and income.
2. It encourages the development of greater skill.
3. It saves time.
4. It lowers production costs.
5. It makes possible the employment of persons who may otherwise be unemployable.
6. It permits the continuous and economical use of tools and equipment.
7. It develops a spirit of interdependence.

Disadvantages of Specialization. Some of the disadvantages of specialization are serious, but they do not necessarily affect the production of wealth. Among the disadvantages are:

1. Workers become greatly dependent on one another.
2. Work may become monotonous and boring.
3. Workers may not have as much pride in their workmanship.
4. Because they are efficient, workers may not be given an opportunity to change to other jobs; whereas, in seeking to find the best assignment for an inefficient worker, the inefficient worker may be given an opportunity to try other jobs.
5. Workers who lose their positions may have difficulty finding or adjusting to other jobs that may require skills and knowledge they have not learned.

Machines, Power, and Productivity

In the struggle to overcome economic scarcity, people have gone through various stages as follows:

Stage 1 — Human energy provided the source of power.

Stage 2 — Human energy was combined with the use of tools.

Stage 3 — Human energy and tools were combined with the use of animals to supply power.

Stage 4 — Human energy, tools, and animals were combined with wind, water, and minerals such as coal and oil to supply power.

Stage 5 — Human energy, improved tools and machines, animals, wind, water, and minerals were combined with electricity as a source of power.

Stage 6 — New sources of energy have been developed and old sources of energy have been improved in effectiveness to provide greater amounts of power.

We sometimes give most of the credit for production efficiency to well-trained workers, good management, and modern machines. We often ignore the great importance of electric power that makes the use of machines possible and work easier. If electric power is scarce and costly, production costs will be high. Some nations suffer from a lack of cheap power because they lack water supply resources and fuel resources from which electric power can be made. We now have atomic and solar power, which help solve the problem of scarce and costly electric power.

Machines multiply a worker's productivity many times.

Productivity is the key to prosperity since a nation improves its level of living through increases in productivity. Future progress depends on raising the output of each worker, and greater production for each worker-hour is possible through increased use of machine power. Machines are now the helping hand of workers in modern industry. A person can make only a very limited quantity of any product manually. With the aid of a few tools, however, the worker can increase production. With the aid of machinery and power, the worker is often able to multiply production ten or twenty times or more.

Increased output or production per worker per day by using machines and power has two favorable results:

1. *Workers have more leisure time.* They can produce more per hour; hence, the number of hours of work per week can be reduced without lowering production.
2. *The worker's daily wage tends to be increased.* Higher production allows greater wages to be paid to the workers because the business is able to make and sell more goods.

Many products that we use today could not be produced at any price if it were not for modern machinery and power. Machines are definitely the muscles of business that lighten the burdens of workers and increase their efficiency so that we all have more and better things for lower prices. Business firms provide the machines that enable employees to produce more than they could by manual methods.

Effects of New Machinery

New machines and new processes invented and discovered, especially during the past thirty years, are great aids to workers, enabling them to produce more per day and often with less effort. This development in industry is referred to as *technology*. With the introduction of automatic machines and processes to factory and office operations, technology has progressed to a new stage known as automation. *Automation* means a continuous operation in production, such as the assembly line, through the use of automatic equipment. This equipment automatically performs routine operations, regulates the flow of materials being processed, and controls the quality of production.

When the effects of technology began to result in many changes in routine factory operations, some workers were fearful of technological unemployment. They felt that machines would be substituted for people or that machines aiding workers would increase output per person to the extent that the number of workers would be reduced. These fears have been largely unfounded.

EMPLOYED PERSONS BY MAJOR OCCUPATION GROUP
Selected Years, 1960–1979
(in thousands)

Occupation Group	1960	1965	1970	1975	1979 (Mar.)
White-Collar Workers	28,522	31,852	37,997	42,227	49,296
Blue-Collar Workers	24,057	26,247	27,791	27,962	30,954
Service Workers	8,023	8,936	9,712	11,657	12,790
Farm Workers	5,176	4,053	3,126	2,936	2,461
Totals	65,778	71,088	78,626	84,782	95,501

Source: U.S. Bureau of Labor Statistics, *Employment and Earnings* (April, 1979).

As you can see from the table above, there was an increase of over 29.7 million jobs in the 19-year period from 1960 to 1979. This represents an increase of 45% in total number of jobs compared with a population increase of only 21% for the same time period. Thus, technology and automation have not eliminated jobs.

Before one jumps to the conclusion that machines create unemployment, one should ask some of these questions: Would I want to give up the use of a shovel and use my hands? Would I want to give up the use of a lawn mower? Would I want to give up the use of a vacuum sweeper? Would I want to give up the use of an automobile and walk instead of ride? Would the worker want to give up an electric drill or drilling machine and use manual labor? All of these items are machines, and they are made by machines.

Many workers now look upon automation in the factory as a competitor to labor. Again there is fear of technological unemployment. Undoubtedly there will be temporary dislocation of labor, and readjustment of workers to new jobs will be necessary. In taking a larger view of industry, however, we find that machines are not competitors of workers and that automation is not a threat to the security of labor. Rather, machines are helpers. They enable the worker to produce more in a shorter period of time with less physical discomfort and strain. In individual cases a machine may be a competitor of a worker for a particular job. Automation may affect a particular worker adversely by eliminating that worker's job entirely. In the long run, however, technology and automation will reduce the number of hours a week a person will need to work to earn the same amount that person would have earned before the changes.

How We Benefit from our Production System

Because Americans are accustomed to a high level of living, they may to some degree fail to recognize and appreciate the importance of our production system in their lives. People often take

---

HOW WE BENEFIT FROM OUR PRODUCTION SYSTEM

1. The economic goods and services that we want and need are provided through our production system.

2. The U.S. economy has given us the highest level of living in the world, and it is still improving.

3. Business converts raw materials into products that are useful to us.

4. Through research, business develops and improves goods that make life easier and more pleasant for us.

5. Business creates jobs.

6. Through specialization and mass production methods, business produces goods at a price lower than would otherwise be possible.

7. We pay lower prices for goods because business provides tools and equipment that increase output per employee.

8. We have available many public services and benefits such as expressways, bridges, schools, and police protection because private business contributes to government through taxes.

the benefits coming to us through our production system for granted. If we are to preserve and improve our economic system and the benefits arising from it, we must recognize and appreciate what it means to us. We must also understand what the free enterprise economy is, what makes it function, and what its benefits are. The first requisite for the protection and constructive change of the free enterprise system is for the people to understand it.

REVIEW QUESTIONS

Section A

1. What are the factors of production?
2. In economics, what do the following terms mean: (a) labor, (b) land or natural resources, (c) capital, (d) management (entrepreneurship), and (e) government?
3. What are some examples of producers of services rather than goods?
4. What is meant when we say that a nation must make a choice whether to produce guns or butter?
5. What four forms of utility are created by production?
6. What is meant by (a) effective demand and (b) consumption?
7. What is the difference between a want and a demand?

Section B

8. What is the law of diminishing returns?
9. (a) What is meant by mass production?
   (b) What is the objective sought in mass production?
10. Why is specialization important in helping us to produce effectively?
11. Why are machines and electrical power important in our production system?
12. What is meant by (a) technology and (b) automation?
13. In what way may machines and automation result in technological unemployment?

DISCUSSION QUESTIONS

Section A

1. How does the role of the entrepreneur in a large corporation differ from the role of the entrepreneur in a small company?
2. (a) How might the government be considered a business?
   (b) Why is the government sometimes referred to as a factor of production?
3. (a) How is consumer economic decision making related to the economic activity of the total economy?
   (b) How is the activity of the total economy related to individual consumer decision making?
4. What happens in a community when the resources being used for one purpose are no longer needed?
5. From your own experience, give an example of how demand has determined production.
6. Why does a clothing manufacturer find it necessary to change styles and designs frequently?

Section B
7. It is still possible for individuals to make cloth and to prepare some of their food. For instance, one could buy a bushel of oats and make rolled oats for breakfast cereal. Rolled oats that you buy in a package in a store cost about ten times as much as the raw oats from which they are made. Would you recommend that every family prepare its own rolled oats? Why?
8. It is sometimes said that electrical power is an index or an indication of the productivity of a nation. Explain why this may be true.
9. How do we as consumers benefit from the American production system?

APPLICATION PROBLEMS

Section A
1. As indicated in this chapter, the four basic factors of production are labor, land (natural resources), capital, and management (entrepreneurship). (a) Give examples of each of these factors. (b) What, in money income, does each factor receive for its contribution to production? (c) List the factors of production in terms of what you think are their relative importance. Compare your list with that of other members of the class.
2. Provide at least two examples of how the value of a good or service is improved through the creation of form, time, place, and possession utilities.
3. Prepare a list of reasons why government might be considered a fifth factor of production. Compare your list with that of other members of the class.

Section B
4. Give your own definition of mass production. Support your definition by statements as to the essential characteristics of mass production.
5. Calculate the percent of increase or decrease in jobs for each occupational group between 1960 and 1979 from the table on page 64. What conclusions can be drawn from these percentage increases or decreases?
6. Compare the results of specialization (or division of labor) in a business with a track team made up of decathlon athletes (those who achieve well in many and varied track and field events as opposed to athletes who specialize in a specific event).
7. Prepare a two-part report on (a) the life and (b) the contributions to the economic development of the United States of one of the following men: Henry Ford, Cyrus McCormick, or Eli Whitney.

COMMUNITY PROJECTS

Section A
1. Select a business in your community. (a) Specifically identify the person or persons who represent each of the factors of production in that business. (b) What economic returns does each factor receive for its part in production?
2. Select a business in your community. (a) Prepare a brief report to show how money invested in capital goods has led to the economic growth of that particular business. (b) Some businesses are said to be "capital intensive." Would you consider the business that you analyzed to fit this category or not? Why?

Section B

3. Provide examples from your own community of each of the following: (a) mass production, (b) the principle of specialization, and (c) the use of machines and power and their relationship to productivity.

4. Using the information entitled "How We Benefit from our Production System" presented on page 65, provide an example of each of the eight points listed as each relates directly to your community.

Marketing in our Free Enterprise Economy

PURPOSE OF THE CHAPTER

Goods and services reach the consumer through the marketing system. Those who participate in marketing provide an economic service. Since much of your contact with business probably consists of selecting and buying goods and services, you will learn from this chapter how marketing serves both producers and consumers in our economy.

After studying this chapter, you will be able to:

1. Define marketing.
2. Explain what functions marketing performs.
3. Explain the problem of costs in marketing.

A. NATURE OF MARKETING

Marketing carries out business activities that direct the flow of goods and services from producer to consumer or user. Marketing is the connecting link between the producer and the consumer or user. The marketing system joins production and consumption.

Significance of Marketing

Approximately one in every six workers is engaged directly in wholesaling or retailing activities. This ratio does not take into account those serving marketing through transportation, communication, and office jobs.

Marketing provides many kinds of job opportunities requiring a wide range of skills and abilities. Although we naturally think of selling as being the primary occupation in marketing, there are opportunities in management, advertising, market and product research, and buying.

The economic well-being of our country is determined largely by productivity, consumption, and employment. The efficiency of the marketing process affects all three. If marketing stimulates demand, people will consume goods at a high rate. High consumption requires high productivity to meet the demand, and high productivity results in high employment. Indirectly, marketing is a key to a high level of living.

What Marketing Is and Does

All people have economic wants. The purpose of economic goods and services is to satisfy those wants. The act of using goods and services to satisfy our wants is known as *consumption*.

Consumption does not take place unless two conditions are met. First, we must know that goods appropriate for satisfying our wants are being produced and are available to us. And second, the goods must in some way reach us at a time and a place in which we can use them. For example, if a scientist in a foreign country were to discover a drug that would cure cancer, it could not be used to cure a cancerous condition we might have unless we or our physician knew that such a drug had been discovered and was available. But knowledge of the drug and its production would not satisfy our want and need for it unless we could obtain it. Marketing fulfills these two conditions.

Marketing includes most of the activities that occur in placing economic goods in consumers' hands. Marketing, like production,

Marketing not only tells us that products are available but also where they can be purchased. Without marketing there would be no consumption.

therefore creates the four basic types of utility: form utility, time utility, place utility, and possession utility. Marketing does not include all the activities that change the form of goods, only those form changes necessary on the spot to complete the transfer from producer to consumer. An example is the alterations a retailer makes on a suit of clothes at the time of the sale. Agricultural productive activities and manufacturing processes are not included in marketing.

Marketing Institutions

In the preceding discussion, we used the term "marketing" to include most of the processes involved in the movement of goods and services from producers to consumers. To businesses, "market" also means the demand that exists for their goods. They say there is a "good" market if the demand is good.

The term "market" may also refer to people and places that perform the marketing functions. Such marketing arrangements are called *marketing institutions*. Common examples of marketing institutions include retail markets and wholesale markets. Other examples include auctions, brokers who act as agents for someone else, and security markets where stocks and bonds are bought and sold.

Geographical Range of Markets

In general, markets are considered to be (a) *local*, (b) *regional*, (c) *national*, or (d) *international*. International markets are frequently referred to as *world markets*.

A large national market encourages production in large quantities. Since large-scale production is usually more efficient, the consumer benefits. For instance, if an automobile manufacturer were limited to a market the size of Michigan, the company could not produce automobiles in large numbers. Both the cost of production and the price to the consumer would therefore be high. Automobile manufacturers, however, have a national market, and some have international markets.

Not all products or services can reach out into the national market. The nature of the product or the service and various other influences tend to restrict the market. Laundries, for instance, are usually confined to local communities. Without establishing branches, a laundry seldom finds it profitable to solicit business at distances greater than 20 or 30 miles. A single retail meat market is necessarily confined to its own neighborhood, although it sometimes enlarges its territory by providing delivery service.

The marketing of vegetables at one time was confined to areas close to the points of production. The marketing areas for these products, however, have been greatly extended through the use of transportation and storage facilities. For example, certain regions, such as the South and the West Coast, have national markets for fresh fruits and vegetables during the seasons when other regions cannot produce these foods.

B. FUNCTIONS OF MARKETING

Some functions of marketing involve the physical handling of goods and others involve the rendering of services. These functions are listed below.

FUNCTIONS OF MARKETING	
1. Assembling and buying	5. Merchandising
2. Storing	6. Transporting and communicating
3. Grading and standardizing	7. Financing
4. Selling and advertising	8. Risk taking

Each function is necessary and must be performed if marketing is to move goods to the consumer.

Assembling and Buying

The assembling of goods is the first step in marketing. *Assembling* means accumulating or gathering goods from various sources. Wholesalers assemble many types of manufactured goods from many manufacturers located in different places and make the goods available to the retailer. The retailer assembles a considerable variety of goods from different wholesalers.

Buying consists of activities pertaining to: (1) agreement on prices and terms of purchase, date of shipment or delivery, and transfer of title; (2) careful determination of needs; (3) selection of sources of supply, that is, from whom to purchase; and (4) determination of the quality and suitability of the goods. Each of these activities is an essential part of the assembling and buying function of marketing.

Storing

At all stages in the marketing process, it becomes necessary to hold goods for varying periods of time. For some goods, production may be geared to demand, thereby reducing the need for storage. Goods, such as wheat, having a fairly steady demand and a seasonal production call for long storage. Some goods need special storage such as refrigeration or air ventilation.

Grading and Standardizing

Grading is the process of separating the supply of a commodity into classes according to established standards. For example, eggs are separated into Grades A, B, and C according to quality. Many agricultural products are carefully graded when they are assembled and marketed. For example, the standards set up by the federal government for wheat include classes or kinds of wheat, amount of moisture present, and percentage of damaged kernels and foreign matter. Most farm products are sold in large lots on the basis of grade. Meat, for instance, is marketed on the basis of inspection and grading.

A useful way to think about grading is to think about the several different ways that grading is done in schools. First, groups of students are often divided into grades; second, the marks that students receive are often in the form of letters or numerical rankings to show a difference in quality or ability. Almost any type of product can be graded. For example, clothing, metals used in making various products, and writing paper are all graded according to quality. Grading, then, takes place in any rank order relating to quality or ability that is established.

Standardizing is the process of preparing a definition or description of the various qualities of a commodity. For example, a No. 1 apple is well-colored, mature, and without blemishes. The federal government and many associations cooperate in promoting the development of standards. Thus, customers are able to buy a commodity again and again with the assurance that the quality of each purchase will meet minimum specifications.

Again you might think of standardizing in a school setting. There are certain minimum standards that a teacher might set before a student is able to pass a test. In marketing, however, a standard is set primarily for the purpose of assuring consumers that they get the same quality of a product time after time once the goods have been classified as to a certain standard. For medical products, for example, it is extremely important that standards are

Grading makes it easier to shop wisely.

set and the consumer is assured of the same quality each time a purchase is made.

Selling and Advertising

The preceding functions deal with gathering and preparing goods for marketing. Those who have collected goods, stored them, and graded them cannot assume that people who want these goods will seek them. It is entirely false to believe that, if you have a good product, "customers will beat a path to your door." One of the primary functions of *selling* is to create or stimulate demand for goods. Creating demand involves informing people that products are available, teaching them how the goods will satisfy their wants, and persuading them to buy.

Elias Howe, sewing machine inventor, had to struggle for years to introduce his invention successfully. Selling and advertising were not used to tell consumers about it and to educate them to its use. Similar stories are frequent in our history. Do you suppose, for instance, that practically every home would have one or more television sets today if selling and advertising had not informed people about television and the availability of sets?

Demand is stimulated in two ways, through personal selling and through advertising. In actual practice, the two methods are usually used together. The manufacturer advertises to the public but also has salespeople who call on wholesale dealers. The wholesaler or manufacturer, in turn, may advertise to the public but will also send salespeople to call on retailers. In recent years, however, large manufacturers have tended to use the mass advertising message, such as television and magazine advertising.

Creating consumer demand directly through mass advertising gives the manufacturer better control over the manner in which the product is presented than is possible when salespeople pass on information about it to prospective consumers.

Selling includes not only creating and stimulating demand but also finding buyers; arriving at terms of sale; determining prices; agreeing upon delivery dates; and, finally, providing for a method of payment and transfer of title.

Merchandising

After demand has been created, it must be satisfied. *Merchandising* is the process of actually filling demand for products. It is particularly important in retail stores where it may include the following:

1. Arrangement of counters and other store facilities.
2. Display of goods in the store.
3. Window displays.
4. Procedure and personnel for showing and demonstrating goods to prospective customers.
5. Delivery service.
6. Systematic credit policy.
7. Installation and repair service for goods.

Not every retailer performs all these functions. For instance, a retailer may have no delivery service and may not need to perform installation and repair service, but probably does have to perform the other functions.

As markets expand and the marketing process becomes more complex, there is an increasing need on the part of wholesalers and retailers for *market information*. Much of this information is collected by manufacturers and by producers' associations and is sent on to wholesalers and retailers. An example of information useful to wholesalers and retailers is the probable future supply of a commodity such as wool or citrus fruits. Another example is the trend in fashions and styles of clothing that may affect the ordering and buying practices of wholesalers and retailers. The possibility of work stoppages due to upcoming labor-management disputes may affect production and, in turn, the supply and delivery dates of many products. Market information may be as helpful to wholesalers and retailers as credit and installation services are to consumers.

Transporting and Communicating

Usually, when ownership of goods is transferred from seller to buyer, there is also a change in the location of the goods. Thus, as goods are sold and transferred from manufacturer to wholesaler, from wholesaler to retailer, and from retailer to consumer, *transportation* is involved. Airlines, railroads, trucklines, pipelines, ships and barges, and other transportation facilities play an important role in our marketing process. Pipelines now transport such items as chemicals, oil, gas, and water. This method has reduced the cost of transportation and lowered the cost of marketing. Modern rapid transportation facilities tremendously expand the markets for fresh foods and many other perishable products.

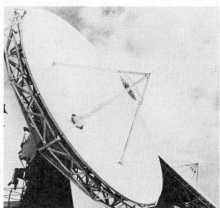

Courtesy of Western Union Corporation, Union Pacific Railroad, and Teletype Corporation.

The marketing process depends on many rapid forms of transportation and communication.

Telephone, telegraph, radiotelephone, and postal services provide the *communication* links between sellers and buyers of commodities and hence, like transportation, play an important role in marketing. For example, orchids ordered by cablegram from Hawaii may be delivered by air to Chicago within 24 hours.

As the distance between the supplier and the consumer increases, the economic significance of transportation and communication in the marketing process also increases.

Financing

The movement of goods from producer to consumer often requires considerable time. The manufacturer may have to store goods in a warehouse before their sale to wholesalers. Wholesalers and retailers must keep an ample supply of goods in storage to meet customer demands promptly. Also, moving goods from one location to another requires time in transit. While goods are in the process of moving to the consumer and while they are in storage, someone has money invested in the goods that cannot be recovered until the goods are sold. At the same time, the owner of the goods needs money to buy more goods and to operate a business. This may mean obtaining a loan. *Financing*, that is, providing the money that is invested in the goods while they are moving from the producer to the consumer, is an important aspect of the marketing process.

The manufacturer provides financing by selling goods to the wholesaler on credit. The wholesaler in turn provides financing by selling goods to the retailer on credit. And the retailer also provides financing by selling goods to customers on credit. Most of the costs of financing by manufacturers, wholesalers, and retailers are passed on to the final users (businesses and individuals) in the form of higher prices.

Risk Taking

Uncertainties and the risk of taking a loss occur in all stages of marketing. *Risks* include fire, theft, breakage, physical deterioration, items becoming obsolete, changes in the price level, and changes in customers' wants and demands. A risk is predictable and insurable. For example, an insurance company can predict the number of automobile accidents per million cars with a great deal of accuracy. *Uncertainty*, however, covers possible events for which one could not make an estimate based on experience. For example, the chance that a new product or technique might make your product or service obsolete is unpredictable. Pianists can obtain insurance against the loss of or injury to their fingers, which is an uncertainty. But most uncertainties are not covered by insurance since by definition they are unpredictable.

Speculation on our organized markets is a form of risk taking that is important in our marketing system. Speculators are willing to purchase a commodity months in advance, even before it is produced. They do this in the belief that the price of the commodity will increase and that they will be able to sell it later at a profit. Other speculators are willing to sell, for future delivery, goods that they do not yet have. They believe that the purchase price of the commodity will decrease; they, too, hope to make a profit.

Some risks, such as loss from fire and theft, can be covered by insurance. Other types of risk may be reduced or eliminated through good management practices. Regardless of insurance coverage and good management, some losses will occur due to uninsurable uncertainties. Owners and operators of businesses attempt, of course, to have their profits outnumber their losses. If they do not, they will not remain in business for long.

C. COSTS OF MARKETING

As you learned earlier, marketing is the connecting link between the producer and the consumer. The marketing services of many people may be necessary to bring goods and services from producers to consumers. The more efficient the marketing services are, the lower the marketing cost will be and the higher the demand for goods and services will be. High consumption leads to high productivity and high employment, which in turn lead to a high level of living. The efficiency of the marketing process, therefore, greatly influences our economic well-being.

Place of Middlemen

Any person or business concern that performs one or more of the eight marketing functions explained earlier in this chapter is a *middleman*. Middlemen are the retailers, wholesalers, agents, brokers, and others whose business is to get the product from the producer to the consumer.

Much criticism is directed at middlemen. Some criticism stems from the increase in the cost of a commodity as it moves from the producer to the consumer. Criticism of middlemen is

Modern transportation performs a middleman function in moving goods from the producer to the consumer.

Trans World Airlines, Inc.

often caused by a lack of understanding of the functions they perform. Many buyers fail to realize that after goods are produced, many additional services are required before consumers can enjoy these goods.

Marketing Channels

As you have already learned, goods move through various middlemen from the producer to the consumer. The route taken by the goods is called the *marketing channel*. It is also called the *channel of distribution* or the *trade channel*. The route is not the same for all goods, and it is not necessarily the same for all goods of the same kind.

When goods flow from producer to consumer through a wholesaler and a retailer or through other combinations of middlemen, the method is frequently referred to as *indirect marketing*. This term is used because the products pass through several hands in going from a producer to a consumer.

Direct marketing is any process by which the producer sells to the consumer directly or through a representative. The Avon Company, distributing cosmetics by house-to-house selling, is an example of direct marketing. Several other well-known manufacturers sell directly to the consumer, such as publishers of encyclopedias and manufacturers of vacuum cleaners.

Producers usually control the first steps in the marketing process; that is, they decide whether their products shall be sold directly or to wholesalers or agents who will control the marketing from that point forward. The numerous marketing channels may be grouped into four major classes shown in the illustration that follows:

Major Marketing Channels

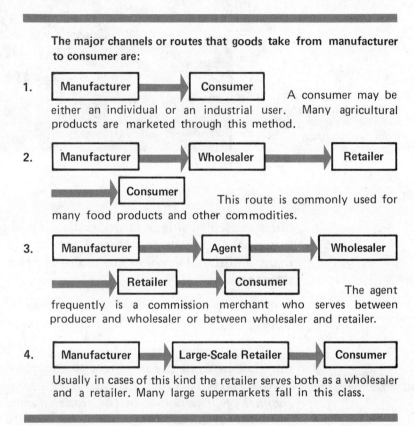

The major channels or routes that goods take from manufacturer to consumer are:

1. Manufacturer → Consumer   A consumer may be either an individual or an industrial user. Many agricultural products are marketed through this method.

2. Manufacturer → Wholesaler → Retailer → Consumer   This route is commonly used for many food products and other commodities.

3. Manufacturer → Agent → Wholesaler → Retailer → Consumer   The agent frequently is a commission merchant who serves between producer and wholesaler or between wholesaler and retailer.

4. Manufacturer → Large-Scale Retailer → Consumer   Usually in cases of this kind the retailer serves both as a wholesaler and a retailer. Many large supermarkets fall in this class.

Cost of Marketing

It is difficult, if not impossible, to determine exactly what part of the dollars spent annually at the retail level represents the cost of producing or manufacturing the goods, what part represents the cost of marketing, and what part is the middlemen's profit. Undoubtedly, more reliable estimates could be made for specific commodities than for all commodities combined.

Recent estimates of average marketing costs indicate that when a consumer pays $1 for a product, about one half, or 50 cents, goes for marketing activities. Of this amount, a relatively small percentage goes for profit. For example, the wholesaler and the retailer together receive an average profit of about 12½ cents on a product for which a consumer pays $1.

In the mid- to late-1970s consumer prices rose dramatically as illustrated in the chart below. During this same time the unemployment rate was going up to a new high of nearly 9% to fall again in 1979 until it reached 5.7% in April, 1979. Increased consumer prices and increased unemployment together often lead people to believe that the middleman is making more money and marketing costs are going up. However, although exact figures are not available for the late 1970s, experts feel that marketing costs still run about 50% of each dollar the consumer pays for a product.

The cost of marketing is thought to be too high by many people. A study of marketing, however, indicates that none of the functions can be eliminated. The hope of reducing marketing costs lies not in eliminating marketing functions but in developing better marketing methods.

Consumer prices rose drastically in the 1970 s.

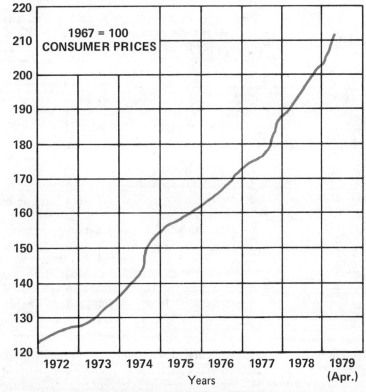

Source: *Survey of Consumer Business* (May, 1979).

FACTS ABOUT MARKETING EVERYBODY SHOULD KNOW

1. Marketing is one of the most important factors in the American economic system; it is one of the keys to a high level of economic living.

2. The marketing process includes everything that happens to economic goods as they move from the producer to the last consumer, with the exception of any significant change in their form.

3. Satisfaction of consumers' wants depends on both the production and the marketing of goods.

4. There are several kinds of markets, each serving a particular function.

5. The functions of marketing can be combined but none can be eliminated.

6. Any person or business concern that performs one or more of the eight marketing functions is a middleman.

7. Middlemen perform necessary marketing services somewhere between the producer and the consumer.

8. Costs of marketing generally are as large as the costs of production. Reduction of marketing costs cannot come from eliminating marketing functions but rather from increased efficiency.

REVIEW QUESTIONS

Section A

1. What is marketing?
2. How does marketing serve both the producer and the consumer?
3. What percentage of our work force is employed in wholesaling and retailing?
4. How does efficient marketing help raise the level of living in our economy?
5. (a) What is consumption? (b) What two conditions must be met before a consumer can obtain and use economic goods?
6. How does marketing create utility?
7. (a) What different meanings does the term "market" have? (b) What are some common examples of marketing institutions?
8. How does a large national market benefit consumers?

Section B

9. What are the eight functions of marketing? Explain each function.
10. What is meant by (a) grading and (b) standardizing?
11. How is demand for goods and services stimulated?
12. (a) What is merchandising? (b) What does it include?
13. What role does financing play in the marketing process?

Section C   14. What is meant by the term "middleman"? Give examples.
15. What is a channel of distribution?
16. What is (a) direct marketing and (b) indirect marketing?
17. What are the four major marketing channels?
18. Are there some marketing services that can be eliminated? Explain.
19. What is the remedy for high marketing costs?

DISCUSSION QUESTIONS

Section A   1. What are some examples from your daily experience of how marketing creates utility?
2. How are demand and possession utility related?
3. What are some examples from your own experience of how wholesale markets help you in making purchases?
4. (a) What is the geographical range of markets? (b) What are some of the products that usually are found in each range?

Section B   5. Of what value to the consumer is the marketing function of standardization and grading? Illustrate by examples.
6. The primary function of selling is to create demand. What is involved in creating demand and how is it accomplished?
7. How does the function of transportation apply in the marketing of citrus fruits?

Section C   8. Are there situations in which we could get along without the services of the wholesaler? Explain your answer.
9. Criticism is often leveled at the middleman. (a) What are the reasons for this criticism? (b) Do you think the criticism is justified?
10. (a) Would it be possible for the middleman to be eliminated on a large scale? (b) What effect would elimination of the middleman have on the economy as a whole?

APPLICATION PROBLEMS

Section A   1. Go to your local discount department store. List 10 products you find on the shelves that are marketed nationally or internationally. Then list 10 products that are marketed on a local, state, or regional basis. If you can't find such goods at one store, try another, not necessarily a department store. What problems did you encounter? What conclusions have you reached while preparing the two lists?

Section B   2. Select a particular product or group of products and describe the marketing process in terms of the marketing functions.

Section C   3. The Mareck Bicycle Repair Shop specializes in repairs and has only a few new bicycles for sale. The retail price of one of them is $75. The cost items related to it are listed on page 84.

Financing of purchase from manufacturer	$ .50
Cost of manufacture	59.50
Transportation	1.50
Uncrating and assembling in shop	1.00
Manufacturer's selling cost (national advertising)	3.00
Insurance in transit	.25
General repair shop operating costs	1.00
Manufacturer's profit	5.00
Advertising in local newspaper	.25

(a) What is the total of cost items that are functions of production?

(b) What percentage of the retail price is this production cost?

(c) What is the total of cost items that are functions of marketing?

(d) What percentage of the retail price is this marketing cost?

(e) Assuming that the items listed are all of Mr. Mareck's costs for the bicycle, what is the amount of his profit if he sells it for $75?

(f) What percentage of the retail price is his profit?

(g) To which of the eight functions of marketing should Mr. Mareck's profit figure be assigned?

COMMUNITY PROJECTS

Section A

1. Among the common types of marketing institutions are (a) wholesale markets, (b) commission markets, (c) auction markets, (d) retail markets, and (e) organized markets (called exchanges) for securities and for commodities. In your area you should be able to find one or more of these five kinds of markets. With the help of your teacher, choose one for study. Begin your study with library materials. Then interview one or more business people involved in the operation of the particular market you chose. Write a report that describes in detail the functions of the market and the special purposes it serves in the marketing process.

Section B

2. Interview a local business person and ask the question "How might marketing costs be reduced through more effective performance of the marketing function?" Provide the business person being interviewed with the list of marketing functions as presented in this chapter. Compare your findings with those of other members of the class.

Section C

3. Make a study of the steps involved in getting a recording by your favorite artist or group to you. Consider what marketing functions have been performed and by whom. Was the artist or group in any way involved in these functions? What kinds of markets were concerned? What marketing channel or channels were used? What was the total cost of the marketing process? Your record dealer may be able to help you answer some of these questions or direct you to other sources of information.

4. Check your local newspaper for direct-to-consumer advertisements, which you will probably find in the classified section. Try to determine if the company offering the goods for sale is actually the manufacturer. Visit a local store or market, if one is available, that claims to engage in direct marketing. Interview the manager to determine if the store is a direct representative of the manufacturer or if some wholesale steps have taken place before the goods reached the store.

Labor-Management Relations in our Free Enterprise Economy

PURPOSE OF THE CHAPTER

Labor and management are two of the most important factors in the successful operation of a free enterprise economy. The success with which they work together will largely determine how well we can all live and have the goods and services we want.

After studying this chapter, you will be able to:

1. Explain what we mean by labor.
2. List the purposes of unions.
3. Define collective bargaining.
4. Discuss how labor and management settle their differences.

A. LABOR MOVEMENT

There are many ideas about what labor is and what the labor movement means. In this section you will have an opportunity to explore these ideas.

Definitions

In economics, the term labor can be viewed in both a broad sense and a restricted sense. Under the broad definition, the term *labor* means all forms of human effort, physical and mental, that provide value to finished products or services. The range of skills involved runs all the way from very unskilled manual or mechanical tasks to such complex skills as those required for brain surgery. The broad definition of labor is the one usually used. Under the restricted definition, however, the term *labor* refers to the kind of labor that is commonly performed by members of organized labor unions. It is the labor involved in the so-called labor movement. The term *labor movement* has gradually come to mean the organization and the activities of labor unions.

Labor Movements and Unions

The labor movement is very old. More than 300 years ago, there were organizations of employees in the simple, small shops of England and other European countries. Paid helpers in these small shops formed organizations to bargain with the owners for better wages and working conditions.

As the labor movement progressed, the goals of employee organizations became greater than simply bargaining with employers. Labor unions sought and succeeded in obtaining political action to gain protection and advantages through legislation. Some of these protections now covered by law involve working conditions, hours of work, and certain other advantages that will be discussed later in this chapter.

Unions are classified in different ways. A discussion of the more common classifications follows.

Guilds. Unions in this country and those in western European nations date back to the stage of industrialization generally described as the guild system. As the agricultural system of large estates crumbled, people moved to towns throughout England and western Europe. They became employed in home workshops where guild organizations developed and gained wide acceptance. There were two types of guild organizations: the *merchant guild* was composed of shopkeepers and retailers, and the *craft guild* was made up of handicraft workers. Craft guilds included three types of members: (1) *masters* — older craftsmen in whose homes the work was performed; (2) *journeymen* — craftsmen employed by masters on a day-wage basis; and (3) *apprentices* — young beginners in the craft, who worked for their room and board while learning about the trade. An apprentice became a journeyman after a period of training. Journeymen could then work for wages in the same shop or in other shops. When they had accumulated sufficient capital, they could set themselves up as masters. Journeymen later formed their own guilds to secure better wages and working conditions from the masters.

Craft or Trade Unions. In a *craft* or *trade union*, the members usually work in a single occupation or in closely related occupations. Plumbers, carpenters, painters, airline pilots, and welders are examples of this type of union. The main advantage claimed for craft unions is that the common interest of members makes for strength and stability.

Industrial Unions. An *industrial union* is composed of all classes of workers in an industry. Examples of this type of union are mine workers, automobile workers, and electrical workers (all types). Industrial unions stress the importance of the underlying interests of all kinds and classes of workers in an industry.

Development of National Labor Organizations

The first permanent national labor oganization, the International Typographical Union, was formed in 1850. It set an example that was soon followed by unions of stonecutters, molders, locomotive engineers, machinists, hatters, and blacksmiths. One of the principal aims of these organizations was to control the supply of workers in the industries represented by the unions.

The formation of unions that developed during the Civil War continued after the war. Many local unions were established in industrial areas. Additional city federations were organized. Several national organizations were established from 1866 to 1881.

AFL, a Federation of Trade Unions. For half a century the underlying ideas of both the American Federation of Labor (AFL) and the railroad brotherhoods (engineers, conductors, firemen, and trainmen) directed and controlled the nature and aims of American unions. This federation of trade unions accepted the idea of a free enterprise economy and did not question the ethical foundations of free enterprise. Except in an incidental way, the Federation and the brotherhoods were not concerned with the social and political welfare of workers and their families, nor were they concerned about the welfare of all workers in general. The Federation sought to further the interests of skilled workers in specific occupations. The railroad brotherhoods restricted their interests to particular groups of workers. Seldom did either organization admit unskilled workers to their memberships.

CIO, a Federation of Industrial Unions. For many years leaders of the American Federation of Labor were divided over the desirability of promoting unions on an industry-wide basis (industrial unions). Some insisted that the guiding aims in the organization of unions should be the nature and characteristics of an industry, not just workers with certain skills. For example, in the automotive industry, it was said that separate unions of machinists, pattern makers, molders, chemists, and toolmakers should not be formed; instead, one union should include all workers in the automotive industry.

A lack of interest on the part of the American Federation of Labor to give more attention to the organization of industrial unions led to the formation of a committee to organize the mass-production industries. It was known as the Committee on Industrial Organization (CIO), and it immediately began a campaign to organize workers in several very important industries. The attempt to organize the automotive, steel, and other industries was successful.

Due to a difference regarding organizational policy, the CIO leaders and their unions were expelled from the AFL in 1938. At this point the committee established an independent federation, which became known as the Congress of Industrial Organizations.

Merger of AFL and CIO. The formation of the CIO in 1938 had several important effects, both on the labor movement and on the public. It caused some of the craft unions in the AFL to liberalize their requirements for admission. Rivalry between the AFL and the CIO caused the leaders of the unions to compete in attempting to win benefits from employers. Competition resulted in jurisdictional disputes (arguments as to which union's members should be permitted to do what types of work) between unions. The jurisdictional disputes led to strikes even though no issue between a union and an employer was involved.

Leaders of both sides recognized that the division among labor unions weakened the strength and progress of organized labor. After a long period of negotiations, a merger of the American Federation of Labor and the Congress of Industrial Organizations was completed on December 5, 1955. Jurisdictional disputes as well as "raiding" of members from one union by another were discouraged. A declared purpose of the AFL-CIO is "to protect the labor movement" from corrupt influence and practices of all kinds, including the efforts of communists to gain control of the unions. The Federation has adopted six Codes of Ethical Practices that apply to the following matters: the issuance of charters to local unions; the handling of health and welfare funds; labor racketeers, communists, and fascists in unions; and the practice of democracy in union affairs.

On the whole, American unions rely on collective bargaining with employers (explained later in this chapter) to achieve their goals. As far as political practices are concerned, unions appear to follow the policy of corporations in rewarding their friends and punishing their enemies.

Local, National, and International Unions

Labor unions are classified not only as trade or industrial unions but also as local, national, or international unions.

Individual members of labor organizations belong to local unions and only indirectly to national and international unions. Some of the large locals include most of the workers in a number of different plants. Many unions employ a *business agent*, who is a full-time employee of the local and acts as its general business manager. *Shop stewards* are usually elected by the departments in unionized establishments. They are not officers of the union. Their chief function is to handle grievances of members with the employer.

Most locals are units in national or international unions. A local union that is a part of the larger union does not have the right of autonomy (independence) that it would otherwise have. The national unions often take the lead in organizing locals. The constitution and the regulations of the locals must observe the general and specific regulations prescribed by the national union. The main functions of the national unions are: (1) to promote and extend union organization by securing additional members for existing locals and to organize new locals; (2) to aid locals in their negotiations with employers; and (3) to represent the local union in the national union, or federation, with which they are affiliated. Some international unions include locals in the United States, Canada, Puerto Rico, and the Canal Zone.

Union Membership

The table on page 90 shows the membership in unions as compared with the total civilian labor force. Union membership increased over the years from about 5 million in 1920 to 21 million in 1977. Over the same time span the total civilian labor force increased from 42 million to 99 million. In 1920 union membership was 12% of the labor force; in 1977 it was 21%.

In early years union membership included only blue-collar trade and industrial union craftsmen. In recent years unions have attracted groups of workers who used to show little interest in unions. For example, about 2.5 million government employees (federal, state, and local) now belong to unions. Workers in white-collar jobs are joining unions in greater numbers, and the number

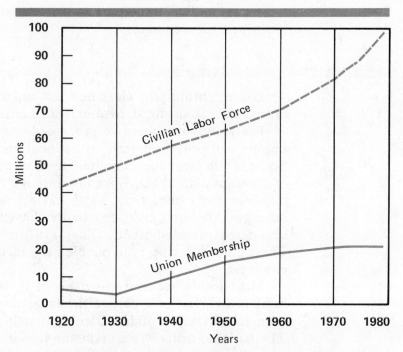

Growth of Civilian Labor Force and Union Membership in the United States, 1920-1977

Sources: *Statistical Abstract of the United States,* 1977.
Survey of Current Business (February, 1978).

of women holding union membership continues to increase. During the 1960s and 1970s a good deal of unionization occurred in the professional occupations, especially in the teaching profession.

Problems Facing Unions in Today's Economic Environment

The primary purpose of unionism in the United States is economics. Unions are designed to provide their membership with higher wages, shorter hours, more vacations, more pleasant work environments, and various fringe benefits such as pensions and health insurance. However, at the national and international level, unions are very active in social legislation. In that sense, unionism extends beyond its membership.

In the late 1970s unions at the local, national, and international level were faced with certain unique problems. Industrial output was down, unemployment was up, and prices were rising. Also, in many segments of the economy, business profits were off substantially. The sluggishness of the economy made it more difficult for unions to achieve the economic advances they would like to have gained for their membership. Consequently, unions argued for a "cost of living adjustment" just as intensely as they did for higher wages, shorter hours, more vacations, and the like. If the cost of living increases 10% in a given year, that, of course, means that a worker's salary must also increase by 10% if the worker is to have the same buying power. Naturally one of the aims of unionism is to retain and improve its membership's earning capacity. Also, when there is a good deal of unemployment, the unions strive to make certain that union members are not laid off their present jobs.

When the economy is growing at a steady or high rate and prices are relatively stable, the unions are in a much better position to bargain with management. During a time of sluggish economic conditions, the unions often have to struggle to keep their membership at an equal level of buying power and to keep the membership employed.

B. COLLECTIVE BARGAINING

Collective bargaining means the bargaining between employers and representatives of organized groups of workers for wages and working conditions. When agreements are lawfully reached, they become binding. Collective bargaining is the central objective of labor unions.

The right to bargain collectively was officially established in 1933 with the passage of the National Industrial Recovery Act. The role of government and the legislation that affects collective bargaining are discussed later in this chapter.

Common Goal of Labor and Management

As indicated previously, labor is interested in obtaining as high a wage as possible (including fringe benefits) under working conditions that are as suitable as they can be. Management, in turn, is also interested in a pleasant working environment as well as in obtaining as much profit as possible. However, both labor and management have a common goal in that they must keep the business operating. If the business is not operating effectively, neither labor nor management will be able to reach its objective. For example, if a business is totally unprofitable, it obviously will be closed down, thus hurting both management and labor. If the business is operated efficiently, then management can share more of the gains with labor. Consequently, it is of common interest to both labor and management to have a well-organized, efficiently operated business.

Collective Bargaining and Industrial Conflict

Why do we have sharp disagreements between employers and employees? Do such arguments indicate a deep-seated, continuing class struggle between property owners and workers? Are such disputes likely to disrupt our society? Who is to blame for them? Are they the result of collective bargaining?

More than 5,000 major disputes occur and about 50 million work-hours are lost each year out of the negotiation or the interpretation of labor contracts. More than 100,000 collective agreements are negotiated each year, an average of almost 300 each day. More than 95% are signed without a work stoppage. Nearly all contracts are carried through to the end of their terms without a strike (work stoppage called by workers) or a lockout (work stoppage called by employers). Although a strike or a lockout is a dramatic form of work stoppage, more labor time is lost in the U.S. by minor illnesses; even the common practice of the coffee break consumes more days each year.

Major Areas for Collective Bargaining

The major areas of collective bargaining include wages, fringe benefits, hours of work, job security, and union security.

Wages. In most bargaining, the central issue brought up by labor is wages. Since prices have, in general, risen throughout the history of the United States, wage increases tend to be a typical part of each new contract that is signed by labor and management.

Wage negotiations are strongly affected by local and national economic conditions. Bargaining points are based on whether cost of living, productivity, and profits are rising or falling; on wages paid in the same general location; and on the national situation. In certain industries that have national significance, such as coal or steel, the government may step in and set certain guideposts for wages and prices.

Fringe Benefits. Not all of the arguments from labor center directly on wages. Labor realizes that it can increase its real level of living by certain fringe benefits such as hospitalization, life insurance, longer paid vacations, pensions, and the like. All of these fringe benefits are discussed as a part of the contract.

The number of fringe benefits has grown rapidly because employers, employees, and public policy favor them. Pensions and other welfare provisions, for example, meet public and individual demands for economic security.

Hours of Work. In recent years the hours of work have also become a factor in collective bargaining. Sometimes a union will be willing to accept a lower rate of pay if the number of work hours per week can be reduced. This approach is particularly true in occupations that pay a relatively high wage and where the labor union membership is willing to make a trade-off of money income for more leisure time.

Also, in recent years it has been common for many labor unions to negotiate for the right to let workers set their own working hours. When such individualization of working hours is not possible, unions have been pushing for a 4-day work week.

Job Security. Job security is of major concern to labor. It is important to unions to be certain that their members will remain employed even at a time when economic conditions are sluggish. Therefore, it is not uncommon for labor to argue against certain types of automation and labor-saving machines that might replace actual laborers. Also, labor is concerned with the procedures for handling grievances, layoffs, disciplinary problems, and possible reinstatement of laborers after they have been laid off.

A contract between labor and management contains specific statements of agreement concerning a number of points.

CONTRACT BETWEEN LABOR AND MANAGEMENT

1. Wages
2. Fringe Benefits
3. Hours
4. Working Conditions
5. Hiring, Firing
6. Procedures for Handling
   A. Grievances
   B. Layoffs
   C. Disciplinary Problems
   D. Reinstatements
7. Contract Negotiations

Union Security. *Union security* means acceptance and recognition of a union by the employer. To achieve as high a degree of security as possible for themselves, unions bargain collectively as to type of representation and type of shop to be in effect.

Type of representation means just which employees are to be represented by the union. The type of representation determines whether the union is the bargaining agent for members only or is the sole bargaining agent for all employees, including non-members.

Type of shop means the status of the business in regard to contractual freedom to employ nonunion workers. The type of shop ranges from the open shop to the closed or union shop. In an *open shop*, the employer is free to hire employees without reference to union membership. In an *agency shop*, all employees in the bargaining unit pay dues to the union, although they do not have to join it. In a *preferential shop*, the employer is required to give special consideration to union members in hiring, layoffs, or promotions. In a *union shop*, any nonunion worker who is employed is required to become a member of the union at the end of a specified probationary period. In a *closed shop*, the employer is not allowed to employ nonunion workers.

WORK STOPPAGES BY MAJOR ISSUES
Work-Days Idle (in 000's) 1973–1978

Issue	Work-Days Idle					
	1973	1974	1975	1976	1977	1978
General Wage Changes & Wage Adjustments	17,115	39,369	22,586	24,341	na	na
Fringe Benefits	1,067	1,104	278	189	na	na
Hours of Work	14	444	10	57	na	na
Job Security	2,445	1,543	3,154	7,187	na	na
Union Security	3,378	1,841	1,488	2,455	na	na
Plant Administration	2,771	2,341	2,884	2,777	na	na
All Other Issues	1,158	1,349	837	853	na	na
Total Work-Days Idle	27,948	47,991	31,237	37,859	35,822	33,714
% of Total Estimated Working Time	.14	.24	.16	.19	.17	.15

The major issues behind most work stoppages relate to wages and security. Despite the large number of work-days idle each year due to stoppages, it represents only a very small fraction (%) of total working time, usually less than 2/10 of 1%.

Sources: Adapted from *Statistical Abstract of the United States*, 1978, and *Monthly Labor Review*, July, 1979.

The Taft-Hartley Act of 1947 made closed shops unlawful for unions that operate in more than one state. In addition, both the closed shop and the union shop were unlawful in 20 states in 1978 under state laws.[1]

Methods Used by Organized Labor

The employment relation between unions and management is friendly most of the time, and differences of opinions are settled by peaceful negotiation. Sometimes the failure of unions and management to reach an agreement results in the use of drastic methods by either side. Both unions and employers have used a number of methods to gain their goals. The methods that have been used by organized labor include: (1) strikes, (2) picketing, (3) boycotts, (4) restriction of output, and (5) propaganda and political pressure.[2]

Strikes. A *strike* is a temporary stoppage of work by a group of employees for the purpose of compelling an employer to agree to their demands. By stopping work, strikers feel they do not cease to occupy the status of employees and do not forfeit the right to return to their jobs when the dispute that led to the strike has been settled. Employers often feel that employees who leave their jobs quit their jobs; therefore, employers should be free to fill the positions with new employees. Any attempt by employers to fill positions vacated by strikers, of course, is opposed by the striking employees.

Upon the expiration of a contract between the union and the employer, the union may adopt the method of "no contract — no work" and refuse to permit its members to work until the employer renews the contract or signs a new one. The union in this case is likely to argue that the work stoppage is not a strike.

A *direct strike* is one that is aimed against the employer and does not involve a third party. A *sympathetic strike* is one that does not arise from a grievance against the employer: its purpose is to assist other employees in a dispute with their employer.

---

[1]The 20 states are Alabama, Arizona, Arkansas, Florida, Georgia, Iowa, Kansas, Louisiana, Mississippi, Nebraska, Nevada, North Carolina, North Dakota, South Carolina, South Dakota, Tennessee, Texas, Utah, Virginia, and Wyoming.

[2]Sit-down strikes, sabotage, hit-and-run strikes, and coercive picketing are not considered since they have been illegal for many years. Sympathetic strikes, general strikes, wildcat strikes, slowdown strikes, mass and cross picketing, secondary boycotts and picketing, and other similar practices are controlled and often are unlawful under the Landrum-Griffin Act of 1959.

A *general strike* is one that involves the workers in all industries in a city, region, or other large area, but it should be distinguished from strikes that are *industry-wide* in their scope. The general strike (as with the sympathetic strike) is conducted to achieve common aims of workers in different industries. The industry-wide strike, however, is carried out for the purpose of achieving or maintaining a system of collective bargaining on some issue in a given industry.

Jurisdictional strikes arise out of a dispute between rival unions, and not because of a dispute with the employer. For example, a dispute between carpenters and steelworkers belonging to different unions may arise as to which union is entitled to perform a certain kind of work. A *wildcat strike* occurs when the members of a local union quit work without authorization by the national union with which the local is affiliated.

A *slowdown* is a form of strike that occurs when employees stay on the job but agree among themselves to restrict the amount of work they perform.

Picketing. A *union picket* is a person stationed near the entrance of a place of employment by a labor organization during a dispute with the employer. The process is called *picketing*. The usual functions of pickets are: (1) to inform other employees, any prospective employees, and the public that a dispute exists; (2) to persuade nonstrikers to join in the strike; and (3) to discourage anyone from entering the place for the purpose of working.

Mass picketing is the parading or assembling of a considerable number of strikers before the workplace for the same purposes as indicated above and in order to emphasize the strike or to provide a display of strength in opposition to workers who refuse to recognize the strike. *Cross picketing* occurs when pickets of rival unions claim to represent a majority of workers in a struck plant. *Secondary picketing* takes place against a second employer who may be doing business with the employer against whom the employees are striking.

Boycotts. A *boycott* is defined as a mass effort to withdraw and to influence others to withdraw from business relations with an employer. Sometimes a distinction is made between a primary and a secondary boycott. The *primary boycott* is one in which the workers agree not to patronize a firm because of their own complaint against the management. The *secondary boycott* is an action by a labor union whereby the union (not involved in the dispute) forbids its members to work for or to have any dealing with a concern whose employees are on strike.

Restriction of Output. *Restriction of output* refers to the withholding of a reasonable amount of effort on the part of workers. *Featherbedding* is the employment of more workers than are needed to perform the work and is usually required by union statutes or safety restrictions. Employees and labor organizations may feel that it is fair to use restrictions for the protection of workers, but employers feel the practice is used for the purpose of cheating them.

Unions may restrict output in various ways. A painter's union may place a limit on the width of the brush its members may use. A bricklayer's union may establish what it considers to be the reasonable number of bricks that a member may lay in a given time.

Regardless of the reasons for restricting output, the result is a reduction in goods and services produced. Consequently, such practices lead to a lower level of living for society as a whole.

Propaganda and Political Pressure. Labor unions make every effort to create favorable public opinion, particularly during a labor dispute. Picketing is one device used, plus public statements, radio and television programs, and handbills. Only when the public suffers inconvenience from a dispute between employers and employees is it greatly concerned. Even then, the primary interest of the public may not be in the cause of the difficulty or in the way the dispute should be settled.

In common with other organized groups, unions attempt to secure the passage of laws that will give labor the legal rights and protection that the unions feel are needed. Both in Congress and in the state legislatures organized labor has striven for the enactment of laws that would guarantee the right of collective bargaining and of engaging in certain labor union activities.

Methods Used by Employers

Although unions generally are the aggressors and employers the defensive unit in collective bargaining, employers have used the following practices in labor disputes: (1) injunctions, (2) lockouts, (3) strikebreakers, and (4) propaganda and political pressure.[3]

Injunctions. An *injunction* is an order from a court commanding an individual or a group to do or to refrain from doing an act or acts. According to the theory of the injunction, damage may

---

[3]The blacklist, yellow-dog contract, company union, and industrial espionage, which were formally used by employers, are not considered because they have been declared clearly illegal. The use of injunctions, lockouts, and strikebreakers is limited under federal and state laws.

result from the acts of individuals or groups for which there would be no adequate remedy, such as economic damages. Those who disobey an injunction are also liable to be sued for any damages to property that they may have caused. The injunction is used when an employer feels that the union is doing or is about to do something that is illegal and that will result in damage to the employer.

Lockouts. A *lockout* is a temporary stopping of the operation of a business by an employer in an attempt to win a dispute with employees. It is the employer's equivalent of the strike. In terms of the number of occurrences, the lockout is a relatively unimportant device because employers seldom shut down their plants in order to force a settlement with labor.

Strikebreakers. A *strikebreaker* is a person hired by an employer to replace a striking employee. Some states have laws that establish certain conditions under which employees may be hired to take the place of striking workers. Under federal law it is illegal to transport strikebreakers across state boundaries.

Propaganda and Political Pressure. Employers and employers' associations seek the help of public opinion in the settlement of industrial disputes. They also seek to secure the passage of laws that will not discriminate against them in their relations with their employees. In the case of a strike that affects a whole community or interrupts business to a considerable extent, employers and associations to which they may belong are likely to place their case before the public in newspaper advertisements.

To secure the enactment or retention of laws, employer groups often distribute printed materials with arguments for or against laws concerning labor relations in industry. Like the large labor organizations, employer groups attempt to prevent enactment of laws that are unfavorable to their own interests and to enact laws that are favorable. A case in point is the so-called "right-to-work" laws in effect in 20 states. Basically, these state "right-to-work" laws eliminate closed shops and union shops by specifying that no one shall be required to join a union to get a job or to keep a job. Employers (and many employees) support "right-to-work" laws; unions oppose them.

Economic Impact of Long Strikes

As indicated previously, most disagreements between labor and management are solved without a work stoppage. The ratio of work hours lost to the total worked has averaged only ¼ of 1%

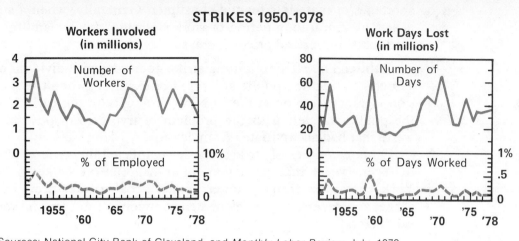

STRIKES 1950-1978

Workers Involved (in millions)

Work Days Lost (in millions)

Sources: National City Bank of Cleveland, and *Monthly Labor Review*, July, 1979.

Over the past 25 years, only 3.3% of employed workers have been involved in strikes and the ratio of work hours lost to total hours worked was only ¼ of 1%.

over the past 25 years. However, when long strikes are involved, there are some significant economic impacts on labor, management, consumers, and the general public.

Labor. The economic impact on labor in a long strike is rather obvious. In time, the funds available through the union disappear and unemployed workers also use up their eligibility for unemployment compensation. Frequently this means that workers will have to take other positions and generally at lower rates of pay than they would be making at their current jobs. A prolonged strike can significantly lower the level of living for the laborer and the members of the laborer's family.

Management. The economic effects of a long strike are equally obvious to management. When no productivity is taking place, the business loses income and profits. More than that, there are certain fixed expenses that must continue to be paid, such as building maintenance, mortgage and debt payments, and property taxes. A long work stoppage might actually force a business firm out of existence.

Consumer. The consumer is affected by all phases of collective bargaining. For example, when it is possible for management to pass on higher wage costs in the form of higher prices for its product, the consumer is directly involved. A long strike means shortages of materials for the consumer. Generally, when a strike is settled after a long period of work stoppage, the demand for the product is higher and prices increase.

Public. The effect of a long strike goes beyond individual consumers to affect the public at large. For example, when the sanitation workers were on strike in New York City in the early 1970s, the public was left with the problem of trying to dispose of the waste that had accumulated from day-to-day living.

Other examples of strikes that have affected the general public in recent years include a general transportation strike in New York City, numerous teacher strikes, coal strike, firefighters' strike, and several instances of strikes involving nurses and medical doctors.

C. PUBLIC POLICY ON LABOR AND MANAGEMENT

Although labor and management are relatively free in the United States to come to their agreements through collective bargaining, public policy sometimes influences the result of the final contract.

National Labor Relations Legislation

In the early years of our country's existence, government tended to take a fairly strong antilabor stand. In 1890, when the Sherman Antitrust Act was passed, it made certain monopolistic restraints of trade illegal. Actually the act did not mention labor unions at all; but until 1914 the formation of a union was often ruled in the courts to be illegal as a "restraint of trade." In 1914, the right of laborers to organize was recognized in the Clayton Antitrust Act, which was an updating of the Sherman Act.

Some of the significant legislation that supported unionization and collective bargaining included the Railway Labor Act of 1926, which established the right of unions to bargain collectively with management. In 1932, the Norris-LaGuardia Act more openly recognized the rights of unions to bargain collectively. In 1935, the Walsh-Healey Act established minimum wage standards for all government contracts. In 1938, the Fair Labor Standards Act sought a minimum wage for most nonfarm workers engaged in interstate commerce.

The most significant act that supported labor's right to unionize and bargain collectively was the National Labor Relations

(Wagner) Act of 1935. This act stated clearly that employees had the right "to self organization, to form, join, or assist in labor organizations, and to bargain collectively through representatives of their own choosing." It also set up the National Labor Relations Board to regulate "unfair labor practices" against labor.

A number of strikes that occurred after World War II led to the Labor-Management Relations (Taft-Hartley) Act of 1947. This act is viewed by most labor representatives as antilabor legislation. The act set forth certain standards of conduct for unions as well as for employers. The act established that strikes which "imperil the national health or safety" may be suspended by an 80-day court injunction. The act also states that unions must give a 60-day notice before any strike. Under the provisions of the act, it also became clear that unions could be sued and held responsible for the acts of their agents.

In 1958, the Taft-Hartley Act was amended by the Landrum-Griffin Act, which took out some of the harshness of the earlier act as it related to labor. The 1960s and 1970s found state and federal legislation expanded to include minimum wage laws, compulsory workman's accident compensation insurance, compulsory unemployment and old-age pension insurance, regulation of working hours, control over the working environment, and the like. In the early 1970s, wage and price increases were "frozen" for a short time; in the late 1970s, presidential "guidelines" for wage and price increases were set.

Role of Government in Labor-Management Relations

In our nation, we have recognized the danger that some of the issues arising out of employment might divide our citizens, create lawlessness and violence, and thus threaten the peace and security of society. We are trying through collective bargaining to develop procedures for settling most differences. Formal grievance procedures, arbitration, conciliation and mediation, and cooling-off periods are examples of these methods. We have tried to minimize the role that government agencies play in actually deciding issues.

To prevent unrest and misunderstanding, there is a way of handling complaints and disputes originated by workers or unions called a *grievance procedure*. A written grievance procedure is often part of the union contract between the employer and the union.

When disputes cannot be settled by mutual agreement or negotiation, the next step is often *arbitration*. In this process the dispute is submitted to a third person or group of persons agreed

Typical Grievance Procedure Under Union Contracts

	8	A government mediator or an arbitrator may help settle the dispute.
	7	Higher union and company officials intervene.
	6	National union agency may negotiate with grievance committee.
	5	Higher authority such as personnel manager intervenes.
	4	If problem is not settled, steward goes to management, chief plant steward, or grievance committee.
	3	Steward and employee talk to foreman.
	2	Steward talks to shop foreman.
	1	Employee reports on complaints to shop steward.

upon by both sides. Such a person is called an *arbitrator*. The arbitrator's decision must be accepted by both labor and management.

In some labor disputes, a government agent, called a *mediator*, meets with labor and management to help reach an agreement. This procedure is called *conciliation* or *mediation*. The mediator has no power but merely attempts to bring both parties into agreement. The federal government in some situations has the legal power to require a *cooling-off period* (delay) before a strike.

To encourage negotiation and reduce conflict, society has tried to narrow the area of possible disagreement between the parties in collective bargaining. We maintain public agencies to establish the general rules and to answer certain types of questions for the parties.

Public agencies are taking an active part in many employment relationships. Representatives of the federal agencies are checking on hours of work and wage rates. State agencies are checking working conditions and the jobs held by young workers. Federal, state, and local fair-employment-practice laws have made it illegal to discriminate in employment based on race, nationality, sex, age, or religion.

ROLE OF GOVERNMENT IN LABOR-MANAGEMENT RELATIONS

1. Interpreting and enforcing the rules of collective bargaining.

2. Assisting in the prevention and settlement of labor-management disputes through conciliation and mediation.

3. Setting standards of minimum wages and maximum hours in both public and private employment.

4. Setting and maintaining standards of safety and health in working conditions by such means as factory inspection and safety programs.

5. Preventing child labor and hazardous employment.

6. Enforcing standards of training for apprentices and assisting in apprenticeship programs.

7. Preventing discrimination based on race, religion, sex, age, or nationality.

REVIEW QUESTIONS

Section A

1. What does the term "labor" mean in economics?
2. What is meant by the term "labor movement"?
3. In the early days of the labor movement, what were some goals of labor in addition to bargaining with employers?
4. What are (a) masters, (b) journeymen, and (c) apprentices?
5. What is (a) a craft or trade union and (b) an industrial union?
6. What is (a) a business agent and (b) a shop steward?
7. What are the main functions of national unions?
8. What is the primary purpose of unionism in the United States?

Section B

9. What is collective bargaining?
10. What are the common goals of labor and management in collective bargaining?
11. What are the major areas of collective bargaining?
12. What are fringe benefits?
13. What is meant by job security?
14. (a) What is meant by union security?
    (b) What are some methods of getting union security?
15. What are some of the methods used by organized labor to gain objectives?
16. What are the usual functions of picketing?
17. What are some of the methods used by employers to oppose unions in disputes?
18. What is the economic impact of long strikes on (a) labor, (b) management, (c) the consumer, and (d) the public?

Section C
19. In what way did labor legislation change from the early days of our country to the present time?
20. (a) What is meant by the term "grievance procedure"?
    (b) What roles do public agencies play in labor relations?
21. What role does government play in labor-management relations?

DISCUSSION QUESTIONS

Section A
1. What is the difference between the term "labor force" and the term "labor movement"?
2. Is there any organization in existence today that might be compared to the old craft guild?
3. What were the main differences that existed between the American Federation of Labor and the Committee on Industrial Organization?

Section B
4. Assume that an employer talks to an employee and offers him or her an inducement not to join a labor union. Is this a legal act? Explain.
5. One of the arguments against collective bargaining is that unions tend to destroy loyalty of employees to the employer. What is your opinion?
6. Under many union contracts all workers are paid the same wage in each classification even though their abilities and productivity may not be the same. What do you think of this practice?
7. Who pays the cost of fringe benefits?
8. From the point of view of economics, is it sound to continue to reduce the length of the workday and the workweek?
9. What are your arguments for or against the union shop?
10. How do jurisdictional disputes hurt almost everyone in society?
11. What are some arguments for and against featherbedding?
12. What is the difference between a strike and a lockout? Indicate the fairness of each.
13. What are "right-to-work" laws?

Section C
14. (a) What are some of the advantages of arbitration?
    (b) What are some of the disadvantages of arbitration?
15. How do economic conditions affect the role of government in labor-management relations?
16. Why do you suppose local, state, and federal governments are more involved in labor legislation today than in the early days of our country?

APPLICATION PROBLEMS

Section A
1. Using the current edition of the *Statistical Abstract of the United States* or any other source available through your school or community library, update the chart on union membership that is presented on page 90. Then answer the following questions:
    (a) What percentage of the civilian labor force is union membership in each year of your update?
    (b) Is union membership as a percentage of the civilian labor force increasing or decreasing? Why do you think this is so?

Section B

2. A machine operator making one small part of a larger product is paid at the rate of $3.10 per hour for an 8-hour day. The employer plans to establish a piecework wage plan whereby the machine operator would receive $.075 for each piece produced. If the operator produces an average of 300 pieces a day, thinking only in terms of income, is it probable that the worker will be happy or unhappy about the change? Why?

3. In a recent year 1,590,000 workers were involved in strikes or other work stoppages related to labor disputes. The work days lost were 22,700,000.
    (a) If the working day was 8 hours, how many hours were lost?
    (b) If the average wage was $2.40 per hour, how much in wages did the workers lose?
    (c) How much did each worker lose (average) based upon the previous figures?
    (d) If each worker gained an increase of 10 cents an hour as a result of the strike, what amount of time must be worked to gain back what was lost?
    (e) From the figures available for the latest year (if directed by your teacher) compute (a), (b), (c), and (d) above.

4. In the Astro Manufacturing Company the fringe benefits average: vacations, holidays, and sick leave, 56 cents an hour; Christmas bonus, 3.4 cents an hour; social security and state benefit programs, 34.6 cents an hour; insurance, pensions, and other welfare programs, 26 cents an hour.
    (a) What is the employer's total cost per hour for fringe benefits?
    (b) If the average wage is $3.20 per hour, the fringe benefits are what percentage of wages?

Section C

5. In a recent year the National Labor Relations Board settled 41,100 cases. These cases were classified as follows:

Unfair labor practices	27,016
Representation	13,542
Union shop deauthorization	192
Miscellaneous	350

What percentage of the total cases settled does each of these classifications represent?

COMMUNITY PROJECTS

Section A

1. Either as an individual assignment or as part of a team, prepare a report on unions in your community. Include types of unions, the number of unions, and the total union membership in your community. Your local telephone directory might provide you with the names and office addresses of unions. If a union office exists in your community, an interview with a labor union official might be an excellent place to begin this research. If you are not aware of any unions operating in your community, you might seek advice from your librarian or from a leading business person as to sources of information.

2. Prepare a report on the current status of the AFL-CIO on a nationwide basis. Include the names of member unions, the latest membership figures, current trends in membership drives, current contract negotiations, or any other current news of union activity.

Section B

3. With the help of your teacher, select a business in your community that offers fringe benefits to its employees. From the owner, manager, or personnel director of that firm, find out what kinds of benefits are provided for its employees. Write a report in which you show how the fringe benefits offered would influence your decision to work or not to work for that firm.

4. Most workers have had problems with job security. They were uncertain whether they could progress at their jobs or even hold onto them. Ask two workers you know whether they have had such problems. Find out if their difficulties were with management, labor, or both. List their reasons.

5. The following practices, which are now illegal, were once used by organized labor to obtain their demands: sit-down strike, hit-and-run strike, sabotage, and coercive picketing. Through library research, identify each of these practices and give an example of when and how each was used.

6. The following practices, which are now illegal, were once used by employers to counter labor demands: the blacklist, yellow-dog contract, and industrial espionage. Through library research, identify each of these practices and give an example of when and how each was used.

Section C

7. As an individual project or as part of a group effort, interview two or more local industrialists or two or more local labor leaders to learn whether arbitration and mediation have been practiced in your community. Make a list of the situations in which arbitrators or mediators were used and the results obtained. Present your findings to the class.

Role of Government in our Free Enterprise Economy

PURPOSE OF THE CHAPTER

Government plays a large role in our economic system. The broad nature of governmental controls and services are discussed in this chapter. Other aspects of the role of government are treated in later chapters.

After studying this chapter, you will be able to:

1. Discuss the growth of government services.
2. Identify who pays for and controls government services.
3. List the special services of government.
4. Discuss how government aids business and agriculture.

A. GROWTH AND NATURE OF GOVERNMENT'S ROLE

In the early days of our country, government services consisted of a few basic but important services designed primarily to protect the individual and the country. Over time, government services have grown to a large number and variety designed to satisfy many special groups of citizens.

Growth of Government Services

When the federal government was established in 1776, its functions were limited primarily to: (1) passing laws for the common good, (2) protecting the rights of every person, (3) maintaining national security through control of foreign affairs and defense, (4) controlling interstate commerce, and (5) coining money and establishing its value. As population increased and business activity grew, demand increased on the part of relatively small groups of citizens for the government to provide special services for them. Some groups wanted government financial aid. Other people wanted regulations to govern competitive practices. Still other people wanted regulations to promote economic growth and stabilization. Today the federal, state, and local governments offer a wide range of services. Some of these services benefit all people and others benefit small groups or individuals.

The growth in government employment and services has shown a steady increase over the years. In 1955 one in every seven jobs was provided through federal, state, and local governments. In 1979 almost one in every five jobs was provided through government. That may not sound like a large increase in government employment of workers, but it is actually an increase of 40% in twenty-five years. The government is the country's biggest employer, consumer, and borrower. In recent years, local and state government employment has been rising at a more rapid rate than federal government employment. Much of this has been due to increased spending for education.

GOVERNMENT EMPLOYMENT
(Civilian only)
(in Millions)

	1955	1965	1975	1979
Local	3.6	5.7	8.8	9.30
State	1.2	2.0	3.2	3.45
National	2.1	2.3	2.8	2.75
Total	6.9	10.0	14.8	15.5

Sources: *Statistical Abstract of the United States*, 1978.
Survey of Current Business (May, 1979).

Who Pays for Government Services? Some people assume that a service provided by government is free because they do not specifically pay cash at the time they use the service. However, such services are not free. The cost must be paid from public income, which comes from taxes paid by both businesses and individuals.

The more services we obtain at public expense and the higher the cost of government services, the more taxes we pay. When we consider buying an article for personal use, we ask ourselves whether we need it and whether we can afford it. However, when we request our legislators to vote for another service or a for a new building or bridge, do we consider the question of whether we and

Jefferson-Pilot Corporation, Greensboro, NC

Payment of taxes for the general good of the people provides for such essential government services as police protection.

other consumers are willing and able to pay for it by paying higher taxes? Some elected legislators promote certain ideas, not because they have been requested to do so, but because of an attempt to get votes. The decision about buying government services faces individuals (citizens) directly when they vote on federal, state, and local tax issues.

As the government's role increases, so does the cost of providing government services. In 1955, 28 cents out of every dollar of the national income was paid to the government to provide services. In 1978, 59 cents of every dollar of national income was paid in taxes to the government to provide services.

Who Controls Government Services? As citizens in a representative form of government, we have the privilege of participating in making the regulations and rules by which we are governed. We participate intelligently in government when we vote for legislators whose points of view about government we know and approve.

Our interest is to see not only that our government provides services for the general good of people, but also that it provides service and special benefits that are essential. Once a government service is provided at public expense, all consumers help pay for it through taxes and sometimes through higher prices even though many of them may not need or want the service.

What Are the Issues? Most Americans believe that government should produce only those services that are not or cannot be provided by individuals and private enterprise. Such services include national defense, police and fire protection, conservation of natural resources, general hospitals, public health, education, and institutions for unfortunate people.

The broad issues relate to: (1) the amount of freedom we want instead of controls, (2) the amount of services and help we want and need instead of self-help, and (3) whether we want to decide how to spend our money or instead let the government take it from us in taxes and decide for us how to spend it. Since we live in a representative democracy, we have the power to decide these issues for ourselves.

Government Performs Many Services

If you were the only person who lived in the United States, you would be entirely independent: your work, your actions, and even your thoughts would not affect anyone else. At the same time you would be wholly dependent on yourself. You would have to protect yourself. You could turn to no one for help, nor could you exchange commodities with others. No need would exist for laws or regulations. Likewise, there would be no need for government services.

Dependence on Government. In a society, people help each other. They cooperate in making and doing things that would be difficult or impossible to accomplish alone. Under a system of specialization or division of labor, people become dependent on one another and on government and business to supply the services and the goods wanted. The more complex the problems of working and living together, the greater is the need for government.

Services for Special Groups. While all government services are intended to serve society in general, some groups of citizens benefit directly from certain services and others benefit only indirectly. Old-age assistance, Medicare, unemployment insurance, subsidies to defense and transportation industries, and price supports for certain farm products are examples of services or benefits to special groups. (Subsidies and price supports are discussed on pages 115–117.) In some instances we have a moral obligation to take care of special groups of people, such as old people and people who for some legitimate reason do not have an income. As will

SERVICES BY LOCAL, STATE, AND FEDERAL GOVERNMENTS

1. Police, fire, military, and coast guard service.
2. Legal title records.
3. Health and sanitation.
4. Garbage collection and sewage disposal.
5. Inspection of goods: weights, standards, quality.
6. Schools, universities, and research laboratories.
7. Flood control programs.
8. Postal service.
9. Public transportation service.
10. Courts, prisons, and jails.
11. Welfare and relief agencies.
12. Mental hospitals and institutions for care of the handicapped.
13. Water, electric, and gas systems.
14. Street lighting and cleaning.
15. Maintenance of streets, sidewalks, highways, bridges, and waterways.
16. Parks and recreational activities.
17. Civic museums, auditoriums, and libraries.
18. Harbors and terminals.
19. Unemployment insurance and old-age pensions.
20. Inspection of building construction.
21. Licensing and regulating for consumer protection.
22. Forestry and reclamation service.
23. Employment service.
24. Price supports and subsidies.
25. Bank deposit insurance.
26. Information and consultation services.
27. Work projects to ease unemployment.
28. Food stamp program.
29. Housing development for low-income people.
30. Financial aid to depressed industries.
31. Tax relief to encourage research and development in certain industries.

be explained later in the chapter, aids by government to special groups of producers, like farmers or aircraft workers, may be for the general economic welfare of the nation.

Services for the Public. Some of the services provided by government are not necessarily for individuals but are provided for all of the people collectively. Inspection of food-processing plants to insure clean and wholesome food is an example of a service for the good of all people. The use by consumers of many government facilities, such as employment service and parks, is voluntary. A few services, such as provisions for social security, are compulsory for those persons to whom the laws apply.

The National Weather Service of the U.S. Dept. of Commerce provides valuable information. Here radar surveillance detects areas of rain within a 125-mile radius.

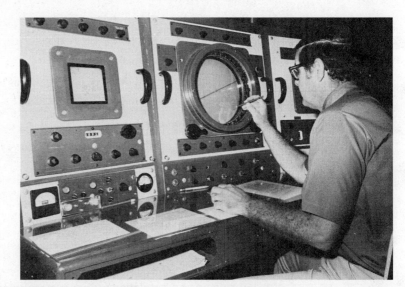

National Weather Service, Greater Cincinnati Airport

Government Engages in Business

Ordinarily we think of commodities and services as being produced for profit under competitive conditions by individuals and private enterprises. Upon examination, however, we find that many services and some commodities are produced by the government without profit and under noncompetitive conditions. For example, local governments often provide transportation services; state governments provide parks and recreational activities; and the federal government provides unemployment insurance and old-age pensions. The list of examples could be greatly expanded. Some of the services provided through government would be very difficult for a private industry to provide. For example, it would be

The federal government develops and operates electric power sources and provides for flood control, irrigation, and land reclamation.

Bureau of Reclamation, Dept. of the Interior

difficult for private industry to provide for our national defense. Certain other services could, however, be provided through private industry if we wished to have them done that way. Transportation services, garbage collection, libraries, museums, and a number of services could be provided through private industry.

In some instances, private business is unable to finance the development of projects, such as the St. Lawrence Seaway or the International Bank. Thus, the development, ownership, and operation of some businesses and facilities is possible only by the government.

The government has sometimes become a producer by doing research and experimentation that developed new products. Aluminum, synthetic rubber, and synthetic gasoline are products that the government has helped to develop experimentally and to produce at least in the initial stages. In many cases private business later bought these businesses from the government.

Also, the government actually owns certain capital goods and operates businesses. For example, it owns much of the capital equipment that is used in the defense industries and a number of dams that are used for irrigation projects. A specific example of government as a producer is the Tennessee Valley Authority, which provides electrical services for a large geographic region in the Tennessee Valley location. Also, one could ask to what degree a firm like Lockheed Aircraft Corporation is really private since more than 90% of its output goes to the government.

B. SPECIFIC AIDS AND CONTROLS

In this section you will be introduced to aids and controls provided to different sections of the economy by the government.

Government Aids to Business and Agriculture

Government aids and controls in business and agriculture are too numerous to permit discussion of all of them. Illustrations of only the major types of aid will be given.

Aids to Management. One type of service to business is the gathering, compiling, and distributing of statistics and information relative to payrolls, wages, prices, volume of production, finance, costs, and many similar aspects of businesses. These data are collected by such agencies as the Department of Commerce, the Bureau of Labor Statistics, and the Federal Reserve Board. Similar aids, such as marketing and research services of the United States Department of Agriculture, are provided for the management of agricultural production and marketing.

Protective Aids to Business and Agriculture. The Bureau of Standards gives an invaluable service to business by testing materials and establishing standards. Many divisions of the Department of the Interior and the Department of Agriculture primarily serve producers. Additional aids to business include navigation

The Bureau of Standards gives invaluable service to business by testing materials and establishing standards.

National Bureau of Standards

services on rivers or lakes, weather reports, financial services through the Federal Reserve Bank, and protection of honest business people from dishonest competitors.

Government Aids for Industrial Development. Following World War II, the Reconstruction Finance Corporation loaned millions of dollars to railroads, banks, insurance companies, and manufacturing companies when loans from other sources were virtually impossible to obtain. During World War II many industries that engaged in war production were *subsidized* (financially helped) by the federal government. In some cases the government has built steamships and leased them to private owners at a price that enabled the owners to operate them. This is a form of *subsidy*. The first synthetic rubber plants were financed by the government and operated by private industry. The rubber was urgently needed; and since private industry could not produce it at a profit, the federal government assisted. Airlines, railroads, and steamship companies have, in some cases, been subsidized in the form of very liberal compensation for carrying mail. More recently, the government has been assisting aircraft manufacturers and bailing out bankrupt railroad companies.

The aids to business paid by the federal government have often been overlooked or taken for granted. It is becoming apparent, at least in the transportation industry, that it is getting harder and harder for private businesses to operate at sufficient profits. In the 1970s, for example, when Pennsylvania Railroad went bankrupt, the government subsidized it to continue certain aspects of its operation. Also, the government very heavily subsidizes mass transit systems in major cities.

When a product or service is subsidized, the consumer supports that subsidy through both higher prices and higher taxes.

Another type of government subsidy is provided through tax relief, which enables businesses to engage in research and development in their own industry. For example, the government has provided tax incentives for oil and gas research and development, pollution control equipment, and automobiles that will operate efficiently while using less gasoline.

Subsidies to Agriculture. Government aid to some phases of business is more direct and more concrete than that of providing statistical information and determining standards. For example, in an effort to guarantee a respectable income to the producers of such commodities as potatoes, eggs, butter, and cotton, the government may regulate the prices of these commodities. The government does this by buying and storing or otherwise disposing of sufficiently large quantities of the products to keep prices at a level satisfactory to the producer. Without government control, if potatoes or eggs are plentiful, the market price drops. As a result, the consumer is able to buy potatoes or eggs at a very low price, but the return to the producer is too low to make a reasonable profit. Under government control of prices, the market price is maintained at a relatively high level, from which the producers of the commodity benefit by realizing a better income. Also, the government stockpiles food to ease world starvation by providing aid in the form of food to poor nations.

Price Supports. The theory of subsidizing business and agriculture is that such aid is needed for the general economic welfare. For example, it is held that the welfare of the whole country is benefited by protecting the farmer. However, business and individuals pay for help to industry and agriculture. They pay taxes that are used for subsidies. They may pay twice: (1) higher prices caused by government support of prices and (2) taxes used by government to support prices.

Price supports and subsidies for special groups of producers, whether farmers or manufacturers or distributors, are of vital interest to the public. They are beneficial to individuals in that some products and services would not be available if the producers were not protected by price supports or did not benefit from subsidies.

However, price supports and subsidies may not always benefit the public. The citizen-voter must decide whether subsidies — for example, to tobacco growers to produce a product that is dangerous to health — are in the best interest of the public.

The issues of particular interest to consumers are many. Shall the producers of some kinds of products and services be subsidized or protected and other producers not? Shall the volume of production of some products be limited to reduce supply and thus hold prices at a certain level for those products but not for others? Is subsidizing the producers of certain products in accord with the basic principle of competition in a free enterprise economy?

GOVERNMENT AIDS TO BUSINESS AND AGRICULTURE THAT AFFECT CONSUMER PRICES AND TAXES

1. Provides owners and managers with statistics and other facts valuable in management.

2. Protects business by offering testing services and by helping to establish commodity standards.

3. Subsidizes and otherwise aids businesses in the development of new types of industries.

4. Subsidizes manufacturers or producers of certain products to enable them to continue in operation.

5. Protects business from unfair competition and from the unethical practices of competitors.

Government Regulation of Business

Laws that regulate business are designed to protect honest business people from unscrupulous competitors and to protect consumers from dishonest business people and from bad business practices among competing businesses. These laws prevent: (1) control of prices and supply by certain businesses, (2) unsatisfactory working conditions, (3) fraud through the mail, (4) adulterated and misbranded foods, (5) false and deceptive advertising practices, and (6) many other undesirable conditions that will be discussed in more detail in later chapters.

Although business owners and managers generally regard government regulation as interference, they recognize that certain regulations are necessary and desirable. Their primary concern is that only necessary regulations be authorized, that these regulations be reasonable, and that they be fairly administered.

Labor, taxes, competition, credit, money, banking, insurance, securities, prices, agriculture, natural resources, transportation, education, safety, health, and almost all aspects of our economic life are regulated by law. You have already seen how labor has been affected by law. In later chapters you will learn more about government laws affecting these other areas.

WHY GOVERNMENT REGULATION OF BUSINESS ACTIVITIES AND PRACTICES IS IMPOSED

1. To curb monopolistic tendencies; to regulate and control prices, rates, and services of enterprises that can operate effectively only as monopolies; and to prevent practices in restraint of trade.

2. To control quality of products and services, primarily to protect consumers.

3. To regulate prices on products and services and to prevent unfair trade practices as protection for consumers.

4. To protect business owners and managers from unfair methods of competition and unfair trade practices.

5. To promote safety, health, and good working conditions.

6. To protect investors by controlling the practices of financial institutions in issuing stocks, bonds, and other securities.

7. To control public utilities, especially as to rates, services, and managerial policies.

8. To guard some aspects of the economy (such as prices of specific commodities) by curbing other aspects, such as production of commodities.

FACTS EVERYONE SHOULD KNOW ABOUT HOW GOVERNMENT REGULATES BUSINESS

1. Control of entry into business by requiring licenses, permits, etc.

2. Government ownership and operation of businesses that are difficult to finance through private sources or where business will not venture because of the cost of the undertaking.

3. Periodic and special investigations of business practices by the officials of government agencies.

4. Control of prices and rates.

5. Regulation of advertising and selling practices.

6. Control of business activity indirectly through taxation.

7. Regulation of interest rates and credit.

8. Regulation of employer-employee relations — hours, wages, safety, and health — through labor legislation.

REVIEW QUESTIONS

Section A

1. What effects have the increase in population and growth of business activity had on the demand for government services?
2. What kinds of demands have been made for government services?
3. Who pays for government services?
4. How may increases in services provided by the government affect the opportunities of private business?
5. What are the basic issues as to whether functions should be performed by private enterprise or by government?
6. What are some groups that receive special benefits from government?
7. (a) Does the government make a profit on the goods and services that it provides?
   (b) Can the government provide goods and services cheaper than could private business?
8. What are some services and products provided by government that probably would never be provided by private business?

Section B

9. How has government aided business and agriculture?
10. How do consumers pay twice for price-support programs?
11. When is a price support or subsidy not justifiable?
12. Do business owners and managers believe that all government regulations are bad?

DISCUSSION QUESTIONS

Section A

1. What will the effect be on the taxpayer if government gets more involved in business?
2. What responsibility does the citizen have concerning government's role in business?
3. What would be the arguments against a plan for education in which public funds would not be used for education and parents would use the taxes thus saved to provide education for their children?
4. If the federal government should increase materially the kinds and extent of the services it now offers to consumers, what might be the effect on businesses that produce similar services and commodities for profit?
5. Would you argue in favor of governments providing police protection as opposed to private police protection?

Section B

6. Since postal rates for the different classes of mail do not provide sufficient income to pay for the costs of operating the postal services, the federal government must bear the remainder of the cost.
   (a) What are the arguments against eliminating postal charges entirely and permitting all mail to be carried free of charge?
   (b) What are the arguments against raising charges to cover the entire cost of this service?
7. What are some of the arguments for and against government subsidy or protection for producers of certain products and services?
8. What are some examples of government regulation of business activities from which consumers may benefit?

APPLICATION PROBLEMS

Section A

1. Prepare a report describing additional government services currently being requested by special groups or for citizens in general. A straw vote could be taken after the report is presented to see if the class would or would not support these requests.

2. Refer to the table on page 108. You will note that there has been just over a 124% increase in total government civilian employment from 1955 to 1979. What has been the % rate of increase in employment from 1955 to 1979 for (a) local governments, (b) state governments, and (c) the federal government?

Section B

3. Prepare a report describing how specific government agencies regulate business and what methods they use to enforce such regulations.

4. Prepare a table with the headings shown below on which you list goods and services that are provided both by private business and by government. Then indicate whether or not the good or service is *competitive* (that is, both business and government provide identical or overlapping goods or services) or *different* (that is, the good or service may appear to be the same but may not be available equally to all citizens). Finally, if the good or service is different, indicate in what way.

Good or Service	Competitive or Different	How Different?

5. Check current newspapers and periodicals for news reports dealing with recommended and proposed legislation pertaining to new consumer protection regulations. If possible, look for evidence in these articles that indicates the expected government costs to enforce such regulations. Present reports to the class for each recommended or proposed piece of legislation. Arrange a bulletin board display utilizing these articles.

COMMUNITY PROJECTS

Section A

1. Make a study of your community to determine the extent to which services are provided by local government and federal government.

2. From the latest *Statistical Abstract of the United States* or from a current almanac, obtain figures showing the amount that your state and the federal government spend in order to provide the many services demanded by businesses and citizens. Prepare pie charts (one for your state and one for the federal government) showing these amounts in relation to each other.

Section B

3. Recently, the nature of the United States Postal Service has been changed. Using your school and/or public library, research the nature of the change. What were the purposes of changing the postal service's structure? What have been the effects? Has the change been successful?

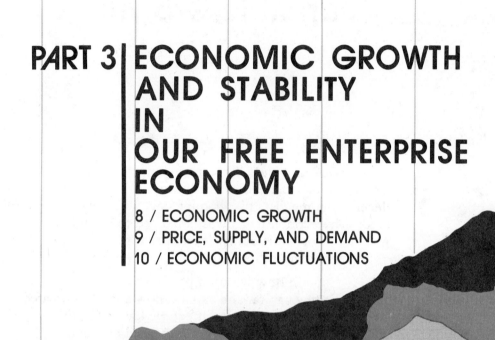

PART 3 | ECONOMIC GROWTH AND STABILITY IN OUR FREE ENTERPRISE ECONOMY

Economic Growth

PURPOSE OF THE CHAPTER

Most of us would like an income that will satisfy our wants, and most of us are disturbed when others are unable to earn a decent income. In this chapter you will have an opportunity to study why economic growth is needed to provide jobs and to help give us a more satisfactory level of living.

After studying this chapter, you will be able to:

1. Explain how we attempt to provide jobs.
2. Define capital and explain how capital is created.
3. Explain how prices affect the level of living.
4. Discuss the benefits of increased production.

A. EMPLOYMENT AND UNEMPLOYMENT

In any society there is a serious problem when people do not have work. They cannot buy goods and services, but they must live by some means — usually by public charity. Public charity is a burden on all other workers and taxpayers. Unemployment can also lead to crime. Therefore, it is important to everyone that unemployment be kept at a minimum.

The Labor Force

Less than half of the total population of the United States is in the labor force, but the labor force is limited by definition. Homemakers, for example, even though they may work as much as or more than many who are in the labor force, are excluded because of the nature of their work and because they receive no pay for it.

The *labor force* simply means all those who are willing and able to work and who are employed or are seeking employment. The *total* labor force includes military personnel. Generally, however, when we speak of the labor force we are referring to the *civilian* labor force. The *civilian labor force* includes self-employed persons but does not include students while in school, unpaid family workers, those in the armed services, retired persons, or those not able to work because of physical or mental problems.

Work force is the term applied to persons actually employed; it does not include those unemployed. The *unemployed labor force* refers to those persons who are able and willing to work but who are unable to find jobs.

Another term often used is *manpower* or *manpower resources*. The term does not refer to the number of persons available in the labor force; it simply means the combined ability or capacity of labor and management to produce goods and services.

Full Employment

The ideal situation is *full employment*, which means full or maximum use of all productive resources, including labor. Usually, we tend to think of it as meaning labor. Even in periods of full employment, 3% to 5% of the civilian labor force will not be working. These are workers who are in between jobs or are changing jobs (labor turnover) plus new workers who have not yet found jobs.

The situation called *underemployment* means part-time jobs for those wanting full-time work or persons working on jobs that do not use their full abilities. Any worker on a job who does not use his or her full abilities is underemployed. For example, a carpenter working as a common laborer is underemployed. Underemployment is part of the total problem of unemployment. For example, a person who is employed only 20 hours a week is underemployed.

Supply and Demand Determine Unemployment

The unemployment problem is a matter of demand for and supply of labor. There may not be enough demand for persons whose skills and knowledge are offered for employment. Demand does not always match supply, either as to numbers of workers or

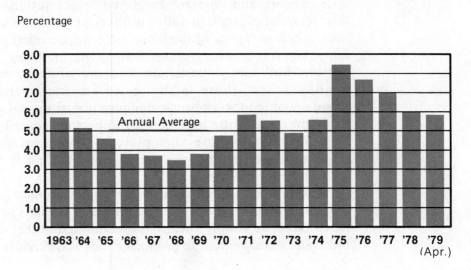

Percentage

Source: *Finance Facts, Statistical Abstract of the United States,* and other sources.

Percentage of the Civilian Labor Force Unemployed

types of workers. For example, even in periods of great unemployment the newspaper advertisements in large cities may show considerable demand for certain types of skilled workers.

In almost all working situations — factories, offices, transportation, communication, farming — jobs have become more complicated because of new machines and processes. Workers with more education and skills are needed. As machines replace unskilled labor, workers without skills find it increasingly difficult to obtain jobs.

One economic problem of unemployment is also a social problem. There is a higher degree of unemployment among some racial groups because of discrimination in hiring. Failure to obtain a job or to obtain wages comparable to other groups is not always because of a lack of education and skill. In 1979, for instance, the unemployment rate for all workers was 5.8%. The unemployment rate for both sexes between the ages of 16–19 was a whopping 16.5%. The rate for men 20 years and over was 4.0% and for women 20 years and over was 5.7%. If we divide the population by color into white and all others, the white population in 1979 had an unemployment rate of 4.9% while all others (by color) had an unemployment rate of 11.8%. It is also significant to look at unemployment by selective groups. For instance, in 1979 experienced wage and salary workers had an unemployment rate of 5.4%. Heads of households had an unemployment rate of 3.6%. White-collar workers had an unemployment rate of 3.4%. Blue-collar workers had an unemployment rate of 6.6%. So as you can see, just giving the unemployment figures for the labor force is sometimes misleading. It is good to look at subdivisions of the labor force as well.

General Solutions to Unemployment

There are two major points of view as to what would solve the problem of unemployment:

1. Education of workers. When employers cannot hire and use profitably the many workers available who lack skills and proper education, the solution is to educate these people and prepare them for the better jobs that are available.
2. Creation of more jobs. When there are not enough jobs available, the way to solve unemployment is to encourage the expansion of business through investment of savings in business enterprises, thus creating more jobs. If there are more jobs, there will be more demand for workers even if they do not possess all the skills and education desired.

There is considerable merit in both points of view. It should be easy to see, however, that the persons with the least to offer in skill and education will understandably be the last to be hired and the first to be fired.

Specific Solutions to Unemployment

Many different methods have been and are being tried to prevent or eliminate unemployment. Some of these methods are discussed below.

Solutions Directed Primarily by Business and Individuals. Among these solutions are:

1. Retraining by industry of workers displaced by machines so that these displaced workers can fill new jobs.
2. Training of apprentices (workers who learn while working) with the cooperation of labor unions and employers to develop skilled workers for special trades such as carpenter, electrician, or machinist.

3. Creation of greater consumption (buying) through easy credit terms, greater advertising and sales effort, and development of new products. Greater consumption means more jobs.

4. Elimination of seasonal unemployment. To avoid seasonal unemployment, some employers have found new methods and new products to keep workers employed steadily. For example, a factory may produce and store goods in a period of low sales for use in a later period of higher sales.

5. New investment by individuals and companies in plants and equipment to increase production and create jobs. New investment depends upon the opportunity to make a profit.

6. Reduction of costs. In some cases wages and other operating costs have become so high that a producer cannot make a profit. The only way for the firm to stay in business and provide jobs is to reduce costs. Producers sometimes move to a more favorable location, leaving workers without jobs. In some of these situations, labor and management have been able to agree on reduced wages and improvements in production so that operations continue in the old location at a profit.

Solutions Directed Primarily by Government. Among these solutions are:

1. More and better technical and vocational education, and keeping students in school until they are qualified to fill jobs in modern industry.

2. Vocational training for school dropouts and other unemployed persons so that they have sufficient skill and education to fill the types of jobs available.

3. Reduction of interest rates through Federal Reserve bank policies to encourage borrowing and the expansion of business and to make it easier for persons to buy on credit.

4. Reduction of taxes to create more demand (spending) for and consumption of goods and services.

5. Stimulation of more savings and investments for the purchase of capital goods to create new jobs by expanding industry. Tax reduction is one method used.

6. Government spending, called *pump priming*, by borrowing and spending instead of increasing taxes. Buying is stimulated because government spending creates new jobs, even though temporary. The idea is to stimulate

UNEMPLOYED PERSONS: 1975–1979
(By Marital Status, Age, Sex, and Race)

Marital Status, Age, Sex, and Race	Males					Females				
	1975	1976	1977	1978	1979	1975	1976	1977	1978	1979
Total, 16 yrs. & over 1,000	4,795	4,140	3,797	2,998	2,902	3,774	3,515	3,655	2,687	2,659
%	8.4	7.2	6.4	5.2	4.9	10.2	9.1	9.1	6.5	6.2
Married, spouse present 1,000	2,016	1,578	1,245	1,165	1,136	1,598	1,431	1,398	1,070	1,118
%	5.0	4.0	3.1	2.9	2.8	7.7	6.7	6.4	4.7	4.7
Widowed, divorced, or separated ..1,000	386	363	326	274	312	596	522	544	535	520
%	10.8	8.3	8.0	6.2	7.0	8.8	7.5	6.4	6.9	6.5
Single (never married) 1,000	2,393	2,238	2,226	1,560	1,454	1,580	1,562	1,713	1,082	1,022
%	17.9	16.2	14.9	11.4	10.2	16.3	15.2	15.4	10.4	9.3
White, 16 yrs. & over 1,000	3,887	3,274	2,975	2,310	2,236	3,017	2,744	2,807	2,040	1,962
%	7.6	6.4	5.7	4.5	4.3	9.4	8.2	8.0	5.7	5.3
Married, spouse present 1,000	1,724	1,316	1,034	985	927	1,348	1,210	1,172	900	925
%	4.7	3.6	2.8	2.7	2.6	7.3	6.3	6.0	4.4	4.4
Widowed, divorced, or separated ..1,000	273	231	253	188	219	451	378	410	383	382
%	9.5	7.3	7.6	5.4	6.0	8.3	6.7	6.8	6.1	5.9
Single (never married) 1,000	1,889	1,728	1,688	1,138	1,090	1,218	1,155	1,225	757	656
%	16.2	14.3	13.0	9.6	8.8	14.6	13.1	12.9	8.5	7.1
Black & Other, 16 yrs. & over ..1,000	908	865	822	687	666	757	771	849	647	697
%	15.4	14.4	13.1	11.2	10.6	15.5	15.1	15.9	11.7	12.1
Married, spouse present 1,000	292	262	211	180	209	250	221	227	170	193
%	8.4	7.5	5.8	5.2	5.8	11.3	9.8	9.6	7.1	7.8
Widowed, divorced, or separated ..1,000	113	92	73	86	93	144	144	134	152	138
%	15.7	12.3	9.7	9.6	10.9	11.0	10.6	9.9	9.9	8.8
Single (never married) 1,000	504	510	538	422	364	363	406	488	325	366
%	29.8	29.0	28.6	23.7	19.9	26.6	27.6	30.0	20.4	21.3
Total, 20–64 yrs. of age 1,000	3,345	2,882	2,502	2,191	2,105	2,633	2,384	2,454	1,998	1,987
%	6.8	5.8	4.9	4.3	4.0	8.4	7.3	7.2	5.6	5.3
Married, spouse present 1,000	1,889	1,461	1,159	1,090	1,063	1,492	1,338	1,305	995	1,052
%	5.0	3.8	3.0	2.9	2.8	7.5	6.5	6.2	4.5	4.6
Widowed, divorced, or separated ..1,000	364	301	321	257	285	548	484	501	490	483
%	11.0	8.3	8.3	6.2	6.8	9.0	7.7	7.4	7.0	6.6
Single (never married) 1,000	1,092	1,119	1,022	844	757	594	563	649	513	452
%	14.0	13.4	11.3	9.2	7.8	10.8	9.5	10.1	7.7	6.4
White, 20–64 yrs. of age 1,000	2,729	2,311	1,964	1,685	1,609	2,114	1,864	1,890	1,508	1,471
%	6.2	5.2	4.3	3.7	3.5	7.8	6.6	6.4	4.9	4.6
Married, spouse present 1,000	1,605	1,216	953	920	864	1,253	1,131	1,084	837	869
%	4.6	3.5	2.7	2.7	2.5	7.1	6.1	5.8	4.2	4.2
Widowed, divorced, or separated ..1,000	259	215	248	177	199	413	343	369	347	352
%	9.8	7.3	7.9	5.4	5.8	8.5	6.8	6.8	6.2	6.1
Single (never married) 1,000	866	880	764	588	547	448	391	438	324	249
%	12.9	12.2	9.8	7.5	6.6	9.7	7.9	8.2	5.9	4.3
Black & Other, 20–64 yrs. of age										
....1,000	616	571	538	505	495	519	520	564	489	516
%	12.1	10.9	9.9	9.2	8.8	12.3	11.7	12.1	9.8	10.0
Married, spouse present 1,000	284	245	206	169	200	239	207	221	156	185
%	8.5	7.3	5.9	5.1	5.8	11.2	9.4	9.6	6.7	7.7
Widowed, divorced, or separated ..1,000	105	86	73	81	86	135	142	132	143	131
%	15.5	12.3	10.2	9.5	10.7	11.1	11.2	10.3	9.9	8.8
Single (never married) 1,000	227	239	258	255	210	146	172	211	189	201
%	21.7	20.6	21.2	19.6	15.5	16.8	17.2	19.7	15.6	15.9

Source: U.S. Bureau of Labor Statistics, *Employment and Earnings* (July 1977, 1978, 1979).

business so that it can carry on without help. If taxes are increased to make government spending possible, however, taxpayers will have less money to spend.

7. Establishment of minimum wages. One purpose of the minimum-wage law is to help assure each worker enough income to live on. If, however, the employer cannot use labor profitably at the minimum wage, the worker will not be hired.

8. Preventing discrimination in employment because of race, age, sex, and religion. Unemployment by sex, race, age, and marital status between the period 1975 to 1979 is presented in the table on page 127.

9. Establishment of state and federal employment offices to help persons find jobs and to help employers find workers.

10. Unemployment insurance. The payment of unemployment insurance benefits (explained in Chapter 19) helps those who are unemployed, usually until they can find jobs. Unemployed workers without money to spend cannot buy goods and services produced by other workers. Therefore, if many workers are unemployed for any great length of time, other workers will lose their jobs because of a decrease in demand. The fact that employers must pay for unemployment insurance causes them to try to provide steady employment, since their insurance costs rise if their employees become unemployed.

11. Controlling immigration and prohibiting temporary workers from entering from such countries as Mexico, Japan, and Canada.

Technology and Employment

The U.S. civilian work force (those actually working) averaged about 95 million in 1979. By 1985, the number employed is expected to rise to 104.3 million. This means that about 1.2 million new workers will enter the work force each year during the next 6 years. Over one half of these new workers will be in the white-collar occupations, one fourth in the blue-collar occupations, and almost one fourth in the service industries. Farm workers, who made up only 3.1% of the work force in 1979, are expected to decline to less than 1% by 1985.

What about the demand for manpower? Two economic factors are largely responsible for determining the number of workers required: (1) the demand for goods and services and (2) the extent of our technology. *Technology* is the extent to which machines or laborsaving methods rather than manpower can be used to produce goods and services. As demand has risen because of more workers and increased earnings, the number of people employed has risen. But progress in technology has caused some of the increase in demand to be met through increased productivity of workers already employed rather than through new workers.

These facts and figures do not tell the entire story. We often have unemployed workers and unfilled jobs at the same time and in the same place because workers do not have the skills and the knowledge required for available jobs.

It is hard to measure the effect of technology on the total demand for workers and to determine whether new technology creates more jobs than it eliminates. There is no doubt that new technology is changing the types of skills and knowledge that workers need. The demand for agricultural skills, for example, has been both reduced and changed. New farm machinery and methods (plus the increase in the size of many farms) have steadily cut the proportion of our labor force required to produce our farm products. In manufacturing, the new production technology of recent years provides for automatic assembly (automation). It replaces many hand functions and reduces the need for semiskilled or unskilled workers.

Technology is changing job opportunities and occupational trends. Of the total work force, blue-collar employment (production worker jobs) declined during the period of 1960 to 1979 by 4.1%. On the other hand, employment in white-collar jobs (clerical, scientific, technical, sales, supervisory workers, and government) increased by 8.3%.

It is clear that demand for workers is increasing most in those occupations that require skill and preparation through longer periods of education and training. The unskilled occupations that require only limited educational qualifications are decreasing or show little if any increase. The decline in need for manpower on the farm, for instance, has caused underemployment of farm workers and has caused a movement of farm workers to city areas. This movement is called *dislocation*. Many of those leaving farm areas are not trained for city employment.

The previous discussion of the labor force and the work force points up the necessity for constantly increasing investment in business to create new jobs so that new workers entering the labor force can find jobs, earn money, and consume the goods and services produced. The increased efficiency through better machines and methods will not help us unless people have jobs.

The changing nature of business through technology also indicates that workers must have better training, and often a new kind of training, in order to fill new types of jobs.

.EMPLOYED PERSONS — PERCENT DISTRIBUTION,
BY OCCUPATION AND RACE: 1960 TO 1979
(Persons 16 years old and over)

OCCUPATION	WHITE				BLACK AND OTHER			
	1960	1970	1975	1979	1960	1970	1975	1979
Total employed...................1,000	58,850	70,182	75,713	84,848	6,927	8,445	9,070	10,678
Percent ....%	100.0	100.0	100.0	100.0	100.0	100.0	100.0	100.0
White-collar workers....................	46.6	50.8	51.7	53.0	16.1	27.9	34.2	38.0
Professional, technical, & kindred workers....................	12.1	14.8	15.5	16.4	4.8	9.1	11.4	12.7
Managers, administrators........	11.7	11.4	11.2	11.4	2.6	3.5	4.4	5.0
Salesworkers	7.0	6.7	6.9	6.9	1.5	2.1	2.7	2.7
Clerical workers........................	15.7	18.0	18.1	18.4	7.3	13.2	15.7	17.5
Blue-collar workers.....................	36.2	34.5	32.4	32.2	40.1	42.2	37.4	35.4
Craft & kindred workers...........	13.8	13.5	13.4	13.6	6.0	8.2	8.8	9.2
Operatives.................................	17.9	17.0	14.6	14.2	20.4	23.7	20.0	18.8
Nonfarm laborers	4.4	4.1	4.4	4.3	13.7	10.3	8.7	7.4
Service workers...........................	9.9	10.7	12.3	12.1	31.7	26.0	25.8	24.7
Private household workers......	1.7	1.3	1.0	.8	14.2	7.7	4.9	3.3
Other...	8.2	9.4	11.3	11.3	17.5	18.3	20.9	21.4
Farmworkers	7.4	4.0	3.6	2.7	12.1	3.9	2.6	2.0
Farmers & farm managers.......	4.3	2.4	2.0	1.6	3.2	1.0	.6	.3
Farm laborers & supervisors ...	3.0	1.6	1.6	1.1	9.0	2.9	2.0	1.7

Source: U.S. Bureau of Labor Statistics, *Employment and Earnings* (July, 1979).

Is the Shorter Workweek the Answer?

Proposals are sometimes made to reduce the length of the workweek and spread the work among more workers at the same weekly pay as for the longer week. Without increased efficiency, such a plan raises the cost of production and raises prices for everyone if the practice is widespread.

It is argued that employers should be required to hire more people instead of working their regular employees overtime at a higher rate. If the workweek were shorter, the overtime rate would begin earlier and, therefore, the employer would find it less expensive to hire more workers than to pay overtime.

Solving unemployment is not that simple. A shorter workweek may not result in hiring more workers if workers with skills are not available and if work schedules cannot be arranged to fit the reduced workweek. Also, if the workweek were shortened, some people might use the available time to work at two jobs and actually make the problem worse. It still may be less expensive to pay overtime than to hire new workers. If the result is higher prices of goods, everyone loses.

The need for better education and training of workers, plus the creation of job opportunities, seems to be the permanent basis for solving unemployment. Two situations emphasize this conclusion:

1. While there are workers unemployed in a community, there are unfilled jobs for which qualified workers cannot be found.
2. While there are unemployed workers in a community, there are workers holding two jobs. This practice is called *moonlighting*. In one community 15% of the workers in a major industry were found to be moonlighting. The average number of hours worked a week on the second job was 21. Approximately 5% of all workers in the United States hold two jobs.

We shall now study the ways in which jobs are created.

B. NATIONAL ECONOMIC GROWTH

In this section we shall discuss capital, economic growth, and the cost of economic growth.

Capital

An economic goal of our society is to provide jobs for all who want to work at wages that will permit them to fulfill their wants for relatively scarce goods and services. We have learned that we can raise our level of living by increasing our production and by increasing our efficiency of production so that each of us has more goods to share.

To create jobs, new capital must be provided constantly. *Capital*, as you learned in Chapter 4, means buildings, equipment, or other physical properties other than raw materials used in a business. It is estimated that the average amount of new capital required for tools and equipment to create a new job in industry is $20,000. This capital investment per worker ranges from about $5,000 in some industries to more than $75,000 in others.

Another term used in business is *working capital*, which means money for day-to-day operations such as wages, materials, and other expenses. Business needs money for working capital in addition to money that is invested in capital goods.

Function of Capital Goods. *Capital goods* are goods used to produce other goods. The goods produced may be consumed or may be used in production. The function of capital goods is to assist labor in production. Capital goods make labor more efficient and make work easier. For example, the tractor and the plow make farming easier and more productive. Machines and all types of power equipment in factories make work easier and more productive. More goods can be produced with less effort. The individual gains from capital goods, and we all gain from more efficient production.

In order to make these gains in the production of capital goods, we must either save by temporarily giving up the use of some of our earnings or we must use resources that are not fully used. For example, when primitive people took time out from crude methods of fishing to make large fishing nets, they were actually using some of the time saved to create new capital, which could then be used to increase the catch of fish.

The time and the resources used for the creation of capital goods temporarily reduce the quantity of consumer goods that can be created. The final purpose of capital goods, however, is greater production.

As individuals and as a society, we must decide whether to use our resources or our savings. Should we use our resources to produce those goods and services that will be consumed immediately? Or should we use some of our savings to create new capital that will, in turn, create new jobs and greater production for future use? An economy grows by increasing its capital and thereby its ability to produce more.

Savings Come from Individuals. To create more jobs there must be new funds (money) for financing new production. Besides the money needed to provide capital, additional money is needed to pay for wages, rent, materials, and other costs of production. The only way that more money can be made available to create capital and to finance other operations is through savings. Savings are needed to produce capital goods, and capital goods are needed to produce consumer goods. Capital increases production and stimulates growth.

Ultimately, all savings that are available for the creation of new capital come from the savings of individuals. Even the profits of a corporation kept by the corporation for creating new capital really could have been paid out as dividends to stockholders. These corporation earnings are actually savings belonging to the stockholders. The decision of the board of directors to keep some of the earnings for capital expansion is a type of savings forced on the stockholders.

People furnish money to business with which other resources needed in the business can be purchased. Even when banks lend money, this money belongs to individuals — the investors in the bank and the depositors.

EFFECT OF SAVINGS ON CAPITAL GOODS

1. Savings are needed to produce capital goods.

2. Capital goods increase the ability to produce consumer goods.

3. Economic growth results from producing more consumer goods per person.

Sources of New Capital. Savings are used in two ways to create new capital. One way is to lend money to those who wish to create capital goods or use it for other business purposes. Savings available for loans to business are known as *loanable funds*. Interest is paid to those who lend the money. The second way to use savings to create new capital is to invest in business. When you invest in a business, you take a risk because you become one of the owners. In economics, you are considered a part of management. You invest hoping to make a profit from the successful operation of a business. Savings available to buy an interest in business are called *investment funds*.

The interest rates paid for the use of loanable funds are determined largely on the basis of supply and demand, just as in the case of goods and services. Sometimes funds are available for loans because the owners of these funds will not use them for investment purposes. They feel that there is not a sufficient chance for profit to take the risk of investing the funds and becoming the part owner of a business.

A single individual who owns a business invests money in that business, but the business as such is separate from the individual who owns it. The investment is made by the individual, not the business. Individuals, therefore, provide the resources or the money needed by business. When we say business buys certain things, we mean that it is the managers of the business who do it. And they do it with the resources or money furnished by others.

Taxes Affect Savings and New Capital. Taxes have a great influence on savings. They therefore have a great influence on the creation of new capital and the creation of new jobs for more people. Taxes reduce the amount of spendable income that people have and reduce the ability of people to save. Taxes also reduce the profits of corporations, leaving less profit to keep in the business for new capital or to divide with stockholders who could save or spend it. Taxes shift the use of savings from individuals and businesses to government. Some taxes collected by government may be used for the creation of new capital, such as roads, bridges, and power dams.

EFFECT OF TAXES ON SAVINGS AND NEW CAPITAL

1. Taxes reduce spendable income.

2. Taxes reduce ability of individuals to save.

3. Taxes reduce ability to buy capital goods.

4. Taxes shift individual and business spending to government spending.

Economic Growth

An individual or a business firm may determine through proper records the value of the economic goods and services it produced in a given year. So too may a nation determine the value of all the goods and services produced by all the people of the nation. As we learned earlier, the money value of the goods and services produced in a year is known as the *gross national product*, sometimes referred to as *national output*.

Meaning of Economic Growth. An increase in per capita (amount per person) output indicates economic progress or growth. In general this means an improvement in economic conditions for people and a rising level of living. A decrease in per capita output may indicate that the economy is in a period of recession. If it is a severe decrease, it might indicate a period of depression. Recessions and depressions are explained in detail in Chapter 10.

In the United States there has usually been an increase in per capita output of economic goods and services over any extended period of time. This increase has resulted in our rising level of living.

In many lesser developed countries, the national output or production always has been low, and the increase per year, if any, is small. In these countries economic growth is taking place slowly or not at all, and the level of living remains low.

Factors in Economic Growth. National economic growth results from the combined effect of many factors. Some of the factors may be controlled by government action; others are not subject to control. Hence national economic growth is influenced by the combined action of business firms, individuals, and government. Some of these factors will be discussed in this chapter and in later chapters.

Population. As the population increases, the labor force tends to increase. It is estimated that the population of the United States will increase from an estimated 222 million in 1980 to approximately 233 million in 1985. On the average 1.2 million jobs must be created each year until 1985 through expansion of business and industry or unemployment will increase. The value of the goods

**U.S. Population and
Growth Rate**

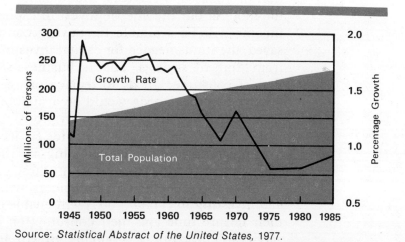

Source: *Statistical Abstract of the United States,* 1977.

and services produced each year by these additional people will increase the gross national product. If economic growth is to take place, the rate of increase in the gross national product per year must be greater than the increase in population.

Cost of Economic Growth

Economic growth does not just happen. It is not free. There are opportunity costs. To get economic growth, certain things of value and other advantages must be given up. The growth may require sacrifices on the part of people. The benefits of economic growth must be considered in relation to the costs of obtaining growth at a desired rate. Two of the more important opportunity costs are the sacrifice of leisure and the curtailment of consumption.

Sacrifice of Leisure. One way to increase the national per capita output or production is through making greater productive use of capital in the form of facilities and equipment. This means that every worker would spend more hours per day using these capital resources. Leisure time would have to be sacrificed for growth. The cost of increased economic growth is determined by the sacrifice of leisure. The opportunity cost of growth depends on the value of the leisure time we give up in order to produce more.

Curtailment of Consumption. One of the economic goals in the United States is to enable people to increase their consumption of goods and services, thus raising their level of living. But the more of our income we invest in capital goods, the less of our income will be available for buying consumer goods. If nobody saved, the funds needed for capital investment would have to come from "forced" savings. That is, business would curtail the production of consumer goods to replace or expand capital. Therefore, fewer consumer goods would be available and prices would rise. So whether people save voluntarily or not, saving is necessary to maintain an economy and to provide for its growth.

Foregoing leisure and spending are the two primary opportunity costs of economic growth. But these costs are only temporary, for the future benefits of economic growth that come from saving and investing in capital goods will enable people to increase again their leisure time and their consumption of consumer goods and services. The costs of economic growth are borne in the present, but the benefits come in the future.

C. ELEMENTS THAT DETERMINE THE LEVEL OF LIVING

In this section we shall examine how levels of living differ from standards of living and discuss how levels of living are increased in the United States.

Level of Living

Most of us would like to buy more goods and use more services than we are buying now. We would like our money to go further. In other words, we would like to live on a higher economic level than we are at present. Our *level of living* is indicated by the quality and the quantity of the goods and services we are able to buy. The level of living is much higher in some countries than in others. It is also higher in some parts of this country than in other parts, and it is higher for some people within a community than for others.

The level of living consists of the goods and services that an individual or a family regularly obtains. A *standard of living* is similar to a goal or a guide. Many of us set standards that we would like to attain. There is really no standard in the true sense of the word; but when we use this term, we usually are thinking of a certain degree of success in satisfying our needs and wants. Thus, a standard of living cannot be measured in dollars and cents like a level of living can. For example, you might set as your goal an increased knowledge and appreciation of music and art. If you achieve this goal, you have improved your standard of living, but the result cannot be measured in dollars and cents.

Our level of living depends not only on our income and our savings but also on how wisely we spend our money in satisfying our wants. Other factors also affect our level of living. For example, if the supply of the goods we want is limited, we may not be able to get what we want. Or, if prices in general are high, our income may not be large enough to permit us to buy what we want. Our level of living is also influenced by inventions of such conveniences as automobiles, dishwashers, and power lawn mowers. Modern manufacturing makes a lot of these products available to us at a cost we can afford. How well our wants for goods and services are satisfied depends on many factors.

We have some control over our income. In general, the harder one works or the better one serves in his or her job, the greater are the earnings. And, of course, we have control over the spending of our income. Both our income and our expenditures affect our level of living.

With the use of skilled workers, such as these workers at an oil well installation, we can increase our individual production and contribute to a higher level of living for all people.

Courtesy of International Paper Company

Raising Our Level of Living. Through our efforts and by our work we produce economic goods and services that people want and are willing to buy. The return we get for our work comes in the form of wages and income. We use our income to obtain the things we need to maintain our level of living. Thus, our level of living is closely related to the work we do or, more accurately, to how much we produce individually. The main way we raise our level of living is by increasing our production (output). We then can earn more and can buy more.

If you receive a wage of $30 a day and give service of equal value, you are helping to maintain the present national level of living. But if you receive a wage of $30 a day and produce less, you are really helping to lower our national level of living. You may feel that temporarily you benefit from receiving more wages than you really earn; but if others take the same approach, prices will have to rise. Consequently, fewer people will be able to buy the goods and services they want, and the national level of living will go down.

If we want to raise our level of living, we must do it by increasing our individual production, which in turn will increase the total production of all people. This means that we must strive for the greatest efficiency. We must have educated and skilled workers. We must take advantage of modern machinery, modern

　　　　　　　　　　　　　　　139

power, and modern science. We must not artificially restrict production except to avoid overproduction to the extent that there is more than can be consumed at established prices. These factors working together for greater efficiency and productivity result in making more goods available at lower prices. This process helps raise our level of living.

Restriction of production may enable a producer (for example, a monopolist) to get a higher price for each unit of what it does produce. There is a limit, however, to the amount any producer can increase its income by raising prices because fewer people will be able to buy its product. Restrictions on output or production, whether by labor or management, tend to lower the level of living for all people by forcing prices up.

Value of a Dollar Affects Level of Living. We are all very much aware of the amount of our weekly or monthly earnings and of how much we have saved. The amount of money we have saved or the amount we earn, however, is not as important as what it will buy. Your wages in dollars are indicated by the amount of your paycheck, but your *real wages* are measured by the amount of goods and services your wages will buy. For example, if five years ago a dollar in wages would have bought four 24-ounce loaves of bread and now a dollar from your current wages will buy only two loaves, the purchasing power of the dollar for buying bread has decreased 50%.

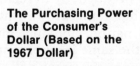

The Purchasing Power of the Consumer's Dollar (Based on the 1967 Dollar)

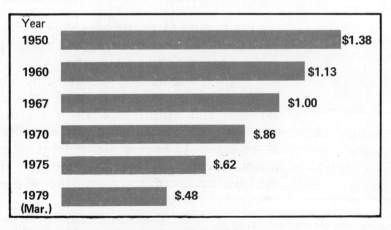

Year	
1950	$1.38
1960	$1.13
1967	$1.00
1970	$.86
1975	$.62
1979 (Mar.)	$.48

Sources: *Statistical Abstract of the United States,* 1977.
Survey of Current Business (May, 1979).

Prices Affect our Real Income. When the prices of goods and services in general increase, our dollars of income buy less; when prices decrease, our dollars buy more. Indirectly, then, the general price level affects our level of living.

Prices of goods and services wanted by consumers generally have increased in the United States. If all goods and services wanted by consumers are considered together, a dollar would buy 48% as much in 1979 as in 1967. This means that a person would have needed an income more than twice as large in 1979 as in 1967 in order to buy the same amount of goods and services.

Prices do not always go up. There are times when prices of goods and services go down. Under such conditions the purchasing power of the dollar increases. As a result, people can maintain their levels of living on less money than when prices were higher.

Production and Its Distribution

In any way that wealth is measured, the United States is the richest nation in the world. Even with this wealth, we are still not producing or distributing enough goods and services for all families to enjoy a comfortable level of living. Almost every person has many unfilled wants. To achieve our goal for all people to dress well, eat well, live in a good home, get a good education, have good medical care, and have their choices of many manufactured articles, we need much greater production of goods and services. We can increase production by greater efficiency and by using all available resources — labor, land, and machines.

Production Must Increase. As indicated earlier, if we expect to have a higher level of living, the gross national product must increase faster than the population.

There is another way of measuring our productivity in relation to the gross national product. As the labor force grows (those available and willing to work), the gross national product must increase at the same rate just to maintain the same level of living. If we expect to have a higher level of living, the gross national product must grow faster than the labor force. The comparison of the labor force with the gross national product is a measure of our efficiency in production.

Productivity and Wages. The problem of productivity of our resources is of great importance to all our leaders in government, and it is certainly important to every individual. Each of us has a selfish interest. We want to earn as much as we can so that we can use our earnings to buy the things we want. From an individual point of view, increased earnings permit a higher level of living provided the prices of all goods and services remain the same. Wage increases, without similar increases in production, merely allow persons with increased wages to buy more compared with those who are not successful in obtaining increased wages.

If everyone has an increase in income, the prices of all goods and services will increase if the supply remains the same. When wages increase faster than production, those with money to spend bid for the scarce goods and services and cause prices to increase. This is what we call *inflation*, which will be discussed in more detail in Chapter 10.

Problems of Distribution. While it is true that efficient production is the key to a high level of living for members of any society, we are still living in an economic society of relative scarcity. At least there is a scarcity of many items and services for many people. There are still many unfulfilled wants. From an individual point of view, the solution to this problem is to use one's resources to fulfill personal wants. The productivity of the individual determines how well that person will share in production. There are many who, because of a lack of education, poor health, old age, or location, do not have the resources or are not able to use their resources to provide a high level of living.

There are many factors that influence wages of individual workers at different times. But in the long run and for all workers, wages depend on the productivity of labor. Producers can pay only wages that are justified by the productivity of workers. Producers cannot continue to operate for any long period of time unless they can make reasonable profits. Therefore, they cannot pay wages that are higher than the productivity that will permit a profit.

Businesses compete for workers just as they compete for sales. Therefore, businesses bid for productive workers in competition with other businesses. The bidding for competent workers will cause wages to reach a level justified by the productivity of the workers.

Some types of workers (labor) are scarce. Since the supply is limited, they can demand high wages because of their education, experience, and special abilities. Some types of workers are plentiful and their productive ability is low because of lack of education, experience, and special skills. These workers are paid low wages because there is a large number of them to satisfy wants. If strong workers willing to do manual labor were limited (scarce), their wages would be higher.

American workers are the highest paid workers in the world. They are paid high wages because of their productivity. The productivity of American workers is high because of their superior education, their skill, their methods of working, the use of modern machines, and expert management. Under our American system, the workers, the managers, and those who have invested money to create the businesses share in production.

One of the great dangers in satisfying our selfish desire for a high income is that all of us may increase our money income, but we may not increase our real income. If prices and the cost of goods produced increase faster than wages, the wage earner loses. If wages and prices rise at the same rate, there is no gain in real wages. If wages rise faster than prices, there is a gain in real wages. Gain in real wages must come from increased efficiency in the productivity of labor.

The role of the government in promoting growth will be discussed further in Chapters 12, 13, and 15.

FACTS EVERYONE SHOULD KNOW
ABOUT JOBS AND PROSPERITY

1. The primary economic goals are to maintain a rising level of living through full employment and a reasonable rate of growth.

2. Capital is made up of savings of individuals, business firms, and government that are invested with the idea of producing something.

3. Economic growth is measured by the increase in per capita gross national product for a given period of time.

4. Economic growth creates jobs.

5. Economic growth is not free. Among the primary costs are the sacrificing of some leisure to provide more time to produce and the curtailment of consumption to increase savings for investment with the idea of producing something.

6. Our share in production is measured by the goods and services that our wages will buy.

7. Productivity or efficiency in production comes from combining all resources so that there is more production per person and at a reduced cost.

8. If we are to make gains in our level of living, production must increase faster than wages.

9. Greater production is the key to solving the problem of scarcity.

REVIEW QUESTIONS

Section A
1. What is (a) the civilian labor force and (b) the work force?
2. What is (a) full employment and (b) underemployment?
3. What are some examples of underemployment?
4. How can education help solve unemployment?
5. What are some examples of how business tries to solve the unemployment problem?
6. What are some examples of how government attempts to prevent unemployment?
7. What do we mean by technology in business?
8. How has technology in industry and agriculture helped to improve our level of living?
9. What happens if workers receive the same pay for shorter workweeks?

Section B
10. What is (a) capital and (b) working capital?
11. How are savings used by business to create new jobs?
12. In what two ways are savings used to create new capital?
13. How do taxes affect savings and the creation of new capital?
14. What is meant by the cost of economic growth?

Section C
15. How is a standard of living distinguished from a level of living?
16. Do we all have the same standard of living? Why or why not?
17. How is our level of living determined by efficient production?
18. What must each individual do in order to raise his or her own and the nation's level of living?
19. How would slowing down or restricting production affect our level of living?
20. What is meant by real wages or real income?
21. What is meant by the purchasing power of the dollar and why does it vary?
22. Which is the more accurate measure of our level of living, real wages or money wages?
23. What is the basic way in which we can raise our level of living?
24. Why is it necessary for our gross national product to increase each year in order for us to maintain our present level of living?
25. From the point of view of economics in a free society, what is the main factor in determining wages?

DISCUSSION QUESTIONS

Section A
1. Under what conditions might a student be included under the definition of the labor force?
2. Why do many economists refer to the economy as being fully employed when 3% to 5% of the labor force is unemployed?
3. Why is increasing emphasis placed on education as a way to reduce unemployment?
4. From your daily experience, what are some examples of jobs that are open and available at the same time other persons are looking for employment and cannot find a job?
5. What are your views on the two general solutions to the unemployment problem mentioned on page 125?

6. How does the government system of "pump priming" help to create jobs?

7. Is the increased use of machines (technology) in business good or bad? Why?

8. Many years ago some workers had a workweek of as much as 60 or 70 hours. A normal workweek now is 40 hours or less. From the point of view of your welfare and the welfare of everyone, what do you think of this trend and should it continue?

Section B

9. In many newspapers, magazines, and government reports, there is a regular reference to the amount of new investment in capital equipment as an indication of our economic growth. Why do economists watch this trend carefully?

10. How may college and training school expenses be classified as investments in human capital?

11. What is the relationship between profits, savings, capital, and jobs?

12. How may taxes affect both the creation of new capital and jobs?

13. If the population increases at the rate of 5% a year and the gross national product increases 2.5% a year, do we have a satisfactory economic growth? Explain your answer.

14. Under what circumstances may the temporary curtailment of consumption create an increase in later production?

Section C

15. (a) Are savings accumulated purchasing power? (b) How does the changing purchasing power of the dollar affect savings?

16. Why cannot an increase in real prosperity be measured in terms of wages?

17. One of the goals of almost every person is to have more income so he or she can live better economically, that is, purchase more of the goods and services wanted. (a) What must a person do in order to raise his or her level of living? (b) To what extent is every person responsible for his or her own level of economic living?

18. What can happen if everyone receives an increase in wages and there is no increase in efficiency or production?

19. There is always resistance to a minimum wage law. (a) Under what circumstances might a minimum wage hurt rather than help workers? (b) What might happen if the minimum wage remained the same while prices continued to rise?

APPLICATION PROBLEMS

Section A

1. The civilian labor force and the number of unemployed in 1965, 1970, 1975, and 1979 are given below.

Year	Civilian Labor Force	Number Unemployed
1965	74.5 million	3.4 million
1970	82.7	4.1
1975	91.4	7.8
1979 (Mar.)	101.6	6.2

Calculate the percentage of unemployment for each of the four years.

Section B   2. The Hastings Manufacturing Company borrowed $320,000 at 8% interest and spent all of it on tools and equipment with which to expand production. As a result of this expansion, 10 new jobs were created.
   (a) How much capital was used to create each of the new jobs?
   (b) How much interest must be paid during the first year on the total investment in tools and equipment? How much must be paid on the investment for each new worker?
   (c) Do you believe that this is the kind of expansion that the Hastings Manufacturing Company should expect to accomplish every two or three years? Why?
3. As measured in constant dollars, the GNP (gross national product) was $620 billion and the population was 190 million one year, and five years later the GNP was $750 billion and the population was 210 million. Was there any real economic growth during the five-year period? Explain your answer.

Section C   4. Assume that a family had an income of $10,000 in 1967. Using the chart on page 139, calculate what income the same family would have to have in each of the years presented in the chart to have the same purchasing power that the family had in 1967.

COMMUNITY PROJECTS

Section A   1. Study the classified advertising section of a newspaper listing job opportunities. Analyze the positions available. Prepare a report under the title "Employment Opportunities" and include a list of the kinds of jobs that are most readily available. You may want to prepare a chart using such categories as white collar, blue collar, skilled or unskilled, and you may wish to itemize particular positions. What kinds of positions seem to be most readily available?
2. The Jacksons had to leave their small tenant farm when it was bought by a large corporation. They were forced to move to the city in order to find work, and Mr. Jackson moved through several temporary jobs in his search for permanent employment. Perhaps you or your family know of an individual or a family that has been similarly dislocated. If so, talk with this person or family about their experiences. Write a report on the problems of dislocation, covering (a) the problems the Jacksons (or the people you know) faced, (b) what steps they might have taken to avoid these problems, and (c) what help is available to them in your community in seeking permanent employment.
3. Generally, unemployment figures are given for the nation as a whole by age, sex, and occupational groupings. However, unemployment figures also vary by geographic region.
   (a) Using the latest available data from the *Economic Report of the President, Statistical Abstract of the United States, Survey of Current Business*, or a local newspaper, determine what the present unemployment rate for the nation is. Then determine the unemployment rate for your particular community. Statistics on the unemployment rate for a particular community are usually available through the nearest government unemployment office. Explain why the unemployment rate for the nation might be different from the unemployment rate for your community.

(b) Make a list of where most of the unemployment exists in your community. Local newspapers and the unemployment office are good sources for this information.

(c) Make a list of the agencies available in your community to help combat unemployment and describe briefly what each agency does.

Section B   4. Three people in a community take the following action. Sarah Hughes buys a new pickup truck for her horse farm. Tim Boyers deposits money in his savings account, which the bank, in turn, loans to a firm that is expanding its building. Floyd Potts pays taxes levied for the purpose of building a public library.

(a) What is the similarity between the actions of Hughes, Boyers, and Potts?

(b) Prepare a list of 10 situations in your own community that show people taking similar action.

Section C   5. Benny Bailey was characterized as a "juvenile offender" when he attended high school. Yet, something happened along the way that made him return to school, going all the way through to a Ph.D. At the age of 30, he and two friends founded the East Kentucky Health Services Center, an innovative medical facility. The case of the "dropout who came back" is not uncommon. Perhaps you or your family know of someone who dropped out of school only to return and succeed. This person's case may not be as dramatic as Benny Bailey's, but perhaps it would be worth talking to the person to find out what changed his or her mind about school. Write a short report on why Benny Bailey (or the person you know) changed from a dropout to a successful and responsible citizen.

Price, Supply, and Demand

PURPOSE OF THE CHAPTER

Everyone is affected by prices. The purpose of this chapter is to help you understand the significance of prices, why prices change, and some of the economic factors that affect them.

After studying this chapter, you will be able to:

1. Define the meaning of the price system.
2. Explain how supply and demand affect prices.
3. Explain how competition and monopoly affect prices.
4. Discuss how prices are controlled by government.

A. NATURE AND SIGNIFICANCE OF PRICES

Both goods and services have value if they are capable of satisfying our economic needs and wants. *Economic value* is the estimate of worth or usefulness that individuals and businesses place on goods and services based on their ability to satisfy wants and needs. Goods that are free, like the air we breathe, have great value because people cannot live without them; but the free air does not have economic value because it ordinarily cannot be bought or sold. If ordinary air were so scarce that the only way a person could get it were to buy it in tanks, it would have economic value. *Price* is the exchange value of goods or services stated in terms of money. For example, the price of wheat is the amount of money required to buy a bushel of wheat.

Price System

In the days of barter, the value of wheat as compared to that of shoes depended largely on the supply and the degree of usefulness

If people had to buy air, it would have economic value.

of each product. When wheat was plentiful and shoes were scarce and difficult to produce, a considerable amount of wheat was required in return for a pair of shoes. When people found that a great many others had wheat to trade but very few had shoes to trade, more people began to produce shoes. As the supply of shoes increased, less wheat was required for a pair of shoes. To a large extent, under the barter system the supply of products regulated their relative value. When the demand for a product increased, it could be traded easily for other products.

The barter system was inconvenient and inefficient for both buyers and sellers. It gave way to the price system in which one's product or labor is exchanged for money and the money is used to buy goods and services. All prices are stated in terms of money. Thus, money serves not only as the medium of exchange, but also as a measure or standard of value for determining prices. Under the price system, a general rise or fall in all prices may occur. A general rise or fall means that the purchasing power or value of

ESSENTIALS OF THE PRICE SYSTEM

1. The product of one's efforts or labor is exchanged for money. The money may be saved or may be exchanged for goods or services.

2. Price is the money value placed on the product resulting from one's efforts. Price is also the money value placed on the goods and services one buys.

3. Thus, price is a common measure of the value both of the products of one's efforts and of goods and services one may desire.

money has changed. Inflation causes higher prices in general, meaning that the value or purchasing power of money has decreased.

Price, Profit, and Production

No business wishes to produce unless it receives enough money to cover costs and make a profit. Costs include wages, raw materials, insurance, rent, transportation, and many other items. Some businesses will continue temporarily to produce goods without profit in the hope that they will eventually make enough to repay previous losses.

Price tends to govern production. For instance, if the price of wheat goes up while the price of corn and hogs remains the same, many farmers will shift to the production of wheat. Then the production of wheat will rise, while the production of corn and hogs will decrease.

Production, in turn, tends to govern price. If too many farmers have shifted to the production of wheat, as indicated above, the supply of wheat will increase and the price will go down. Because of the decrease in the supply of corn and hogs, the price of corn and hogs will rise. Then there is likely to be a new shift in production. These examples serve to illustrate the fact that there is a constant interplay of price and supply, each influencing the other.

The fluctuation in price and supply, however, will be steadied by a basic factor — the cost of production. If price long remains much above the cost of production, new competitors will usually enter the field, supply will increase, and the price will be driven

If price remains much above cost of production, new competitors will enter the field.

down. On the other hand, if price falls below the cost of production and remains there long, some producers will drop out or will decrease production, supply will be curtailed, and the price will rise.

Production cannot be continued indefinitely unless the selling price is greater than the cost of production. More efficient methods of production permit the lowering of the selling price. It is for this reason that the least efficient producers are the first to be driven out of a field. Their departure may cut the supply enough to steady prices above the production costs of the more efficient producers.

PRICE AND PRODUCTION

1. Prices must be high enough to make a profit possible; otherwise there will be no production.

2. Prices influence the kind of products that are produced. No one will produce a product that is too costly to be of practical use; no one will produce a product that is so valueless that it has no price.

3. Prices above the cost of production of a given commodity tend to increase the quantity of production; prices below the cost of production lower it.

4. High volume of production of a commodity tends to lower prices; low volume tends to raise prices.

Price and Supply

The amount of goods and services offered for sale is governed considerably by the price. If the price is favorable to the producers, they will offer large quantities of their products for sale. If the price is not favorable, they will not produce. Similarly, a farmer may have harvested 10,000 bushels of wheat. If the price of wheat is $3 a bushel, the farmer may sell all the wheat. But if the price is only $2 a bushel, the farmer may sell only enough to provide sufficient cash until the rest can be sold at a better price. A southern cotton grower may have harvested 1,000 bales of cotton. If the selling price is 50 cents a pound for cotton, the grower may sell all the bales. But if the price is only 20 cents a pound, the grower may be willing to sell only 500 bales. In both examples the wheat and cotton growers have created an artificial supply shortage in the

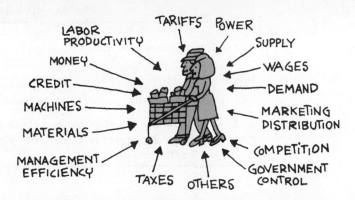

Your prices are affected by many forces.

hope that this will cause prices to rise. Price therefore tends to regulate supply.

Theoretically, *supply* represents the quantity of goods offered for sale at a given time and price. If the supply increases — in other words, if more goods are offered for sale — the price tends to be lowered. If the supply continues to increase, the price will eventually reach a level that is close to the cost of production. When the price goes below this point, producers frequently fail or go into bankruptcy, for they cannot continue to produce without profit. The supply then tends to decrease, and the price becomes more stable. As the supply decreases, the price rises.

SUPPLY AND DEMAND

1. Supply of a commodity is the amount offered for sale at a given time and price.

2. Demand for a commodity is an indication of the desire for that commodity by people who have the money to buy and who are willing to pay the price; it is the amount that will be purchased at a given price.

An opportune time to buy is when the supply is great and the demand is low. This condition is called a *buyer's market*. When the demand is high and the supply is low, the condition is referred to as a *seller's market*. In the first case the buyer has the bargaining advantage; in the second, the seller has the advantage.

PRICE AND SUPPLY

1. The available supply of a commodity depends on its price and on the prices of products that could be produced instead.

2. An increase in the supply of a commodity tends to make its price fall; a decrease in the supply tends to make the price rise.

3. If the quantity supplied is greater than the quantity demanded, prices will fall; if the quantity demanded is greater than the quantity supplied, prices will rise.

Price and Consumption

People who buy goods want to pay the lowest price possible. This is because they are interested in getting the most for their money. Businesses usually have to buy this way to make a profit.

As the price of a commodity increases, the number of people who buy that commodity at the price asked decreases. Take the example of clothing. Normally, an increase in the price of clothing will reduce the amount purchased unless incomes are increased.

PRICE AND QUANTITY OF COMMODITY USED

1. In general, as the price of a given commodity rises, the quantity of it used will decrease. In general, as price decreases, the quantity used will increase.

2. If the quantity demanded is greater than the quantity produced, the price will rise. If the quantity demanded is less than the quantity produced, the price will decrease.

Price and Demand

Usually people think of demand as simply how much of some given commodity is wanted. But in economics the term *demand* refers to the amount of a product or service that people would buy at several different prices, assuming that their income remains the same. Ordinarily, people will buy less of a product or a service at a high price than they will at a low price. For instance, people will buy fewer T-bone steaks at $3 a pound than at $1.50 a pound. Furthermore, when the demand for a product increases, the price may go up also. Using food as an example again, if the price of eggs has been approximately 85 cents a dozen for some time and the demand for eggs increases 10% per month for 5 consecutive months, it is probable that the price of eggs will go up also.

Factors Affecting Demand. Three things may affect the demand for a product or a service. (1) The amount of money people have to spend may change. If it increases, demand will increase; and if it decreases, demand will decrease. (2) The habits and desires of people may change, affecting their willingness to buy the product or service. For instance, water sports may become increasingly popular, thus increasing the demand for boats, water skis, and other similar equipment. On the other hand, the popularity of water sports may decline, thus decreasing the demand for equipment. (3) People may substitute one article for another. For example, margarine is a substitute for butter. If the price of margarine goes up, the demand for butter may increase. Likewise, if the price of margarine goes down, the demand for butter may decrease.

If the price is favorable to the producer, large quantities of the product will be offered for sale.

Elasticity of Demand. A commodity is said to have an *elastic demand* when a change in price will bring about considerable change in the amount of that commodity that will be purchased. The demand for a commodity is *inelastic* when a change in price will bring about little or no change in the quantity of the commodity purchased.

As an example of elastic demand, let us consider the case of automobiles. Many car manufacturers have discovered that, by reducing the price of their cars, a much larger number can be sold. The sale of a larger number will enable the manufacturer to produce cars at lower per unit cost. The reduction in price in many instances has resulted in the manufacturers making more profit than they made at the previous higher price.

A hypothetical case about the demand for automobiles will serve to illustrate the general principle of elastic demand.

THE PRINCIPLE OF ELASTIC DEMAND

Price per Car	Number That Can Be Sold	Total Receipts from Sales	Profits from Sales
$6,000	75,000	$450,000,000	$16,200,000
5,600	125,000	700,000,000	28,000,000
4,800	175,000	840,000,000	38,400,000
3,400	250,000	850,000,000	30,000,000

It is evident from this analysis that the reduction in price proves profitable up to the point where the price is approximately $4,800 a car. Any further reduction in the selling price of the car results in a decrease in the total profit.

As an example of inelastic demand, a decrease in the price of bread may cause only a slight increase in the demand. The profit becomes less at the reduced price if the cost of production remains about the same. A hypothetical example will serve best to illustrate the principle of inelastic demand.

THE PRINCIPLE OF INELASTIC DEMAND

Price per Loaf of Bread	Number of Loaves That Can be Sold	Total Receipts from Sales	Profits from Sales
75¢	6,000,000	$4,500,000	$120,000
65¢	6,250,000	4,062,500	90,000
59¢	6,500,000	3,835,000	12,000
25¢	6,750,000	1,687,500	Loss, $30,000

From these analyses we see that demand and price are interrelated and that demand has an important effect on price. Demand for a commodity tends to increase the price when the supply of the commodity is limited.

PRICE AND DEMAND

1. Demand for a product is *elastic* when a change in its price has considerable effect on the quantity used.

2. Demand for a product is *inelastic* when a change in its price has little or no effect on the quantity used.

3. In general, an increase in demand for a product having an elastic demand tends to make its price rise; a decrease in demand makes its price fall.

4. Price increases when the supply of a commodity is limited in relation to the demand for it.

Even in the case of an inelastic demand, these rules do not hold strictly true when prices get too high. Although the demand for bread, regardless of price, is relatively inelastic, if the price were to go high enough relative to the price of potatoes, people with limited income would shift to the buying of potatoes as a substitute. This represents *substitution* as a principle of economics.

PRINCIPLE OF SUBSTITUTION

The amount of a commodity used becomes smaller when the price of a substitute product is reduced.

Price and Competition

An essential feature of a free enterprise or market economy is the competition among producers of economic goods for the favor of the consumer. The rivalry is of two kinds: (1) price competition and (2) nonprice competition. Through *price competition*, producers or distributors attempt to take business away from their competitors by offering their goods or services at lower prices than their competitors. Some producers and distributors also offer nonprice incentives, such as higher quality of goods, latest styles, inventions and innovations, free delivery service, and installation and maintenance services. These nonprice inducements to attract consumers are collectively referred to as *nonprice competition*.

Nonprice competition is based on factors other than price.

Price competition is based on selling price.

Price competition tends to force prices down to the lowest possible level that will still permit full coverage of the costs of production plus a reasonable profit for the industry as a whole. More efficient firms will make a better profit; less efficient firms will make a lower profit or might suffer a loss.

Competition is one means of protection for the consumer, for it helps to minimize prices, to promote efficiency, and to assure buyers that they can obtain what they want at the time they want it. Fundamentally we operate on the basis of a competitive system; but as will be discussed later, we also have some regulated monopolies and occasionally price controls, which set the maximum prices allowed on various goods.

Under free competition, no producer can persistently sell goods at prices that are much higher than those of competitors. If producers make excessive profit — in other words, if they charge prices that are relatively high — their customers will buy from competitors that sell at lower prices. New competitors may also enter the field. As a result of this competition, the high prices that were formerly charged will be reduced.

Efficient businesses may make more profit than inefficient ones. Inefficient producers who cannot succeed in keeping costs low find it impossible to compete with efficient producers. When inefficient producers try to lower prices to compete with efficient producers, they fail to make a profit and have to quit business.

Through competition, buyers tend to get goods at the lowest prices at which the goods can be produced.

The economic principle of substitution is also an important factor in the competitive system. If prices of cotton go to a high level, there is likely to be a shift to substitutes such as rayon.

PRICE AND COMPETITION

1. Free competition among producers of a commodity tends to assure efficiency in production, high-quality products, and low costs of production.

2. Free competition among retailers and wholesalers of a commodity tends to cause the consumer price to fall towards the cost of production plus handling charges.

B. ECONOMIC FACTORS RELATED TO PRICE

Demand, supply, and competition are factors that directly affect price. In addition, monopoly, the value of money, credit, and taxes are factors that indirectly affect price.

Price and Monopoly

In a few instances, a producer free from competition may have absolute power to determine the selling price of a certain product or service. By releasing for sale a supply of goods or services that is less than the amount that would be purchased, the producer keeps prices high. This is a situation known as *monopoly*. As there is no competition, the monopolist may try to charge what it pleases. The monopolist usually limits production to keep prices artificially high. The monopolist also tries to create and maintain demand in order to get the prices asked. In a monopoly, prices are not necessarily determined by the cost of production; rather, as has been explained, they may be determined by the monopolist.

Telegraph and telephone companies provide interesting examples of monopolies, or at least partial monopolies. If one telephone company has a monopoly on telephone service in a particular city, it has control over the supply of that service. In the absence of any local control, the telephone company could set its own rates. A rise in the rates might cause some people to discontinue telephone service. If the rates were to continue to rise, the telephone company might lose so many customers that it would not be able to make a profit. State governments, however, reserve the right to regulate the rates, or prices, charged by such companies.

The production of diamonds is controlled largely by monopoly. The monopoly governs the price and keeps it high. As a result of a restriction in the supply, diamonds are in constant demand. The volume of sales is limited, however, by the high price. At the high price at which diamonds are sold, a large profit is made. If the price were lowered, the rate of profit would decrease, although the amount demanded would increase. If the price were lowered still more, it would eventually reach a point at which the total sales would not pay the producers as much profit as they made at the former high price.

PRICE AND MONOPOLY

1. In monopolies not regulated by government, supply and price are manipulated in relation to demand to yield the maximum profit.

2. Government regulation, rather than supply and demand, determines price for some monopolies such as public utilities.

Price and Money

Money is our medium of exchange. It also serves as the basis for establishing the relative values of goods. The value of money is determined by the amount of goods that a dollar will purchase. When the value of a dollar is low, the dollar will not buy as much as when its value is high. In other words, money is cheap if it buys little, and it is dear if it buys much. When money changes in value, prices in general change.

Two factors that affect the price level are (1) the quantity of money and (2) the rapidity with which money is used. The amount of money in the United States is less than the total value of goods being exchanged at a particular time. It is estimated that the total quantity of money in the United States changes hands from 20 to 40 times a year. The quantity has been increased several times during the history of the United States by the issue of new paper money in the form of representative money or credit money. When there is an increase in the money available to buy goods and this money is used rapidly, prices tend to rise. The supply of dollars is

The amount of money available to consumers affects both demand and price.

greater, and the increase in rapidity with which money is used has the same effect as an increase in the amount. The general rise in price is not always in proportion, however, to the increase in the supply of money or to the increase in turnover.

As a simple example, let us consider an island on which there is a certain amount of money and a relatively elastic demand for certain goods. The people who have money will soon establish the values of goods. If the total supply of money is suddenly doubled, however, everyone is in the same relative position. Each person has twice as much money as formerly but cannot buy twice as much goods because all the people want the goods in the same proportion as before. If a person attempts to buy goods with the same amount of money formerly used, that person will find that other people are willing to pay more because they have more money. He or she will therefore have to pay just as much as anyone else. Prices in terms of money will rise because of the increase in the supply of money. In other words, increasing the supply of money has caused inflation of commodity prices.

Price and Credit

Increases and decreases in credit affect price in much the same way as increases and decreases in the supply of money. Since credit expands the use of money, it serves to increase the rapidity with which money is used. If a person has $100 to spend and borrows $100, he or she has a total purchasing power of $200. If, at the same time, the supply of products and services remains unchanged, prices will increase because there is an increased amount of money and credit with which to buy products and services. Of course, prices won't rise if just one person borrows money; but in the United States thousands of people are borrowing money daily.

When money and credit are increased, however, the supply of products and services may also increase. If the purchasing power continues to increase faster than the supply of goods and services, prices will continue to rise. When credit decreases, prices tend to decrease.

Price and Taxes

Generally, high taxes on producers and distributors tend to increase prices, for taxes make up part of the cost of producing any article or providing any service. If a high tax is levied on a building, it must be included in computing the rent of the building. If a sales tax is levied on any item, such as gasoline, clothing, or drugs, it is a part of the cost of the product regardless of the person against whom it has been assessed. Part or all of the taxes are usually passed on to the consumer, either directly or indirectly. Therefore, the levying of a tax against a particular product will eventually cause a rise in the price of that product.

Federal, state, and local taxes levied on the incomes of individuals reduce the purchasing power of consumers. This tends to decrease the demand for goods and services and therefore tends to lower prices.

Price Controls by Government

The preceding discussion of prices has assumed that there would be no control of prices. However, prices are controlled to a certain extent by government, by business, by farmers, and by workers. Organized groups representing various aspects of production, distribution, and consumption attempt to obtain government protection or regulation on their behalf. Labor, professional, business, and farm groups practically all seek some kind of federal legislation primarily to give them an economic advantage. Some of the legislation is undoubtedly desirable, and some is necessary. However, from the early days of the Roman Empire to the present, attempts to control price and to regulate income have created many other problems.

As citizens, we vote in state and national elections on economic issues. It is highly important that we understand clearly the

issues having to do with prices, subsidies, and government ownership of industry so that we may have a basis for intelligent voting.

Goods and Services. The federal government owns and operates some industries. Sometimes it sets the prices of its commodities or services at less than cost and sometimes at more than cost.
Among the industries owned by the federal government in which
prices are controlled are the United States Postal Service and the
Tennessee Valley Authority. Some states also engage in production and distribution. States and municipalities own and operate
many industrial and commercial enterprises, most of which have
some of the characteristics of monopolies. In many government-
owned enterprises, prices are set without reference to costs. Deficits are paid from funds derived from taxation.

The rates for services provided by public utilities, not government owned, are usually regulated or controlled by the state or the
federal government. For example, the rates for telephone service
are under the control of the government. Likewise, railroad pas-
senger rates and freight rates are government controlled.

Economic Emergencies. At various times, primarily since
1930, the federal government has extended its power to control
prices because of either a real or an assumed economic emergency.

Minimum prices. During the depression years of 1933 to
1936, the National Industrial Recovery Act regulated minimum
prices of certain commodities and determined the volume of production of some industries by restricting the quantity of raw materials available. The purpose was to aid in recovering from the economic depression. About the same time, the Secretary of
Agriculture was empowered to set up a quantity restriction on the
production of certain farm crops. If this quantity restriction on
production was agreed upon by the growers of the crop, then the
government would make subsidy payments to the farmers if the
market price of the crop fell below the established minimum price,
called *parity*. This agreement to limit production and this guarantee of a specified minimum price constitute control through price
supports.

Maximum prices. During World War II, the Emergency Price
Control Act regulated maximum prices for most goods. The maximum prices allowed were called *price ceilings*. The regulations
affected the producers of raw materials, manufacturers, wholesalers, and retailers but did not include farm commodities, wages

of labor, or the compensation of professional workers (wages and salaries were restricted through the War Labor Board). The regulations were administered by the Office of Price Administration, commonly known as OPA.

Wage-price freeze. Starting in August of 1971 and continuing for three years, President Nixon imposed direct controls on wages and prices. Actually, the price controls went through four distinct stages, starting with wages and prices, then moving to the larger area of the economy, and then eventually phasing out. The purpose of the wage-price freeze was to stop inflation, which had been increasing rapidly at that time.

Until the controls were put into effect, the major method used to reduce inflation was a "tight money" policy imposed by the Federal Reserve System. The Federal Reserve System made less money available to the economy in an attempt to reduce prices. This approach was an indirect method, and the Nixon Administration decided to attack the problem more directly. However, the type of direct method used needed to be stopped before the mid-1970s since it was affecting the supply of goods. For example, under the price phase it was impossible for most steel companies to make products such as barbed wire. Consequently, they shifted their products to other areas and barbed wire simply was not available. Many more examples of this type could be cited. As a result, the use of more indirect methods became the standard practice by the mid-1970s. For example, in 1974 President Ford imposed a tax per barrel on imported fuel oil, which indirectly increased gasoline prices.

Government controls do, however, still exist on most forms of transportation, financial institutions, and natural gas. Sometimes the direct controls work against their intent. Thus, in recent years the trend has been to drop as many regulations as possible.

Interest rates. For many years, the various states have had regulations as to the maximum interest rates that may be charged for borrowing money. In more recent years, the Board of Governors of the Federal Reserve System has exercised the power of control over the discount or interest rates that Federal Reserve banks may charge member banks. This control influences the rates of interest that banks charge to customers.

Wage rates. With the enactment of laws regulating minimum wages per hour and maximum hours per week for labor, a control of the price of labor has been in effect. Not all workers are covered by the laws, but all wages are influenced by this legislation.

Credit. From time to time the federal government may exercise control over prices by means of credit policies designed to prevent inflation and rapidly increasing prices. The federal government seldom exercises direct control over prices by means of credit policies, but the authority does exist. It has been used at different times in the past. For example, when larger down payments are needed for major appliances or homes, fewer of these goods will be sold. Also, if the payment period is reduced from a long period of time to a short period of time, buyers tend to reduce their purchases.

However, the Federal Reserve Board does exercise a good deal of control over credit through its monetary policy, which is discussed in detail in Chapter 15.

Price Indexes

Business managers and consumers have an interest in the trends in production, wages and salaries, prices, costs of production and distribution, and similar factors that reveal economic and business conditions. A system of price index numbers has been developed to measure the price level and to make trends more easily observed and understood. Many trade organizations or retailers, wholesalers, manufacturers, and others prepare index numbers for their commodities and services.

Index numbers are percentage figures to measure such economic activity factors as industrial production, consumer prices, and wholesale prices. A *price index* compares the average of the prices of a group of goods and services in one period with the average of the prices of the same goods or services in another period. A *base period* is arbitrarily selected as the period with which current prices or current production is to be compared. The one currently in use is 1967. The index number for 1967 is 100.

Consumer Price Index. The most widely used price index is the *Consumer Price Index* (CPI). There are actually two CPIs. The first index (CPI-W) has been used since 1919 and represents only urban wage earners and clerical workers making up less than 45% of the population. The second index (CPI-U) was created in 1978 and represents all urban residents (salaried workers, self-employed workers, retirees, some rural families, and unemployed persons, as well as wage earners and clerical workers) making up 80% of the population. The remaining 20% of the population (military, people in institutions, and most rural families) is not represented in either index. Generally most wage earners (and especially union employees) will want to use the CPI-W; others (especially renters, self-employed, and retired persons) will want to use the CPI-U.

The CPIs include a market basket of purchases in eight major groups (see table below). These indexes measure the change in the average price of a representative sample of nearly 400 goods and services.

PERCENT DISTRIBUTION OF THE CPI MARKET BASKET

Major Group	% Distribution	
	CPI-W	CPI-U
Food and alcoholic beverages	20.4	19.5
Housing	39.8	42.9
Apparel	7.0	7.0
Transportation	19.8	17.0
Medical care	4.2	4.6
Entertainment	4.3	4.5
Personal care	1.8	1.7
Other goods and services	2.7	2.8
	100.0	100.0

The CPIs are stated in terms of index numbers. For example, the index number for CPI-W prices in April, 1978, was 190.6. This means that the average of consumer prices in April, 1978, was 90.6% higher than the average of consumer prices in the base

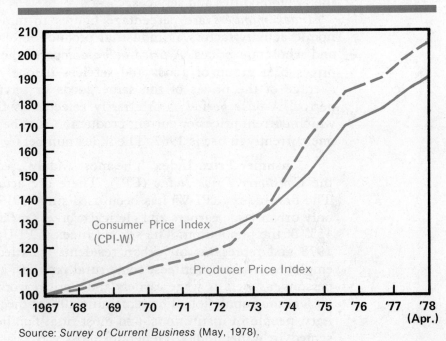

Price Indexes, 1967-1978 (1967 = 100)

Consumer Price Index (CPI-W)

Producer Price Index

Source: *Survey of Current Business* (May, 1978).

period of 1967. In other words, what a person could buy in 1967 for $1, by 1978 cost $1.91. As can be seen from the illustration on page 164, during the 1970s the CPI rose very rapidly.

Cost-of-living adjustments in wage contracts and pension plans are frequently tied to the CPI. When the CPI changes, so do the amounts paid for wages and pensions. For example, if the CPI rises, wages or pensions automatically go up according to the terms of the agreement.

Producer Price Index. Another index that is watched by some economists is the *Producer Price Index* (PPI), formerly known as the Wholesale Price Index (WPI). This index measures basically farm products, processed foods and feeds, and industrial commodities. An increase (or decrease) in the Producer Price Index is usually reflected at a later date in the Consumer Price Index. Retailers often watch the PPI in order to set prices on goods to be sold at a later date. For most consumers, however, the CPI is of more importance than the PPI.

WHAT EVERYONE SHOULD KNOW ABOUT VALUES AND PRICES

1. The price system is the process by which people exchange labor or products for the goods and services they need through the medium of money.

2. High prices tend to increase production, whereas high production tends to decrease prices.

3. As the supply of goods increases, the price tends to be lowered.

4. The greater the demand for goods in relation to the supply, the higher prices tend to be.

5. The price of a commodity influences consumption.

6. Competition tends to force a reasonable relationship between (a) the cost to produce and (b) the price asked.

7. When money is plentiful and credit relatively easy to obtain, prices tend to be high.

8. Taxes on producers tend to increase the cost of goods and therefore to increase prices. Taxes on consumers reduce purchasing power and therefore tend to decrease consumption.

9. Some prices are partially or completely controlled by governments.

10. Price indexes indicate price changes over a period of time. The two most common ones are the Consumer Price Index (CPI) and the Producer Price Index (PPI).

REVIEW QUESTIONS

Section A

1. When does a good or service have economic value?
2. How does price relate to economic value?
3. Under what circumstances would water have economic value?
4. What determines economic value in the barter system?
5. What is the relationship between price and money?
6. Under what condition would a business continue to produce goods without making a profit?
7. What is the relationship between price and production?
8. How does the cost of production affect the price of a product in the long run?
9. What do we mean by supply?
10. What are the two characteristics of a buyer's market? Of a seller's market?
11. What do we mean by demand in economics?
12. When does a commodity have an elastic demand? An inelastic demand?
13. Under what conditions would a consumer substitute one product for another?
14. What do we mean by nonprice competition?

Section B

15. What is the main feature that identifies a monopoly?
16. What really determines the value of a dollar?
17. What effect does credit have on prices?
18. How do taxes affect prices?
19. What is an example of a government service operated in such a manner that the prices charged for services do not cover all expenses?
20. What government agency has the responsibility of regulating interest rates?
21. What are index numbers?
22. What does a price index do?
23. What is measured by the Consumer Price Index? By the Producer Price Index?

DISCUSSION QUESTIONS

Section A

1. How does the price system work in a free enterprise or market economy?
2. If we are to have an ideal economic society, why is it absolutely necessary for the prices of goods and the prices of wages to remain relatively stationary or to fluctuate together?
3. What is the relationship between production and price in a free enterprise or market economy?
4. What is the relationship between production and profit?
5. The consumption of frozen orange juice in the United States has increased rather rapidly within the last twenty years. Why do you think the increase has taken place?
6. (a) What would be the effect on prices if the supply of a commodity (such as pencils) increases but the demand for it remains approximately the same? Why?
   (b) What would be the effect on prices if the demand for a commodity increases but the supply remains approximately the same?

7. What conditions would be necessary for a buyer's market to exist for the buyer of fresh fruits and vegetables?

8. What are the principles of elastic and inelastic demand? Give several examples other than those in the chapter to illustrate each of the principles.

9. If you were a retailer, would you prefer to sell products with an elastic demand or to sell products with an inelastic demand? Why?

10. The history of most newly introduced products, such as air-conditioning equipment and the automobile, shows that the products first sold at high prices, although they were not nearly so good as they were later. How do you account for the reduction in price?

11. How can automation affect prices?

Section B

12. Is there a need for regulation of public utility rates? Why?

13. What logical reasons can be given for the governments of diamond-producing countries not to regulate the production of diamonds?

14. What would be the effect on prices of goods if all installment sales and all charge sales were to be discontinued?

15. How do you think a sales tax affects prices?

16. How can the federal government affect prices of goods through control of wage rates?

17. (a) What are some examples of prices of consumer goods and services that you think should be regulated by government? State the reasons for your point of view.

    (b) What are some examples of prices of consumer goods and services that you think should be regulated by competition? State the reasons for your point of view.

18. Refer to the table on page 164. Why are food, housing, and transportation weighted so heavily among the 8 major expenditure groups in constructing the CPIs?

APPLICATION PROBLEMS

Section A

1. Conduct a panel discussion on the immediate and long-range effects of a rapid rise in prices in general on: (a) farmers, (b) wage earners, (c) policemen, (d) retired persons, (e) government expenses, and (f) retail merchants. Each person on the panel should represent one of the categories listed.

2. Analyze the prices advertised in an edition of your local newspaper for common food items such as bread, sugar, potatoes, bananas, milk, head lettuce, bacon, and potato chips. Compare the prices advertised by different stores, and report the differences in prices that you find. Why do such differences exist? What keeps the differences from becoming greater?

3. In studying this chapter, you have learned that when the price of a commodity increases, the number of people who buy that commodity at the price asked will ordinarily decrease. In an attempt to deal more thoroughly with this idea, prepare three lists of items: (a) things people will buy with almost no regard for price, (b) things people will tend not to buy if prices are sharply increased, and (c) things people will stop buying if substantial price increases go into effect. Study the three lists you have

prepared and in general terms describe or characterize the items in each list. What conclusions can you reach regarding the relationships between prices, demand for various commodities, and the nature of people's needs?

Section B

4. Using the following table, determine the relative changes in the prices of food, housing, apparel, and medical care for the years given. Which items increased the most? Which the least? Note that 1967 = 100.

CONSUMER PRICE INDEXES FOR SELECTED
PRODUCTS IN SELECTED YEARS (1967 = 100)

Year	Food	Housing	Apparel	Medical Care
1950	74.5	72.8	79.0	53.7
1960	88.0	90.2	89.6	79.1
1970	114.9	118.9	116.1	120.6
1979 (Apr.)	226.3	219.8	165.4	235.1

5. In your school or public library, locate the latest copy of *Economic Indicators*, the *Federal Reserve Bulletin, Survey of Current Business*, or some other source of government statistics. Study and analyze the tables showing the Consumer Price Index, the Producer Price Index, and other statistics on consumer prices, producer prices, and prices received and paid by farmers. Prepare a report indicating such observations as general trends in prices, rapid increases and decreases in prices, and effects of prices on consumer goods.

COMMUNITY PROJECTS

Section A

1. Make a study in the stores in your community and gather evidence that the prices for comparable products vary in numerous ways. Make a list of the stores that offer trading stamps, door prizes, coupons, credit premiums, and other "rewards" that in effect make prices different. Ask several merchants to describe their efforts to meet the price competition provided by other merchants. Make either an oral or a written report of your findings.

2. Ask the librarian in your public library to show you the files of newspapers from your local area. In the financial section of the newspapers you will find quotations (prices) on agricultural products such as wheat, corn, beef, and eggs. Select five items for the study of prices. Look up the prices of the five selected items for the corresponding month for each of the last five years. Prepare a table of the price trends of the selected items for five years. What changes in prices did you observe? What do you believe to be the reasons for the changes in prices?

Section B

3. The business sections of the Sunday issues of large city newspapers, *The Wall Street Journal, Business Week, Newsweek*, and other sources frequently contain articles about the prices consumers pay. Make a study of such materials, going back about six or eight weeks. Search out the reasons given for the price increases and/or decreases during that time. Then prepare a report to the class on the trends in consumer prices and the reported reasons for their changes or lack of change.

4. In 1979 the U.S. government began phasing out its price controls on domestic oil production, thus enabling U.S. oil companies to raise prices of domestic oil to compete with OPEC prices. This deregulation greatly increased profits of U.S. oil companies. Against these increased profits, the government was considering a "windfall profits" tax. From reports in newspapers, weekly business magazines, radio and television news reports, and interviews with people in your community, obtain responses to the following questions:

    (a) How did the government propose using the "windfall profits" tax?

    (b) Was the "windfall profits" tax just another form of government price control?

    (c) What was the reaction of American oil companies to the "windfall profits" tax?

    (d) How did the American oil companies say they would use the increased profits from deregulation?

    (e) Would the "windfall profits" tax help to counteract the increased domestic price of domestic oil and also help to reduce inflation?

Economic Fluctuations

PURPOSE OF THE CHAPTER

Income, prices, and profits are affected by the level of business activity, which in turn affects each of us. This chapter is intended to help you understand business fluctuations and cycles and to acquaint you with economic indicators.

After studying this chapter, you will be able to:

1. Describe the business cycle.
2. Explain the nature of inflation and deflation.
3. Explain how measurement of business activity helps individuals, owners, and managers in planning future operations.
4. Discuss what economic indicators are available and how they are used.

A. FLUCTUATIONS IN BUSINESS ACTIVITIES

Business conditions are almost always changing. There are periods of great activity and of less activity. The changes occur in the total amount of goods produced, total employment, average prices, income, and other business activities. Fluctuation or change in business activities is desirable, for economic growth cannot take place without it. Change may be predicted, but knowing the severity of the change and when it will take place constitute problems for all engaged in business.

The Business Cycle

In an earlier chapter, economic activity was defined as any procedure or act that is concerned with satisfying people's wants and needs for goods and services through production, distribution, and consumption. It was pointed out that we speak of the combined or total production of all goods by all people and all business firms in the country as *aggregate production*. Likewise, *aggregate income* refers to the combined or total income earned in the country, *aggregate supply of goods* refers to the total supply of goods for the country, and so forth. Applying this idea, it may be said that the business cycle is a fluctuation in aggregate (total) economic activity. Ordinarily, fluctuation in one business activity, such as production, is accompanied by fluctuation or change in other basic economic activities, such as employment.

The *business cycle* may be defined as alternating periods of expansion and contraction in production, employment, income, and other economic activities. Once an expansion or contraction of economic activity gets under way, it spreads from firm to firm, from area to area, and from process to process until a peak or a bottom in aggregate (total) activity is reached.

Phases of the Business Cycle. Wide economic fluctuations seem to be characteristic of free markets. If we are to control wide fluctuations, we must first understand them. To better understand business fluctuations, economists study a model they call a business cycle. Business activity does not normally follow the business cycle exactly, but the model is helpful in understanding business fluctuations under free market conditions. Also, a study of the business cycle helps one to understand how wide fluctuations might be controlled.

If management were able to forecast with certainty the business activity in the period ahead, then it would be much easier to plan how much to produce, how much to buy, what prices to charge, and other similar activities. It would help management in its planning to know whether a business is about to enter a period of general increase or decrease in activity.

Each major business cycle has four phases or periods, as follows:

1. *Prosperity* — During this phase all economic activity is at a relatively high level.
2. *Recession* — During this phase there is a marked decline in the level of economic activity.
3. *Depression* — During this phase economic activity drops to a level as low as it will go during the business cycle.
4. *Recovery* — During this phase the level of economic activity begins to increase.

The length of the business cycle is the number of months or years from the peak of one period of prosperity to the peak of the next period of prosperity.

The following illustration shows the four phases of a business cycle. The usual characteristics of each of the four phases are given in the chart at the bottom of the page.

Phases of the Business Cycle

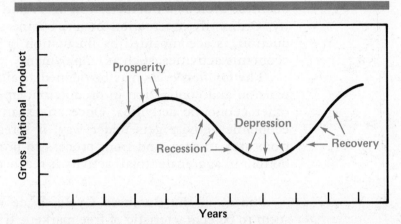

Source: Thomas J. Hailstones and Michael J. Brennan, *Economics* (2d ed.; Cincinnati: South-Western Publishing Co., 1975), p. 176.

USUAL CHARACTERISTICS OF THE BUSINESS CYCLE

Prosperity	Recession	Depression	Recovery
1. Wages increase.	1. Business stops investing and begins paying off loans.	1. Spending declines.	1. Interest rates are low.
2. High level of employment is reached.	2. Borrowing is reduced.	2. Prices become lower.	2. Most debts are paid.
3. People are overly optimistic.	3. Inventories accumulate.	3. Unemployment increases.	3. Banks are willing to lend.
4. Demand for consumer goods increases.	4. Demand for goods decreases.	4. Inventories decline.	4. Production increases.
5. Demand for loans increases.	5. Average hours worked declines.	5. Buying is for immediate purposes only.	5. Employment increases.
6. Interest rates increase.	6. Profits decline.	6. Borrowing is low.	6. Prices begin to increase.
7. New businesses start.	7. Prices decline.	7. Business failures increase.	7. Profits increase.
8. New construction and expansion of business nears completion.	8. Banks are unwilling to make loans.	8. Banks accumulate excess reserves.	8. Construction begins.
9. Prices increase further.	9. People become pessimistic.	9. Interest rates fall.	9. Incomes increase.
10. Banks loan all their excess reserves.	10. Volume of business declines.	10. Operating costs decline.	10. Demand for goods increases.
11. Profits are high.	11. Business failures increase.	11. Production is efficient, but low.	11. Consumer goods are produced.
12. Production is high.	12. Number of jobs decline.	12. Wage rates are low.	12. Capital goods production increases.
	13. Business expansion is limited.		13. Installment sales increase.

Causes of the Business Cycle. People are aware that business conditions change, but they are not always aware of the causes or the significance of the changes. Even experts disagree on the analysis of the business cycle.

Business people and economists give many explanations for changes in business conditions. Their explanations vary widely. Some explanations credit or blame the current state of business activity on the political party in power, on labor troubles, on communism, or on conditions brought about by the weather. No completely satisfactory or reliable explanation for the cyclical changes in business activity has ever been given.

There will always be a certain amount of fluctuation in profits, in the total amount of business, and in the incomes of individuals. If we could prevent the extreme fluctuations, we would have the cure for depressions.

Inflation

The first phase of the business cycle is known as prosperity. Sometimes prosperity is incorrectly referred to as inflation.

The essential characteristics of a period of *prosperity* are: (a) high production, (b) high employment, and (c) stable prices. In contrast, prices in a period of *inflation* increase not only to unreasonable heights but also at alarmingly rapid rates. In periods of inflation the purchasing power of the dollar declines rapidly.

Inflation occurs when the total demand for goods and services is greater than the supply available at a given time. This situation usually produces a shortage of goods, which ordinarily results in an increase in prices. Inflation also may occur when wage increases cause the prices of goods to rise.

General price increases are often followed immediately by a demand for wage increases on the grounds that the cost of living has increased. Likewise, a general increase in wages is often closely followed by increases in prices of commodities and services on the grounds that the cost of producing goods and services has risen because of increased wages. Thus, as prices tend to increase, wages also tend to increase; and as wages increase, prices rise. This relationship of price increase and wage increase is called either the *wage-price spiral* or the *price-wage spiral*. In the long run an alternating increase in wages and in prices (when a spiral has been created) causes the purchasing power of the dollar to decrease.

Rapid increases in prices and in wages and rapid decreases in the purchasing power of the dollar tend to be harmful to our economy. Inflation can be harmful to business and to many groups of people unless it is kept under control. Several ways to halt or control inflation are given in the chart below. Further discussions of some of these methods are presented in Chapters 12 and 15.

WAYS TO HALT OR CONTROL INFLATION

Government
   Control money and credit supply, thus avoiding overexpansion of business activity.
   Increase taxes, thus reducing private spending power.
   Avoid further increases in the national debt, except for grave emergencies such as war.
   Reduce nonessential government expenditures.

Business Firms
   Keep production geared to reasonable demand.
   Avoid unnecessary stockpiling of raw materials and semifinished products.
   Increase productivity per employee.
   Postpone construction as much as possible.
   Maintain present prices, increasing them only as necessary.
   Be content with reasonable profit.
   Cooperate with labor and government in stabilizing prices.

Labor
   Increase productivity per man, thus decreasing costs, hence prices.
   Give a full day's service for a day's wages; wages collected for work not done increase costs, hence prices.
   Cooperate with management in controlling the wage-price spiral.

Consumers
   Engage in productive effort of some kind; work, earn, produce.
   Increase personal savings.
   Reduce personal spending.
   Participate actively in civic and political activities with a view toward halting continuous rise in prices.

Government-Business-Labor-Consumers
   Before making any economic decision, weigh its ultimate effect on the price-wage (wage-price) spiral.
   Cooperatively attack with strength and foresight the task of preventing further inflation.

During inflation some firms can adjust to rapidly rising prices. They attract capital and labor from other businesses which become lost to the economy as a result.

Deflation

A rapid fall in general prices and income extending over a period of a few months results in *deflation*. This means that noticeably more goods and services may be obtained for a dollar than was true before deflation took place.

Deflation and economic depression are not the same but they are related. If deflation is rapid and continues over several months, business activity is curtailed sharply. This means that not only do prices fall but production of goods and services decreases and, therefore, unemployment increases.

WAYS TO HALT OR CONTROL DEFLATION

Governments
    Encourage credit expansion, which will stimulate business activity and employment.
    Decrease federal taxes, leaving more money in the hands of people.
    Increase federal spending on public works, relief, subsidies, national security, etc., which tends to stimulate business activity.

Business Firms
    Extend credit to consumers to stimulate consumer buying.
    Improve service, thus stimulating demand for goods and services.
    Encourage people to spend more of their savings.

Consumers
    Use personal savings for purchase of needed goods.
    Increase personal spending within reasonable bounds.
    Cooperate with civic and government movements to increase business activity.

There are advantages to deflation. Money that has been saved prior to deflation will buy much more than it did in periods of inflation. Likewise, a dollar of income from investments from savings that were made under conditions of inflation will also buy more than was true under inflation.

Although some advantages of deflation are recognized, deflation can reach a point that is very harmful to business activity in general. It is necessary to have some ways to control deflation.

The Problem of Fluctuating Business Conditions

Extreme changes in business activity resulting in rapid changes in prices may be detrimental to both business firms and individuals. The problem is to find effective means of reducing, if not eliminating, the effects of changes in business conditions.

The Employment Act of 1946 provided for a Council of Economic Advisers. The Council's primary purpose is to recommend to the President economic policies for the maintenance of employment, production, and purchasing power and to avoid the extreme fluctuations in business activity that lead to periods of inflation and depression. Each year in December, the Council is required to make a report to the President on the economic conditions of the nation. The recommendations of the President in his Economic Report to Congress are ordinarily based on, or at least greatly influenced by, the report of the Council of Economic Advisers. The

---

FACTS EVERYONE SHOULD KNOW ABOUT FLUCTUATING BUSINESS CONDITIONS, CHANGING PRICES, AND INFLATION AND DEFLATION

1. Ordinarily, extreme fluctuations in general business activity are caused not by one factor but by a combination of several factors.

2. Sharply rising prices result in lowering the purchasing power of wages and income, an economic condition known as inflation.

3. In periods of decreasing prices, the purchasing power of savings and wages increases, but chances to earn wages or an income decrease. This economic condition is known as deflation.

4. Inflation has been ruinous to many nations: rapid deflation can harm both individuals and business firms. In the long run, everyone is hurt by both severe inflation and severe deflation.

5. The combined efforts of government, business firms, labor, and all consumers are required to halt inflation and deflation.

Council of Economic Advisers thus becomes the central government agency for analyzing and interpreting business conditions for the guidance of Congress.

B. MEASURING BUSINESS ACTIVITY

In operating either a small individually owned business or a large corporation, managers are aware that their success depends on many factors that affect the profits they make. Among these factors are: (1) demand for their product, that is, the kinds of products people want and the amount or quantity they will buy; (2) price level, such as the cost of raw materials; (3) wage rates for employees; (4) rates of interest on borrowed funds; (5) expenses, such as taxes; and (6) the income that the business may expect. These are all economic matters that affect individuals, local businesses, and corporations of national and international scope.

Managers of both large and small businesses have to make decisions, most of which will affect the profits in the year or years ahead. They know that their business activities will be affected by general business conditions. If they had the answers to certain questions, they probably would make wiser decisions than they would without the answers. Some of these questions are: Is it probable that expansion and growth in business activity in general will hold steady, increase, or decrease? Will the total demand for all goods and services change? Will the average level of all prices hold steady, go up, or go down? Will the total income for the country tend to remain about the same, rise, or fall?

The level of business activity affects inventories.

The answers to the questions that are concerned with business conditions in general are found by measuring and analyzing the *aggregate* (total) economic activities for the country as a whole.

Government Surveys and Statistics

The federal government undertakes the complex task of gathering, recording, and classifying the statistical information needed to study business conditions for the country as a whole. Among the federal agencies that prepare information on business conditions are the Bureau of the Census, Department of Commerce, Department of Labor, Department of Agriculture, Securities and Exchange Commission, Council of Economic Advisers, and Federal Reserve Board. The system and the process used by the government for recording statistical information about the total economic activity of all people, business firms, and government is known as *national income accounting* or *social accounting*.

The governments of some states and a few private agencies, such as foundations, trade associations, and chambers of commerce, also gather and prepare economic information. These data are useful in measuring changes occurring in business conditions.

Types of Economic Information

Information pertaining to business activity includes such items as population, employment, production, personal and national income, wages, prices, finance, and foreign trade. By comparing current statistics with those of the past month and previous years, the trend of general business conditions may be determined. Among the most commonly used indicators are:

1. *Gross national product (GNP)*, which is the dollar value of all goods and services produced in a year in the United States.
2. *National income*, which is the total income earned by those who contribute to current production. It represents the gross national product remaining after deductions are made for indirect taxes, depreciation, and business transfer payments.
3. *Consumer prices*, which is the cost in dollars of nondurable goods used by consumers, such as food, clothing, and rent.
4. *Wholesale prices*, which represent the dollar cost to producers and distributors of farm products, processed foods, and industrial commodities.

5. *Consumer credit*, which is the total amount of debt owed by consumers on installment purchases and charge accounts.
6. *Industrial production*, which is roughly the quantity of durable and nondurable products manufactured and of minerals mined.
7. *Employment status and wages*, which indicate the number of persons employed and unemployed and the average hourly, weekly, and monthly wages of employees.
8. *Sales and inventories figures*, which show the dollar value of goods sold to consumers and of inventories of merchandise that business has on hand.

Other figures that may indicate general business conditions are statistics dealing with such items as prices of stocks, amount of bank loans, new construction, farm income, and imports and exports.

Economic Indicators

The records from which GNP and national income are derived are made up of many parts, each of which is a factor representing an economic activity. Each of these factors may be useful as a measure of business activity and a predictor of business conditions for the immediate future. Selection of the factors to use in prediction of future business activity depends partly on the nature of one's business.

The indicators of change in general business conditions are numerous. Individuals interested in business conditions generally may select the indicators they wish to use. Some indicators of change in business activity that may be used under appropriate circumstances are:

Gross national product (GNP)
National income (NI)
Personal income (PI)
Disposable personal income
Personal consumption expenditures
Personal expenditures for durable goods
Personal expenditures for nondurable goods
Personal expenditures for services

Personal savings
New plant and equipment expenditures
Compensation of employees
Corporate taxes
Corporate profits (before taxes and before inventory adjustment)
Dividends
Population
Median family income
Total employment

Rate of unemployment   Total consumer credit
Agricultural employment   Amount of new construction
Manufacturing employment   Retail sales
Government employment   Wholesale sales
Total time deposits in banks   New housing starts
Total installment debt   Exports and imports

The economic indicators selected by an individual may be figures for one month, or one quarter, or one year to show immediate current positions and trends. However, a comparison of selected indicators over a period of years is useful in showing the trend of change in those economic activity factors and is an aid in determining general business conditions. The table below shows changes in selected economic indicators for a five-year period.

CHANGES IN INDICATORS OF BUSINESS CONDITIONS IN FIVE YEARS

Item	Billions of Dollars		Increase	
	1972	1977	Amount	Percent
GNP	1,171.1	1,889.6	718.5	61.3
National Income	951.9	1,520.5	568.6	59.7
Personal Income	942.5	1,536.7	594.2	63.0
Disposable Personal Income	782.4	1,309.2	526.8	67.3
Personal Consumption Expenditures	733.0	861.2	128.2	17.4
Personal Expenditure for Durable Goods	111.0	138.2	27.2	24.5
Personal Expenditure for Nondurable Goods	299.0	333.7	34.7	11.6
Personal Expenditure for Services	322.0	389.2	67.2	20.8
Personal Savings	49.4	67.3	17.9	36.2
Compensation of Employees	715.1	1,156.3	441.2	61.7
Corporate Profits (before taxes and inventory adjustment)	96.2	171.7	75.5	78.5
Dividends	24.6	41.2	16.6	67.5

Source: Adapted from *Survey of Current Business* (May, 1978).

From this table the trend of change in each indicator for a five-year period can be observed easily. The trends shown can then be used by an individual or a business in making plans for the future.

FACTS EVERYONE SHOULD KNOW ABOUT MEASURING ECONOMIC ACTIVITY AND PREDICTORS OF BUSINESS CONDITIONS

1. The federal government gathers, classifies, and publishes statistical information useful in studying general business conditions.

2. Many departments and agencies of the federal government participate in the complex task of recording and publishing statistics on business activities. The system used is known as national income accounting.

3. Several basic measures of total business activities have been designed. The two most commonly used are the GNP and national income.

4. The GNP and national income totals and the factors of which they are comprised are useful to individuals and business owners and managers in planning their operations for the next year.

5. The goods and services that comprise the GNP are purchased and used by individual consumers, investors in business, governments, and foreign customers. Consumers use about 63% of all goods and services produced.

6. National income represents the sum of all incomes received by individuals for their contributions to the production of all goods and services.

7. Many economic activity indicators are available for studying general economic conditions. A selection of those to use should be made by each individual who is interested in general business conditions as a basis for planning operations.

8. The use of economic indicators singly or in combination to determine business conditions for the future is not infallible.

REVIEW QUESTIONS

Section A

1. What do we mean by (a) *aggregate* production and (b) *aggregate* income?
2. (a) What is the business cycle?
   (b) How is the length of the business cycle measured?
   (c) What are the phases or periods of the business cycle?
3. How will an understanding of the business cycle help the manager of a business enterprise?
4. What conditions ordinarily exist when an upswing of business activity toward a period of prosperity takes place?
5. Why are general price increases usually followed by a demand for wage increases?
6. Why is a general increase in wages usually followed closely by an increase in the price of commodities and services?

7. We all like prosperity but we would like to avoid uncontrolled inflation. Who can help to halt inflation?

8. What business conditions usually exist when there is a period of deflation?

9. What are some of the ways in which governments can help to halt or control deflation?

10. What is the primary responsibility of the President's Council of Economic Advisers?

Section B

11. On what main factors does profit-making in business depend?

12. What is national income accounting?

13. What items of information pertaining to general business conditions are available to business managers and the public?

14. How can information about business conditions be used by business managers?

15. What are the most commonly used indicators of general business conditions?

16. How can a comparison of selected economic indicators over a period of several years be useful to an individual or to a business?

DISCUSSION QUESTIONS

Section A

1. What effect does each of the four phases of the business cycle have on each of the following factors: (a) wages, (b) prices in general, (c) business profits, (d) employment opportunities, and (e) volume of production?

2. The recession and depression phases of the business cycle usually cause some business firms to discontinue operations. What characteristics or problems did the firms that went out of business probably have?

3. What are the differences between a period of prosperity and a period of inflation?

4. How does a wage-price (price-wage) spiral work?

5. Excessive installment selling is sometimes given as one of the main reasons for the beginning of a business depression. Why?

6. Why is production generally more efficient during recessions than during periods of prosperity?

7. Why does a wage-price (price-wage) spiral cause the purchasing power of the dollar to decrease?

8. Some people yearn for a return of the days when $2 would buy plenty of food for the average family for one week. Did people live any better in those times than they do during periods of high prices?

9. Refer to the box summary on page 174, which deals with the ways to halt inflation. In your judgment, which of the five groups named in the box summary can be the most effective in halting inflation? Give reasons to support your answer.

10. How does deflation work to the advantage of individuals who made investments from their savings during inflation?

Section B

11. What are some of the common economic indicators used to predict future business activity?

12. Which of the various economic indicators listed on pages 179 and 180 would probably be of greatest value to business managers engaged in the

following businesses: (a) a wholesale food distributor, (b) a construction firm that builds houses, (c) a manufacturer of children's shoes, and (d) a bank in a small rural community?

13. From what source or sources may a business manager get information about general business conditions that will help him or her in planning for the future and in managing the business?

APPLICATION PROBLEMS

Section A

1. With the help of your teacher and librarian, look for information concerning how tax cuts, tax increases, and government spending have been used in recent years for stabilizing the economy of this country. (a) What specific devices did the government use to halt inflation or to halt deflation? (b) What is the government now doing or planning to do in the near future to stabilize the price structure or to stabilize the general economy?

2. Assume that you bought a utility bond costing $1,000 and kept it for 20 years. Assume also that the price level increased 16% over the period of 20 years. How much of the original investment of $1,000 would you have lost over the period of 20 years?

Section B

3. From the *Survey of Current Business*, the *Federal Reserve Bulletin*, or some other source suggested by your teacher or librarian, obtain data for the past year for the business indicators shown in the table on page 180. Then prepare similar tables comparing these amounts for the past year with the amounts for 1972 and 1977. Show the increase or the decrease for each item both in dollars and as percentages.

4. In April of a recent year, government economists were predicting that the annual rate of growth of the GNP would be $5 billion to $6 billion for that year. In late June, the annual rate of growth was reported to be about $8.5 billion. The increase was attributed primarily to a boost in consumer spending for nondurable goods, a rise in business inventories, and an increase in exports. (a) Write a statement in which you explain the meaning of each of the three reasons given for the increase in growth of the GNP. (b) From reports of business trends in *Newsweek, Business Week, U.S. News and World Report*, or *The Wall Street Journal*, determine whether the GNP is now increasing or decreasing. (c) Write a second statement in which you explain the meaning of each of the reasons given for the current increase, decrease, or stable condition of the GNP.

COMMUNITY PROJECTS

Section A

1. Is the present a good time to buy real estate as an investment, or would it be wiser to save money now in anticipation of buying real estate later? Write your answer in a report incorporating the principles discussed in this chapter.

2. In the first half of the 1970s, the United States was in a recession following the longest period of prosperity in our history. The economy exhibited most of the characteristics of recession indicated in this chapter, with the exception that inflationary conditions continued to exist. What changes have occurred in the business cycle since 1975?

Section B

3. In this chapter we spoke a lot about the forces affecting general business conditions and the economic indicators about which data can be obtained. With this information in mind, arrange to talk with two owners of businesses. Ask them how they make use of various kinds of available information. Find out how they determine what and how much to produce or how much to purchase for resale. Prepare an oral report of your findings for class presentations.

4. At present, there is much disagreement about which phase of the business cycle currently describes the economy. Using the latest edition of *Economic Indicators, The Economic Report of the President*, the *Statistical Abstract of the United States, Survey of Current Business*, and/or other sources of economic data available in your school or city library, determine the current status of the economy. Analyze present employment conditions and wages. What trends are revealed in the various indexes that will affect business conditions in the coming months?

PART 4 | FACTORS INFLUENCING NATIONAL INCOME IN OUR FREE ENTERPRISE ECONOMY

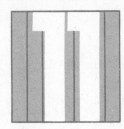

National Income and Its Distribution

PURPOSE OF THE CHAPTER

National income represents the total income received by all who contribute to the production of goods and services of the country for one year. Individual wage earners, investors, businesses, and government are included. The purpose of this chapter is to show how national income is divided among people and why some receive more than others.

After studying this chapter, you will be able to:

1. Define gross national product.
2. Explain what national income is.
3. Discuss what entitles a person to a share in national income.
4. Discuss what affects the share of total income received by each of the following: (a) owners of land or other natural resources, (b) labor and managers, (c) lenders of money, (d) owners of business, and (e) government.
5. Explain why some persons receive more income than others.

A. GROSS NATIONAL PRODUCT, NATIONAL INCOME, AND PERSONAL INCOME

We describe economics as being concerned with how people satisfy their needs and wants for economic goods and services. We may approach the study of economics in two ways. One is to study production, distribution, and consumption from the standpoint of the individual or family, the business firm, or an industry. In such a study we are concerned with economic problems affecting individuals and businesses, such as supply and demand, prices, savings, profits, and investments in capital.

Another approach to economics is to study economic and business activities for the nation as a whole as they affect all citizens as a group and all businesses as a group. This approach deals with the *national economy* in total rather than the personal or business economy. It is concerned primarily with production, income, distribution, and consumption for the nation as a whole. This chapter deals primarily with the national economy.

Gross National Product

Gross national product (GNP), as defined earlier, is the total current market value of all final goods and services produced in the nation as a whole during a given year. By *final goods* we mean a product or a service as it is when sold to its final purchaser. However, GNP does include business inventories at an estimated market value. If the goods and services that are produced are to be used, they must be bought and paid for by those who will use them. These goods and services are purchased by consumers, business investors, government, and foreigners. The GNP includes what we export but subtracts what we import.

The Office of Business Economics, U.S. Department of Commerce, compiles the statistics from which the GNP is determined. These statistics are drawn from many sources, and they include all business activities. The users or purchasers of the products and services produced fall into four groups:

1. *Individual consumers* — This group uses two kinds of goods. One kind is known as *durable goods*, including

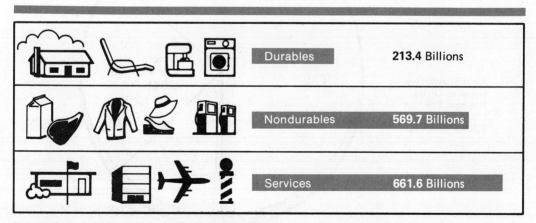

Durables	213.4 Billions
Nondurables	569.7 Billions
Services	661.6 Billions

Source: *Survey of Current Business* (April, 1979), p. 6.

What Consumers Bought in 1979

long-lasting items such as automobiles, household appliances, and furniture. The other kind is known as *nondurable goods*, including items that are consumed quickly, such as food, clothing, and gasoline for our automobiles. Individual consumers also buy many services. These include items such as rent, private education, medical care, legal advice, haircuts, and transportation. The amount of services used by individual consumers is greater than the amount of nondurable goods they buy.

2. *Business investors* — Business investors buy products such as new homes, factories, shopping centers, and public utilities. This group also buys factory machinery, tools, and equipment that are used in the production of other goods and services. Some of the purchases of this group are in the form of raw materials, semifinished and finished goods used in manufacturing, and inventories in wholesale and retail business firms. The level of purchases for business investments indicates the level of growth of our economy.

3. *Government* — Local, state, and federal governments purchase a wide variety of goods and services. The items range from such things as equipment for national defense,

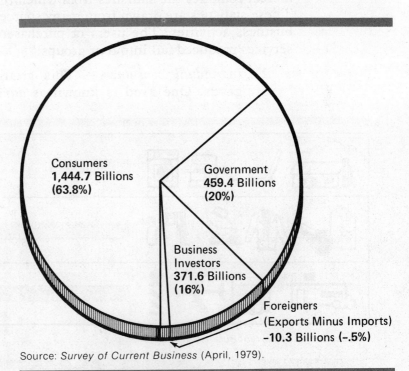

Final Purchasers or Users of Gross National Product (1979 GNP = 2,265.6 Billions)

Consumers
1,444.7 Billions
(63.8%)

Government
459.4 Billions
(20%)

Business Investors
371.6 Billions
(16%)

Foreigners
(Exports Minus Imports)
-10.3 Billions (-.5%)

Source: *Survey of Current Business* (April, 1979).

public buildings, roads, and dams to such things as pensions for veterans, health services, education, and welfare.

Total state and local government purchases of goods and services are almost twice as large as the total purchases of the federal government as shown in the table below. Approximately one fifth of the total goods and services produced in a year are used by local, state, and federal governments. Government purchases are extremely important in determining business conditions.

4. *Foreign purchasers* — The people and businesses of other countries buy many of our products, and we buy many of theirs. The goods we sell to other countries are called *exports*; the goods we buy from them are called *imports*. The difference in dollars between our total exports and our total imports represents our *net exports*, and it increases our GNP. If the value of our total imports exceeds the value of our total exports, the net difference decreases our GNP.

GROSS NATIONAL PRODUCT
(Billions of Current Dollars Seasonally Adjusted, Annual Rate)

	1971	1972	1973	1974	1975	1976	1977	1978	1979
Personal Consumption Expenditures	667.1	729.0	805.2	876.7	968.8	1,094.0	1,211.2	1,403.9	1,444.7
Gross Private Domestic Investment	153.7	179.3	209.4	209.4	179.1	243.3	294.2	364.0	371.6
Government Purchases	234.2	255.7	276.4	309.2	343.5	361.4	395.0	454.5	459.4
Net Exports	−.2	−6.0	3.9	2.1	13.0	7.8	−10.9	−7.6	−10.3
Total GNP	1,054.9	1,158.0	1,294.9	1,397.4	1,504.4	1,706.5	1,889.6	2,214.8	2,265.6

GOVERNMENT PURCHASES OF GOODS AND SERVICES
(Billions of Current Dollars Seasonally Adjusted, Annual Rate)

	1971	1972	1973	1974	1975	1976	1977	1978	1979
National Defense	71.2	74.8	74.4	78.7	86.1	86.8	94.3	102.1	103.9
Other Federal	26.5	30.1	32.2	38.2	44.4	43.3	51.1	60.4	60.7
State & Local	136.6	150.8	169.8	192.3	213.0	231.2	249.6	292.0	294.8
Total	234.2	255.7	276.4	309.2	343.5	361.4	395.0	454.5	459.4

Source: *Survey of Current Business* (April, 1979). (Because of rounding off, the figures for the total GNP do not always add up exactly.)

The importance of foreign trade in our economy will be discussed in Chapter 13.

The chart on page 188 shows the final purchasers or users of the gross national product in 1979. Of the $2,265.6 billion of goods and services produced, people as consumers used $1,444.7 billion; business investments accounted for $371.6 billion; local, state, and federal governments used $459.4 billion; and net exports (purchases by foreigners) was −10.3 billion. This unfavorable balance of trade actually lowered GNP in 1979. Changes in the purchase and use of the total products and services by consumers, business investors, government, and foreign interests may indicate changes in business conditions in general.

Net National Product

The gross national product, we have noted, is the total current market value of all final goods and services produced in the nation for a given year. In producing these goods and services, a certain amount of capital goods is used up. Buildings, machinery, and

RELATION OF GROSS NATIONAL PRODUCT, NATIONAL
INCOME, AND PERSONAL INCOME
(Billions of Dollars)

	1975	1977	1979
Gross national product	**1,516.3**	**1,889.6**	**2,265.6**
Less: Capital consumption allowances	161.3	197.0	231.7
Equals: Net national product	**1,355.0**	**1,692.6**	**2,033.9**
Less: Indirect business tax and nontax liability	138.7	165.2	186.2
Business transfer payments	6.3	9.0	11.7
Statistical discrepancy	4.4	−.1	-----
Plus: Subsidies less current surplus of government enterprises	2.0	2.0	2.0
Equals: National income	**1,207.6**	**1,520.5**	**1,834.0**
Less: Corporate profits & IVA	91.6	139.9	165.3
Contributions for social insurance	109.7	139.0	184.3
Plus: Government transfer payments to persons	168.9	197.9	226.4
Interest paid by government (net) and by consumers	36.1	47.0	57.6
Dividends	32.1	41.2	54.0
Business transfer payments	6.3	9.0	11.7
Equals: Personal income	**1,249.7**	**1,536.7**	**1,834.1**

Sources: *Statistical Abstract of the United States*, 1977, and *Survey of Current Business*, April, 1979, p. 12.

equipment depreciate with use, become obsolete, and lose their value. For this reason, the GNP must be reduced by the amount of depreciation and obsolescence, generally called *capital consumption allowances*. When the capital consumption allowances are subtracted from the GNP, the result is the *net national product* (NNP). The table on page 190 shows how the net national product is derived from the gross national product.

National Income

To those who buy the goods and services included in the GNP, the amount spent is a cost or expenditure. To those who receive a payment for goods or services, the amount received is income. Now, let us look again at income and who receives it.

National income is the amount of annual earnings derived from the production of goods and services. It represents the sum of all the incomes received by individuals for their contributions to the production of all goods and services. National income arises only from productive effort. This means that national income excludes such items of income as your weekly allowance if you do not work to earn it, interest received on government bonds, and pensions.

The national income is closely related to the GNP and the NNP. The value of the national income can be obtained by subtracting from the NNP the indirect business taxes, such as sales taxes, and a few other minor allowances. The table on page 190 shows how the national income is derived from the net national product.

The national income of the United States for 1979 was $1,834.0 billion. This is the total amount earned by all individuals, such as laborers and managers, owners of plants and equipment, lenders of money, and owners who originate ideas and assume the risks of business.

Personal Income

As individuals we are more concerned with personal income than with national income. *Personal income* is the annual income received by persons from all sources. Personal income can be determined by subtracting from national income (1) all corporate profits and inventory valuation adjustments, (2) all contributions for social insurance, and (3) wage accruals less disbursements. Then the following must be added: (1) government transfer payments to persons, (2) interest paid by government and by consumers, (3) dividends, and (4) business transfer payments. A *transfer payment*, as defined earlier, is a payment of money for which no current goods or services are produced, such as a business or government pension received by a retired person. The table on page 190 shows how the personal income amount is derived from national income.

We all know there is quite a gap between our earnings and our take-home pay. This gap is caused by the fact that we must pay taxes on our income. *Disposable personal income* is the amount of income that people have left after all local, state, and federal income tax payments have been deducted from personal income. Disposable personal income is really what people have left to spend or to save.

Who Earns a Share in National Income?

The main problems that concern us in this chapter are: (a) who earns the national income and (b) what percentage of the total national income is earned by each class or group of individuals who have a part in the production of goods and services?

In industry, the results of *production* are divided among those who represent the factors involved in the production of goods and services. These factors, usually classified as natural resources, labor, capital, management, and government, were discussed in

The economic problems: (1) Who earned a share in national income? and (2) What portion of the total national income should each group of contributors to production receive?

Chapter 4. The results of *productive effort* are divided into classes or categories known as rents, wages, interest, profit, and taxes. These are various forms of income. Rents go to the owners of land or other natural resources; wages go to the workers; interest goes to the lenders of money; profits go to the owners of business or industrial enterprises; and taxes go to the government.

A person may earn income by contributing to more than one of the essential aspects of the production of goods and services. For instance, Mr. Hunt, who owns a garage, has a house that he rents. In this way he earns rent. He has some money in a savings bank and earns interest on it. From the business that he operates, he probably draws a weekly or monthly salary, thus earning wages. Since he owns the business, he earns the profits if there are any after all the expenses of operating the business have been paid. If he owns some stock in a corporation, he shares also in the profits of that business.

B. DISTRIBUTION OF NATIONAL INCOME AMONG PRODUCERS

A study of the income and the expenses of the business in the following example shows the ways in which those who represent the various factors of production share in the income from production. The Wizard Manufacturing Company, a corporation, was organized to produce educational toys and games. The stockholders, through their board of directors, hired a manager, Joan Bowles, to operate the business. Ms. Bowles rented a building and land. She borrowed money from a bank in order to buy equipment and to help pay the expenses that would be incurred in manufacturing and in selling. She also hired people to do the work in the factory and in the office and to sell the goods.

At the end of the first year, the manager prepared the income and expense statement shown at the top of the next page. From the data on the statement one can readily determine how those who contributed to the production of the toys and games were rewarded by receiving earnings.

This statement briefly illustrates that rent, wages, interest, profits, taxes, and miscellaneous expenses claim rights to the income of the Wizard Manufacturing Company. After all other deductions have been made, the balance of the income, or net profit, goes to the stockholders who own the business. If there is a net loss, the owners are the ones who lose.

WIZARD MANUFACTURING COMPANY
INCOME AND EXPENSE STATEMENT FOR THE YEAR 19—

Income from sales..	$945,000	
Cost of merchandise sold...	340,000	
Gross profit		$605,000
Rent of land and buildings[1].......................................	$ 14,600	
Wages of clerks and factory workers[2].......................	310,000	
Interest on borrowed money[3]..................................	7,400	
Salary of manager[2]..	18,000	
Taxes[4]..	115,000	
Other expenses (supplies, insurance, etc.)[5]	45,000	
Total expenses...		510,000
Net profit (to owners)[6]...		$ 95,000

Statement Showing
the Sharing in the
Fruits of Production

[1]Earnings of landlords for use of land and buildings.
[2]Earnings of employees (labor and managers) for services.
[3]Earnings of lenders of money.
[4]Income to government for protection and services.
[5]Income and earnings to suppliers of materials and services.
[6]Earnings to owners who originate ideas and assume risks.

Rent — Income Earned by Landowners

In an economic sense, *land* includes all natural resources. Farms, urban building sites, minerals, forests, and water are all natural resources. In many instances, people have made improvements on the land, such as buildings, permanent equipment, or dams. These improvements increase the usefulness of the land and hence its value.

Ordinarily, *rent* is the contract price received from a tenant for the temporary use of land including buildings and other improvements. In a more restricted sense, *economic rent* is that portion of income which is due solely to the land without buildings and other improvements. The more productive the land is, the greater the economic rent. In the usual sense, however, we speak of rent as income earned for the use of land and the buildings and other improvements on it.

What Regulates the Rent on Land? Rent depends on the usefulness, the productivity, and the desirability of the property. For example, a piece of land that will produce 50 bushels of wheat per acre is theoretically worth at least twice as much as land that will produce only 25 bushels per acre. Richness of the soil, mineral deposits, and location with regard to water or transportation facilities are some of the factors that have a bearing on land value.

The law of supply and demand applies to land just as it does to wages and interest. A person who has land available for rent can

The amount of rent for land depends on its productivity.

U.S. Dept. of Agriculture

obtain rent only in proportion to the productivity of the land measured in comparison with that of competing land.

Rent and Prices. Only a slight relationship exists between the rent producers pay for the use of the land in production and the price they charge for their product.

Merchants sometimes advertise that, because their rent is lower, they can sell merchandise at a lower price than other merchants. Their statements are sometimes, but not always, true. Other factors, such as the quantity of merchandise, affect the price at which it can be sold.

Merchants in a shopping center of a large city pay high rent, but they have many more customers than merchants in outlying districts. Those in the shopping center sell goods faster and therefore need less borrowed capital to finance purchases. Merchants in outlying communities or small towns have fewer customers and sell their goods more slowly. Their rate of profit is not any higher, and usually is lower, than that of the city merchant.

Wages — Income Earned by Labor

Wages make up that part of income from production belonging to those who perform either mental or physical labor. Wages are the prices paid for the labor and management factors. The price of labor in terms of money is the value of labor.

The price of labor is determined in the same way as the price of any other economic good or service. Supply of and demand for labor are the primary factors that influence wage rates. The supply consists of the working force that is available at a given time. The demand consists of the needs of employers for workers.

Supply of Labor. The supply of labor is indicated by the number of workers who are seeking employment in each kind of work at each of the wage rates offered in the occupation. If the wage rate for an occupation is low, it is usually because of a large supply of workers (such as unskilled workers). When wages are high, it is usually because the supply of labor for those jobs is limited or scarce (such as skilled labor). Workers compete for the better jobs, and employers compete for workers when labor is scarce. Competition for employment and wages is just as active among workers as it is for sales among businesses.

The fact that many occupations are available for a large number of qualified persons can affect the supply of labor. The attractiveness and the working conditions of certain jobs also affect the supply. Many persons choose clerical work over manual labor, even at lower wages, because they prefer the working conditions. The desire to live in the city or the country affects the supply of labor. Many other factors, such as minimum working age, economic conditions of older workers who may retire, amount and cost of training, and policies of organized labor, influence the supply of labor.

Demand for Labor. The demand for labor reflects the demand for the products of labor. If, for any reason, the demand for a product or a service declines or disappears, the demand for the labor that produces that product or service will likewise decline or disappear. Workers will therefore become unemployed unless they are able to shift to a new type of work. The creation of demand for a new product or service may result in abnormally high wages for the comparatively few workers able to produce the product or provide the service. Wages tend to decrease, however, as more persons prepare to perform the type of work that is rewarded so highly.

Factors Affecting Labor Supply and Demand. Wage rates, above the minimum required by law, are determined by supply and demand; but many conditions may affect either factor. Demand may fall because of lack of consumer purchasing power. Supply, too, may be affected in many ways. One common method of regulating supply is through the unionization of workers and the closed shop. Unions often attempt to maintain a closed shop in a

Since the supply of highly trained workers is often limited, these workers command high wages.

The President's Committee on Employment of the Handicapped

given business, which means that only members of the unions representing the workers in that business may be hired. Thus, nonmember workers are prevented from being employed. Other factors that may affect demand and supply are the substitution of other types of labor and the substitution of machines.

Wage Differences. Why does one worker get $20 a day and another $40 a day? Why are those who do some of the more disagreeable work of the world rather poorly paid?

Education and training are two of the most important factors causing wage differences. Natural ability is another. The supply of people who can handle the low-paying positions is greater than the supply of those who can handle the better positions. If a certain kind of work demands more training and knowledge than another, an employer is willing to pay more for someone to do this work. Essentially, however, the wages in each group are determined according to the supply of labor in that group. The supply of labor becomes smaller as the training and knowledge required for the job becomes greater.

Legislation Affecting Wages. The Fair Labor Standards Act, commonly known as the Federal Wage-Hour Law, regulates wages and hours of work. The act covers employees in enterprises engaged in commerce or in the production of goods for commerce.

The act was originally passed in 1938 and was amended several times. The principal provisions of the present act are:

1. Minimum wage rate of $2.65 an hour (1978), $2.90 an hour (1979), $3.10 an hour (1980), and $3.35 an hour (1981).
2. Regular time of 40 hours a week.
3. Overtime pay provisions. Any number of hours beyond 40 per week requires an hourly overtime rate that is 1½ times the regular rate. For certain positions, time worked on Sundays or holidays requires an overtime rate that is 2 times the regular rate.
4. Wage discrimination prohibited. Basically, wage discrimination is now prohibited on the basis of race, creed, religion, sex, national origin, or age.

In general, the Fair Labor Standards Act and its amendments apply equally to men and women, to homemakers as well as factory and office workers, and usually regardless of the number of employees of an employer. The Fair Labor Standards Act is enforced by the U.S. Department of Labor. Many states have their own wage or hour rates to supplement the federal regulations.

The Walsh-Healey Act and the Davis-Bacon Act supplement the Wage-Hour Law by regulating the minimum wages that may be paid by a producer under contract to the federal government.

Interest — Income Earned by Lenders

The amount paid for the use of borrowed funds is called *interest*. Another concept of interest is that it is that portion of national income traced to the use of capital, not including land. Usually interest is considered payment for the use of money borrowed.

The *interest rate* is the price that one must pay in order to obtain the use of money. The rate is quoted either as a percentage or as so many dollars for every $100 borrowed. For example, an interest rate of 8% per year means that the price of borrowing $100 for one year is $8. The rate of interest is determined by supply and demand in the same way that wages are determined by supply and demand. However, government agencies, such as the Federal Reserve Board and the United States Treasury, also influence interest rates as described in Chapter 10.

Suppose that Robert Lopez, the owner of a department store, needs to borrow $5,000 to buy a stock of goods for the season. He goes to an individual or a bank and inquires about the rate that is being charged on loans made at that time. If the rate quoted seems too high, he may go to another individual or bank. Frequently, the rate of interest asked by one bank may be the same as that asked by another in the same community. In some cases, however, one bank may have more money on hand to lend than another and may therefore be willing to take a lower rate of interest in order to make the loan. When large loans are being negotiated, the bargaining for rates of interest is frequently prolonged and carefully considered on a competitive basis.

When banks have plenty of money available for which there is no immediate need, they are usually eager to lend it. When few businesses wish to borrow money, there is a lack of demand for loans in relation to the available supply. As a result, the interest rates on loans are low. On the other hand, when banks already have lent most of their funds and there is an active demand for loans, the interest rates are high.

The simple laws of supply and demand, however, do not work just exactly as described because of governmental controls and psychological factors. When profits and the prospects of profits are good, borrowers are willing to pay higher rates of interest if necessary. The banks are willing to lend money because they can charge good rates and because they are reasonably sure that the borrowers will have the ability to repay the loans.

Interest Is Paid to Make a Profit. If money is to be borrowed for business purposes, the amount that can be paid for its use is determined by the amount of profit that can be made from business operations. If interest rates are high, businesses are less likely to borrow; but they will borrow if there is sufficient chance for a profit. The borrower's willingness depends on the intensity of the needs and on available alternatives. For example, a restaurant owner estimated that the installation of new fixtures would increase gross profits by $90 monthly. But the interest costs on the money needed to pay for the fixtures would cost $100 monthly. Therefore, the owner decided to postpone installation of new fixtures until interest rates declined.

Risk in Lending Money. Those who lend money take a risk that the borrowers may not be able to repay the loans when they become due. If the money is not repaid, the lenders suffer a loss. Those who lend money are entitled to a reasonable return for the services performed by the money and also as compensation for the risk. If the risk is great, the interest rate will be high; if the risk is low, the interest rate will be low.

Profit — Income Earned by Owners

Profit is a portion of the income earned by owners of businesses; it is the remaining portion of income after all expenses have been paid and all claims of those who have contributed to production have been met.

Rent is paid to the owner of the land, buildings, and equipment that have been leased. Wages are paid to laborers and employed management. Interest is paid to the one from whom funds have been borrowed. Taxes are paid to local, state, and federal governments. Anything left over out of income after these claims have been paid is the property of the owners. It is their profit. If the income in a given period is not large enough to pay the claims of rent, wages, interest, taxes, and other expenses, the loss must come out of previously accumulated surplus or must be paid by the owners.

The economist and the accountant do not compute profit the same way. *Pure profit*, as computed by the economist, is the income remaining after all expenses have been deducted. These expenses include economic rent for the use of land owned by the business and interest for the use of capital goods, that is, the equipment and buildings owned by the business. *Net profit*, as computed by the accountant, is the income remaining after paying all expenses that require money to satisfy. These expenses do not include economic rent for land and interest on capital investment owned by the business, as no money is required to satisfy them. They do include depreciation, which is a loss in value of property due to use and age.

In order to induce people to invest in a business and to devote their time and energy to its management and operation, the business must have the possibility of profit after allowances are made for a normal return on the investment and for the wages of management.

Competition and Profits. On the average, the profits of a business are limited to a fair return on the investment and a reasonable compensation for risk. Sooner or later, competition slows the increase in profits. Competition always tends to appear when someone makes a success of a business.

If one business has a secret that will enable it to operate at a profit that is greater than the profits of competitors, it has an important advantage. If its competitors learn the secret and become as skillful, it will lose the advantage.

Owners' Rights to Profits. A business must build up a surplus to take care of times when there may be no profits. In order to build a surplus, a reasonably high rate of profit must be earned when business is good. If a firm has no surplus, bad times may cause the firm to fail. Building a surplus out of profits from income will enable the business to take the risks involved in ownership and management.

If state and federal governments demand taxes that make accumulation of profits impossible or if labor demands wages that take too great a portion of the employer's income, a business may be forced to discontinue operations. This, of course, would mean not only a loss of the goods or services it produces but also the disappearance of jobs for labor. In a competitive economy, the right of business to make a profit and the actual making of a profit over a period of time are both imperative.

Taxes — Claim of Government on Income

Every business benefits in many ways from services provided by local, state, and federal governments. The costs of these services are met by taxes. Furthermore, the general welfare of the

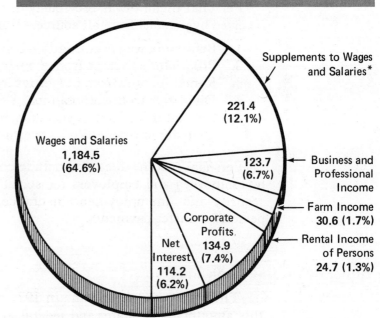

Supplements to Wages and Salaries*

221.4 (12.1%)

Wages and Salaries 1,184.5 (64.6%)

123.7 (6.7%) ← Business and Professional Income

Farm Income 30.6 (1.7%)

Rental Income of Persons 24.7 (1.3%)

Corporate Profits 134.9 (7.4%)

Net Interest 114.2 (6.2%)

Distribution of $1,834 Billions of National Income in 1979

*Includes employer contributions to social insurance, pensions, and employee welfare funds.

Source: *Survey of Current Business* (April, 1979), p. 13.

people as a whole is promoted by government through research activities and public work. Governments, in turn, claim a portion of the income or earnings of individuals and of businesses.

It will be recalled that the motive of business is to make a profit and that profits are necessary in order to provide new capital for replacement, growth, and expansion. Hence, there is a close relationship between profits and taxes. If taxes become large enough to absorb most or all of the income of business after other expenses are paid, there will be no growth or expansion, hence no new jobs. And unless a profit is earned in at least some of the years, a business will not be able to withstand losses in poor years.

C. DISTRIBUTION OF PERSONAL INCOME AMONG INDIVIDUALS

As individuals we are interested not only in the distribution of the total national income but also in the distribution of that part of the national income that we receive as personal income.

What Is Included in Personal Income

Personal income was previously defined as the annual income received by persons from all sources. It includes:

1. Before-tax wages currently received by individuals.
2. Proprietor's income from a business or farm.
3. Rental income from properties leased.
4. Dividends from corporations.
5. Interest from savings accounts, bonds, and loans.
6. Transfer payments from government and business.

Personal income does not include contributions to government by employees and employers for social insurance, such as social security and unemployment insurance. Neither does it include personal transfer payments.

How People Use Their Income

The total personal income in 1979 was $1,834.1 billion. From this amount local, state, and federal taxes of $270.6 billion were paid, leaving the people of the United States $1,563.5 billion as disposable personal income, which they could spend or save as they chose. As shown by the chart on the next page, they spent $1,444.7 billion on personal consumption expenditures and $36.8

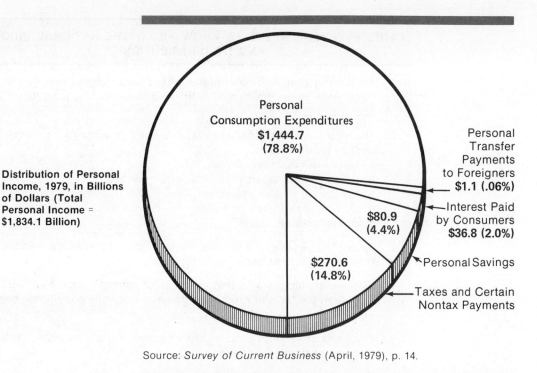

Distribution of Personal Income, 1979, in Billions of Dollars (Total Personal Income = $1,834.1 Billion)

Personal Consumption Expenditures
$1,444.7
(78.8%)

Personal Transfer Payments to Foreigners
$1.1 (.06%)

Interest Paid by Consumers
$36.8 (2.0%)

$80.9
(4.4%)

$270.6
(14.8%)

Personal Savings

Taxes and Certain Nontax Payments

Source: *Survey of Current Business* (April, 1979), p. 14.

billion for interest, they sent $1.1 billion abroad to foreign friends and relatives, and they saved $80.9 billion.

Differences in Personal Income

The total personal income varies from year to year according to the production of the nation. It is influenced by business conditions in general. Since 1929, the personal income (in 1979 dollars) has ranged from a low of $47.0 billion in 1933 to $1,834.1 billion in 1979. If equally divided among all men, women, and children in the United States, the 1979 income would give each person an income of approximately $8,347 (before taxes) for the year or about $160.50 a week ($8,347 divided by 52 weeks).

Of course, many people received more than the average (per capita) income and many received less. Numerous factors account for the differences in income distribution among people. Among these factors, personal traits, habits, and abilities are the most important. Such facts as general economic conditions in the geographical area in which one lives and works, education, accumulated savings, and employment opportunities also affect the amount any one person may earn.

FACTS EVERYONE NEEDS TO KNOW ABOUT THE NATIONAL INCOME AND ITS DISTRIBUTION

1. Annual national income consists of the total income received in a given year by all the people who contributed to the production of goods and services.

2. The total annual national income is received as earnings for contributions to production by:
   a. Land owners, in rent.
   b. Labor and management, in the form of wages.
   c. Lenders of money, in interest.
   d. Owners of business, in profits.
   e. Government, in taxes.

3. Managers, owners, and lenders are entitled to a just share in income for the risks they assume.

4. The primary factors affecting the share of national income earned by owners in the form of profits are general economic conditions, competition, and managerial ability.

5. The costs of services performed by government are paid for through taxes on businesses and individuals.

6. The primary causes of inequality in receiving shares in personal income are differences among people in personal traits, habits, and abilities.

REVIEW QUESTIONS

Section A

1. From what two approaches may economics be studied?
2. How is gross national product (GNP) defined?
3. What is meant by "final goods"?
4. Who are the users or purchasers of the products and services included in the GNP?
5. How are durable goods distinguished from nondurable goods?
6. How does the amount of services purchased by individuals compare with the amount of nondurable goods purchased? How does it compare with the amount of durable goods purchased?
7. How does the amount of purchases by state and local governments compare with the purchases of the federal government?
8. How does the government's use of goods and services compare with the total amount of goods and services produced in a year?
9. What is meant by "net exports"?
10. Of the four groups of final purchasers or users of GNP, which group uses the most goods and services?
11. What is net national product (NNP)? How is it derived?
12. What is national income?
13. What is the difference between personal income and disposable personal income?

14. What are the major classes or categories of national income?
15. Who receives each class or part of the national income?

Section B

16. What is rent?
17. What regulates the cost of rent?
18. What factors sometimes affect the labor supply?
19. How are the wages of labor determined?
20. What relationship exists between the amount of schooling someone has had and the money income or wages that person receives?
21. What are the principal provisions of the Fair Labor Standards Act?
22. What is interest?
23. What factors influence the rate of interest charged borrowers at a given time?
24. What is profit?
25. Why do governments claim a portion of the income or earnings of individuals and businesses?

Section C

26. What is included in personal income?
27. How do people typically use their personal income?
28. What accounts for the difference in income distribution among the people of the United States?

DISCUSSION QUESTIONS

Section A

1. How can the budget items of the federal government affect the GNP?
2. Why are capital consumption allowances subtracted from the GNP?
3. How may the value of goods and services be an expenditure for some and an income for others?
4. Why are such items as weekly allowances, interest received on government bonds, and pensions excluded from national income?
5. How is national income related to the GNP?
6. What conclusions can you reach regarding the relationship between the amount of education of a nation's people and that nation's GNP?
7. An increase in the level of purchases for business investments indicates an increase in the level of growth of our economy. (a) Under what conditions might an increase in business investments be misleading? (b) Would you favor a regulation or law making it compulsory for everyone who receives income to invest a certain percentage in business? Why?

Section B

8. A store in a large shopping center advertises that it sells a large volume of goods and that therefore it can sell at lower prices than competitors. Could this be true? Discuss.
9. Would you favor paying the same wage to all workers who are in a particular occupation, such as stenography or over-the-counter retail selling? Why?
10. Since the passage of the original Fair Labor Standards Act, the minimum wage has been raised several times. (a) What are the arguments in favor of raising the minimum wage and what are the arguments against? (b) Do you believe a minimum wage per hour should be established for all workers? Why?
11. How do the laws of supply and demand work on the interest rate on loans?

12. Does a dividend paid to a stockholder represent a share of income in the form of wages, rent, interest, or profits? Explain.

13. Assume that there is only one hardware store in a city of 10,000 population. Since there is only one store, the owner charges very high prices and makes an exceptionally large profit. What natural economic controls are likely to remedy this situation?

14. Why do some companies earn a higher rate of profit than others?

15. Why may the income that an owner-manager receives from the operation of a small business not be all profit?

16. In recent years, the federal government has used tax cuts to stimulate the economy. (a) In what way does this action affect the economy? (b) Why not eliminate all taxes in order to stimulate the economy?

Section C

17. Why are government and business transfer payments to persons included in personal income but not personal transfer payments?

18. The average total income received per person will vary widely from state to state or from one geographical area to another. What accounts for this wide variation in per capita income?

APPLICATION PROBLEMS

Section A

1. The *Statistical Abstract of the United States* is published annually by the United States Department of Commerce. In the latest edition, locate the table titled "GNP and National Income — Summary: 1929-latest year," and find answers to the following questions:
    (a) What major economic or other conditions can you associate with the GNP for the years provided in this table which you feel was the probable cause for the size of the GNP for those years?
    (b) Which industry divisions enjoyed the greatest percentage gain in productivity between 1929 and the latest year?
    (c) How do you account for these particular industry divisions enjoying the largest percentage gains?

Section B

2. Consult the latest edition of the *Statistical Abstract of the United States* and find answers to the following questions:
    (a) What was the national income for each of the last five years for which data are given?
    (b) For both the first and fifth year data, compute the percent of the national income that represented (1) wages and salaries, (2) supplements to wages and salaries, (3) income of unincorporated businesses, (4) rental income of persons, (5) corporate profits, and (6) net interest.
    (c) What net percentage change resulted between the first and fifth years in each part's share of the national income? How can you explain these changes?

3. Find for the latest year the percentage of profits for a variety of leading corporations such as drug, food, petroleum, automobile, electrical, farm machinery manufacturing, and processing firms. (Weekly business magazines, almanacs, and government publications publish such information.) Compare these various profit rates with the rate of interest you could get by investing your money in a local savings and loan association. Considering the total risks involved, how would the two compare?

Section C   4. In the latest edition of the *Statistical Abstract of the United States*, find the answers to the following questions:
    (a) What was the per capita personal income for the United States as a whole for each of the last five years for which figures are given?
    (b) What was the per capita personal income for your state for each of the last five years for which figures are available?
    (c) What was the average net income for each of the last five years for physicians, dentists, and lawyers?

COMMUNITY PROJECTS

Section A   1. Almost daily some mention is made of GNP in the newspapers. Popular news magazines carry frequent in-depth coverage about GNP figures. Locate at least three current articles either from newspapers or magazines that refer to the GNP. Based on what you read in these articles, prepare a brief report indicating why GNP information is important to a community and to individuals.

Section B   2. The United States Employment Service has an office in most large towns and cities. Businesses seeking employees inform the office as to the kinds of jobs that are open, what the qualifications are, and what the rate of pay will be. Unemployed persons file statements of their experience and qualifications and the kind of job they seek.

Go to or write the nearest Employment Office to obtain a list of the open jobs and inquire about the number of people who are seeking employment. Compare the supply (persons seeking employment) and the demand (jobs that are open). How does the total supply match the total demand in numbers? How well do the qualifications and experience of the unemployed people on record meet the requirements of the open jobs?

3. (a) Investigate the hourly wage rates in your community for various workers, such as carpenters, painters, lawn-care workers, and typists. What is the present trend in wages? How do present wages compare with wages five years ago?
    (b) Next, compare the present local rates with the national averages for such workers. The national figures can be found in the *Occupational Outlook Handbook*, which should be in your school library or guidance office. What explanation can you give for the difference in rates?

4. Talk with a local proprietor or someone you or your family know who owns a business. Find out from this person as many risks as you can that are a part of running this business. Write a report on business risks based on your discussion with this person.

Section C   5. On an outline map of the United States, enter the per capita personal income for each state for the latest available year. Obtain the figures from the latest issue of the *Statistical Abstract of the United States*. Study the map to locate areas of the country that tend to have a higher or lower income distribution pattern than the average. Write a brief report on the reasons for these regional differences.

Taxation, Fiscal Policy, and National Debt

PURPOSE OF THE CHAPTER

Everyone benefits directly or indirectly from many of the services provided by local, state, and federal governments. Taxes are collected and spent to provide these services. By means of controlling taxation and government spending (called fiscal policy), governments can increase or decrease national income.

After studying this chapter, you will be able to:

1. Define taxation.
2. List the principles of taxation.
3. Explain the kinds of taxes.
4. Explain how fiscal policy works.
5. Discuss national debt.

A. TAXATION — SOURCE OF GOVERNMENT INCOME

Local, state, and federal governments provide protection and services that are for the common good of all citizens, organizations, and businesses. Expenses and costs are incurred by governments in providing protection and services. These expenses and costs must be paid. The device or plan that a federal, state, or local government has for raising funds to pay these expenses and costs is known as *taxation*.

Tax Systems

A *tax* is a compulsory contribution of money made to a government to provide for services for the common good. This definition distinguishes taxation from payments to government agencies. For instance, a postage stamp pays for a service, but its use is not compulsory unless the service is desired. Citizens who violate laws have to pay fines as penalties. The fines are compulsory, but they are not taxes; they are penalties. Every person in a state may pay a tax for some general improvement in the state, but an assessment on certain property for the construction of a street or sewer does not constitute a tax. It is a payment for the improvement of the property.

In some instances a government may use several devices or plans for raising funds. All of these fund-raising devices and plans considered together are known as a *tax system*. For example, the tax system of a town or city may include collection of taxes from citizens and businesses on the basis of the value of property they own, the amount of annual income they have, and the cost of goods they buy.

ESSENTIALS OF A TAX SYSTEM

1. The plan or system must produce sufficient income to pay the costs of the government.

2. It must be relatively simple to understand and easy to administer.

3. The tax each individual should pay must be determined by a formula or rule, not arbitrarily.

4. The tax must be just, that is, based upon a plan that is considered to be fair to all taxpayers.

5. The system should make tax evasion difficult, if not impossible.

Fair Taxation

Public services and public facilities such as schools, streets and roads, parks, and city halls cost money whether they are produced by private enterprise or by governments. The money must come from citizens and business enterprises; there are no other sources. The question is, how may the costs of government services and public facilities be divided among citizens and businesses so that each pays a fair share? What is a fair basis for charging each citizen and business? Several different ideas on how to charge the costs of government have been developed. Let us consider two of the most popular theories.

Cost-of-Service-Received Theory. One theory of fairly apportioning the tax burden is that taxpayers should be assessed according to the cost of the service or benefit received. The cost-of-service-received theory would charge taxes to citizens and businesses on the basis of the amount of services received or the benefit gained from government services and facilities. For example, a family with four children in elementary school would be assessed taxes for educational purposes at twice the rate charged to a family having only two children in school. In theory, individuals would pay for the upkeep of streets according to how much they use the streets. They would be taxed for police protection on the basis of the numbers of persons in their families and according to the value of the property being protected.

In one sense the cost-of-service-received plan of taxation is based on the principle that the more property, such as real estate, you own, the more protection and benefit of government services you receive; therefore, you should pay taxes proportionate to the service you receive. This principle is followed in a tax that is based on a percentage of the appraised value of real estate.

The difficulty in the cost-of-service-received plan of assessing taxes is that it is practically impossible to determine the amount of service or benefit a person or business has actually received from government services.

Ability-to-Pay Theory. The ability-to-pay theory is the most widely accepted tax plan in use. It is based on the principle that individuals and businesses with large amounts of property or large incomes are more able to pay taxes than are individuals and businesses with little property or small incomes. For example, it is assumed that an individual having property worth $100,000 is more able to pay $5,000 a year in real estate tax (that is, 5% of the value) than an individual owning property worth $10,000 is able to pay $500 (also 5%). The question is whether or not the sacrifices made by the two individuals are the same. Some people argue that the individual paying $500 tax on property worth $10,000 is making a greater sacrifice than the individual paying $5,000 tax on property worth $100,000.

What should be the basis for determining the ability of an individual to pay for government services through taxes? Does the amount of real estate an individual owns indicate ability to pay? Does the amount of stocks and bonds and the amount of life insurance an individual has indicate ability to pay? Or is ability to pay indicated more accurately by an individual's annual income? These are difficult questions to answer.

The federal income tax, which applies a progressively higher rate as the amount of taxable income increases, is based on the ability-to-pay theory. For example, according to the federal income tax rates for 1979 income for a single person, the tax rate increases as taxable income increases, as shown in the following table.

Taxable* Income	Amount of Tax	Percentage of Taxable Income
$ 3,000	$ 154	5.1
5,000	422	8.4
10,000	1,387	13.9
20,000	4,177	20.9
50,000	18,067	36.1
100,000	50,053	50.1

*Taxable income is income after all allowances for personal deductions have been subtracted.

Classification of Taxes

Taxes are frequently classified according to their nature as direct taxes, indirect taxes, and hidden taxes.

Direct and Indirect Taxes. A *direct tax* is a tax that is levied directly on a particular group of persons or businesses and that is not passed on to others. An example is the income tax a person pays on salary. An *indirect tax* is a tax that is levied on a group of persons or businesses but that is passed on indirectly to others. An example is the tax on gasoline, which is passed on to consumers through an increase in the retail price.

It is often difficult to make the distinction between direct and indirect taxes because they may overlap. For example, a tax on real estate is usually considered to be a direct tax because it must be paid by the owner of the real estate. Nevertheless, the tax on real estate can be passed on to a renter by charging higher rent. From this point of view, it may be considered as an indirect tax.

Some sales taxes are direct and others are indirect. If a sales tax is charged on the total sales of a merchant, it will probably be passed on indirectly to the individual customers through increased prices. If the sales tax is added to each sale, it is a direct tax to the consumer because it is paid by the consumer. It is, however, called an indirect business tax since it is collected by businesses and paid by them to the government.

Whenever the cost of a product is increased to include a tax, the tax is being passed on to the consumers. This process is referred to as *shifting the tax burden*. Legislators have discovered that the least "painful" taxes are the ones that arouse least opposition. Indirect taxes are in this class.

Hidden Taxes. Many taxes are referred to as *hidden taxes* because most people are not aware of the fact that they are paying those taxes. For example, one may pay a sales tax when buying a new radio. The purchaser is aware of paying the sales tax but is not aware of paying many other taxes that are included in the selling price. For instance, taxes have been paid on the labor that was required to produce the radio or on raw materials that were needed in manufacturing the radio. Taxes have been paid on the factory in which the radio was manufactured. Transportation costs have been included in the selling price; the transportation companies that handled the radio have included a certain amount of taxes in their charges. Many of these taxes cannot be traced definitely to their original sources, but it has been estimated that hidden taxes represent almost 20% of every dollar of retail sales.

Kinds of Taxes

Taxes are levied and collected by local, state, and federal governments. The major kinds of taxes are: property; individual income; corporation profits; sales and gross receipts; excise; social security; and others, including estate, inheritance and gift, licenses, and permits.

Property taxes are levied primarily at the local level. Individual and corporation income taxes are primarily federal taxes, although they are used some at the state and local level. Sales and excise taxes are used extensively by local, state, and federal governments.

Property Taxes. A *property tax* is one levied on real estate or any personal property that has value and that can be bought and sold. This tax is based on the assumption that the ownership of property is an indication of the owner's ability to pay taxes.

One of the most important arguments for a property tax is that since property receives various types of government protection such as police and fire, the owners should be required to pay for the protection. In the early days when our tax system was established, the ownership of real estate was a reasonably good index of the ability to pay taxes. Now, however, there are many persons who do not own real property but who have much larger incomes than some other people who own real estate. The ownership of real estate, therefore, should not be the only criterion of one's ability to pay taxes.

Individual and Business Income Taxes. The principal source of revenue of the United States Government is the income tax. In 1979 approximately 44% of the revenue of the federal government came from the individual income tax, 17% from corporate income and profits tax, 33% from employment taxes such as social security taxes, 4% from excise taxes, and the remainder from miscellaneous sources.

Sales and Excise Taxes. A *sales tax* is a tax on sales. An *excise tax* is any tax that is levied on commodities, facilities, privileges, or occupations within a country. The sales tax and the excise tax are very similar. Basically, the only difference is that sales taxes tend to be more general in nature, such as a retail sales tax or a wholesale tax. Excise taxes tend to be levied on a selected basis, such as on luxuries, amusements, or gasoline.

Business or Service Taxes. Business or service taxes are based on the idea that a business should pay for the privilege of existing and operating. It is argued that a business benefits from the services of government and, therefore, should pay its share of the costs of government. Among the common business or service taxes are *licenses, permits,* and *franchises* that give the business a right to operate. Other types are based on the quantity of natural resources sold (called a *severance tax*); on the amount of capital stock of a corporation; or on some aspect of the business' operations, such as its payroll. A tax on gasoline is sometimes classified as a *benefit tax*. This is based on the idea that those who use the roads should be taxed to build and maintain them.

Inheritance and Gift Taxes. During the 20th century, estate, inheritance, and gift taxes have grown rapidly. Such taxes, commonly referred to as death taxes, are now levied under federal and state laws.

Two general types of inheritance taxes are: (1) the estate tax and (2) the inheritance tax. The federal government largely employs the estate tax, whereas most states use the inheritance tax.

Estate tax. The *estate tax* is calculated on the entire amount of the net estate before the property passes to the heirs, regardless of the interests of the beneficiaries.

Inheritance tax. The *inheritance tax* may be taken out of each share of the will, provided the will so specifies. In the absence of specification, the tax is taken out of the part of the estate remaining after specific bequests have been distributed. The rate of this tax may vary according to the individuals who share in the estate. Under some state laws, portions of an estate that go to distant relatives are subjected to higher taxes than portions going to close relatives.

Gift tax. A *gift tax* is levied by the federal government on a gift from one person to another. Ordinarily, gift taxes are levied to prevent avoidance of estate and inheritance taxes. The object of this tax is to make it impossible for an estate to escape taxation because it is given to heirs by the owner before death.

Social Security Taxes. The federal government collects payroll and self-employment taxes to provide partial financial support for three social security insurance programs that are commonly known as: (1) unemployment insurance; (2) old-age benefits, including disability, death, support of children and surviving spouse, and monthly pension; and (3) health and medical assistance insurance for the aged. These taxes are discussed in detail in Chapter 19.

Special Taxes. Various special taxes are levied by the federal government, state governments, and local governments. Many of these, such as the tax on legal papers (deeds, notes, and mortgages), are *stamp taxes*; that is, they are collected through the use of revenue stamps. Some are customs taxes on imports. Others are excise taxes in the form of automobile, dog, and hunting and fishing licenses. Still others are special licenses for conducting certain types of businesses.

Sources and Distribution of Government Income

Analysis of the budgets of local, state, and federal governments will reveal the sources of government funds and the kinds of services for which these funds are spent. The chart on the next page shows the annual average percentage of federal government receipts and outlays for the fiscal year 1978.

You will note from the chart that the main source of federal government income is individual income taxes. The second largest source is social insurance taxes and contributions, but the income from these insurance programs is more than offset by transfer payments for health and income security. Therefore, the federal government must rely primarily on personal, corporate, and indirect business taxes to pay for goods and services it uses,

The Annual Federal Budget, 1978

(Average annual percent distribution by function for fiscal year ending Sept. 30)

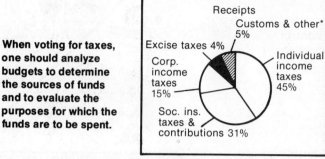

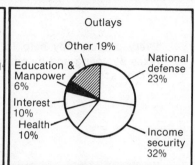

Source: Adapted from *Federal Reserve Bulletin* (May, 1979), p. 31.

*Other includes estate and gift taxes and other receipts.

When voting for taxes, one should analyze budgets to determine the sources of funds and to evaluate the purposes for which the funds are to be spent.

for aid to state and local governments, for subsidies of various types, and for interest payments.

Citizen Control Over Taxes

The average citizen considers taxes a burden and something to be avoided if possible. If there were a better understanding of the purposes and the uses of taxation, citizens might have a different attitude toward being taxed. Every person and business benefits from services provided by government. Few, if any, of us benefit directly from the use of all government agencies, but each of us benefits directly from the use of some of the agencies and indirectly from the use of many, if not all.

As our nation develops in size and complexity, citizens are demanding more and more public services from government. Citizens rarely realize, however, what additional tax burdens these demands cause. Services, whether provided by governments or by private enterprise, cost money. Any additional service rendered by a government must be paid for by some group of citizens. The real questions to the citizen (or taxpayer) are: How can I get the service most economically and effectively? Does my tax money produce more service in the hands of government than it would in the hands of private enterprise? These questions are not answered easily. Most taxpayers consider only how much they pay in taxes. A much more basic consideration is how tax money is spent.

Every person may help to control taxes by voting and by participating in civic activities.

People who vote for taxes should weigh the advantages of each particular tax in light of the benefit to the entire community. It should be remembered that no public service is free; someone has to pay. The person who ultimately bears the burden is the taxpayer.

B. FISCAL POLICY — GOVERNMENT CONTROL OF SPENDING AND TAXATION

In addition to providing the public with many services, the government is also concerned to see that the nation has high employment and economic growth without price inflation. By making decisions to spend more or to spend less, to tax more or to tax less, the government can help to control the economy. Government decisions affecting spending and taxation are known as *fiscal policy*. Fiscal policy, though influenced by the Administration, is the responsibility of Congress, which must pass the laws regarding spending programs and taxation (budget). This means that sound fiscal policy actually rests with the voters who elect senators and representatives and who tell them what the voters want.

Government Spending

Government, like businesses, families, and individuals, finds it necessary to set up budgets. Income and expenditures are estimated, and the budget is prepared as a spending plan to be followed during the fiscal year. The Administration presents its yearly budget to Congress for approval.

Federal Budget Receipts and Outlays for Fiscal Years 1960 to 1980

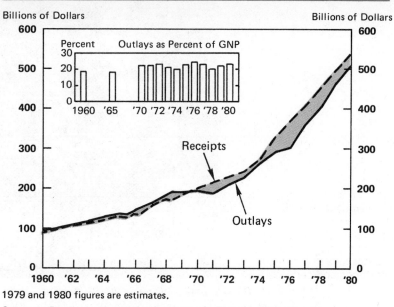

1979 and 1980 figures are estimates.

Sources: Based on chart prepared by U.S. Bureau of the Census.
Additional statistics from *Economic Indicators* (May, 1979).

Deficit Budget. If business activity slows down and unemployment rises, the Administration will probably submit a deficit budget to Congress. In a *deficit budget*, the government expects to spend more than it expects to receive. Such increased expenditures might pay for public projects (such as road building, slum clearance, and new government buildings) and/or welfare projects (such as larger social security payments). Public projects create employment opportunities and provide people with more income.

When more people have more money to spend, they are then able to buy more goods and services. Business activity is increased in order to provide the goods and services demanded by people who now have money to spend. If the demand is great enough, businesses may have to hire more workers, and this will create even more income which can be spent for still more goods and services. In order to spend more than the amount of income it has, the government will have to borrow money, thus increasing the national debt.

Surplus Budget. If business activity is increasing too rapidly and there is full employment and a danger of price inflation, the Administration will submit a surplus budget to Congress. In a *surplus budget* the government expects to spend less than it expects to

Government spending provides needed improvements for taxpayers and at the same time creates jobs and demand for goods and services.

Southern California Visitors Council

receive in income. In effect, the government says that it will wait awhile before spending money since the economy is already quite active. The excess income can then be used to reduce the national debt (discussed later in the chapter).

Transfer Payments for Pensions, Subsidies, and Interest. Some of the spending by the federal government is not in payment for purchases of goods and services. Examples of such payments are pensions to veterans and others, social security payments, subsidies to farmers and others, and interest on the national debt. These are known as transfer payments because they are payments of money for which no current goods or services are produced.

When the government spends funds for food for the armed services, construction of a bridge or building, or paper for use in government office operations, it purchases goods and services produced as a part of GNP. When it makes payments for pensions, subsidies, or interest, it is merely transferring funds out of tax collections. However, the individuals who receive the transfer payments may use them to buy goods and services. The transfer payments therefore have the same effect on business activities in general and on employment as government payments for goods and services that were produced as a part of GNP. The total spending of federal, state, and local governments in 1979 was $459.4 billion for the purchase of goods and services plus $205.2 billion for transfer payments, making a total of $664.6 billion.

Social security payments by the government are from funds accumulated from employees and employers. They are known as transfer payments.

Total Spending. Total spending in the United States is comprised of the payments made by both the private sector and the public or government sector of the economy. Some economists believe government spending, including both purchases of goods and services and transfer payments, to be highly important in maintaining favorable business activity and employment. In case the spending in the private sector of the economy decreases, government spending may be increased to maintain a satisfactory level of business activity and employment. If the government decreases its spending, income and employment are forced downward. In a way, government spending in a given period of time provides balance by adjusting its spending upward or downward to maintain total spending (private and public combined) on an even keel at a level that maintains favorable income and employment.

Government Taxation

The federal government also uses taxation as another important control to stimulate or reduce economic activity. Taxes on incomes (both individual and business) and on the sale, manufacture, and buying of certain goods (excise taxes) provide the bulk of income received by the federal government. Therefore, if the government raises taxes, it reduces the amount of money individuals and businesses have available to spend. This act will tend to reduce business activity and prevent price inflation.

If business activity is slow, the government could reduce corporation income taxes with the idea that businesses will use this extra money to modernize, expand, and replace old equipment. In this way the government encourages businesses to buy more goods and perhaps to hire more people. If personal income taxes are also reduced, the wage earner will have more money to spend on goods and services. This act, too, should create more business activity and eventually create more jobs.

In most instances, the government will use both controls (spending and taxation) together in the best possible combination. For example, a large government spending program (deficit budget condition) may not act quickly enough to offset downward business activity because it takes time to draw up blueprints, survey land, purchase land, and award contracts to get a road building project underway. Therefore, it might be necessary to combine increased spending programs with tax cuts since tax cuts usually get money into circulation more rapidly.

When the economy becomes quite active again, the government may feel that it must continue some major projects it has started, but that to do so may cause inflation because of too much government spending. It may then raise taxes in order to bring the budget into a balanced or surplus condition. The raising of taxes should offset the continued government spending on major public projects and thereby hold down excess spending by business and consumers and prevent price inflation.

C. NATIONAL DEBT — RESULT OF GOVERNMENT SPENDING

The *national debt* is the amount of money that the federal government has borrowed from individuals and business firms (including banks). The federal government owes individuals, businesses, and others who hold government securities. In the approximately 200 years that our government has been in operation, it has spent nearly $670 billion more than it has received in revenue. As the table on the next page shows, most of this indebtedness has been incurred in the last 39 years.

Growth in National Debt

The growth of the public debt, as shown in the chart on the next page, has taken place particularly at five different periods since 1930. These periods coincide with the following events in history:

1930–1939	The Great Depression
1939–1945	World War II
1950–1955	Korean War
1957–1964	Cold War
1965–1973	Vietnam War

NATIONAL DEBT
SELECTED YEARS 1930–1979
(Billions of Dollars)

Fiscal Year	Public Debt
1930	16.2
1940	43.0
1945	258.7
1955	272.8
1965	313.8
1970	382.6
1975	544.1
1979	804.0

Source: *Statistical Abstract of the U.S.*, 1977, and *Economic Indicators*, May, 1979.

Per Capita National Debt

The per capita debt for the federal government represents an accumulated excess of expenditures over revenue received by the

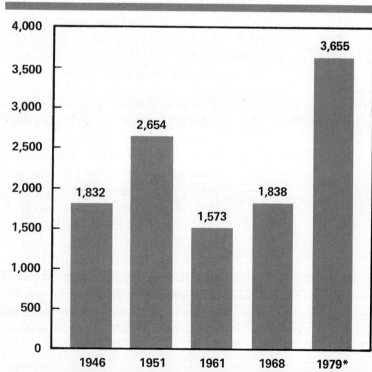

Per Capita Share of National Debt (At End of Selected Years, 1946-1979)

Source: U.S. Department of Commerce, 1970, and *Survey of Current Business*, April, 1979.

*Estimate based on a population of 220 million.

government. The per capita share of the debt is determined by dividing the total accumulated debt by the population of the country. The illustration on page 221 shows the per capita national debt for selected years.

Concern About National Debt. Some economists have expressed fear that the value of money will decline if the national debt is permitted to rise still higher. They believe that the country is facing continuously rising prices leading to more inflation. Others are concerned that the interest on the national debt now exceeds $50 billion each year or about 11% of the total federal budget. Some individuals believe we can never pay off the present debt. Others believe that the size of the public debt is not a serious threat to the economic well-being of the nation. They argue that many individuals and businesses have debts that would require their total income for several years to pay off, but that the public debt could be paid off with approximately one third of the total production in the United States for one year.

Essential Facts About National Debt. There are many issues and problems arising from the national debt. An understanding of the national debt is important to all of us because of its influence on the economic life of the nation. Consider the following essential aspects of the national debt:

1. The dollar amount of the national debt increased at an accelerated rate during World War II. It has increased more slowly but continuously since World War II.
2. From 1945 to 1979 the population of the United States increased about 50%, but the federal debt increased about 200% in the same period. As a result, the per capita debt increased from approximately $1,832 in 1946 to an estimated $3,655 in 1979. However, the median yearly earnings of all civilian (nonfarm) employees increased nearly 400%. Note that these dollar amounts *are not* corrected for inflation or for increases in the GNP.
3. The annual GNP, that is, the dollar value of the goods and services produced, is an indication of the ability to pay off the debt. In 1946, the national debt was 116% of our GNP; in fiscal 1979, the national debt had dropped to 35% of our GNP.
4. The growing economy adds to our ability to pay the annual interest on the national debt and to reduce the total amount by paying off the debt gradually.

5. In order to pay off the national debt, the total receipts must exceed the total expenditures of the federal government. This means that debt reduction is possible only when there is a budget surplus.

6. The interest on the national debt, estimated at about $57 billion for the 1979 fiscal year, is approximately 11% of the total estimated expenditures. These interest dollars received by individuals and businesses help the economy.

Management of National Debt. The national debt cannot be paid off at one time. To do so would upset the economy. It would place an additional sum of money in the hands of individuals and

---

FACTS EVERYONE SHOULD KNOW ABOUT
TAXATION, FISCAL POLICY, AND NATIONAL DEBT

1. Taxation is a device or plan by which funds are raised to pay the costs of operating local, state, and federal governments.

2. The more services and benefits people want from government, the more government costs and the higher taxes become.

3. In order to make taxes fair to all, the tax each individual and each business should pay must be determined by a formula or rule, not arbitrarily.

4. The only agency that has the power and right to tax is government.

5. Taxation plans are based on ideas such as fairness to the taxpayer, cost of service given, benefit from the service, and ability to pay.

6. Tax payments require approximately one third of the income of the typical individual. Every individual has a vital stake in taxes.

7. Fiscal policy is the decision of government to spend and to tax in amounts that help the economy grow, increase employment, and prevent price inflation.

8. Heavy government spending and low tax rates usually reflect a deficit budget; moderate to low government spending and high tax rates usually reflect a surplus budget.

9. The national debt has been created largely by wars and economic depression. One measure of the ability of the nation to pay its debts is the dollar value of the goods and services it produces each year. The national debt was 116% of GNP in 1946 but only 35% in 1979.

10. The only way the national debt can be paid is through budget surplus (excess of federal income over federal expenditures).

businesses equal to over one third of the total GNP for a year. Good management of the national debt will require an honest effort (1) to maintain a healthy balance between government receipts and expenditures and (2) to retire bonds and other indebtedness when possible through budget surpluses without hampering sound economic growth.

REVIEW QUESTIONS

Section A

1. What is taxation?
2. What is the difference between a tax and a payment to a government agency?
3. What are the essentials of a tax system?
4. Why is it not really possible to apportion the tax burden according to the cost of the service or benefit received?
5. What is the most widely accepted theory for apportioning taxes? Why?
6. Upon what theory of taxation is the federal income tax based?
7. What is (a) direct tax? (b) indirect tax?
8. Under what conditions are the following taxes direct and indirect: (a) real estate and (b) sales?
9. What is meant by "shifting the tax burden"?
10. What is meant by the term "hidden taxes"?
11. By what process is the amount of a property tax determined?
12. What is the principal source of revenue of the U.S. Government?
13. On what theory are business or service taxes based?
14. What are the two general types of inheritance taxes?
15. What are the most common special taxes?
16. (a) What are the chief sources of income for the federal government dollar? (b) What are the chief expenditures of the federal government dollar?
17. How can consumers help to control taxes?
18. Who ultimately pays for public services?

Section B

19. What do we mean by the term "fiscal policy"?
20. What is (a) a deficit budget and (b) a surplus budget?
21. (a) What two controls does the government use to stimulate or reduce economic activity? (b) How does each work?

Section C

22. To whom is our national debt owed?
23. What relationship is there between the increase in national debt and historical events?
24. What does good management of the national debt require?

DISCUSSION QUESTIONS

Section A

1. In what ways should taxpayers help determine how tax money is spent?
2. (a) How may a tax on gasoline used to pay for roads in all parts of the state be distinguished from an assessment on adjoining property used for a new sewer?
   (b) What are the benefits derived in each case?
   (c) Why is one a tax and the other not a tax?

3. (a) Two major plans for apportioning or charging taxes to individuals and business firms are the cost-of-service-received plan and the ability-to-pay plan. On what principle does each plan work?

    (b) What are the major problems encountered in using each of these plans?

4. A new expressway and an overpass are constructed from the center of a city into an outlying district. Part of the cost is paid from a general tax fund and part is obtained through the assessment of adjoining property owners. Some taxpayers believe that the entire cost should be paid by the adjoining property owners. Would this plan be fair or unfair?

5. What are the advantages and the disadvantages of property tax as a source of government income?

6. Is it fair or not fair to charge a single person who has a taxable income of $5,000 a year, $283 in federal taxes and a single person who has a taxable income of $20,000 a year, $3,999 in federal taxes?

7. A single person pays a considerably higher rate of federal income tax than a married person. Is this practice fair? Why or why not?

8. Suppose a sales tax of 2% were levied by a state on all commodities and services. If this were the only state tax, why would it be fair or unfair?

9. What is the theory or purpose of inheritance taxes?

Section B

10. In times of national emergency such as a war, why might fiscal policy demand a deficit budget?

11. How do transfer payments of the federal government for pensions, subsidies, and interest affect business activities?

Section C

12. Assume that the Administration is about to present a balanced budget to Congress but at the last minute decides to spend $5 billion more for a major slum clearance program. Would this additional expenditure automatically call for a $5 billion deficit budget? Why or why not?

APPLICATION PROBLEMS

Section A

1. The assessed valuation of the real estate in a certain city is approximately 33⅓% of the market value. The tax rate is $8.20 per $100 of assessed valuation. Mr. Hershey builds a house that costs $20,000 on a lot valued at $3,500. What is a reasonable estimate of the taxes on this property that he will have to pay each year?

2. Assume that you are a single taxpayer earning $125 a week in wages before taxes and other deductions. You pay $195 a year in state income taxes, $538 in federal income taxes, $70 in state sales taxes, $65 in property taxes on your car, $62 in state gasoline taxes, $393 in social security taxes, and $70 in all other taxes (excise, licenses, and fees). How many weeks must you work just to pay taxes?

Section B

3. In 1975, tax rebates were granted to individuals. Research the background of the rebate, explaining its purposes and how the money was to be apportioned. Then talk with several heads of households about what they did with the money. Did their actions fulfill the government's intentions? Were the rebates successful?

Section C   4. From data found in the current issue of the *Statistical Abstract of the United States*, prepare a series of charts showing (a) the total amount and sources of revenues for your state; (b) the expenditures for various functions (education, highways, public welfare, natural resources, etc.) by your state; (c) kinds of taxes and amount received from such taxes in your state; and (d) the amount and purpose of the state debt (if any) for your state.

COMMUNITY PROJECTS

Section A   1. Prepare a report on the early history of taxation in this country. In your report make references to such items as the Constitution and the limitations it imposed on the federal government with respect to taxation; the purpose for imposing excise taxes on certain items (tobacco, liquor, cosmetics) as opposed to other consumer items in the early history of our country; when the graduated income tax came into existence and who proposed it; the first attempt to tax personal incomes and why it was dropped and then resumed.

2. A tax calendar giving dates on which the various local, state, and federal tax payments and reports are due for your state usually can be obtained from the local or state chamber of commerce. Your instructor will give you a tax calendar or will instruct you in how to prepare or obtain one.

   Using the tax calendar for your state, prepare a list of tax reports and payments that need to be made each year by:

   (a) An individual who is employed as a toolmaker by a manufacturer.

   (b) A retail grocer who owns a store building, equipment, delivery trucks and merchandise, and who employs six full-time and four part-time people.

   (c) A local manufacturing firm that owns its plant, all equipment and necessary trucks, and that employs 500 people.

Section B   3. Obtain a copy of the budget for your city, county, or parish. From the budget, prepare two financial statements. One should show the total estimated expenditures classified under such topics as schools, police protection, city or county administration, and payments on indebtedness. The other statement should show the sources of income and the estimated amount of income from each source.

   Based on the statements of estimated expenditures and estimated income, what recommendations would you make regarding: (a) the expenditures? (b) the sources of income and the kinds of taxes used to obtain the income?

Section C   4. From the current edition of the *Statistical Abstract of the United States* prepare a chart showing the per capita share of the national debt from 1915 to the present. Note the rise and fall of per capita share of the debt throughout this period of time. Key the per capita share of the debt for selected years to historical events that could have accounted for the size of the per capita shares, such as wars, depressions, post-war recovery, and recessions. Then check population growth figures and salary comparison figures for various types of employment for selected years against the current year. What generalizations can you draw from these data?

 **International Trade**

PURPOSE OF THE CHAPTER

International trade is of great cultural, political, and economic significance to the nations of the world. The volume of international trade grows continuously and has a direct bearing on the national income of the countries involved. The major problem confronting a nation in its financial dealings with other nations is maintaining approximately the same money income as money outflow.

After studying this chapter, you will be able to:

1. Explain why international trade is important to a country.
2. Discuss the effect on a country if its total payments to foreign countries substantially exceed its total receipts from foreign countries for a given year and for several years in a row.
3. Explain the significance of international trade agreements.
4. Discuss the arguments for and against tariffs.
5. Explain international monetary policies used to reduce trade surpluses or deficits among countries.

A. BUYING AND SELLING ABROAD

International trade, or *foreign trade* as it sometimes called, is the buying, selling, and exchanging of goods and services by individuals and business firms between nations. Many American citizens and businesses transact a great volume of trade with other nations. Their international trade consists of imports, exports, private investments abroad, and the establishment of manufacturing and distribution branches abroad. Foreign nations and their citizens carry on similar activities in the United States.

Ships of many nations transport goods in international trade. The exports of one nation are the imports of the nation to which they are brought.

The Port Authority of NY & NJ

Our government also gives direct and indirect economic aid to underdeveloped nations. The direct aid consists of dollars and materials. The indirect aid consists of technical assistance and other means of helping those nations to help themselves. In addition, our government maintains several military bases abroad.

International Trade Affects Relationships Among Nations

International trade has an important bearing on the relationships among nations. On the positive side, trade among nations promotes the sharing of cultural traditions, particularly in literature, the arts, and inventions. It helps the people of the participating nations understand each other. It provides the basis for both individual and international friendships. And through trade, the peoples of the participating nations can enjoy the benefits of many commodities and services that otherwise would not be possible for them.

From another view, international trade gives rise to economic problems between nations that in some instances lead to wars, revolutions, and political crises. International trade is probably the most important single factor in promoting lasting friendships between nations. Nations, like individuals, are highly sensitive to the treatment they receive in business transactions with others. It is highly important that we understand the economic problems of the world and how those problems affect the nations with whom we trade. Our welfare, security, and prosperity are affected by those problems.

Importance of International Trade

No nation is self-sufficient. Many things are needed to supply individuals with the products they need for satisfactory living. The United States is particularly fortunate in having many of the essentials needed for security and for the welfare of our people.

The United States Imports Many Essential Commodities. Goods and services that we buy from other countries are called *imports*. We find it necessary to import many products either because we do not have them at all or because we do not have

Strategic Imports Essential to Our Industry

The United States produces only a small portion of many products that are essential to our industry.

Platinum 95%
Nickel 92%
Cobalt 90%
Beryllium 96%
Antimony 90%
Manganese 98%
Natural Rubber 100%
Industrial Diamonds 100%
Fluorspar 71%
Bauxite 90%
Tin 100%
Chrome 90%

Imports ■
U.S. Production □

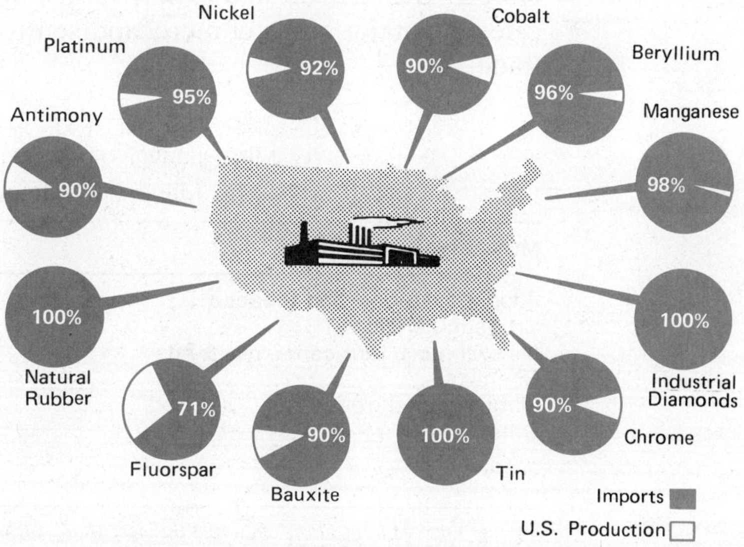

Source: *ABC's of Foreign Trade,* Department of State, Publication 7713.

enough to supply our needs. For example, we must import such products as coffee, tea, spices, industrial diamonds, ore from which aluminum is made, chrome, cobalt, copper, tin, wool, and zinc. Some of the products we import are for the use of individuals or are used in the manufacture of goods for individuals. Others are particularly important in national defense, especially metals and minerals used in the manufacture of many kinds of weapons.

Foreign Nations Need our Exports. Goods and services that we sell to other countries are called *exports*. The nations from which we import products have need for our wheat, machinery, and many other products that we extract from the earth or manufacture. They buy some of our products and we buy some of theirs. Many groups of items of merchandise may be both imported and exported by the same country. For instance, the United States and Japan import small compact automobiles from western Europe. At the same time the United States exports both small and large automobiles to the countries of South America. Another illustration of importing and exporting the same class of product is food. The United States exports wheat and at the same time imports rice. Precision instruments, manufactured in western Europe and Japan, are imported by the United States. At the same time machinery and transportation equipment manufactured in the United States are exported to Asia and Africa. The following table of U.S. import and export values by merchandise group indicates the major kinds of merchandise involved in our international trade.

U.S. IMPORT AND EXPORT VALUES
BY MERCHANDISE GROUPS, 1978
(In Millions of Dollars)

Merchandise Group	Imports	Exports
Food, beverages, and tobacco	$ 15,742	$ 20,626
Crude materials	9,334	15,553
Mineral fuels, lubricants, oils & fats	42,616	5,400
Chemicals	6,427	12,618
Manufactured goods	93,925	81,865
Other goods	3,981	5,007
Total	$172,025	$141,069

Source: Adapted from *Survey of Current Business* (April, 1979).

International Trade Is Essential to the U.S. Economy. International trade of merchandise for the United States represents about 5% of all business activity in this country. These figures include only merchandise and exclude military grants, aid, interest, and other considerations. This ratio of foreign trade to domestic trade may seem relatively small when compared to amounts as high as 40 to 50% in some countries. However, the volume is highly important from the standpoint of the employment of our people and prosperity in general. For example, approximately 5% of our labor force works in the export industry. Trade is even more significant in our relations with the nations of the world, for they need our products and we need theirs.

Basis for International Trade

Every nation wants the opportunity to export its goods and services to other countries. A foreign outlet for sales permits a manufacturer or a distributor to increase the volume of business activity, thus leading to increased employment, profits, and opportunities. Every nation wants the chance to buy from foreign countries those products and services that are scarce or unavailable at home. In short, every nation wants foreign trade as a means of raising the level of living for its people.

Most nations could not import goods and services unless they could also export their goods and services to others. Without exports it would be difficult, if not impossible, in the long run to pay for goods and services that a nation would like to import. This means that the factors which enable a nation to build a volume of export trade are important.

Factors in Export Competition. Manufacturers and merchants within a country such as the United States compete for business in several ways. They compete on the basis of price asked, quality of merchandise or service offered, and usefulness and serviceability of the product or service to consumers. Business firms and individuals within a country compete with business firms and individuals in other countries for exporting their products and services. The businesses and individuals in some nations have more favorable conditions than others with which to meet the competition of international trade. The essential factors in determining the ability to meet export competition are summarized on the next page.

The factors that determine ability to compete with other nations for export trade must be considered collectively in making decisions about entering the international trade market. Rarely will there be a situation in which all the factors are favorable. Even though some factors are only partially favorable to engaging

---

FACTORS THAT DETERMINE A NATION'S ABILITY TO COMPETE FOR EXPORT OPPORTUNITIES

---

1. Raw materials from which consumer goods are made for export trade are readily available at a reasonable cost.

2. The production and distribution operations of businesses are efficiently managed.

3. Management is imaginative, creative, and resourceful in inventing, innovating, and designing useful products that have strong appeal to consumers.

4. The competencies and skills of available labor are adequate for and compatible with the work to be performed in the production and distribution of the goods to be produced for export.

5. Labor is available at a cost that is fair to employees and that enables a producer or distributor to compete in the export market.

6. Transportation of the finished goods from the exporting country to the importing country is available at costs that make it possible for the exporter to compete.

7. High quality products are available at low production costs due to improvements through technology.

8. The quality of the product is compatible with the quality needed for the use to be made of it.

9. The product in total is acceptable to the people of the importing country from the viewpoint of total cost, quality, usefulness, and service.

10. Trade regulations and restrictions of the exporting country are favorable.

---

in export trade, the factors collectively may merit entering the international trade market.

Absolute Advantage. A nation is said to have an *absolute advantage* in production when it can produce a product more efficiently than another nation. Absolute advantage as a basis for engaging in international trade may be shown by the following situation. Assume a situation in which (a) free trade (no duties or tariffs) exists between the nations, (b) products produced by one country are equal in quality to the same products produced in the other country, and (c) there is no national prejudice between the nations involved. Further assume that costs to produce are as follows:

Product	Nation A Cost to Produce	Nation B Cost to Produce
Bicycle	$20.00	$19.00
Roller skates	2.00	2.50

Manufacturers of bicycles in Nation B can compete favorably for export business with Nation A. Manufacturers of bicycles in Nation A must find a way of reducing costs to produce a bicycle. If this cannot be done, they may be forced to shift to another product if they wish to engage in international trade.

The situation is reversed in the case of roller skates. Manufacturers of roller skates in Nation A can compete favorably with manufacturers of roller skates in Nation B. Manufacturers of roller skates in Nation B will have to find a way to reduce costs to produce roller skates or they will have to shift to some other product.

Nation A has an absolute advantage over Nation B in producing roller skates. Nation B has an absolute advantage over Nation A in producing bicycles. But what would happen if one of the nations had an absolute advantage in producing bicycles *and* roller skates? Would trade be profitable for either or both countries? The answer is yes, both countries would benefit from international trade. The answer is found in what economists call comparative advantage.

Comparative Advantage. A nation is said to have a *comparative advantage* in production when it has an efficiency advantage or a cost advantage between two products. Let us change our trade example to show what happens when Nation A can produce bicycles and roller skates for less than what it costs Nation B to produce these items.

Product	Nation A Cost to Produce	Nation B Cost to Produce
Bicycle	$20.00	$30.00
Roller skates	2.00	5.00

In Nation A, without trade with Nation B, a bicycle is worth 10 pairs of roller skates. In Nation B, without trade with Nation A, a bicycle is worth 6 pairs of roller skates.

Now assume that the two nations are free to trade without duties or tariffs. What happens? If Nation A produces only roller skates, it can, for instance, produce 30 pairs for $60. Since a bicycle in Nation B costs 6 pairs of roller skates, Nation A can use, say, 12 pairs of skates to buy 2 bicycles from Nation B. Now Nation A has 2 bicycles and 18 pairs of skates for a cost of $60. Without trade, 18 pairs of skates would have cost $36 and 2 bicycles would have cost $40 for a total expenditure of $76.

If Nation B produces only bicycles, it can produce 2 for $60. If it trades one of these bicycles to Nation A, it can get 10 pairs of roller skates. Therefore, for a cost of $60 Nation B has 1 bicycle and 10 pairs of roller skates. Without trade, one bicycle in Nation B would cost $30 and the 10 pairs of roller skates would cost $50 for a total expenditure of $80.

Both nations are better off because of trade even though Nation A has an absolute advantage (can produce both items for less) in producing bicycles and roller skates. The reason, of course, is that the comparative advantages in producing bicycles and roller skates are different in the two nations. Nation A is 50% better at producing bicycles than Nation B, but it is 150% better than Nation B in the production of roller skates.

When each nation produces those goods and services that it can produce most efficiently and trades freely with other nations, the level of living in each country rises.

A simple example from daily experience might help to highlight the principle of comparative advantage. Suppose that an artist can earn $50 for painting a picture. It takes the same time to do one picture as it takes to mow the lawn. The artist can hire someone to mow the lawn for $10. Even if the artist were more skilled at mowing the lawn than the person hired and could do it at a cost of, say, $5, would it be profitable to take painting time to mow the lawn? Would it be profitable for a skilled surgeon who is an excellent typist to take time from a medical practice to do typing? Might not the surgeon be better off hiring a secretary?

Stated simply, the principle of comparative advantage states that trade is mutually profitable for two nations if each specializes in the production of products in which it has the greatest relative efficiency. This is true even if one nation is absolutely more efficient in the production of every product produced.

Balance of Trade

The term *balance of trade* refers to the balance between a nation's exports and its imports of goods. The balance of trade is said to be *favorable* if the value of exports exceeds the value of imports. This means that the nation receives more in payment for goods sold to foreign countries than it paid for goods imported from foreign countries. An *unfavorable* balance of trade means that a nation has imported more than it has exported. The balance of trade for the United States was generally favorable until 1971, as shown in the following table. Except for 1973 and 1975, the United States had an unfavorable balance of trade during the 1970s.

U.S. BALANCE OF TRADE
(In Millions of Dollars)

Year	Exports	Imports	Net Balance
1967	$ 30,666	$ 26,866	$ 3,800
1968	33,626	32,991	635
1969	36,414	35,807	607
1970	41,947	39,788	2,159
1971	42,754	45,476	−2,722
1972	48,768	55,754	−6,986
1973	71,379	70,424	955
1974	98,309	103,567	−5,277
1975	107,184	98,139	9,045
1976	114,694	124,047	−9,353
1977	120,585	151,644	−31,059
1978	141,069	172,025	−30,956

Sources: *Statistical Abstract of the United States*, 1977, and *Survey of Current Business*, April, 1979.

We should be aware that a favorable balance of trade (excess of exports over imports) does not tell us how well a nation fared financially in all of its transactions with foreign countries. In the discussion of balance of payments in the next section of this chapter, you will learn about other foreign transactions that affect a country's international financial status.

B. U.S. BALANCE OF PAYMENTS

The meanings of "balance of trade" and "balance of payments" are sometimes confused. "Balance of trade," which you have just studied, is concerned only with the import and export of goods. If the value of exported goods exceeds the value of imported goods for a nation, that nation is said to have a favorable balance of trade. On the other hand, "balance of payments" includes all financial transactions that take place between one country and the rest of the world during a given year. For the United States, balance of payments includes both receipts and payments for export and import of goods, foreign tourist spending in the United States and American tourist spending abroad, amounts received and spent on shipping services involving other nations, and amounts received and paid on interest and dividends. Other financial transactions with foreign nations that are included in our balance of international payments are support of troops and military bases overseas; transfer of gold in foreign exchange; and gifts, loans, and assistance to foreign countries.

Definition of Balance of Payments

The U.S. *balance of payments* is the difference between total payments to other nations and the total receipts from foreign nations. The U.S. balance of international payments in recent years is shown in the following table.

U.S. BALANCE OF PAYMENTS
ON GOODS, SERVICES,
AND REMITTANCES
(In Millions of Dollars)

Year	Net Balance
1967	1,273
1968	−1,313
1969	−1,956
1970	− 281
1971	−3,879
1972	−9,710
1973	335
1974	−3,357
1975	11,916
1976	4,339
1977	−15,221
1978	−15,960

Source: *Federal Reserve Bulletin* (May, 1979).

In 8 of the 12 years for which the U.S. balance of payments is given in the table, there was an excess of payments over receipts. This indicates an unfavorable net balance of payments. However, the balance of trade (excess of exports over imports) was unfavorable only 6 years during the same time period.

Deficits and Liquid Liabilities

The deficit created by an excess of payments over receipts can be measured by the outflow of gold and an increase in liquid liabilities held by the people of foreign nations. A *liquid liability* is a financial obligation on which payment may be requested at any time. The U.S. liquid liabilities held by foreign nations consist primarily of U.S. dollars that we have paid for goods we have imported. These dollars are held in banks by foreigners or are invested in U.S. assets that can be converted into cash on short notice. In 1978 our short-term liabilities to foreigners exceeded $14 billion. Our ability to deal in international exchange depends on the confidence foreigners have in the U.S. dollar. This confidence will exist if we take steps to (1) check inflation in the U.S., (2) keep our prices of goods competitive in the foreign markets, (3) maintain a favorable balance of trade and a favorable balance of payments most years, (4) practice conservation and restraint in use of energy, and (5) balance the federal budget.

U.S. Payments To and Receipts From Foreign Countries

The U.S. balance of payments for any given period of time is the net result of many financial transactions with foreign countries. The question arises as to what these transactions were. The financial transactions resulting in payments to and receipts from foreign countries in 1978 are summarized by classes or kinds in the following table.

U.S. BALANCE OF PAYMENTS, 1978
(In Millions of Dollars)

Payments		Receipts	
Merchandise Imports	$175,988	Merchandise Exports	$141,844
Gifts, Pensions, & Other Transactions	2,048	Net Military Transactions	531
U.S. Gov't Grants (direct foreign aid)	3,028	Net Investment Income (income from U.S. investments overseas less payments to foreign investments in U.S.)	19,915
Total Payments	$181,064		
Balance of Payments Deficit	−15,960	Net Other Services	2,814
		Total Receipts	$165,104

Source: Adapted from *Federal Reserve Bulletin* (May, 1979).

Solving the Deficit Problem

Despite the favorable balance of payments during 1973, 1975, and 1976, the United States has been plagued with very large deficits between 1968 and 1978. An unfavorable balance of payments, particularly when it occurs often, is a problem of major concern to our government and to us as individuals. The U.S. government has been studying each item of the balance-of-payments account to scale down the outward flow of international payments and to increase the inward flow of receipts from foreign financial transactions.

Some of the steps that may be taken to reduce or eliminate a balance-of-payments deficit are:

1. Expand our exports under the leadership of industry and government.
2. Encourage our military establishments abroad to buy U.S. goods rather than foreign goods; promote the selling of military equipment to our allies rather than lending the equipment to them; and encourage other industrial nations to assume a greater share of the cost of trying to keep world peace.
3. Attract foreigners to visit the United States as tourists; encourage American citizens to travel at home first and abroad second, which probably would reduce the volume of American tourist traffic abroad.
4. Adjust interest rates to compete with those of foreign countries to encourage American investors to invest at home.
5. Stimulate the sale of U.S. goods abroad by including a provision in agreements for U.S. foreign aid grants and loans requiring the country to buy U.S. goods and services.
6. Reduce U.S. aid to foreign countries.
7. Reduce our military operations in foreign countries (for example, by closing military bases or reducing the number of personnel there).
8. Periodically adjust the value of the dollar in relation to foreign currencies.

C. INTERNATIONAL TRADE CONTROLS

Almost all nations want foreign trade for at least two reasons. First, they are dependent on imports for some goods that are essential to the well-being and lives of their citizens. Second, exports of their goods and products provide the opportunity for increased employment and additional income. These same nations are also interested in maintaining a control over trade to provide a favorable balance between exports and imports. Ordinarily, a greater volume of exports than imports is considered favorable to economic growth and stability of business activities.

How Nations Control Trade

Numerous controls are used by governments to limit imports or to increase exports. Among the most commonly used controls are:

1. Place high tariffs (import taxes) on imports.
2. Require import licenses that limit the volume and the values of goods that each merchant may import.
3. Set national limits or quotas on the total value or volume of a product that may be imported in a year.
4. Require licenses for obtaining foreign currencies (money) by people who want to use foreign currencies to buy goods abroad, thus limiting the amount of foreign goods they may buy for import purposes.
5. Subsidize selected export products by making payments to the producers, thus enabling them to sell at lower prices abroad and hence to encourage foreign sales.

Nations often attempt to control foreign trade to avoid a balance-of-payments deficit or to protect industries at home against the competition of foreign goods. Some nations enter into trade agreements with other nations to remove trade barriers and to promote trade among the participating countries.

Tariffs

Tariffs, sometimes known as *customs duties*, are taxes levied on exports or imports, usually the latter. Tariffs are levied on two bases: *ad valorem* and *specific*. The former is a percentage of the value of a commodity; the latter is a given payment on a unit of the commodity, as per bushel or per ton.

Purposes of Tariffs. Tariffs may be levied for purposes of (a) revenue, (b) protection of an industry or of labor, or (c) both. While tariffs produce a revenue, the amount of revenue from tariffs is relatively small in relation to the total revenue necessary to run the federal government. Most of our tariffs are intended to protect business interests and labor. They are sometimes used to protect industries that are vital in our national defense. Tariffs are also used to protect infant industries and certain other industries that might be destroyed by competition of foreign goods.

Tariffs Affect Markets. The common practice of placing tariffs on foreign products is the result of the desire of domestic producers to have the national market to themselves. While a tariff on an

The World Trade Center in New York City provides a central office location for importers, exporters, and others associated with world trade.

The Port Authority of NY & NJ

import gives the domestic producers some control over the market, it also tends to limit their foreign markets. Foreign countries tend to retaliate by placing tariffs on products produced in a country with high tariffs, such as the United States. Of course, a high tariff policy affects various producers differently. From the viewpoint of a manufacturer whose entire market is in this country, a high tariff is desirable. But from the viewpoint of a manufacturer whose main market is abroad, a high tariff may be unfortunate.

Tariffs Affect Prices. From the consumer's point of view, a tariff on a foreign product is simply a tax. Tariffs that protect certain domestic manufacturers or other producers necessarily result in higher price levels. Most consumers are quite unaware of the fact that they have to pay high prices daily for certain commodities or have to accept similar inferior products simply because of the existence of tariffs.

A tariff is a hidden tax. For example, woolen blankets are manufactured in certain foreign countries and are sold at prices much lower than the prevailing prices in the United States. A person in this country who wishes to purchase a woolen blanket that was produced abroad must pay the foreign price of the blanket plus the tariff. That person, however, may purchase a similar blanket produced in this country, but will have to pay a price that is approximately the price of the foreign-produced blanket plus the tariff. The consumer also has the alternative of purchasing a lower-grade, domestic blanket at a price approximately the same as the price of the foreign blanket without the tariff.

Tariffs Affect Labor. One of the most frequent statements favoring a high tariff is that such tariffs protect workers from the competition of foreign countries where labor is cheap and levels of living are low. Whether or not this argument has a basis of fact depends on (a) the purchasing power of the American worker's dollar and (b) whether or not the tariff is to the benefit of the worker or the manufacturer. If a general high tariff results in a high price level, obviously the worker's wages will not purchase as much as they would if the price level were lower.

Tariffs Affect Agriculture. Tariffs affect farmers in two ways. They affect (1) the manufactured products farmers must buy and (2) in some cases, the products that farmers sell. In the United States, major farm crops have been protected by high tariffs, although tariffs on some agricultural products have been reduced. There have also been tariffs — and resulting higher prices — on clothing, machinery, and other products that a farmer must have. Thus the advantages that farmers might gain from higher prices on crops are frequently offset by higher prices they must pay for needed products.

Tariffs Affect Manufacturing. Very early in the history of the United States, certain manufacturers, notably in the textile field in New England, sought government protection by the encouragement of high tariffs. They argued that infant industries and industries necessary for our defense in case of war would be protected and encouraged. They also defended the idea that high tariffs brought about high levels of living. Manufacturers whose markets are largely domestic are the chief gainers from tariffs. Other manufacturers may actually be injured and their foreign markets destroyed if foreign nations react against high tariff policies.

Tariffs Affect the Consumer. Although an individual as a producer may gain from tariffs, as a consumer that person suffers because high tariffs are generally injurious. From the consumer's point of view, tariffs result in (a) high prices and (b) a narrower range of choice. In some few instances tariffs may protect a consumer from cheap and shoddy goods. In general, however, the competition of foreign products would make domestic manufacturers more efficient in order to compete with foreigners; otherwise, they would have to withdraw from the market. As productive efficiency is always to the consumer's advantage, tariffs indirectly serve to discourage efficiency and therefore penalize the consumer. In general, it may be said that high tariffs decrease the consumer's purchasing power.

Conflicting Theories. The tariff problem has long been a source of political and economic debate. Economists have generally agreed that low tariffs or no tariffs are desirable from a national and a consumer point of view, but political representatives have usually been powerful enough to overcome the opposition to tariffs. There are many pros and cons with respect to tariffs. Advocates point out that tariffs keep out cheap foreign products made by low-paid labor; that they maintain industries necessary in case of war; that they promote young and weak industries; and that they help to make the nation self-sufficient. Economists and others point out that tariffs reduce productivity by limiting specialization and markets; that they penalize the consumer; that they help, not labor, but only particular groups; and that they create international ill will.

The dominant point of view seems to be that tariffs are undesirable. But in a world in which national rivalries are increasing, it is difficult to reduce tariffs. If tariffs are reduced, certain industries, especially those in which foreign competition is strong, will be affected adversely.

D. POSITION OF THE UNITED STATES ON FOREIGN TRADE

The United States is one of the largest buyers and sellers of goods on the world market. The economic welfare not only of the United States but also of the other countries of the free world is affected by the volume of world trade in which the United States engages annually. The United States and its citizens, therefore, have a great interest in stimulating foreign trade.

Trade Reform Act of 1974

In December, 1974, Congress passed the Trade Reform Act of 1974 to replace the Trade Expansion Act of 1962. The Act is designed to encourage foreign trade and to stimulate economic growth in the United States. According to the Act, the President may:

1. Reduce or raise U.S. tariffs during negotiations.
2. Impose an import surcharge (additional tax) up to 15%.
3. Reduce or eliminate nontariff barriers, such as export subsidies, import quotas, investment restrictions, health and safety codes, and pollution standards, subject to approval of Congress.
4. Retaliate against unreasonable foreign restrictions on U.S. trade.

The Act permits the President to extend "most-favored-nation" treatment to certain communist nations. The Act also makes it possible for firms and workers who suffer a financial loss because of increased imports to receive various forms of financial help from the government.

Deficits

In the late 1960s and 1970s, international trade of the United States changed significantly. The favorable balance of payments of the past became unfavorable deficits. As you will note from the figures presented on page 236, the United States ran a deficit in its balance of payments each year (except 1973, 1975, and 1976) since 1968. Some of these deficits were extremely large. In 1977, for example, the deficit was over $15 billion.

Obviously something had to be done to wipe out the large deficits experienced by the United States. Two of the steps taken are discussed in the following paragraphs.

Suspension of Gold Payments. The first action, and probably the most significant, taken by the United States to reduce its international trade deficit was taken in August, 1971. At that time the United States announced that it would no longer exchange gold for dollars held by foreign monetary authorities.

Following that announcement, major exchange rate changes took place. Many people felt that the dollar was of less value to them since they could not exchange it for gold at an established rate. Therefore many bankers and foreign traders preferred to hold currencies other than the U.S. dollar. The demand for the dollar declined. The fall in demand for the U.S. dollar made it worth less in other countries. Therefore, Americans wishing to buy foreign goods had to pay more in terms of U.S. dollars. At the same time, currencies of other countries rose in value as a result of an increase in demand. These currencies could, therefore, buy more in the United States. The end result was to reduce U.S. buying abroad and at the same time increase selling abroad. The policy was, of course, aimed at reducing the international U.S. deficit.

Devaluation. The U.S. dollar is defined in terms of gold. For many years $1/35$ ounce of gold was defined as worth one U.S. dollar. In December of 1971 and again in February of 1973, the U.S. redefined the value of the dollar in terms of gold. The price of one ounce of gold was increased by 7% in 1971 and by another 10% in 1973. This action made the U.S. dollar worth less in terms of gold since in 1973 it took 17% more dollars to buy the same amount of gold. The process of increasing the price of gold in terms of dollars is called *devaluing the dollar*.

Since most countries define their currency in gold, the value of the U.S. dollar was less in their countries too. Thus it took more U.S. dollars to buy goods abroad. Also, it took a lesser amount of foreign currency to buy goods in the United States. Devaluation, therefore, encouraged exports and discouraged imports. Obviously, this was the intent of the United States in an attempt to reduce its international deficit.

Worldwide Inflation

In the 1970s major industrial countries experienced the worst inflation they had known in 20 years. At the same time, *real* economic growth (actual growth after inflation has been taken into account) declined. Consequently, large shifts in funds took place to settle buying and selling among countries. In terms of dollars, international transferal of funds increased by 50% in one year alone, 1973–74.

A new word, *stagflation*, was introduced into the language in the 1970s to describe the situation. Stagflation is a shortened form of stagnation (decline or economic slump) and inflation (rapidly rising prices). Generally stagnation and inflation had not occurred at the same time in the past. Therefore new and sometimes drastic economic policies had to be used to deal with the situation. The U.S. decision not to convert dollars to gold and the devaluation of the U.S. dollar serve as examples.

Energy Crisis

International trade became further complicated in the 1970s when countries belonging to the Organization of Petroleum Exporting Countries (OPEC) raised crude oil prices. Crude oil prices increased over 400% in 1974 alone. Between 1975 and 1980 crude oil prices increased another 35%.

The oil crisis led to many changes in the economy in the 1970s, all of which cost U.S. citizens dearly in higher prices and unemployment. Some of these changes were: conversion of power plants from oil to coal, which raised the price of domestic coal; increased demand for small, energy-saving cars, which increased foreign imports and reduced domestic production; construction of the Alaskan pipeline; a step up in costs for pollution control devices caused by using more coal; and a tariff imposed on OPEC imported oil, which raised oil prices even more. The results were further stagnation.

In 1979 President Carter froze oil imports to 1977 levels, encouraged every citizen to practice conservation, ordered the nation to explore immediately new energy sources (solar, oil shale, biochemical products), and recommended the use of even more coal. His aim was to make the U.S. self-sufficient in fuel by 1985. These measures meant that all citizens would need to change their life styles and make personal sacrifices.

Some people have suggested that the U.S. counter OPEC countries by raising prices of agricultural and industrial products which these countries need. Others believe that such a measure would only create new international crises. These crises could take the form of (1) increasing inflation even more, (2) causing the OPEC nations to cease exporting oil to the U.S. completely, and (3) perhaps cutting off diplomatic relations with the countries in the Middle East.

International Monetary Reform

Most of the measures discussed above, which are aimed at solving the international monetary crisis, are temporary at best. In

FACTS EVERYONE SHOULD KNOW ABOUT INTERNATIONAL TRADE, BALANCE OF PAYMENTS, AND TARIFFS

1. International trade has an important bearing on the relationship between nations.

2. International trade has cultural and political as well as economic implications. The goal of a nation entering into international trade is to provide a higher level of living for its citizens.

3. Nations compete for export sales, just as merchants at home compete, through producing a better product at a lower price.

4. Trade is mutually profitable for two nations, even if one nation has an absolute advantage in the production of all products, if each nation specializes in the production of those products in which it has the greatest relative efficiency.

5. The value of exports and the value of imports of goods and services for any country must be approximately the same; otherwise an unfavorable balance of trade is created.

6. The balance of trade is the balance between a nation's exports and imports of goods. The balance of trade is favorable if the value of exports exceeds the value of imports; it is unfavorable if the value of imports exceeds the value of exports.

7. The balance of international payments for a nation is the difference in the total amount received from and the total amount paid to foreign nations for all purposes including exports and imports.

8. The balance of trade of a given nation may be favorable and the balance of payments unfavorable.

9. An unfavorable balance of payments for a given country may be corrected by encouraging its citizens to buy domestic products, reducing purchasing and spending abroad, and promoting more exports.

10. Many countries enter into trade agreements with other countries to promote the free flow of goods and services among the countries. The European Common Market is an example of such an arrangement.

11. Tariffs and other trade barriers tend to retard international trade. At the same time they may protect new business, employment opportunities, high wage scales, and the development of defense industries.

12. The international trade problem became extremely complicated in the 1970s and certain temporary measures (such as discontinuing the conversion of dollars into gold and devaluing the U.S. dollar) were undertaken. The Committee of Twenty (C-20) is attempting to find a more lasting solution to international trade problems.

1973 a group of major countries, including the United States, joined together to form the Committee of Twenty (C-20). The C-20 has been examining all aspects of international financing and hopes to come up with a workable long-run solution. The work of the C-20 was handicapped in the mid-1970s because of the energy crisis when additional temporary measures needed to be taken.

One development in international financing that many people feel has promise is the creation of Special Drawing Rights (SDRs). SDRs are held by an organization commonly called the World Bank and are used as money to settle international accounts. Some people refer to the SDRs as "liquid gold" since they tend to replace gold to a major extent in settling international trade accounts.

At present, most countries let their currencies "float" in response to supply and demand. Floating exchange rates tend, over time, to reduce surpluses and deficits in international trade accounts.

REVIEW QUESTIONS

Section A

1. What do we mean by international or foreign trade?
2. What major types of merchandise does the United States import more than export? What types does it export more than import?
3. What are some examples of products imported by the United States?
4. In the table on U.S. Import and Export Values on page 230, does the United States import more or less merchandise than it exports, and how much?
5. Approximately what percentage of business activity does international trade of merchandise for the United States represent?
6. How is it possible for a nation to import annually 40% or more of the goods and services used in that country?
7. What do we mean by absolute advantage? Give an example.
8. If Nation A produces a bicycle at $20 and Nation B produces a comparable bicycle at $19, which nation will be the more likely to export bicycles?
9. What do we mean by comparative advantage? Give an example.
10. What is meant by "balance of trade"?
11. What has been the trend in the balance of trade for the period from 1968–1978?

Section B

12. What is meant by the term "balance of payments"?
13. What is a liquid liability?
14. What does "balance-of-payments deficit" mean?
15. What are some of the steps that may be taken to reduce or eliminate a balance-of-payments deficit?

Section C   16. Why do nations want foreign trade?
    17. Why do nations who want foreign trade also want to maintain control over it?
    18. What are the ways by which nations attempt to limit imports and increase exports?
    19. What is a tariff and what are its purposes?

Section D   20. What two steps involving the dollar has the United States taken to wipe out the balance-of-payment deficit?
    21. What is meant by devaluation of the dollar?
    22. What is stagflation?
    23. What is the C-20 and what is its purpose?
    24. What are SDRs?

DISCUSSION QUESTIONS

Section A   1. Why is international trade important to the United States?
    2. What would be the effect on the United States if all imports were discontinued?
    3. Which is more important to a nation — the ratio of its domestic trade to its foreign trade or the ratio of its exports to its imports? Why?
    4. Assume that two nations are both highly productive in producing goods and services, but one of them is able to sell great volumes of its products to foreign nations and the other is able to make very few sales abroad. What conditions make foreign trade opportunities more favorable to the one nation than to the other?
    5. How does the principle of comparative advantage promote international trade and raise the levels of living in the countries involved?
    6. What is the meaning of "favorable" and "unfavorable" balance of trade?
    7. In 1975 the United States exported about $1.11 of goods for every dollar of goods it imported. What would have been the effect on business conditions in the United States if the United States had imported more goods than it exported?

Section B   8. In 1970 the U.S. balance of trade was just over a $2 billion surplus (exports of goods exceeded imports) and in the same year the balance of payments resulted in an approximate $300 million deficit. How is this possible?
    9. How does the ability of the United States to deal in international exchange depend on the confidence foreigners have in the U.S. dollar?
    10. What kinds of business transactions do foreign countries conduct with the United States that would result in those nations making payments to the United States?

Section C   11. Many United States business firms make substantial investments in foreign branches or in the establishment of separate foreign firms. These investments result in the outflow of U.S. payments to foreign nations. Would it be possible for the United States government to prohibit such investments? What would be the effect of making such a regulation?

12. American tourists spend money abroad each year. Would it be desirable to limit the amount American tourists could take with them to spend?

13. What are the reasons for and against high tariffs?

Section D

14. What actions has the United States taken to help solve world trade problems and what might be some possible future actions?

15. In addition to the completion of the Alaska pipeline, what other measures did the government take to make the U.S. less dependent on oil imports?

APPLICATION PROBLEMS

Section A

1. Select 10 foreign countries, identify the currency they use, and determine the official exchange rate in terms of U.S. dollars. Assume that you wish to purchase a $10 pair of shoes with foreign currency. How much would the shoes cost in each of the 10 foreign currencies?

2. Compile a list of minerals the United States imports annually, and prepare a report on the uses of these minerals.

3. Assume that in Nation A, one unit of food can be produced by exerting one day's labor and one unit of clothing can be produced for two days' labor. In Nation B, one unit of food costs three days' labor and one unit of clothing costs four days' labor. Prepare a simple chart similar to the one on page 233 to illustrate how and why international trade would be beneficial to both Nation A and Nation B.

Section B

4. From recent issues of publications such as the *World Almanac* and the *Statistical Abstract of the United States*, prepare charts showing the top 10 exports and imports of the United States, the leading countries receiving the exports, and the total dollar values of each of the imports and exports.

Sections C and D

5. Prepare a report on one of the following topics: (a) The Export-Import Bank, (b) The European Common Market, and (c) The World Bank — International Bank for Reconstruction and Development. Include in your report a complete description of these agreements or institutions, when they were established, the countries or agencies involved, and the purposes for such agreements or institutions.

COMMUNITY PROJECTS

Sections A–D

1. Visit a local department store and make a list of some of the foreign-made products offered for sale. Some stores have import gift departments. Compare the prices of these products with similar products made in the United States. How many kinds of products have you found that are not manufactured in this country?

2. Find someone in your community who has recently made a trip to a foreign country. Discuss with this person the difference between the official exchange rate and the unofficial exchange rate. Determine whether or not U.S. citizens can make purchases with U.S. dollars when they are in foreign countries.

3. Investigate local manufacturing industries in your city to find out what, if any, goods are being exported to other countries. Try to find out specifically what is being exported, to what countries, and the approximate percent of production that exports represent for the business.

4. From information provided by your state's Department of Commerce and from recent issues of various almanacs, prepare a chart or graph showing the role your state plays in world trade (goods exported and imported and the dollar value).

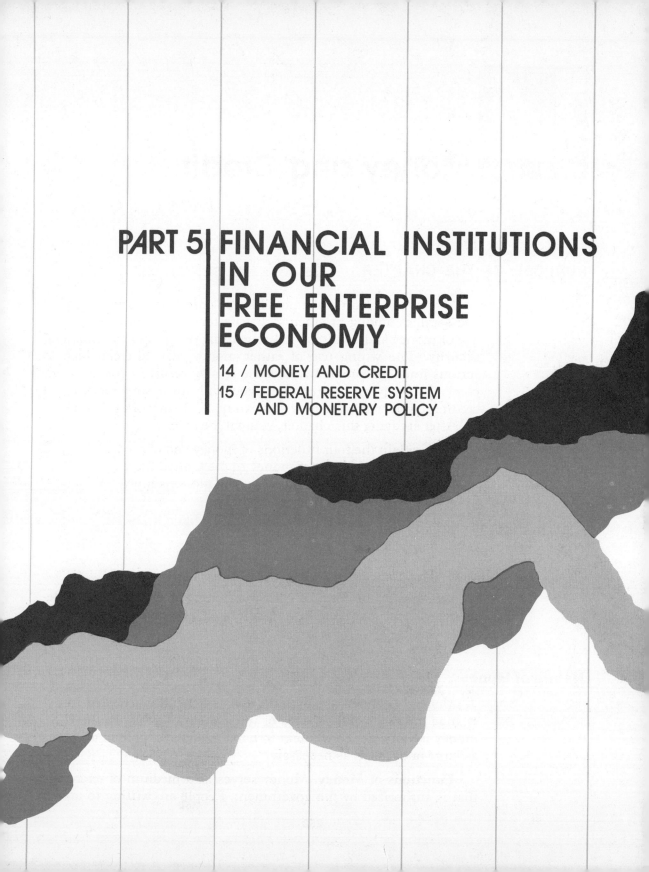

PART 5 FINANCIAL INSTITUTIONS IN OUR FREE ENTERPRISE ECONOMY

14 / MONEY AND CREDIT
15 / FEDERAL RESERVE SYSTEM
AND MONETARY POLICY

14 Money and Credit

Money and credit make possible the orderly exchange of goods and services among producers, distributors, and consumers. Wise use of money and credit is vital to gaining happiness and financial security. The wrong use of either money or credit can lead to serious financial problems, because it may result in losses of income. In studying this chapter, you will learn why money and credit are important and how you can make them work for you.

After studying this chapter, you will be able to:

1. Explain the four functions of money and of credit.
2. Identify the kinds of money in the United States.
3. Explain how credit increases the money supply.
4. Explain what consumer credit is.
5. Define buying power.

A. MONEY

Whether in the form of coins, currency, or checks, money demands careful management regardless of how much or how little of it one has.

Nature of Money

Money is defined as anything that is generally accepted in exchange for goods and services or in payment of debts. In the U.S., money is valuable, convenient to handle, and available in amounts as large or as small as necessary.

Functions of Money. Money serves as a medium of exchange that is authorized by the government. People are willing to take it as payment for their labor, for the goods they have for sale, or for the services they render. Money provides a measure of the value of labor, goods, and services. Money also serves as a means of building up the power to purchase goods and services, and it makes credit possible. What makes money valuable is the work it does in helping economic growth and development of individuals and the nation.

FUNCTIONS OF MONEY

Money serves us in four major ways:

1. *Medium of exchange* — Money lets you exchange your services (such as mowing Mr. A's lawn or working in a restaurant) for goods (such as a new jacket at X Department Store).

2. *Measure of value* — Just as scales measure weight in pounds and ounces or kilograms and grams, money measures the value of a good in dollars and cents. The X Department Store may price a white sweater at $19.95, which indicates that the store judges it to have that value to a customer. You, as a customer, may or may not agree.

3. *Store of value* — Wages or other income received may be saved or may be exchanged immediately for goods and services. Wages are usually saved in the form of money or bank deposits. The wages saved really are purchasing power that you have earned but not yet used. Thus, money is a store of value.

4. *Standard of future payments* — Money becomes a standard of future payment when someone buys a good and promises to pay for it in the future. For example, a neighbor who purchases a home and promises to pay a certain sum each month for a 12-year period is using money as a standard of future payments.

Acceptability. The basic standard for judging the value of money is *acceptability*. Any money becomes acceptable when it performs the functions that are demanded of it. In economic usage, true wealth consists of goods capable of being bought, sold, or stored for future use. Through the use of money it is possible to build up wealth without having to collect and store goods. Money, except metallic money that has some real value, is only a right or a claim to wealth and must, therefore, be acceptable to those who have things to sell. When any item used as money ceases to be acceptable in the buying and selling of goods and services, it is no longer considered to be money. Whenever you have saved a large amount of money, you are wealthy as long as the item used as money can be exchanged for goods and services. If your money ceases to have value, you are no longer wealthy. In such a case only those who have their wealth in the form of usable goods are wealthy.

Kinds of Money

Money, you will recall, is defined as anything that people will accept in exchange for goods or services. There are three forms of money in common use in the United States: coins, currency, and checkbook money.

Coins. Money made of metal (called coins) is made for convenience in paying small amounts. The U.S. Treasury has the responsibility for minting coins; the money is then issued by the Federal Reserve banks. All coins now in circulation in the United States are made of alloys (mixtures) of metals. Thus the face value of a coin is more than the value of the metal of which it is made. No gold coins have been made since 1934. The last silver coin minted was the 1971 Eisenhower dollar.

Currency. The Congressional Committee on Banking and Currency has defined currency as paper (or folding) money. In the past, currency has been issued by national banks, Federal Reserve banks, and the U.S. Treasury. Today nearly all of the currency in circulation consists of Federal Reserve notes, which are issued by each of the twelve Federal Reserve banks.

Silver certificates, which were backed by silver held by the U.S. Treasury, were formerly issued in $1 and $5 denominations but are no longer issued. Most silver certificates have been taken out of circulation by banks and collectors.

Checkbook Money. Checks drawn on demand deposits (money deposited in checking accounts) in commercial banks are accepted by people in exchange for goods or services. Thus, according to the definition of money by the Committee on Banking and Currency, checks are money. Demand deposits account for about 80% of all money circulating in the country. It is estimated that the total number of checkbook dollars used to make payments is more than $2 trillion a year. This would mean that on the average each person in the United States receives and issues checks totaling $10,000 yearly. If you received $6,000 in salary checks during the year and wrote $4,000 in checks to pay for goods, services, and debts, the $10,000 average would be met.

MONEY IN CIRCULATION IN THE UNITED STATES
(In Millions of Dollars)

Year	Coins in Circulation	Currency (Paper Money) in Circulation	Demand Deposits in Banks (Checkbook Money)	Total
1950	1,554	26,190	92,272	120,016
1955	1,927	29,232	109,914	141,073
1960	2,427	30,441	115,200	148,068
1965	4,027	38,031	131,200	173,258
1970	6,281	50,130	166,900	223,311
1975	8,959	72,700	221,700	302,659
1978	10,355	97,500	263,700	371,555

Sources: *The World Almanac*, 1979, and *Federal Reserve Bulletin*, June, 1979.

There are three ways in which you may build up checkbook money in the form of demand deposits. (1) You may deposit coins and/or currency in a checking account in a commercial bank; (2) you may deposit a check that has been given to you; or (3) you may borrow from the bank and have the amount deposited to your account. Since banks make loans to individuals and businesses, they actually create new money in bank deposits. As loans are repaid, demand deposits are decreased. Since banks are able to increase or decrease the amount of money available, it is said that they "create and destroy" money as the need for it changes.

Most people receive their wages in the form of checks that are soon deposited in banks. Through the use of checking accounts, people simply write and mail checks in payment of bills. The can-

Nearly four fifths of all financial transactions are handled by checks.

celed checks serve as receipts. For businesses, demand deposits are even more valuable. A business that receives many checks can quickly deposit them in a bank, which is the way most business transactions are completed. Thus the bother of handling, storing, and possibly losing large sums of money is reduced.

It is well to note here the use of the term "cash" as it relates to kinds of money. In general, *cash* is any ready money that a person or business firm actually has, including money deposited in a checking account. Therefore, the total supply of cash available for financial transactions is the sum of the paper money and coins in circulation plus the total of the balances in checking accounts.

What Backs U.S. Money?

You learned earlier that whatever is used for money must be acceptable to both the buyer and the seller. For money to be acceptable worldwide, most people feel that there should be something of real value available for exchange in case one doesn't want to buy goods and services. This item of exchange is called a *backing*.

Formerly Backed by Silver or Gold. The currency of a country is said to be on a silver standard or a gold standard when the paper currency is backed by silver or gold dollars or by bullion (uncoined silver or gold).

Before 1873, United States currency could be converted into either gold dollars or silver dollars upon request to the United States Treasury. From 1873 to 1933, the United States had a gold standard, and currency could be exchanged for gold.

In 1933 the United States went on a limited gold standard. In other words, each dollar was backed by only 25 cents in gold bullion. United States citizens could no longer exchange their currency for gold. Only foreign nations could exchange American dollars for gold. In 1973 the United States went off the gold standard completely. This means the United States no longer has to exchange gold even for U.S. dollars held by foreign countries.

Backed by Faith and Confidence. It was stated earlier that for money to have value, it must be acceptable. Some people and nations may feel safer if money is backed by a precious metal (such as gold) that always has value. However, if you have faith and confidence in the person or the nation that issues money, you do not worry about backing.

The United States government and its people have had a long

history of being a high-producing, wealthy nation. We grow more food crops per person per acre than any other nation. We produce more cars and farm machinery, for example, than any other nation. As a nation we own more cars, television sets, radios, and telephones than any other nation. We have valuable natural resources. All these things help our people and other nations to have faith and confidence in our currency. As long as we continue to manage our lives and our country in a responsible way, everyone will have faith in our currency. Thus we have come to believe that we do not need any other form of backing for our currency.

Managed Paper Currency. Checkbook money is created when a bank loans someone money, with that person's valuable assets pledged as security (backing). Businesses pledge their inventories and machinery to get loans from banks. Farmers pledge their farm assets to get loans. Many citizens pledge their homes or life insurance contracts to get loans. Thus you could say that checkbook money is created and backed by inventories, machinery, farm assets, and homes — all of which have value.

Granted, if more dollars were created than the value of the real assets pledged, the value of those dollars would be in question. What safeguard is there to stop too many dollars being created in this way? The answer is that the Federal Reserve System (described in Chapter 15) carefully decides just how much money can safely be created by bank lending. Thus checkbook money is created only if there are enough valuable assets backing the loans. You could say, then, that the amount of money created (our money supply) is controlled through the Federal Reserve System.

B. CREDIT

Like money, credit demands careful management. Unwise use of credit can cause people, businesses, and even governments to go bankrupt.

Nature of Credit

Credit in the form of a debt occurs whenever cash, goods, or services are provided on a promise to pay at a future date. Most people and business organizations use credit in one form or another. Consumer credit is the financial tool with which most citizens buy what they want when they want it and pay for it out of future earnings. Based on the faith of one individual in another, credit, like money, represents immediate buying power. A person or a firm has ability to buy now when a promise to pay at some time in the future is acceptable to the seller.

Credit Increases Purchasing Power. Like money, credit is valuable because it provides purchasing power. If everyone, including business firms and the federal government, had to pay cash for everything bought, business would slow down almost to a standstill. Like money, the value of credit is determined by its acceptability. When credit is used wisely, it performs useful functions just as money does.

FUNCTIONS OF CREDIT

Credit serves us in four major ways:

1. *Stabilizes the economy* — Credit steadies economic activity as it lets individuals and businesses buy goods and services even when income is temporarily limited. Through borrowing, the government may help the economy as it spends money for roads, schools, unemployment benefits, and so forth.

2. *Promotes business formation* — Many people start new businesses and thousands of others continue in business through the use of credit. For example, wholesale firms grant credit to retailers, thus letting them operate with less money.

3. *Expands production* — Business firms may increase the production of goods and services by means of long-term loans from banks, insurance companies, and other financial institutions. By borrowing, you, too, may increase your productive (earning) power by getting more education or by investing borrowed money at a rate of return greater than the cost of the borrowing.

4. *Raises the level of living* — The general level of living is raised as such things as homes, automobiles, furniture, appliances, insurance, and health service are bought on credit. Through credit, demand is created without money, production is increased, and jobs are created. Today a young family does not wait for savings to build up before buying those things that make for a comfortable life.

Wise Use of Credit. Proper use of credit has a steadying effect on the economy in helping to avoid unusual increases and decreases in business. However, a major problem is that unwise use of credit can cause violent changes in business conditions.

For example, if credit is too easy to get and is used too much, debts may not be paid when due. When this situation occurs on a national scale, many lenders suffer losses. Buying then decreases, causing a weakening of business conditions and a drop in production and jobs. For that reason, those granting credit and those using it have a basic responsibility to society and to themselves to use it wisely.

Credit may sometimes let persons start businesses that really should not have been started. Industrial expansion that takes place largely on the basis of consumer credit depends on the consumer's future earning power. Should this future earning power fail to grow, these industries are likely to have great losses in their businesses. Because businesses can be expanded or reduced rapidly through the use of credit, they are sometimes overconfident. Credit causes a business to rely on others. A business must often use credit and offer credit. In order to offer credit, it must have faith in others and faith in the future.

Effect of Credit. The ease with which credit may be used increases the flow of goods to consumers. If the head of a household has a job and can expect to continue to earn money, the family can buy now on credit.

If a family uses credit wisely, it can plan carefully to meet all payments and enjoy many goods without having cash at the time of purchase. But goods bought on credit should last beyond the time the final payment is made.

If people fail to meet their legal and moral obligations of credit and cannot pay their debts, they may get into serious legal trouble. They will lose their credit standing, and their buying power and level of living will decrease.

Kinds of Credit

Credit comes in many forms and may be grouped in many ways. Three groups quickly come to mind: government credit, business credit, and consumer credit. The instruments of credit most often used include bonds, drafts, promissory notes, conditional sales contracts, and real estate mortages.

Government Credit. Governments build highways, schools, hospitals, and many other projects for public use. Often a government will pay only part of the full cost of a project from tax funds already collected. Thus governments, like individuals, borrow when they spend more than their current income. The usual practice is to sell bonds, with the interest and the principal amount to be paid back out of future taxes. A *bond* is a written promise to pay a specified amount plus interest at a certain time.

A local government will usually levy enough taxes to pay its police, fire fighters, and teachers and to cover the cost of other operating expenses. It will, through the sale of bonds, use credit when it must build a new school, a courthouse, or a city park.

GOVERNMENT CREDIT OUTSTANDING
1970–1978
(in Billions of Dollars)

	1970	1972	1974	1976	1978
Federal Government	$340	$382	$437	$597	$ 761
State and Local Governments	145	178	211	236	264
Total Government Debt	$485	$560	$648	$833	$1,025

Business Credit. Businesses use *commercial credit* to cover the cost of producing and marketing goods. A manufacturer buys raw materials and gives a promise to pay for them in 30, 60, or 90 days. A retailers buys goods from a wholesaler on similar terms. A farmer may buy seed or fertilizer and pay for it when the crop is harvested.

Businesses also use commercial credit in buying productive resources such as land, buildings, and machinery. Through borrowing, a restaurant can obtain land for a parking lot, an automobile manufacturer can acquire a new building, and an oil company can set up a new refinery. Bonds, maturing over periods of ten or more years, are often sold for such purposes.

CORPORATION AND FARM PRODUCTION
CREDIT OUTSTANDING
1970–1978
(in Billions of Dollars)

	1970	1972	1974	1976	1978
Corporation Debt	$797	$ 975	$1,223	$1,415	$1,621
Farm Production Debt	58	68	89	108	120
Total Corporate and Farm Production Debt	$855	$1,043	$1,312	$1,523	$1,741

Consumer Credit. Use of *consumer credit* helps many people to buy the goods and services needed to satisfy their immediate wants. You may borrow money from a bank or a finance company so that you can pay cash for a car or for modernizing your home. You may use installment buying in which you make a down payment on a washing machine and pay the rest in 12 or 18 months. Also, you may frequently use your credit card or charge-a-plate for buying at service stations or your favorite department store. Many people prefer credit buying to paying cash simply because it is handier. Some find it easier to pay for things by means of regular installment payments than to save up the same amount of money. Also, the danger of losing money or having it stolen from you when shopping makes the use of credit attractive to many people.

CONSUMER CREDIT OUTSTANDING
SELECTED YEARS, 1955–1978
(In Millions of Dollars)

Year	Total Consumer Credit Outstanding
1955	$ 38,830
1960	56,141
1965	89,883
1970	127,163
1975	172,353
1978	275,640

Source: *Federal Reserve Bulletin* (June, 1979).

Another important type of credit is the *home mortgage* — a loan that is backed by real estate. Though usually not called consumer credit by the *Federal Reserve Bulletin*, this type of credit is used frequently by consumers. Mortgage loans are a part of the total outstanding consumer debt picture. You may pay only a small portion of the full cost of your home in cash. You then borrow the rest from a bank or a savings and loan association. The borrowed money, plus interest, is paid back in monthly payments spread over a period of 10, 20, or even 40 years. In the meantime, the house and lot serve as backing for the loan. If you cannot meet your monthly payments, the bank or association can sell the property and get its money back. The total amount of real estate mortgage debt outstanding early in 1978 was approximately $611.0 billion.

On March 31, 1978, the total amount of consumer debt outstanding, including mortgage credit, was about $923.0 billion. At the same time, total consumer assets were estimated to be over $4.6 trillion. Thus, the ratio of all consumer assets to all consumer debts was about 5.1 to 1.

Credit lets people buy expensive items before they have saved the cash price. In 1978 consumers owed $1 for every $5.10 worth of assets owned (houses, cars, furniture, appliances, TV sets, campers, etc.).

C. EFFECT OF MONEY AND CREDIT ON BUYING POWER

If money and credit are not carefully managed, consumer buying power will be reduced. If too much money is created without assets to back it up or if too much credit is used, the buying power of the dollar will suffer.

Nature of Buying Power

Production today is very specialized. Most people produce goods and services that they themselves do not use. The exchange of goods and services they produce for goods and services they can use involves two transactions in which money serves as the medium of exchange. People are paid money for the goods and services they produce; they use this money to buy other goods and services for their own use.

The *buying power* or value of money is measured by the quantity of goods that a given amount of money will buy. The amount of goods a dollar will buy depends on the price of the goods. When prices are high, it takes more money to buy the same amount of goods than it does when prices are low. If prices begin to fall, we say that the buying power of money increases; the dollar will buy more than it would before. With this in mind, it may be said that prices of goods and services vary in reverse manner with the buying power or value of money.

The value of a dollar affects the level of living. Problems can arise when there is too much or too little money. Some control must be kept over the value of money, the amount of it available, and the rate at which it is spent. Such control must influence the flow of money payments in order to help the money supply adjust to the changes in the flow of goods and services. By increasing or decreasing the amount of money available, the Federal Reserve System tries to bring about this type of control.

The buying power of the dollar at one time is often compared with the buying power of the dollar at another time. The *price index number* is a device to compare the buying power of the dollar at various times. The United States Department of Commerce and the Bureau of Labor Statistics prepare price index numbers on many groups of goods and services.

The figures in the table below mean that in 1979 the consumer had to spend $211.80 to buy the same goods that $100 would have bought in 1967. And in 1965 the consumer's dollar had 5½ cents more buying power than in 1967. Roughly, a dollar in 1979 was worth less than half of what it was worth in 1967. In other words, in 12 years the buying power of the dollar was reduced by 53% through inflation. (A more detailed explanation of inflation was given in Chapter 10.) A rising price index means a fall in the buying power of the dollar.

BUYING POWER OF THE DOLLAR
SELECTED YEARS 1955 TO 1979
(1967 = 100)

Year	Monthly Average as Measured by	
	Producer (Wholesale) Prices	Consumer Prices
1955	87.8	80.2
1960	94.9	88.7
1965	96.6	94.5
1967	100.0	100.0
1970	110.4	116.3
1975	178.2	164.6
1979 (April)	226.3	211.8

Source: *Federal Reserve Bulletin* (June, 1979).

The Producer Price Index is a good clue to what will happen to the Consumer Price Index. If the Producer Price Index rises, the Consumer Price Index will soon rise. The reason is simple: producers pass on their higher prices to consumers. When the Producer Price Index drops, the Consumer Price Index will usually drop shortly afterward.

Expanding Buying Power with Credit

Assume that all the people of a community or city had five or ten times as much money as they now have. Suddenly their wants for goods and services would increase greatly. They would buy many more goods than they did before. Expanding credit, or increasing the amount of debts that individuals or businesses may have, has the same effect as increasing the amount of money that they have. Expanding credit is a process banks use to increase their ability to make loans to customers.

The money that banks can loan to customers usually comes from the deposits other customers have made. People who deposit money expect to be able to get it when they ask for it. Experience has shown, however, that all depositors do not ask for their money at one time; thus the bank may make loans to other customers from the deposits. Banks must keep a certain cash reserve as required by law.

Creditor and Debtor Relationships in Expanding the Use of Money

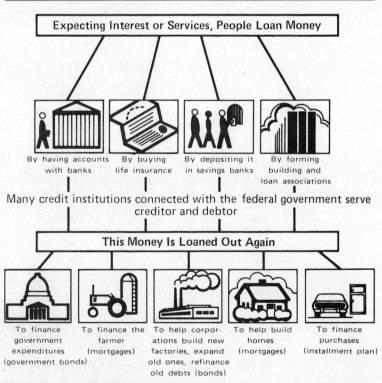

Expecting Interest or Services, People Loan Money

By having accounts with banks　By buying life insurance　By depositing it in savings banks　By forming building and loan associations

Many credit institutions connected with the federal government serve creditor and debtor

This Money Is Loaned Out Again

To finance government expenditures (government bonds)　To finance the farmer (mortgages)　To help corporations build new factories, expand old ones, refinance old debts (bonds)　To help build homes (mortgages)　To finance purchases (installment plan)

Source: Maxwell S. Stewart, *Debts-Good or Bad?* The Public Affairs Committee, Inc., New York City.

A bank cannot by itself greatly increase its ability to make loans; but if it can sell some of its customers' notes to another bank, it may obtain money that in turn it can loan to other customers. Hence, bank credit can be expanded.

Expanding a member bank's credit by discounting (selling) customers' notes at the Federal Reserve bank is explained in Chapter 15. The following illustration will explain the effect of discounting customers' notes on increasing a bank's ability to loan more money to customers, thereby creating more credit.

The following simple balance sheet shows the status of the Central National Bank at a specific time:

BALANCE SHEET OF CENTRAL NATIONAL BANK

Assets:		Liabilities and ownership:	
Cash	$ 80,000	Amount due depositors	$100,000
Bonds	120,000	Capital stock	150,000
Deposits in Federal Reserve bank	20,000	Surplus	50,000
Equipment	20,000		
Building	60,000	Total liabilities and	
Total assets	$300,000	ownership	$300,000

The American Manufacturing Company, a customer of this bank, gets a loan of $10,000 for 3 months at 9% interest and gives as backing its promissory note. A *promissory note* is a written agreement to repay the borrowed money at a specified future date. The bank deducts its interest of $225 in advance and gives the customer credit for $9,775 in its account. The latter may use this credit by writing checks to the amount of $9,775. The note, which is a credit instrument, has become an asset of the bank. It represents a promise of the American Manufacturing Company to pay $10,000 at the end of the 3 months. After the loan has been made, the balance sheet of the bank appears as shown below.

BALANCE SHEET OF CENTRAL NATIONAL BANK

Assets		Liabilities and ownership:	
Cash	$ 80,000	Amount due depositors	$109,775
Bonds	120,000	Capital stock	150,000
Deposits in Federal Reserve bank	20,000	Surplus	50,000
Loans to customers	10,000	Undivided profits (interest)	225
Equipment	20,000		
Building	60,000	Total liabilities and	
Total assets	$310,000	ownership	$310,000

It is clear that there has been no increase in the amount of money, but there has been an increase in the use of money. The deposits are almost 10% larger than they were previously.

Since this bank is a member of the Federal Reserve System, it can sell (discount) the note of the American Manufacturing Company at a Federal Reserve bank. The Federal Reserve Board sets the discount rate. Suppose that the note is discounted in this case at 7%. The bank discount of $175 is deducted in advance. The Central National Bank accepts Federal Reserve notes (lawful money) for $5,000 and leaves the balance of $4,825 on deposit in the Federal Reserve bank. The Central National Bank's balance sheet is then:

BALANCE SHEET OF CENTRAL NATIONAL BANK

Assets:		Liabilities and ownership:	
Cash	$ 85,000	Amount due depositors	$109,775
Bonds	120,000	Capital stock	150,000
Deposits in Federal Reserve bank	24,825	Surplus	50,000
Equipment	20,000	Undivided profits	50
Building	60,000	Total liabilities and	
Total assets	$309,825	ownership	$309,825

The Central National Bank now has $5,000 more cash that can be loaned to customers. It has $4,825 more on deposit in the Federal Reserve bank, which also increases its ability to make loans to customers. Its undivided profits are reduced from $225 to $50 because of the bank discount paid.

This process of expanding the use of money by means of credit could be continued. Under present laws the expansion of credit can continue until the reserve in the Federal Reserve bank drops to a stated percentage of the bank's deposits.

Other Aspects of Credit and Debt

For the country as a whole, the total debts owed are equal to the total credit extended. When an individual, a business firm, or a government borrows money, credit is expanded. Credit expansion has the same effect on the economic activities of the country as increasing the amount of money that people, businesses, and government have to spend. Debts must be repaid. Therefore, credit expansion must always be kept within reasonable bounds. During the process of expansion, prices tend to rise and the buying power of the dollar decreases. In other words, prices are inflated. If debts become too large so that many of the debtors are unable to pay them when they fall due, business is faced with depression. Depression means that production is slowed down or stopped, jobs decrease in number, wages fall, and everyone in the economy is in poor financial shape.

As you have learned, credit means that someone has borrowed money. Where does the money that one borrows come from? One may say it comes from a bank, a loan company, or some person who has great wealth. But where did these agencies get the money? Money available for loans comes from the savings of people. Banks receive customers' deposits of funds saved. Insurance companies receive life insurance premiums from the savings of people. Wealthy people have wealth because they or members of their families did not spend all of their income. It would be impossible to borrow money if no one had ever saved a part of one's income. Credit, therefore, is based on the savings of others.

Idle money does not stimulate business. If money is used to buy goods or is lent for productive purposes, production is in-

WHAT EVERYONE SHOULD UNDERSTAND ABOUT MONEY AND CREDIT

1. Money and credit require wise use, no matter what size one's income is, if financial goals are to be reached and satisfaction is to be gained as the result of spending.

2. Authorized by the government, money represents purchasing power in terms of prices so that values can be set in the production of goods and services.

3. Money makes it easy to bring together the factors of production and to organize markets so that goods may be distributed to consumers.

4. Based on faith, credit is available to individuals at almost all income levels. Credit, therefore, tends to make up for some inequalities arising from differences in amounts of income.

5. Use of credit tends to increase buying and thus increases the production and the use of goods and services.

6. Productive power is increased for both the individual and the nation, as the use of credit aids economic growth and a higher level of living.

7. Personal financial honesty and responsible business practices are a must if credit is to work well in our economy.

8. The banking system provides the basis for our monetary system and for control over the amount of money and credit available.

creased, more workers are needed, and business is improved. The illustration on page 264 shows how the money of individuals is lent to various institutions and is then loaned out again for various productive purposes.

In summary, it is almost impossible to overstate the importance of money and credit in our society. As tools of exchange, they are needed for efficient production, distribution, and consumption. They aid in the achievement of personal happiness and security. They promote economic growth and development for both the individual and the nation. Without money and credit, the present high level of living in the United States would not have been possible. Only by wise consumer use and careful institutional control of the money and credit supply will the high level of living continue or be made even higher.

REVIEW QUESTIONS

Section A

1. What is money?
2. What are the functions of money?
3. (a) What is true wealth? (b) If money ceases to be of value, who are the only persons who possess wealth?
4. Of what is the supply of money principally composed?
5. What backs up or makes valuable the currency of the United States?
6. In general, money is accepted and paid out without regard to the value of the material in the coin or paper. Why?
7. What is meant by "managed paper currency"?
8. What happens to the amount or supply of money when a borrower from a bank draws checks against demand deposits?

Section B

9. (a) What is credit? (b) In what ways are money and credit alike? (c) What makes money and credit truly valuable?
10. How widespread is the use of credit today?
11. (a) What are the three most common kinds of credit? (b) How do they differ?

Section C

12. How is the purchasing power of the dollar measured?
13. Why is the ability of banks to expand their credit important?
14. Whenever credit is given, a debt has been contracted that must be paid at some time in the future. This means that someone has borrowed money. Where does the money come from?

DISCUSSION QUESTIONS

Section A

1. What advantages are there in using checks to conduct business affairs?
2. When would a person not be wise to use money as a store of value?
3. Why are prices likely to increase or decrease as the supply of money available changes?
4. Why are balances in checking accounts a part of the available money supply?

5. Since the United States no longer backs its currency in gold, what guarantees do foreign nations who sell us goods have that our currency is good?

Section B

6. There are people who use too much credit and use it unwisely. It has been said, however, that this does not show the use of a bad thing, but the abuse of a very good thing. What do you believe?

7. Individual bankers must make decisions about who shall have loans. How do such decisions affect the quality and the quantity of the money supply?

8. No one should use mortgage debt or consumer debt beyond that person's ability to pay. What, then, decides the amount of debt that an individual or a family may use wisely?

9. What are the main functions of credit? How are they related?

Section C

10. Why do you think some bankers need to keep more cash than others in order to be sure they have enough to pay depositors on demand?

11. What are the functions of banks in expanding purchasing power through credit?

APPLICATION PROBLEMS

Section A

1. Refer to the table on "Money in Circulation in the United States" on page 255.

   (a) What percentage of the total money supply was checkbook money in 1965? In 1978?

   (b) What economic conditions may have caused this shift in the nature of the money supply?

Section B

2. The following table shows consumer credit by types for selected years:

CONSUMER CREDIT
(in Billions of Dollars)

Type of Credit	1970	1975	1978
Installment credit:			
Automobile loans	$ 35.1	$ 53.0	$ 86.0
Mobile home loans	2.5	12.2	15.2
Home improvement loans	5.0	8.0	13.7
Bank credit card	3.8	9.5	14.5
Bank check	1.3	2.8	3.9
Other	54.2	76.7	94.3
Total installment credit	$101.9	$162.2	$227.6
Noninstallment credit:			
Single-payment loans	$ 9.7	$ 13.1	$ 15.9
Charge accounts	8.0	9.9	11.9
Service credit	7.4	12.0	15.8
Total noninstallment credit	25.1	35.0	43.6
Total consumer credit	$127.0	$197.2	$271.2

(a) What percentage of total consumer credit was total installment credit in 1970, 1975, and 1978?

(b) What percentage of total installment credit were automobile loans in 1970, 1975, and 1978?

(c) What percentage of total consumer credit was total noninstallment credit in 1970, 1975, and 1978?

(d) What was the percentage increase in use of bank credit card charge accounts in 1978 over 1970 and 1975?

(e) What was the percentage increase in use of total consumer credit in 1978 over 1970 and 1975?

(f) What conclusions about consumer buying habits can you reach from the percentages calculated above?

Section C

3. We do not all earn the same income or spend our income for the same things. Thus there is a personal way to look at the buying power of the dollar for our own income. That would be to see how many minutes or hours we would have to work to buy things today as compared with a time in the past. A sample of one person's comparison from 1965 to 1975 is given below.

(a) What was the percentage increase of income for this person from 1965 to 1975?

(b) How much longer did the person have to work in 1975 than in 1965 to get the same goods and services?

(c) Disregarding housing, did this person have more buying power or less buying power in 1975 than in 1965?

Item	($2.45/hour) 1965	($4.25/hour) 1975
1 lb. hamburger	13 min.	14 min.
Single-family home	12,224 hr., 54 min.	12,783 hr., 32 min.
1 gal. gasoline	8 min.	8 min.
Bicycle	20 hr., 25 min.	16 hr., 57 min.
Movie admission	37 min.	39 min.
Hospital room (semiprivate)	12 hr., 14 min.	19 hr., 30 min.
Electric bill	4 hr., 5 min.	3 hr., 38 min.
Property tax	40 hr., 49 min.	38 hr., 43 min.

4. Refer to the table on page 263. Approximately how much more consumer goods could have been purchased for $1 at retail prices in 1960 than in 1967? How much less in 1979 than in 1967?

COMMUNITY PROJECTS

Section A

1. Prepare in one column a list of five things you own that vary widely in value (for example, a frisbee, a football, a sports jacket, a bicycle, and a transistor radio). Then select five additional things you own and list them in a second column so that each item is about the same value as the item opposite it in the first column. Indicate in a brief explanation how you arrived at your decisions as to which items were of the same value.

Section B

2. Make a study of several issues of *The Wall Street Journal, Business Week, Newsweek,* or the financial pages of a city newspaper for information relating to money and credit. Look for articles that deal with topics such as expansion of credit, control of interest rates, home financing, consumer price changes, and so forth. What are the money and credit trends shown in these sources of information? Write an explanation of what these trends mean to individuals and to families.

3. List and give explanations or examples of all the different types of credit (that is, debts to be paid in the future) that each of the following may have: (a) you or a classmate, (b) a young family, (c) a neighborhood retail store, (d) your local government.

4. Many retail stores permit customers to open charge accounts. Prepare a list of questions you would like to ask the credit manager of a large retail store. For example, you may wish to inquire about the average size of a credit purchase, the period of time taken to pay for it, the number of people who ask for extension of time in making payments, and similar questions. You probably will want to ask for advice from the credit manager about how you should plan for use of credit. Your teacher may invite the credit manager of a large department store to discuss your questions or may ask you to make a report to the class.

Section C

5. Scan your daily newspapers or current issues of *Business Week* and *Newsweek* in the school library to find the most recent Producer Price Index and Consumer Price Index figures. (These indexes are published monthly.) Compare these new figures with those in the table on page 263 for trends regarding the status of the economy.

6. Construct a consumer cost of living index for your own community. Select 15 items (for example, a loaf of bread, a quart of milk, a pound of hamburger, a pair of jeans, and a pair of sneakers) and price them at current prices. One month later, price the identical 15 items to see what change in cost of living took place, if any.

15 Federal Reserve System and Monetary Policy

PURPOSE OF THE CHAPTER

The Federal Reserve System has been called a central banking system, or in other words, a bank for bankers and for the government. Such a bank has one main function — to control the nation's supply of money and credit. This chapter will help you understand how the Federal Reserve System determines monetary policy.

After studying this chapter, you will be able to:

1. List six important functions of the Federal Reserve System.
2. Define monetary policy.
3. Explain the necessity for monetary policy.
4. Describe how the Federal Reserve System controls monetary policy.
5. Describe the effect of money supply on credit.

A. FEDERAL RESERVE SYSTEM

The Federal Reserve System is made up of 12 Federal Reserve banks, 25 branch banks, and 5,613 member banks. These banks handle the majority of banking activities in this country.

Organization of the Federal Reserve System

The banking system that is the outgrowth of the Federal Reserve Act passed in 1913 is called the *Federal Reserve System*. Under this Act, the country is divided into twelve Federal Reserve districts. In each district there is a Federal Reserve bank. Each

Organization of the Federal Reserve System

bank is a separate and distinct organization and is managed by a board of directors of nine persons. These nine directors are divided into three classes of three each, referred to as Class A, B, and C.

Class A directors are elected by member banks and represent these banks. Class B directors also are elected by member banks but at the time of their election must be engaged in their district in industry, commerce, or agriculture. No Class B director may be an officer, director, or employee of any bank. Class C directors are appointed by the Board of Governors (which consists of seven members all appointed by the President of the United States and approved by the Senate). No Class C director may be an officer, director, employee, or stockholder of any bank.

For the purpose of electing Class A and Class B directors, the member banks are divided into three groups representing large, medium-sized and small banks. Each group elects one Class A and one Class B director.

The board of directors of each Federal Reserve bank selects one member each to serve on the Federal Advisory Council. This Council confers with the Board of Governors on business conditions and makes advisory recommendations on the affairs of the System. The Federal Open Market Committee (discussed later in this chapter) is made up of the seven members of the Board of Governors and five members elected by the twelve Federal Reserve district banks. (See the organization chart on page 275.)

Member Banks

All national banks are required to belong to the Federal Reserve System. State-chartered banks, known simply as state banks, may join the System if qualified and accepted by the Federal Reserve Board. Member banks must abide by the many provisions of the Federal Reserve Act, some of which are: (1) they must place legally required reserves either on deposit without interest at the Federal Reserve bank or as cash held in their own vaults; (2) they must honor checks drawn against them at par (that is, no charge may be deducted for processing checks) when presented by a Federal Reserve bank for payment; (3) they must submit to examination and supervision by the Federal Reserve System; (4) they cannot pay more interest on deposits than the rate set by the Federal Reserve Board; (5) they must abide by loan and investment limitations stated by the Federal Reserve Board; and (6) they must abide by other specified conditions, all of which are designed for the protection of the public interest. Also, every member bank is required to buy stock of the Federal Reserve bank of its district in an amount equal to 6% of the member bank's capital and surplus. Thus, the Federal Reserve System is owned by its member banks.

In July, 1978, there were 14,713 commercial banks in the country, of which 5,613 were member banks. Though representing only 38% of all commercial banks, member banks held over 77% of all demand (checkbook) deposits, which along with coins and currency serve as our money supply. As a result, Federal Re-

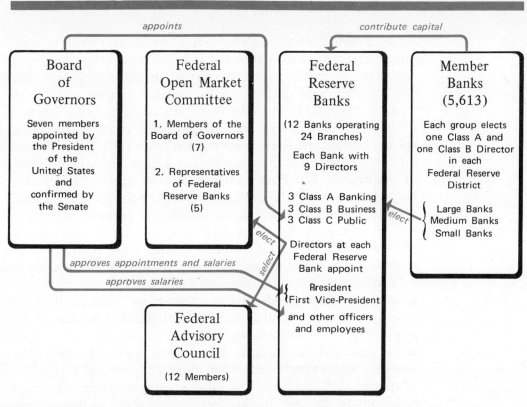

Source: *The Federal Reserve System: Purposes and Functions,* 5th ed., 1967.

The Federal Reserve System

serve Board policies have a direct influence on financial institutions holding most of the country's money supply.

Member banks enjoy many privileges, some of which are: (1) they can borrow from the Federal Reserve banks when temporarily in need of extra funds; (2) they can use Federal Reserve banks for collecting and clearing checks and transferring funds to other cities; (3) they may obtain currency whenever needed; (4) they share in the vast amount of business and economic information provided by the Federal Reserve system; (5) they take part in the election of six of the nine directors of the Federal Reserve bank for their district; and (6) they receive a cumulative dividend of 6% on the paid-in capital stock (the amount of shares of stock purchased by the member banks) of the Federal Reserve banks. This dividend totaled about $62 million in 1977.

Functions of the Federal Reserve System

In many respects, a Federal Reserve district bank is similar to any ordinary state or national bank. Both are corporations operating under a charter, both issue stock, both receive deposits, both pay checks drawn on deposits, both discount (buy and sell) promissory notes, and both make loans according to law. However, the Federal Reserve banks deal largely with member banks. Under special conditions they make certain types of loans to responsible business enterprises, but they do not accept deposits of individuals or businesses. The Federal Reserve banks may rightfully be called bankers' banks, for their stock is owned by the member banks.

The Federal Reserve System makes it possible to shift money and credit rapidly from one district to another to take care of supply and demand. It also controls money and credit so as to promote economic growth and stability. Making a profit is not one of its chief goals. However, through discounting notes, making loans to member banks, and earning interest on Treasury bills (short-term government bonds), the Federal Reserve banks do make a profit. The Federal Reserve banks keep a surplus out of profits to equal their paid-in capital. The paid-in capital is the amount of shares of stock purchased by the member banks. In July, 1978, this amounted to $1,057 million. After paying operating expenses and dividends to member banks, the Federal Reserve banks turn over the remaining profits to the Treasury of the United States. Since 1947 the Federal Reserve has paid most of its net earnings to the U.S. Treasury. In 1977 this payment amounted to nearly $6 billion.

The important functions of the Federal Reserve System are: (1) issuing notes (paper currency), (2) maintaining centralized bank reserves, (3) making loans to member banks, (4) discounting notes, (5) aiding in the clearing and collecting of checks, and (6) regulating business activity.

Issuing Notes (Paper Currency). The Federal Reserve System issues one type of currency, the *Federal Reserve note*. This is our main type of currency. It serves as credit money and is accepted in all business channels as legal tender. *Legal tender* is any kind of money (coin or currency) that by law must be acceptable in paying debts and taxes. The Federal Reserve banks act as agents of the United States government in issuing this type of note. The Federal Reserve note and other types of currency were discussed in Chapter 14.

Maintaining Centralized Bank Reserves. A member bank must maintain a deposit in the Federal Reserve bank equal to a fixed percentage of its own deposits. This percentage is governed by the Federal Reserve Board and may be changed from time to time. This deposit is known as a *required reserve*. Banks, of course, may and often do deposit more than the Federal Reserve Board requires. In this case these additional deposits are known as *excess reserves* or *free reserves*. It is from these excess reserves that banks can make personal and business loans and make investments for their stockholders. The combined deposits of all member banks make up a centralized reserve in a Federal Reserve bank.

Member banks must keep on hand enough cash to take care of the day-to-day demands of their customers. The deposits in the Federal Reserve banks make it unnecessary for member banks to keep a great amount of cash on hand. These deposits are like checkbook money and can be withdrawn very quickly when needed. This system causes a Federal Reserve bank to act more or less as a money pool for its district. Each member bank can draw

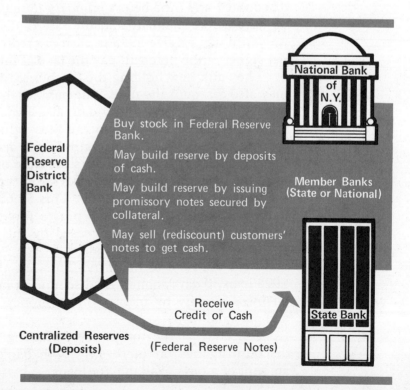

Relations of Federal Reserve Banks with Other Banks

Federal Reserve District Bank

Buy stock in Federal Reserve Bank.

May build reserve by deposits of cash.

May build reserve by issuing promissory notes secured by collateral.

May sell (rediscount) customers' notes to get cash.

National Bank of N.Y.

Member Banks (State or National)

State Bank

Receive Credit or Cash

Centralized Reserves (Deposits)

(Federal Reserve Notes)

upon the pool or reserves. The pooling of a portion of the funds of each member bank serves to strengthen every bank in the district.

Making Loans to Member Banks. A member bank may get a loan from the Federal Reserve bank by giving its promissory notes to the Federal Reserve bank. These notes are backed by government bonds, notes, or other bonds to guarantee the payment of the loan when it is due. When used for this purpose, bonds, notes, or other negotiable paper are known as *collateral*. The Federal Reserve bank gives the local bank credit either by increasing its reserve or by issuing to it Federal Reserve notes (paper money). Most loans to member banks are made this way.

Discounting Notes. Another way a member bank may get funds from its Federal Reserve bank is to sell to the federal bank the notes it holds. Let us say that a customer gives a business firm a 60-day, $1,000, non-interest-bearing note in payment for goods. The business firm, not wishing to wait 60 days for its money, may take the note to a bank and *discount* (sell) it. The note may be discounted any time before *maturity* (due date). If it is discounted 30 days before maturity and the rate of discount is 6%, the business firm will receive $995 in cash or credit. At maturity, the original signer of the note will pay the face of the note, $1,000.

The bank now holding the discounted note in this illustration may also discount the note. The bank exchanges the note for cash or credit before its maturity date at a Federal Reserve bank. The amount received is equal to the face value of the note less the interest from the date of discount to the date of maturity. Assume that the member bank discounts the note on the day it is received from the business firm. If the Federal Reserve discount rate is 3%, the bank would receive $997.50. This $997.50 represents the $995 it originally paid for the note plus a profit of $2.50. The bank's lending power has been increased by the amount of this profit. Also, the bank has its original $995 back 30 days sooner than if it had held the note to maturity. This lets the bank make another $995 loan 30 days sooner. By discounting notes, banks can expand business activity by making more money available for business and personal loans.

The table at the top of the following page shows the effect discounting has on increasing both bank profits and the total amount of money available for loans.

EFFECT OF DISCOUNTING ON MONEY SUPPLY
(60-day, $1,000, Non-Interest-Bearing Note)

Note discounted by business firm at 6% and held to maturity by member bank		Same note discounted by member bank after 30 days with Federal Reserve bank at 3%	
Bank pays business firm	$ 990	Reserve bank pays member bank	$997.50
Business pays bank (after 60 days)	1,000	Less amount bank paid	
Bank's profit (60 days)	$ 10	business firm	990.00
Original $990 can be loaned		Bank's profit (30 days)	$ 7.50
6 times a year for a total of	$5,940	Original $990 can be loaned	
+ Total profits ($10 × 6)	60	12 times a year for a total of	$11,880
Total money available for loans	$6,000	+ Total profits ($7.50 × 12)	90
		Total money available for loans	$11,970

Clearing and Collecting Checks. You have already learned that the Federal Reserve banks act as major clearinghouses for the collection and return of checks. The Federal Reserve banks provide this service free to member banks. In a recent year the Federal Reserve banks collected and cleared over 6 billion separate checks, amounting to nearly $5 billion a day.

Regulating Business Activity. One of the most important functions of the Federal Reserve System is to regulate business expansion and contraction. This regulation, called *monetary policy*, will be discussed in Part B.

FACTS EVERYONE SHOULD KNOW ABOUT THE FEDERAL RESERVE SYSTEM

1. The Federal Reserve System consists of 12 districts with 12 Federal Reserve banks, 25 branch banks, and 5,613 member banks.

2. The Federal Reserve System is owned by its member banks.

3. Member banks control over 81% of our money supply.

4. Federal Reserve banks are bankers' banks.

5. The primary objective of the Federal Reserve System is to achieve economic stability through the control of money and credit.

6. The Federal Reserve System issues paper currency.

B. MONETARY POLICY

You have just learned of the many activities carried out by the Federal Reserve System. Now you will study the major function of the Federal Reserve System that is so important to economic stability. This function is the controlling (expanding or reducing) of the nation's supply of money and credit.

What Monetary Policy Is

Monetary policy is a plan to promote economic growth and to maintain a stable economy through control of the supply of money and bank credit. The plan may be changed when current conditions indicate it is desirable to do so.

If business activity is slowing down and unemployment begins to rise, the Federal Reserve banks will try to expand the money and credit supply. To do this, Federal Reserve banks might encourage member banks to borrow money from the Federal Reserve banks at low interest rates. Hopefully, such an "easy money" policy will in turn encourage businesses to borrow money from member banks to expand their operations. It would also encourage wage earners to borrow money to buy more goods and build more homes. On the other hand, if business activity expands too rapidly (prices are rising, there is too much borrowing and spending by businesses and consumers, there is full employment and job vacancies), the Federal Reserve banks will try to reduce the money and credit supply. This "tight money" policy will discourage businesses and consumers from borrowing. If the money supply is limited, the interest rates will rise higher than most businesses and people are willing to pay.

Effect of Supply of Money on Total Spending

Economists do not always agree about the effect that controlling the supply of money has on the total spending of individuals and business firms. Some believe that causes other than supply of money may affect total spending. For example, the invention of a new, reasonably priced product that everyone wants may cause total spending to increase very rapidly for a period of time. Monetary policy probably would have little or nothing to do with total spending in this case. Also, a depression or a war may create such fear of immediate danger that it causes people to reduce total spending even though the supply of money is plentiful. All econ-

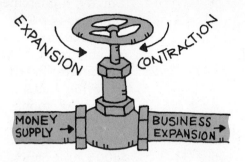

Federal Reserve monetary policy may control business expansion or contraction, depending on the level of business activity.

omists would probably agree that the amount of money created by banks through monetary policy is related to total spending; economists may differ, however, about the degree of effect that control of money supply has on spending.

Major Monetary Controls

There are three major ways by which the Federal Reserve System can expand or contract the supply of money and credit: (1) changing the legal reserve requirements of member banks, (2) changing the discount-rate policy, and (3) engaging in open-market operations.

Legal Reserve Requirements. You learned that a member bank must keep a percentage of its customers' deposits on deposit in the Federal Reserve bank. This is a safeguard against a member bank investing (making loans and buying government securities) too much or all of its customers' deposits. The banks need to have enough money on hand in case a large number of customers wish to withdraw their funds at the same time. Experience has proved that about 3% of the demand deposits (checking account money) would be enough to handle the day-to-day business activities or customer withdrawals. Congress has set a much safer margin, a 7% reserve requirement. However, Congress has given the Federal Reserve Board the power to demand an even higher reserve requirement (up to 22%) of member banks' demand deposits. A higher reserve requirement would be put into effect if economic conditions would seem to demand such action.

Let us see how the legal reserve requirement operates. For ease of computation, assume that the Federal Reserve Board has set a 15% reserve requirement of member banks' demand deposits. Thus, if a customer deposited $1,000 in a member bank, the bank must deposit $150 (15% of $1,000) in the Federal Reserve bank under required reserves. The balance, or $850, can be used by the member bank for investment purposes, that is, to make loans or to buy interest-bearing government securities.

If the Federal Reserve Board felt it necessary to reduce the amount of money member banks could invest from deposits, it could raise the reserve requirement to 20%. Thus, the member bank that received the $1,000 deposit would now have to deposit $200 (20% of $1,000) with the Federal Reserve bank instead of $150 under the 15% rate. Now the member bank would have only $800 to invest or loan.

If the Federal Reserve Board wanted to ease credit, it would do the opposite of the above. For example, if the reserve requirement were 10%, only $100 (10% of $1,000) of the original $1,000 deposit would have to be placed on reserve with the Federal Reserve bank. This would leave a balance of $900 ($1,000 less $100) that a member bank could invest or loan.

Discount-Rate Policy. Banks, like other businesses and wage earners, find it necessary at times to borrow money. The Federal Reserve banks make loans to member banks through a process called *discounting*. Member banks "sell" securities they own (government and other types) and their customers' promissory notes to the Federal Reserve bank at a discount from the face value in order to receive borrowed funds. (An example of discounting notes was given in Part A.) If the Federal Reserve bank's discount rate is low, say 3%, member banks find it profitable to discount their se-

High Federal Reserve discount rates create even higher interest rates for business and consumers.

curities and promissory notes to get extra cash. The member banks can then lend this money to customers at 5%, thereby making 2% gross profit on borrowed money.

If the Federal Reserve bank wishes to discourage member banks from borrowing, it will raise the discount rate to member banks. Assume the discount rate is raised from 3% to 6%. Member banks would have to charge their customers 8% on loans in order to make the same 2% gross profit seen earlier. Customers may not be willing to pay member banks such high interest and, therefore, may refuse to borrow money. When this happens, the Federal Reserve bank's discount-rate policy has worked. The member banks won't sell their securities and notes to the Federal Reserve bank at 6% if they can't find customers willing to pay 8% on borrowed funds.

Open-Market Operations. The most important of the major monetary controls available to the Federal Reserve System is the use of open-market operations — the buying and selling of government bonds in the open market. The Open Market Committee is composed of the seven-member Board of Governors and five members selected by the twelve Federal Reserve banks. The Committee meets weekly to decide whether to buy or sell government securities. Selling government securities reduces the lending ability of member banks. Buying government securities increases the lending ability of member banks. For example, by selling government securities the Federal Reserve bank takes money from deposits that member banks could use for lending. If the Federal Reserve bank buys government securities, it puts money back into deposits that can be loaned by member banks.

Let us use a simple example to see how the open-market operation works. Assume that the Open Market Committee wishes to reduce lending activities of member banks. The Committee would decide to sell a $5,000 Treasury bill (short-term government bond). The buyer pays for the bond by a check drawn on a member bank. The Federal Reserve bank in turn presents this check for payment to the buyer's member bank. The member bank immediately loses an equal amount of its required and excess reserve balances with the Federal Reserve bank because its demand deposits have been decreased. This loss means the member bank has less money available to loan. The illustration on the next page will help you to see this more clearly.

If the Open Market Committee wishes to increase a member bank's ability to loan money, the Committee will buy government securites. For example, if the Federal Reserve bank gives a check

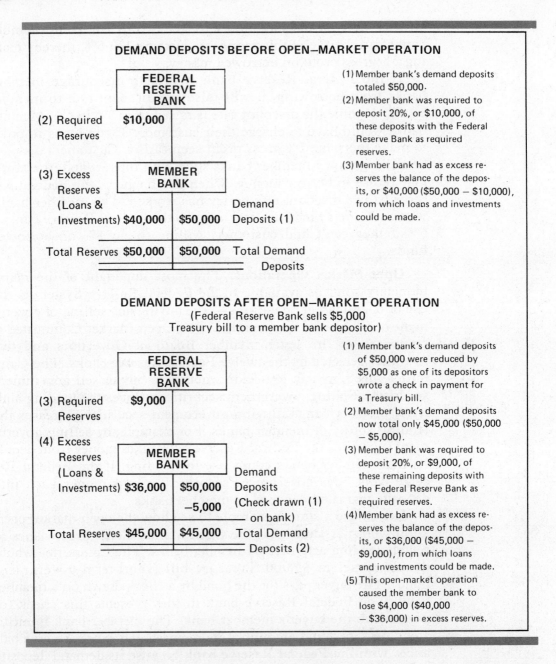

DEMAND DEPOSITS BEFORE OPEN—MARKET OPERATION

FEDERAL RESERVE BANK

(2) Required Reserves $10,000

MEMBER BANK

(3) Excess Reserves (Loans & Investments) $40,000 $50,000   Demand Deposits (1)

Total Reserves $50,000 $50,000   Total Demand Deposits

(1) Member bank's demand deposits totaled $50,000.
(2) Member bank was required to deposit 20%, or $10,000, of these deposits with the Federal Reserve Bank as required reserves.
(3) Member bank had as excess reserves the balance of the deposits, or $40,000 ($50,000 — $10,000), from which loans and investments could be made.

DEMAND DEPOSITS AFTER OPEN—MARKET OPERATION
(Federal Reserve Bank sells $5,000
Treasury bill to a member bank depositor)

FEDERAL RESERVE BANK

(3) Required Reserves $9,000

MEMBER BANK

(4) Excess Reserves (Loans & Investments) $36,000 $50,000   Demand Deposits
−5,000   (Check drawn (1) on bank)

Total Reserves $45,000 $45,000   Total Demand Deposits (2)

(1) Member bank's demand deposits of $50,000 were reduced by $5,000 as one of its depositors wrote a check in payment for a Treasury bill.
(2) Member bank's demand deposits now total only $45,000 ($50,000 − $5,000).
(3) Member bank was required to deposit 20%, or $9,000, of these remaining deposits with the Federal Reserve Bank as required reserves.
(4) Member bank had as excess reserves the balance of the deposits, or $36,000 ($45,000 − $9,000), from which loans and investments could be made.
(5) This open-market operation caused the member bank to lose $4,000 ($40,000 − $36,000) in excess reserves.

to the U.S. Government for $5,000 to pay for a Treasury bill, the government will deposit this check in a member bank. This transaction immediately increases the member bank's required and excess reserves; thus, it can make loans with the funds placed in the excess reserves. If the required legal reserve is 20%, the member bank deposits $1,000 (20% of $5,000) in the Federal Reserve bank. This would leave 80%, or $4,000, in excess reserves with which the member bank can make business loans.

Effects of Major Monetary Controls on Borrowers and Depositors. Through the use of major monetary controls, the Federal Reserve Board helps to determine the amount of money that a bank has available to lend. These controls also help to determine the rate at which a bank can afford to lend money. Policies that create more money and that lower the cost of borrowing or discounting permit banks to lend more money to businesses at lower rates. This action encourages expansion on the part of business, creates more jobs, and increases production. Policies that reduce the money supply and that raise the cost of borrowing or discounting cause banks to lend less money and to charge higher lending rates. Thus, it becomes more difficult for businesses to borrow from individual banks. They must pay a higher rate of interest, and therefore it is more difficult for them to expand, increase jobs, and produce at a profit.

The supply of money and the interest rates on money also have an effect on consumers. For example, if money is scarce and rates are high, it is difficult for families to buy or build a home; therefore, fewer homes are built and there are fewer jobs for workers. If money is plentiful and interest rates are low, it is easier for families to buy homes; therefore, the demand for new homes creates jobs for construction workers and suppliers of materials.

Commercial banks do not borrow funds from a Federal Reserve bank only to make more business loans. They also borrow to prevent a crisis if many depositors should suddenly want to withdraw their deposits at one time. This feature of the Federal Reserve System has the effect of stabilizing business in the communities served by the commercial banks. This in turn helps to stabilize the economy of the nation as a whole.

Minor Monetary Controls

The Federal Reserve System has some minor monetary controls that it can use to strengthen the major monetary controls. Some of these minor monetary controls are moral suasion, margin requirements, consumer credit controls, and real estate controls.

Moral Suasion. Sometimes the Federal Reserve Board will simply appeal to bankers to use more than an average amount of self-control and common sense and to pay heed to current business conditions. The Federal Reserve bank may send word to member banks that economic conditions are such that bankers should cut back on making loans. If they don't, the Federal Reserve Board might threaten to raise the legal reserve requirement or raise the discount rate or both.

Usually member banks will pay attention to the warnings of the Federal Reserve banks. For one thing, they don't want to endanger their relationship with such an important institution. Not to follow the wise directions and warnings may result in the Federal Reserve bank's unwillingness to make loans to member banks when funds are really needed.

Margin Requirements. The Securities and Exchange Act of 1934 gave the Federal Reserve Board the power to control speculation on common and preferred stocks. Prior to 1934 one could buy stock by paying as little as 10% down and borrowing the rest. Today, however, the Federal Reserve Board can require down payments of as much as 40% of the market price, and, if necessary, as high as 100%. Thus, if the Federal Reserve Board wishes to reduce credit and speculation with respect to stock purchasing, it simply requires a higher down payment. If it wishes to encourage stock purchasing, it will lower the size of the required down payment and encourage buyers of stocks to borrow the balance needed.

Consumer Credit Controls. Though not now in effect, the Federal Reserve System has had for many years the power (called Regulation W) to set certain terms on installment contracts. For

Tight consumer credit controls can delay consumer purchasing.

example, consumers could be required to pay 10, 20, or 33⅓% down when buying cars, furniture, and other goods. The time which the consumer had to repay the balance could also be regulated. Regulation W also could require a charge account customer to pay the account in full before buying additional goods on credit. Such a monetary control could help to tighten money and credit and help to prevent price increases and inflation.

Real Estate Controls. For a short time (1950–1953) the Federal Reserve System exercised a right granted to it by Congress to set mortgage terms. The Federal Reserve banks could say how much a home buyer had to have for a down payment and how many years the buyer had to pay off the mortgage. Thus, through "Regulation X," as it was known, the Federal Reserve banks could reduce housing construction and buying. They could do this by raising the size of the down payment required and reducing the number of years over which a mortgage is to be repaid.

For example, assume that Regulation X required a down payment of 25% of the value of a $20,000 home (or $5,000) instead of 10% (or $2,000). A person could not buy or build a $20,000 home until another $3,000 had been saved. If this example were multiplied by many thousands of cases, you can see that home building and buying would be greatly reduced. By reversing the action, the Federal Reserve banks could expand housing construction and buying.

C. CREATION OF BANK DEPOSITS

The major and minor controls on bank deposits have been shown to be quite powerful tools wielded by the Federal Reserve System. The real strength lies, however, in the multiplier effect that initial bank deposits create.

Banks Create Money

You will recall that for any given demand deposit, a member bank has the right to make use (invest and extend loans) of the excess reserves. As an example, assume that excess reserves amounted to 80% of each deposit and that required reserves amounted to 20%. This can be illustrated by the simple balance sheet on the next page for a $1,000 demand deposit.

INITIAL BANK DEPOSITS

Assets:		Liabilities:	
Required Reserves (20%)	$ 200	Demand Deposit	$1,000
Loans and Investments (80%)	800		
Total	$1,000	Total	$1,000

Thus, it can be seen that the bank actually created an extra $800 of money or credit. This was done by lending the $800 rather than holding it in reserve or in the vault.

If the $800 that was used in making loans is deposited in the same or another member bank by the borrower, still more money or credit can be created. Another balance sheet would show this new deposit as follows:

SECOND BANK DEPOSIT

Assets:		Liabilities:	
Required Reserves (20%)	$160	Demand Deposit	$800
Loans and Investments (80%)	640		
Total	$800	Total	$800

Thus, we see that the member bank created out of this second deposit an extra $640 of money or credit.

We can also expect this $640 to be deposited by the new borrower. The multiplier effect continues: $128 is held in reserve (20% of $640), and $512 is put out in loans or other investments by the member bank. The cycle continues until there is not a penny left to deposit. By this time the original $1,000 deposit will have enabled member banks to "create" $4,000 in extra money or credit.

Now one can see the real importance or effect of the tools used by the Federal Reserve System for monetary control. Banks can create extra money or credit from deposits. If more money is deposited, banks can create that much more money or credit. When the Federal Reserve banks buy Treasury bills, for example, more money is deposited in member banks. Also, more money or credit can be created if required reserves are lowered; less if raised.

What Affects Amount of Money Created

You have just seen how a single demand deposit of $1,000 can actually create an extra $4,000 in new money or credit. If the legal reserve rate were increased, then the multiplier effect for creating new money or credit would be reduced. This would be known as a "tight money" policy. If the legal reserve rate were reduced, then the multiplier effect for creating new money and credit would be increased. This would be known as an "easy money" policy.

Economic conditions and personal behavior can prevent the multiplier effect from reaching its full force. For example, if the economy is in a period of inflation and interest rates are quite high, businesses and consumers may not wish to borrow money. Thus, the lack of demand for money would mean that member banks could not loan all the excess reserves available and the multiplier effect would be stopped. If the economy is in a period of recession, businesses and consumers may be afraid to borrow even though interest rates are low. This, too, would stop the multiplier effect from reaching its full potential, since banks are not able to make loans. The multiplier effect in creating new money and credit can reach its full potential only when the demand for money (loans) equals the supply (excess reserves).

Another condition that can stop the multiplier effect from reaching its full potential is personal behavior regarding money and banks. There still are some people who do not trust banks and thus hoard their money by hiding it around the house or by locking it up in home safes or safe-deposit boxes. If this money does not get into circulation (through spending or depositing the money in banks), then the multiplier effect is stopped.

FACTS EVERYONE SHOULD KNOW ABOUT MONETARY POLICY

1. Monetary policy is a means of controlling (expanding or contracting) the nation's supply of money and credit.

2. Monetary policy is necessary to achieve economic stability — to enable economic growth at stable prices.

3. The major monetary controls are legal reserve requirements, discount-rate policy, and open-market operation.

4. The minor monetary controls used by the Federal Reserve are moral suasion, margin requirements, consumer credit controls, and real estate controls.

5. Bank deposits enable member banks to "create" new money and credit by making use of excess reserves through loans and investments.

6. Economic conditions, the monetary controls, and personal behavior regarding money and banks all determine the amount of new money and credit that can be created by bank deposits.

REVIEW QUESTIONS

Section A

1. What benefits or privileges do member banks enjoy by being members of the Federal Reserve System?
2. What do we mean when we say that a Federal Reserve bank is a bankers' bank?
3. What are six important functions of the Federal Reserve System?
4. What notes are issued by Federal Reserve banks and circulated as currency?
5. How is the currency issued by the Federal Reserve System obtained by a member bank?
6. How do member banks build up reserves in the Federal Reserve bank?

Section B

7. What is monetary control?
8. Under what conditions would the Federal Reserve Board decide to contract (reduce) the money supply? expand the money supply?
9. What happens to money supply if the legal reserve requirement is raised? lowered?
10. What happens when the Federal Reserve Board increases the discount rate? decreases the discount rate?
11. Why does the selling of government securities by the Federal Reserve banks decrease the money supply in member banks?

Section C

12. How do banks "create" money?
13. What affects the amount of new money and credit banks can create?
14. If the required legal reserve were increased, what effect would this have on creating new money and credit?

DISCUSSION QUESTIONS

Section A

1. The raising of the discount rate by the Federal Reserve Board is supposed to restrict business expansion. Can you think of any cases in which this action by the Federal Reserve Board would not be very effective? Explain your answer.
2. In order to encourage business expansion, the Federal Reserve System reduces the discount rate. Can you explain any situation when you think that a reduction in the discount rate would not be effective?

Section B

3. If there were no monetary controls, what steps could the federal government take to slow down business activity?
4. Why do you suppose Congress has set a minimum rate for required legal reserves at 7% even though typical banking experience has shown that 3% is usually adequate?
5. It has been said that lowering the discount rate to member banks may not result in the expected outcome of encouraging banks to borrow from the Federal Reserve banks. Why might this statement be true?

6. Why would the Federal Reserve System decide to use moral suasion rather than exercise some of the major and other minor monetary controls available to it?

7. Under what economic conditions would the Federal Reserve System be apt to raise or lower the margin requirements on stock purchases?

Section C   8. What is the relationship of the multiplier effect to the creation of money?

APPLICATION PROBLEMS

Section A   1. Total assets and demand deposits for all commercial banks (both member and nonmember banks) in a recent year were as follows:

CLASS OF BANK	ASSETS*	DEMAND DEPOSITS*
All banks	1,166.0	382.9
National banks	651.3	211.6
State member banks	210.4	81.2
Nonmember banks	304.3	90.1

*In billions of dollars

(a) What percentage of total bank assets is held by member banks?

(b) What percentage of total demand deposits is held by member banks?

(c) What conclusions can you draw from these figures regarding the influence of the Federal Reserve System on banking activity?

Section B   2. Prepare an illustration complete with itemized explanations similar to the one on page 284 showing the effect of a Federal Reserve bank buying a $10,000 Treasury bill.

Section C   3. Assume that the required legal reserve rate on demand deposits is 12%. If a customer deposited $500 in a member bank, how much new money and credit could be created for loans and investments by a member bank from this deposit? (Let X equal the total amount of demand deposits resulting from initial deposit, and then use the algebraic formula: 12% of X = $500.)

COMMUNITY PROJECTS

Section A   1. Obtain from a local bank a statement of its capital worth (balance sheet) to see what kinds of assets it has and how much capital stock it owns in the Federal Reserve bank in its district. (a) How much larger is the bank's asset "Loans" compared with its liability "Demand Deposits"? What does this difference tell you? (b) Assume that the Federal Reserve bank will pay a 6% dividend on the capital stock owned by your local bank. How much income for the year would your local bank earn from ownership of this stock?

Section B   2. You learned that it is possible to buy stocks "on margin," paying down only a percentage of the market value in cash and borrowing to pay the rest. Find out from a local stockbroker or an officer in the bank who buys stocks for customers what advice they would give regarding this practice. When and for whom would they recommend buying "on margin"?

Section C   3. Check with a local bank in your community to find out what is the required legal reserve rate on demand deposits. From this information determine the amount of money that could be "created" from a $100 customer deposit.

PART 6 | FINANCIAL PLANNING IN OUR FREE ENTERPRISE ECONOMY

16 Managing Income

PURPOSE OF THE CHAPTER

Any successful person, regardless of income, must do some financial planning. Financial planning includes setting up a spending plan, keeping certain records, and providing for savings. Financial planning can be difficult or simple. This chapter provides some simple guidelines.

After studying this chapter, you will be able to:

1. Define a spending plan.
2. Explain how income and expenditures (payments) can be estimated.
3. Prepare a spending plan and maintain a daily cash record.
4. Identify what records should be kept for financial planning and for income tax purposes.
5. Describe how money can work for you.
6. List places where savings can be placed.

A. FINANCIAL PLANNING

In order to enjoy the highest possible level of living from one's limited income, financial planning is necessary. In this section you will learn what is required for proper financial planning.

Developing a Spending Plan

A *spending plan* (also called a *budget*) is a guide for spending and saving one's income. Such a guide or plan helps us to get as many of the things we need and want as possible. Spending plans will seldom be the same for any two individuals or families. Since each of us (either as an individual or as a family) has different wants and different life goals, each of us should set up our own spending plan.

Operating without some kind of spending plan is like trying to drive a car without a steering wheel. A spending plan involves (1) determining immediate, short-range, and long-range goals, (2) estimating how much cash (income) will be available to spend or save, and (3) planning the expenditures (payments).

Determining Goals. This is the first step in building a spending plan or budget. One should think first of the immediate goals for the coming year. Obviously, everyone's immediate goals are to provide the basic needs of food, clothing, and shelter. In addition to these basic needs, a high school student, for example, may plan to buy a class ring, take a vacation, or buy a used car. A newly married couple may need to buy a piece of furniture or start a reserve fund for emergencies.

Short-range goals (for the next 5 years, for example) also need to be considered. A high school student may plan to go to college or plan to buy a new car. A newly married couple may plan to save for a down payment on a home or to buy expensive appliances such as a stove, a refrigerator, and an automatic washer and dryer.

Long-range goals are usually planned by families and adults who have completed their education and training. Such long-range goals might include (a) providing a college education for one's children, (b) having a debt-free home, (c) having retirement income, and (d) helping newly married sons and daughters set up housekeeping. Setting goals helps one who is building a spending plan to know how much money should be set aside or saved for each month and year.

In preparing a spending plan, the first step is to set immediate, short-range, and long-range goals.

Estimating Cash Available. The second step in building a spending plan is to estimate the amount of cash that will be available. This consists of cash on hand at the beginning of the spending plan period plus all income for the period. *Income* includes: (a) wages or salary received; (b) interest on savings; (c) dividends on stocks; (d) money received from other sources such as gifts, allowances, and bonuses; and (e) money one plans to borrow. The total of all these items is the amount of cash available for the spending plan period.

Cash on hand includes money in your possession and in your checking account. Do not count money in savings accounts, which was set aside for emergencies or some special purpose (goal). However, if you plan to spend some of your savings, you should include this amount in your estimated cash available.

When including wages or salary, list only the net amount of *take-home pay*, which is the amount available after the employer has withheld deductions for taxes and other purposes. Wages or salary may be estimated fairly well for the next year by considering the wages or salary received last year and adjusting for any expected increase or decrease.

The best way to estimate the amount of interest, dividends, gifts, allowances, or bonuses is to assume that it will be the same as last year. If you know of any expected increases or decreases in such amounts, however, the adjusted amount should be used.

Money that is borrowed will be part of the cash available to spend. When the borrowed money is repaid, the payments are fixed expenditures.

Planning Expenditures. After you have figured how much available cash you will have, then you need to estimate your expenditures. *Expenditures*, for the purposes of a spending plan, include payments not only for actual expenses (money spent for items that will be used up and never recovered) but also for items that will last a long time and for money placed in savings or investments. Expenditures also include payments on homes and repayments of loans.

A method of setting up a cash spending plan on a monthly basis is illustrated on page 297. Note the two groups of expenditures: fixed payments and variable payments. Note also that there are three columns for each month, one showing the amounts spent last year, one showing the estimated amounts for this year, and one for the actual amounts spent this year. The first two columns are filled in when the spending plan is made up. The third column

YEARLY CASH SPENDING PLAN

Cash Received and Paid	January			February		
	Last Year	Estimate this Year	Actual this Year	Last Year	Estimate this Year	Actual this Year
Cash available						
Cash at beginning (checkbook)	$100.00	$100.00	$110.00	$119.00	$110.00	$ 63.00
Net wages (take-home pay)	480.00	500.00	500.00	480.00	500.00	500.00
Interest and dividends	3.00	3.50	3.50	3.00	3.50	3.50
Borrowed						
Other:						
Bonus or cash gift						
Total cash available	583.00	603.50	613.50	602.00	613.50	566.50
Fixed payments (expenditures)						
Rent or payment on mortgage	100.00	150.00	150.00	100.00	150.00	150.00
Life insurance	50.00	50.00	50.00			
Homeowners insurance				35.00	40.00	40.00
Auto insurance				75.00	75.00	75.00
Real estate taxes						
Payments on debts		25.00	25.00		25.00	25.00
Contribution to church	10.00	11.00	11.00	10.00	11.00	11.00
Savings	10.00	15.00	15.00	10.00	15.00	15.00
Other:						
Total fixed payments	170.00	251.00	251.00	230.00	316.00	316.00
Variable payments (expenditures)						
Water	8.00	8.00	9.00	8.00	9.00	10.00
Heat	18.00	20.00	24.00	20.00	20.00	25.00
Telephone	6.50	6.50	6.50	6.50	6.50	6.50
Gas and electricity	18.00	18.50	19.00	18.00	18.50	20.00
Medical	25.00	20.00	25.00	25.00	25.00	12.00
Food	114.00	120.00	125.00	116.00	120.00	120.00
Clothing	35.00	30.00	32.00	50.00	25.00	
Car operation and repair	35.00	30.00	29.50	30.00	30.00	26.50
Recreation and education	20.00	20.00	15.00	20.00	20.00	15.00
Personal	15.00	15.00	14.50	15.00	15.00	15.00
Other:						
Total variable payments	294.50	288.00	299.50	308.50	289.00	250.00
Summary						
Total cash available	583.00	603.50	613.50	602.00	613.50	566.50
Total payments (fixed and variable)	464.50	539.00	550.50	538.50	605.00	566.00
Cash balance at end	$118.50	$ 64.50	$ 63.00	$ 63.50	$ 8.50	$ .50

is filled in at the end of each month when the actual expenditures are known.

In estimating your expenditures, first record those payments that you know have to be made. These are the *fixed payments*, many of which represent large expenditures. For example, you

Mortgage payments, home insurance, and real estate taxes are examples of fixed payments to be included in a family spending plan.

know that you have to pay the rent or make a payment on your home. You will have various kinds of insurance policies and will know in advance when the payments are due and how much they are. Note that savings are included in this group of fixed payments. If you do not plan your savings in advance before you allow money for the many optional items, you will probably never save any money. Savings should, therefore, be taken out of each paycheck and put away before the money is spent.

The fixed expenditures should also include payments on money borrowed, interest on money borrowed, church contributions, and installment payments that come due.

The *variable payments*, those that are smaller in amount or more subject to change, may be estimated on the basis of past experience but adjusted to fit anticipated needs. Water, heat, telephone, gas, and electricity are included in the variable payments group because many of these payments are small. The time of payment is known, but payments may vary. In most cases, in setting up your spending plan you must decide whether you spent too much last year or whether you will have to spend more. This decision is a matter of judgment. You may decide that food prices have gone up and you will have to spend more, that the children are growing older and you will have to spend more, or that more must be budgeted for personal expenses and school allowances. If you expect any major repairs on the automobile, this amount should also be included in your spending plan.

A high school student would have different expenditures than those in the illustration, but the spending plan would be prepared in the same way. Typical expenditures for a high school student

Careful, systematic record keeping is important to the proper maintenance of the spending plan.

include clothes, personal items, recreation, school lunches, school supplies, transportation, gifts, and church contributions.

Daily Cash Record

A *daily cash record* is a form on which to record actual receipts of income and actual expenditures on a daily basis. One form of daily cash record is shown in the illustration on page 300. This form provides a column for cash available and a column for each fixed payment and each variable payment listed in the cash spending plan on page 297.

An entry is made in the daily cash record each day that money is received or paid. Sources for daily entries include checks received, sales slips, grocery receipts, ticket stubs, and checkbook stubs if you use a checking account.

At the end of each month, the columns of the daily cash record are totaled. These monthly totals are then transferred to the column in the yearly spending plan labeled "Actual this Year." A comparison of the estimated figures with the actual figures shows how well the estimated spending plan is being followed. If too much money is being spent, it may be necessary to reduce the estimated planned expenditures in the future.

Another method of keeping the daily cash records is to use a

Daily Cash Record

Date	Explanation	Cash Available	Rent	Life Insurance	Home-owner's Insurance	Auto Insurance	Real Estate Taxes	Payments on Debts	Church	Savings	Other Payments	Water	Heat	Telephone	Gas and Electricity
												(VARIABLE PAYM)			
			FIXED PAYMENTS												
Jan 1	Cash Available	110 00													
2	Life Insurance			50 00											
4	Groceries														
6	Gasoline														
7	Dental Bill														
8	Dress for Mary														
9	Mr Tenlot	3 50													
10	Accident Insurance														
11	Groceries														
15	Personal Allowance														
15	Magazines														
15	Salary	250 00													
18	Groceries														
19	Theatre Tickets														
20	Gasoline														
21	Church								5 50						
22	Trousers for John														
23	Paid Dr. Smith														
24	Rent		150 00												
25	Groceries														
26	Installment Payment							25 00							
30	Salary	250 00													
31	Church								5 50						
31	Heating Bill												24 00		
31	Savings Account									15 00					
31	Gas and Electric Bill														19 00
31	Groceries														
31	Telephone													6 50	
31	Totals	613 50	150 00	50 00				25 00	11 00	15 00			24 00	6 50	19 00
Feb 1	Cash Available	63 00													
3	Fire Insurance				40 00										
4	Rent		150 00												
5	Groceries														
6	Auto Insurance					75 00									

A Partial Illustration of a Daily Cash Record for January and February, 19—

notebook in which one page is devoted to each kind of income and expenditure. From this notebook you can determine the monthly totals and insert them in the "Actual" column in your cash spending plan.

Statement of Assets and Liabilities

Occasionally, it is desirable for a family or an individual to determine how much is owned (*assets*) and how much is owed (*liabilities*). A *statement of assets and liabilities* will show what the real net worth or ownership value is.

Below is a statement of assets and liabilities for a family. The family had to estimate the value of the household equipment, the furniture, and the automobile. By looking at their life insurance policies, they were able to determine their cash value. The value of the United States savings bonds was determined by examining the table on the bonds.

L. D. KOZLOWSKI FAMILY
STATEMENT OF ASSETS AND LIABILITIES
DECEMBER 31, 19--

Assets Owned by the Family		Liabilities Owed by the Family	
Cash in checking account.	$ 232.00	City Savings Bank (due on	
Cash in savings account....	305.70	refrigerator).....................	$ 100.00
U.S. savings bonds.............	250.00	Cranley Department Store.	25.00
Life insurance (cash value)	391.33	First Federal Savings and	
Household equipment........	950.00	Loan Association	
Furniture	1,000.00	(amount still owed on	
Automobile.........................	1,000.00	house and lot)................	11,000.00
House and lot......................	15,000.00	Total liabilities	$11,125.00
		Net worth (ownership)	8,004.03
		Total liabilities and net	
Total assets........................	$19,129.03	worth..............................	$19,129.03

(Total assets, $19,129.03 − Total liabilities, $11,125.00 = Net worth, $8,004.03)

Records Needed for Income Taxes

The records required for the cash spending plan and the statement of assets and liabilities should be saved during the year. In addition, records that will provide information in filling out income tax returns should be saved during the year.

At the end of the year, an employer is required to furnish each employee a statement (Form W-2) that shows the total amount earned and all deductions for federal, state, and city income taxes withheld. In preparing a federal income tax return, an individual is required to list the total amount earned before deductions from wages. Other types of income must also be listed, but not money from gifts or from borrowing.

A taxpayer who wishes to itemize expenses instead of taking a standard deduction is entitled to itemize deductions for: (a) state and local taxes; (b) interest paid on loans and installment contracts; (c) contributions to church and charity, but not personal gifts; (d) a certain proportion of medical expenses if they are great enough; and (e) certain losses and thefts not covered by insurance. Thus, it is important to have receipts (canceled checks are acceptable) as proof of one's having paid these expenses. A spending plan and a daily cash record will not be acceptable as proof for income tax purposes.

Other Financial Records Needed

A record of items having value, such as furniture, appliances, books, jewelry, and silverware, should be kept to provide an inventory in case of loss by fire or theft. Dates of purchase, from whom purchased, and cost should be shown on the record.

Though deeds to property, stock certificates, bonds, and insurance policies should be kept in a safe-deposit box, a record of these items should always be kept at home for ready reference.

B. A SAVINGS PLAN

A savings plan requires one to set immediate, short-range, and long-range goals. It also requires one to have knowledge as to where and how a part of one's income should be saved.

Savings and Financial Management

In the discussion of financial planning, it was stressed that a spending plan should include regular amounts for savings. Unless savings are planned, there usually will be no savings. Unless there are savings, an individual or a family can never look forward to having the really important things that they want.

The savings of millions of people, when used for financing business, create new capital, new jobs, and greater production for the benefit of all. Therefore, as people save and put their money to work where it will draw interest, they are helping their country as well as themselves.

Saving Can Be Rewarding

Setting aside a part of income regularly is known as *saving*. A regular plan of saving is a mark of good money management. Saving can be fun if you will look forward to some greater future pleasures by giving up some of your present spending for foolish or unnecessary things. The question before you is whether you are willing to make a plan that will enable you to reach a desirable and pleasant goal. Some of the decisions that you must make in planning a savings program are discussed in the following sections.

SOME DECISIONS THAT MUST BE MADE

For immediate or short-range pleasure		For permanent value or longer-lasting happiness
1. Should I spend 50 cents a day on little pleasures?	or	Should I save 30 cents a day and have $100 for a summer vacation?
2. Should I wear the latest styles?	or	Should I wear good clothes longer?
3. Should I be satisfied with a limited education?	or	Should I save and go to college?
4. Should I spend foolishly on dates now?	or	Should I save to have money to furnish a home after marriage?
5. Do I really need a car now?	or	Should I buy life insurance or invest the money?
6. Should I drive or take a bus?	or	Should I walk and save for new clothes?
7. Should I buy lots of new clothes now?	or	Should I save for a down payment on a home after marriage?
8. Should the family spend all and live lavishly now?	or	Should the family plan to educate the children and prepare for old age?
9. Should we "keep up with the Joneses"?	or	Should we live our own lives and save for the future?
10. Should we rent a home and spend the rest?	or	Should we buy a home and invest all we can?
11. Should we buy now on the installment plan and pay more?	or	Should we save and pay cash?
12. Should we let the future take care of itself?	or	Should we build a savings, investment, and insurance program?

Setting Goals for Savings

Most people have some definite goals in life, some things toward which they are striving. Some of these goals are really ideals and ambitions, and some are desires for material things that will add to the comfort of living. Regardless of the kind of goals we may have for ourselves, money is usually a factor in achieving them. Most of us have to set aside a little at a time from our income in order to save enough to fulfill our goals.

WORTHWHILE GOALS OF SAVING

1. Further education.

2. Marriage and furnishing a home.

3. Buying a home.

4. Starting a business.

5. Buying insurance for protection and future income.

6. Investments in securities for future income.

7. Buying major comforts and luxuries for better living.

8. Providing for emergencies, such as unemployment and hospital bills.

9. Paying cash to save on the purchase of important items instead of buying on the installment plan.

10. Retirement.

11. Vacation.

Making Money Work for You

Very few people realize the added power of compound interest. Interest is a very faithful worker, but it will work for you only if you have savings. This fact explains why many people live comfortably after retirement. Although they cease to work, their money continues to work for them by earning interest.

Let us see how a savings program will grow. The table on the next page shows how much will be accumulated if $1 is deposited each week in a savings account at various rates of interest. In this table the interest is *compounded* quarterly. *Compound interest* means that interest is paid on accumulated interest as well as on

One of the most important goals of a savings program is the provision for an education for a chosen occupation.

City Colleges of Chicago, photo by Sy Friedman

the principal. Assume that a young person starts saving $1 a week in the third grade and that interest is compounded quarterly at 5¼% a year. At the usual age of graduation from high school, that person would have $682.87. The amount saved during these 10 years was $520; interest amounted to $162.87.

GROWTH OF REGULAR SAVINGS IF $1 IS DEPOSITED WEEKLY AND INTEREST IS COMPOUNDED QUARTERLY

Amount of Savings at End of	Annual Rate of Interest		
	5%	5¼%	6%
1 year	$ 53.31	$ 53.40	$ 53.58
5 years	295.13	297.16	302.85
10 years	673.51	682.87	710.75
15 years	1,158.61	1,183.50	1,260.12
20 years	1,780.52	1,833.30	1,997.63

Where To Put Savings

The average person saves only a few dollars a month. Hence, a place is needed to put the monthly savings until enough builds up to invest in bonds, stocks, real estate, or some other form of permanent investment. In deciding on a place to put savings where they will earn income, consider these questions:

1. Will the savings be safe?
2. Will the savings earn a reasonable rate of interest?
3. Will the savings be available at any time?
4. How often is interest compounded?

Commercial Banks. Most commercial banks have savings departments. These banks generally pay a fixed rate of interest.

Banks usually are conveniently located, making it easy to deposit savings at the time of cashing a paycheck. The interest on savings may be credited quarterly, semiannually, or annually. Some banks require 30 days' notice before withdrawing a savings deposit. This right is seldom exercised, but it may be if necessary. The savings departments of commercial banks will usually accept time deposits at a slightly higher rate of interest than is paid on regular savings accounts. A *time deposit* is usually made for six months, one year, or longer; and a certificate is issued to the depositor indicating that the deposit, plus interest at the agreed rate, may be withdrawn at the end of the specified time. Usually a minimum of $1,000 is required to purchase a time deposit certificate.

Each deposit account in all national and in many other banks is insured by the Federal Deposit Insurance Corporation to the extent of $40,000. Like savings accounts, savings certificates are also insured up to $40,000.

Savings Banks. Some savings banks are organized as stock companies in which the owners invest money and also accept deposits in savings accounts. Interest is paid on these deposits. Usually these savings banks make loans only to consumers. Some savings banks, however, operate as trust companies and in other ways are similar to commercial banks since both institutions lend to businesses. Besides accepting regular savings account deposits, savings banks also accept time deposits in the same manner as commercial banks.

Mutual Savings Banks. A mutual savings bank is a slightly different type of bank because it is owned by the depositors. The depositors are not promised a fixed rate of interest. If there is a profit, each depositor is paid a dividend instead of interest. But if no profit is earned on the operations of the bank, the depositors do not get a dividend. In most other respects, however, a mutual savings bank is operated the same as the savings department of any other bank.

A regular savings plan helps you reach your financial goals.

Mutual savings banks permit a depositor to withdraw funds on demand or after giving notice. The laws of most states require notice of 30 to 90 days, but usually withdrawals may be made instantly on demand. Mutual banks do not ordinarily accept checking accounts, but in a few states they do.

The accounts in most mutual savings banks are insured by the Federal Deposit Insurance Corporation up to $40,000. In a few states all deposits are insured under the state banking laws.

Industrial Banks. Industrial banks are owned and controlled by stockholders who invest their money. Most industrial banks accept regular deposits and time deposits in the same manner as commercial banks, and they pay interest on these deposits.

Savings and Loan Associations. A savings and loan association is organized for the purpose of lending money to people who do not have enough money to buy or to build a home. The money that the association lends is obtained from depositors. In most states, when people make deposits in a savings and loan association, they really buy shares and become part owners. These shares earn income, generally a slightly higher rate of interest than that on a savings account in a bank.

Many savings and loan associations will also accept time deposits at a slightly higher rate of interest or dividend than is generally paid on passbook savings deposits. In this respect, the practice is similar to that of savings departments of commercial banks.

Most savings and loan associations are mutual associations and in this respect are similar to mutual savings banks. Those who have money deposited in the savings and loan association receive dividends, which are the earnings. There usually is no guaranteed dividend rate, but the expected rate is announced from time to time. A few savings and loan associations are organized as stock companies. In this case the owners invest money and accept deposits in a manner similar to that of a stock savings bank. Interest is paid on these deposits.

All federal savings and loan associations are members of the Federal Home Loan Bank and operate under regulations established by the federal government. The accounts of these associations are insured by the Federal Savings and Loan Insurance Corporation up to $40,000. All state-chartered savings and loan associations may have their accounts insured with the Federal Savings and Loan Insurance Corporation. To do so they must be members of the Federal Home Loan Bank and must pass rigid insurability tests.

Under normal conditions, withdrawals may be made from savings and loan associations on demand. However, under most state laws the institution is allowed 30 days in which to fill a request for a withdrawal. In times of economic stress, state laws impose additional restrictions for the protection of both the institution and the depositor.

In New England, savings and loan associations and savings banks are permitted to offer NOW (negotiable order of withdrawal) accounts. These are interest-bearing deposits on which you can write checks. Congress is considering legislation to permit all financial institutions throughout the U.S. to issue NOW accounts.

United States Savings Bonds. One of the safest and most popular methods of saving is to buy United States savings bonds. Several types of government bonds may be purchased by investors; the most popular are discussed below.

Series E bonds have been the most popular bonds among people who are saving small amounts regularly. Series E bonds were bought at a discount of 25% of their face value (the amount printed on the front of the bond). If held to maturity (the end of the stated period of 5 years), they can be redeemed (cashed in) for the full amount of the face value, which includes interest at 6%. For example, a $50 Series E bond bought for $37.50 would be redeemed at maturity by the government for $50. The difference, $12.50, is the interest earned. If Series E bonds are held beyond maturity, the interest continues to accumulate.

Beginning on January 2, 1980, the new *Series EE* bonds have replaced the Series E bonds. The Series EE bonds — so named because they will double in value between their purchase and maturity dates — are available in denominations of $50, $75, $100,

$200, $500, $1,000, $5,000, and $10,000. The purchase price is one half of the face value, the term to maturity is 11 years and 9 months, and the interest rate is 6%. For example, a $50 Series EE bond bought for $25 would be redeemed at maturity by the government for $50.

Another popular type of United States savings bond was the *Series H* bond. These bonds were purchased at their full face value, and interest was paid semiannually by check. Beginning on January 2, 1980, the new *Series HH* bonds have replaced the Series H bonds. The Series HH bonds can be purchased in denominations of $500, $1,000, $5,000, and $10,000. They have a 10-year term to maturity, and interest at 6% is paid on them semiannually by check.

The rate of interest earned on Series E, EE, H, and HH bonds is reasonable in comparison with the rate of earnings on some other savings and is usually higher than that earned on regular savings accounts. The main difference between E bonds and H bonds is in the method of paying interest. In the case of Series E and Series EE bonds, interest is paid only when the bond is redeemed. In the case of Series H and Series HH bonds, interest is paid semiannually by check.

United States post offices sell United States savings bonds. Banks and some savings and loan associations also sell United States savings bonds without any charge or commission for this service. A person may also use a payroll savings plan as a convenient way to invest in Series EE bonds. Under this plan, the employer deducts a small amount from each paycheck and buys a bond for the employee when a sufficient amount has been saved.

Credit Unions. *Credit unions* are cooperative associations operating both as savings and as lending institutions for the benefit of their members. Credit unions are usually formed by large groups of people with common interests. For instance, they may be formed by such groups as teachers in a large school system, workers in a large factory, store employees, and members of a church.

In most states, credit unions operate under state laws, but some credit unions operate under a federal charter. While the credit unions established under the laws of the various states are by no means uniform, there is uniformity in the organization of federal credit unions. A member of a federal credit union must buy at least one $5 share and may buy a larger number of shares if desired.

The purchase of one or more shares makes a member eligible for a proportionate share of the annual dividends that may be declared. These dividends represent interest earned on the money deposited with the credit union and loaned to others. Dividends (interest) can vary from 4 to 6% depending on the size and the success of the credit union. Federal credit unions are now allowed to issue share drafts, a type of checking account service that is interest bearing.

Endowment Insurance. In Chapter 19 you will learn more about life insurance. Most life insurance policies provide not only protection but also savings. Endowment insurance policies combine life insurance with a high degree of savings. An endowment policy is purchased over a stated number of years, such as 10, 20, or 30. The cash value of such policies builds up rather rapidly. Many people use endowment policies as a combination of protection for the family while saving for some specific purpose. For example, a young person in high school may buy a $5,000 endowment policy at age 16. When the person is 26 years of age, the face value of the policy will become due. Then the person will have $5,000 to make a down payment on a home.

Annuities. If one has a certain sum of money, for example $3,000, one can purchase a life insurance *annuity*. At a stipulated age the money will be paid back to the person in monthly payments with interest. Annuities can also be purchased on the installment plan, which is a method of saving that will build up an income for retirement. At retirement, the amount of the policy will be paid back in guaranteed monthly installments with interest. If the annuitant dies before the stipulated date, the face value of the annuity is paid to the beneficiary just like a life insurance policy.

Economic Problems of Savings Programs

There is always some risk in any savings or investment program. That is why it is important to put savings in a safe place.

Interest rates may change from time to time and the amount of dividends declared may vary, depending on economic conditions. For example, if banks have more money than they can invest at a profit, they will reduce the interest rates they pay on deposits.

There is another economic problem involved in saving. Let us assume that you have $5,000 in a savings account on which you are drawing interest or dividends. Also assume that prices and the cost of living increase at a rate greater than the interest rate you are receiving on your savings. In such a case, the purchasing power of your savings will be decreased. For example, assume that the $5,000 you had in a savings account drew interest at 5% compounded semiannually. At the end of 5 years your savings would have accumulated to approximately $6,400. Assume also that during those same 5 years the cost of living index had risen to 135.10. This means that it would take $135.10 today to buy what $100 would have bought 5 years ago. Thus, today you would need $6,755 (rather than your $6,400 accumulated savings) to buy what $5,000 would have bought 5 years ago. As a result, your savings were decreased in value through inflation by $355 ($6,755–$6,400) during these 5 years.

To protect yourself from this inflationary situation, you might diversify your investment. Diversifying investments means dividing your savings among different investment options. This practice is also called *hedging* against inflation. For example, some options in which the rate of return is fixed and the principal invested is always in the form of money (such as savings accounts, life insurance, and government, municipal, and corporate bonds) will not increase in value with inflation. Other options (such as some real estate, growth stocks, art objects, and small businesses) often grow in value, keeping pace with or exceeding the rate of inflation. In these growth instances the principal invested is always in the form of property (such as land, buildings, shares of ownership, rare coins) that can be converted to money (sold) at its inflated value.

FACTS EVERYONE SHOULD KNOW ABOUT A SAVINGS PROGRAM

1. Choices must be made between immediate spending or saving for later substantial spending.

2. A spending plan is desirable in any savings program.

3. Goals for saving should be established.

4. Savings of a small amount each week are worthwhile and will grow at compound interest.

5. There are several safe places to put savings where interest will be earned.

REVIEW QUESTIONS

Section A

1. What three major items does a spending plan involve?
2. For purposes of a spending plan, what is meant by income?
3. For purposes of a spending plan, why should you consider only take-home pay?
4. What are some examples of (a) fixed payments and (b) variable payments in a family spending plan?
5. In addition to the regular spending plan, why is it necessary to keep a daily record of income and expenditures?
6. In what two ways may you keep a record of daily expenditures?
7. What are some possible assets a family renting an unfurnished house may record in a statement of assets and liabilities?
8. From a statement of assets and liabilities, how can one determine net worth or ownership?
9. Besides the information needed for a spending plan and a daily cash record, what information will be needed for income tax purposes?

Section B

10. From the point of view of economics in our society, why are the savings of people so important?
11. What are some decisions that you must make daily to determine whether to spend for immediate pleasure or to save and spend for greater values and longer-lasting happiness?
12. What are three important goals of saving?
13. What facts should be considered in selecting a place to open a savings account?
14. What is a time deposit?
15. What is the primary purpose for which savings and loan associations are organized?
16. (a) How does the price paid for a Series EE United States savings bond differ from the price paid for a Series HH bond?
    (b) How does the interest paid on a Series EE bond differ from the interest paid on a Series HH bond?
    (c) What amount will be paid at maturity to the redeemer of a $1,000 Series EE bond and the redeemer of a $1,000 Series HH bond?
17. Why is endowment insurance considered a method of saving?

DISCUSSION QUESTIONS

Section A

1. Why does information gathered from past experience help in establishing a spending plan?
2. If Mr. Murphy finds that, according to his spending plan, he is not going to have enough cash in his checking account to take care of expenses, what can he do to avoid this situation?
3. Why is it recommended that savings be classified under fixed payments in the cash spending plan?
4. Why would a carefully prepared spending plan and daily cash record not serve as proof of one's income and allowable deductions for income tax purposes?
5. According to the cash spending plan in this chapter, how would the receipt of a Christmas gift of $50 be recorded, and how would it be handled

if it were placed in savings?

6. If a comparison of actual expenditures with estimated expenditures in the spending plan shows that one month's expenditures for food exceed the spending plan, what would you recommend be done?

7. If income proves to be less than was originally expected, what must be done with the spending plan?

8. Why is it necessary to correlate a spending plan, savings, and buying a home?

Section B

9. Why can commercial banks and savings and loan institutions pay higher interest on time deposits than on regular passbook savings accounts?

10. Suppose a young person finds it possible to save $50 a month. After 10 months this person has $500 and decides to use this amount as a down payment on an automobile. It will cost $50 a month to complete the payments on the automobile. Is this person justified in buying the automobile?

11. Many people like to keep up with the Joneses; therefore, they borrow money and buy many things on the installment plan in order to live like their neighbors and friends who may have larger incomes. What advice would you give to a person of this kind?

12. Why is a payroll savings plan a convenient way to invest in Series EE savings bonds?

13. If prices and the cost of living increase and we have inflation, how does this affect savings in a savings account or in U.S. savings bonds?

APPLICATION PROBLEMS

Section A

1. List a number of immediate (within one year) and short-range goals you have for yourself. Do these goals require money to fulfill? If so, estimate how much for each goal. Then estimate how much you would have to save each month in order to fulfill these goals.

2. Itemize a list of expenditures you make during one school year. Which of these expenditures would you classify as "fixed" expenses and which as "variable" expenses?

Section B

3. Suppose you wish to finance the purchase of a used car priced at $600. After financing charges have been added to the cost of the car, you find that you must make 12 monthly payments of $54.
   (a) How much do the financing charges cost?
   (b) If you had invested the $54 monthly for 12 months at 6% compounded semiannually, how much would you have saved at the end of the year?
   (c) If you had financed the purchase of the $600 car, what would have been the total cost of such a transaction?

4. Assume that you have been saving $1 a week for 10 years at 5¼% compounded quarterly. During these 10 years prices and the cost of living have risen 15%.
   (a) From the table on page 305, how much would your savings be after 10 years?
   (b) How much less (in dollars and cents) would your total savings buy at the end of the 10 years?

(c) After you had saved for 10 years, what effect would the 15% inflation rate have had on the total interest earned on your deposit?

(d) From these findings would you say that saving is quite risky and perhaps not worthwhile?

COMMUNITY PROJECTS

Section A

1. Using the cash spending plan and the daily cash record in this chapter as models, prepare (a) a spending plan of your own based on your past experience and (b) a daily cash record with columns that will meet your own needs. Keep a record of your income and expenditures for at least 2 months.

Section B

2. The table on page 305 illustrates regular weekly savings of $1 and annual rates of interest from 5 to 6% compounded quarterly. Inquire at a local bank and a savings and loan association to see if they can supply you with similar tables where interest is compounded more frequently (monthly or daily). From comparing these tables, what can you conclude with respect to compounded interest?

3. (a) Check with the various types of savings institutions in your community to obtain information about the interest or dividend paid by the different programs in each institution.

   (b) If you had $1,000 to put in a savings account or in United States savings bonds, where would you place the money in view of your own goals? Why?

4. Check your newspaper or latest edition of the *Statistical Abstract of the United States* in your library to see what the annual inflation rate is. Then assume you had $100 in a savings account that paid interest at 5% compounded quarterly. How was the purchasing power of your savings and interest affected by inflation?

Buying Wisely

PURPOSE OF THE CHAPTER

In a free enterprise economy, there is an abundance of goods and services for which people can spend their money. It is important, therefore, that people spend their money wisely. Spending wisely means allocating one's income so as to provide for those necessities everyone needs (food, clothing, shelter, medical care), to provide savings for emergencies, and to provide for some luxuries. This chapter will give you a few guides in buying wisely.

After studying this chapter, you will be able to:

1. Explain why buying is considered choice making.
2. Define price cycles.
3. Explain what kind of sale is a bargain.
4. Describe how advertising helps in consumer decision making.
5. Describe differences between standards, brands, and labels.

A. GENERAL GUIDES IN BUYING

Buying wisely is important to the economic well-being of the individual and the family. The following general buying guides will help you to spend your money more advantageously.

Buying Is Choice Making

Buying is always a matter of making choices. Choices must be made (a) between wants and needs, (b) between one product and another of the same kind, (c) between two entirely different kinds of products, or (d) between spending your money now or saving it.

No product is worth buying unless it is worth more to the buyer than the money spent for it. If you think carefully about every purchase you make, there will be less chance of buying unneeded and unwanted luxuries instead of filling the real needs of yourself and your family.

BEFORE YOU BUY, ASK YOURSELF THESE OR SIMILAR QUESTIONS:

1.   Do I really need it? If so, why?

2.   Is it worth the cost in terms of my effort to earn the money?

3.   Is there a better use for the money?

4.   Am I buying it to do as others do? To show off? To make someone envious? To make myself feel important?

The real needs of the average family are usually limited, but wants can be increased almost without limit. Because of high-pressure advertising and selling as well as our rising levels of living, there is a tendency on our part to want to "keep up with the Joneses." We try to tell ourselves that what actually is a luxury is instead an urgent need.

The vast majority of families do not earn enough money to enjoy unlimited purchases of luxuries. In fact, many families cannot purchase all their real needs without practicing self-restraint when buying. In the average family the tendency is to follow individual selfish urges in filling emotional wants rather than to practice individual self-restraint for the benefit of the whole family. A parent may buy something either on an emotional urge or without consulting the family. If children want something, they may spend their own money without much thought or they may put pressure on parents to buy the things they want. If family buying is considered from the point of view of unselfish group needs, most families can get the most out of their income.

A great amount of money can slip through the fingers of every member of the family in buying little things that merchants call *impulse items*. These are the little things in the nature of luxuries that sit by the cash register and are easy to pick up for 5 to 25 cents or more. Because buyers have a little money in their pockets, they buy these items on impulse (without thinking whether they need the items).

A Plan for Spending

Very few people earn so much money that they can buy all they want without considering whether they have enough money to pay for all their purchases. Therefore, a spending plan is necessary. You have just learned that a *spending plan*, or *budget*, is a guide for spending and saving. The plan will help a person to decide how much to spend and how much to save for a given period of time. When the actual spending is broken down into months and weeks, it should be checked with the spending plan to be sure that over-spending is not taking place. The spending plan may have to be changed to take care of unforeseen problems as they arise.

ADVANTAGES OF A SPENDING PLAN

1. It will help you live within your income.

2. It will help you save.

3. It will help you decide what you can and must have so that you will not spend your money for foolish things and deprive yourself of things you really need.

Quality, Economy, and Value

There are two extremes of thinking in regard to prices. One is that the highest-priced item is the best; the other is that the lowest-priced item is the best bargain. Neither viewpoint is correct. The price of an item must be related to its quality, its economy, and how it satisfies your needs and wants.

Many things determine quality for different people. For some people, beauty is what they want; for others, long-wearing economy is sought; still others want special features, such as a timer on a stove.

What is quality? It may be many things to many people. In general it is a combination of design, color, workmanship, beauty, wearing quality, and economy. The best bargain may be the product that is the best buy for the money. It could be the cheapest, but it might be the highest priced.

Service May Be Important

Price may not be the most important consideration in buying, even when buying the same product or brand of product. When buying mechanical or electrical equipment, as well as many other products, the main consideration is to obtain a product that will operate without trouble. However, when trouble occurs, you must be sure you can get good repair service.

When to Buy

The timing of purchases can be an important factor in buying wisely, for prices may vary widely at different times of the year. For example, at the beginning of a season, style goods sell at their highest prices. As the season progresses, prices are gradually lowered, since merchants hope to dispose of goods before the season's end.

There are important price cycles for many other products. For instance, in cities in which coal is used for heating purposes, it is usually sold at its lowest price in April and May and at its highest price during the winter months. If fuel oil tanks are filled in the summer, the price may be lower than in the fall.

Fresh fruits and vegetables usually sell at their cheapest prices during the summer. As one might guess, goods that are hardest to store have wide differences in price. The prices of canned goods are lowest soon after the canning season.

During periods of generally high prices, wise consumers will avoid buying anything they do not really need. Wise consumers will save their money and wait until prices are lower. Of course, families have to eat regularly. Purchases of food cannot be put off until prices fall. However, one can watch prices and buy the kinds of foods that are currently being sold at the most attractive prices.

Quantity Buying

People who buy in the smallest units usually pay more than those who buy in larger units. For example, an 8-ounce (227-gram) can might sell for 30 cents, but a 16-ounce (454-gram) can may sell for 50 cents. Besides buying in larger units, it is often possible to buy more units at a reduced price. For example, one unit might sell for $1; two for $1.80; three for $2.50. But buying more than needed or a larger size than can be used without waste is not economical.

Special Sales and Bargains

All retail stores have special sales during which prices are lower than at any other time. Some sales include standard items

One can save money by buying larger quantities and by taking advantage of bargains.

that are kept in stock regularly. Other sales are clearance sales to close out styles, models, or items at the end of the season. Some are sales of special goods brought in for the sale.

In almost every community a pattern is followed yearly by most stores, such as sales of housewares in March, school clothes in August, furniture in August, toys after Christmas. Bargains can be found and money saved by waiting for sales.

The list at the top of the next page indicates some types of sales in which one can often purchase bargains. This is especially true when merchants sell their regular merchandise at reduced prices. However, some merchants bring in special merchandise for special sales and do not reduce the price on their regular merchandise. Some of the special merchandise may be good, but it should be compared with the regular merchandise normally sold by the store.

EXAMPLES OF BARGAIN SALES

1. Remnant sales of merchandise of odd lengths, sizes, and assortments.

2. Sales of soiled goods that may be returned goods, shopworn goods, or sample merchandise.

3. Preseason sales in advance of the regular season.

4. Preinventory sales to reduce stock of merchandise on hand.

5. Out-of-season sales of merchandise left over at the close of a season.

6. Odd-lot sales of merchandise, such as irregulars or seconds.

7. Surplus stock sales resulting from overbuying of a merchant or overproduction of a manufacturer.

8. Anniversary sales as a special event to stimulate business.

9. Special seasonal sales that offer bargains in season.

Trading Stamps and Premiums

Nothing is free in this world. Somebody pays. If you receive premiums or trading stamps, the cost of these is included in the prices you pay. Buying at a certain store only because it offers premiums and stamps is a poor reason. You should check to see if you are paying fair prices on all items you purchase. *Unit pricing* is one way of checking. In unit pricing you divide the cost by the weight in grams or ounces. This gives the price per unit of weight. You then can compare the price of one product with that of another of the same kind. To check quality, consumers may read test results of many brands of products that are published by independent testing laboratories.

Usually trading stamps have a cash value of $\frac{1}{10}$ of a cent per stamp (10 stamps equal 1 cent). Thus, if a product with trading stamps costs 1 cent more per dollar purchase than the same product without stamps, you are paying for the stamps.

Buying from Discount Houses

In almost every community there are stores commonly called *discount houses* that try to sell goods at prices lower than those of anyone else. Discount houses operate in almost all fields of con-

Because of large sales volume and self-service, discount houses offer merchandise at low prices.

sumer merchandise. Sometimes these firms sell standard merchandise like that sold in other stores, but very often they sell unknown brands. Some of the brands may be good, but others may be of questionable quality. A discount house attempts to sell a great deal of merchandise at a low margin of profit in the hope that there will be a large total profit on the operations.

Some discount houses provide delivery service and repair service on equipment, but often they do not. Many times there is an extra charge for such services. If you buy a piece of equipment from a discount house, you may find it necessary to obtain service from an independent repairer. On some products you may be able to obtain the same guarantee from a discount house as from any other source.

In buying from a discount house, you should make sure that you are getting good merchandise and that the saving in price makes up for any possible lack of service.

B. SPECIFIC GUIDES IN BUYING

In order to make wise buying decisions, consumers need information and knowledge. The following specific buying guides will help you to make wise consumer decisions.

Advertising

Have you ever studied advertising in general to discover whether it is really of value to you? If it is of no value to you, then it is wasteful. If advertising is of value, you should learn how to use it wisely.

FOLLOW THESE GUIDES IN ANALYZING ADVERTISEMENTS

---

1. Do you need the item advertised?

2. What does the product contain and how is it made?

3. Is the product beneficial?

4. How economical is the product?

5. How long will the product last?

6. How does its price compare with the prices of similar products?

7. Does the item carry any seals identifying its quality or any evidence of authoritative scientific tests?

8. What proof is used to back up the statements?

9. Are there any service or maintenance problems?

10. Are any of the advertising statements evasive or misleading?

11. Does the advertisement appeal to your intelligence or your emotions?

12. Does the advertisement make you feel confident that, if you buy, you will be a satisfied customer?

Advertisements should be studied from two points of view: (1) for information about the product, and (2) for deceptive or misleading statements. Some advertisements are neither informative nor deceptive. They are simply evasive or general, or they merely appeal to the emotions. The intelligent consumer will look for helpful information. Learn to recognize the difference between emotional appeals and rational appeals. Learn to evaluate testimonials about products to distinguish facts from false or misleading statements.

From a consumer's point of view, an advertisement may be considered to be good if it provides facts in regard to quality, standards, specifications, performance, and uses. It cannot be consid-

---

THE VALUE OF ADVERTISING IN GENERAL

A study of the following questions should indicate how useful advertising is to consumers.

1. Could you get all the information you want about the latest automobile without referring to advertisements?

2. What facts and other information about the latest developments in home appliances and equipment have you obtained through advertising?

3. What can be learned about foods from newspaper advertisements?

4. What new products have you learned about through advertising in the past two years?

5. What information of an educational nature about health, recreation, or sanitation have you received through advertising?

6. If all home appliances were sold without trade names and trademarks, how would you select them?

7. If canned foods did not carry labels and trademarks, how could you select canned goods wisely?

8. How do you benefit by reading the advertisements of local stores?

9. How is attendance at your school events, such as plays, athletic contests, and operettas, promoted? Is advertising involved?

---

ered to be good if it fails to provide this information and instead appeals only to the emotions.

A more detailed discussion of advertising from the point of view of the consumer is given in Chapter 21.

Brand Names

A *brand name* or *trademark* is used for one purpose: to encourage people to ask for the product again after using it the first time. Without information that would permit comparison, the recognized brands of reputable producers are often more reliable than other brands. If other information is available, however, the brand on a product should not be used as the only means of comparison.

Brand names or trademarks, however, can be important guides for a consumer. Once you have tried a certain product, you can ask for the same brand again with reasonable assurance that you will get the same quality as before. Reputable manufacturers try to

By means of brand names, consumers are able to purchase the same brand again and again and be reasonably certain that each time the quality will be the same as before.

maintain standards for products carrying their brand names. Nearly all products carry a brand name now, but some branded products are not reliable. The manufacturers do not try to maintain standards, and quality may vary greatly from time to time. However, the manufacturer who advertises a product intensively with the idea of building a reputation for the brand usually tries to maintain a satisfactory standard.

Trial use is an important means of buying any product. This is true whether it is trial use from a sample, trial of merchandise bought by a friend, or trial use from a small purchase before making a large purchase.

Standards

Imagine trying to get along without standards. A *standard* is a unit of measure. A pound or a gram is a measure of weight. A foot or a meter is a measure of distance or length. A gallon or a liter is a measure of liquids. How would we buy coffee, or fabrics, or milk without these standards of quantity? How could prices be set? How could you indicate how much of a product you want?

There are other standards too. We identify the size of a shirt by neckband size and sleeve length; shoes, by length and width; and some articles, such as hats and sometimes dresses, by arbitrary numbers. Other kinds of standards pertain to performance, such as the octane rating of gasoline or the heat units, known as British thermal units (Btu's), in coal.

A standard ordinarily is thought of as a measure of quantity, weight, or extent, and sometimes of quality. A standard for consumer goods is usually a definition that states fully what the measuring stick is.

Grades

With the exception of foods, standards usually define a single level of quality of a satisfactory product. A drug, for example, either complies with the formula of the official United States Pharmacopeia, which is known as the USP standard, or it does not. There are no degrees of conformance to the drug standard. But when applied to foods, standards often are established to define several levels of quality, each of which is known as a grade. For example, there are four grades of butter, each of which is defined by a standard. A *grade*, then, is a term applied to standards of quality when more than one quality of a particular food is defined. The federal government agencies sometimes refer to the definitions as *standards of identity*, because the definition describes or identifies the standard or grade so that it is recognizable.

Labels

Back in the days when practically all food, clothing, and other necessities were prepared and made in the home, there was little need for standards and grades. Consumers purchased raw materials from which to make the things they needed. Processed goods and ready-made clothes were practically unknown. Purchasers could see what they were buying and even taste food before buying. There were few choices to make, for the merchant usually had only one kind of coffee, shoes, or furniture for sale.

Most of the food, drugs, clothing, and other things we buy are finished products and ready to be used. Thus, merchants keep in stock a variety of each kind of product from which we choose the one that appeals to us. Many goods, such as food and drugs, are in cans or otherwise packaged so that we do not actually see them until we use them. Standards and grades thus are very important to modern consumers. Standards indicate to us what the product really is, what it is made of, and what its characteristics are. If there are several qualities of a product, such as there are in foods, grades indicate the level of the quality.

A *label* is a written statement attached to an article or a product describing its main characteristics. Standards and grades, as

Study the labels and identify standards and grades. A label must be truthful, and a standard requires the contents to be as labeled.

well as other information of importance to consumers, may be indicated on the label. Consumers should learn to recognize standards and grades. Consumers should carefully read the labels on merchandise to learn the characteristics of the goods that they are thinking of buying.

Informative Labeling. Good informative labels can provide the kind of information one wants and needs for the selection of products. Good labeling gives not only quality standards and grades but also important facts that you, as a consumer, may want.

Informative labeling applies to many products, including appliances, clothing, and fabrics. In the case of fabrics, there are various terms used to indicate shrinkage, such as "preshrunk." If this term is used, the fabric should not shrink more than 2%. Other information on fabrics and clothing may indicate the type of fiber used, the weave, the water repellency, the finish, the crease resistance, and the proper method for cleaning.

Industry Standards for Informative Labeling. Some canners and distributors have developed a more descriptive type of labeling that they believe is better for the consumer than the A, B, C, or other grade labeling. It is often referred to as *descriptive labeling*. Descriptive labels for foods, for instance, would contain such information as: (a) style of the pack; (b) degree of maturity of the food; (c) number of units in the can, such as the number of halves of peaches; (d) quantity in terms of weight (ounces or grams or liters); (e) quantity in terms of servings; (f) size of the can; (g) description of the raw product and the method of processing; (h) suggested methods or ways of serving.

Government Requirements for Informative Labeling. In recent years the federal government has required some definite labeling practices that are meant to help the consumer. For example, if a food product claims or uses the words nutrition or nutrient, the manufacturer must display nutrition information on

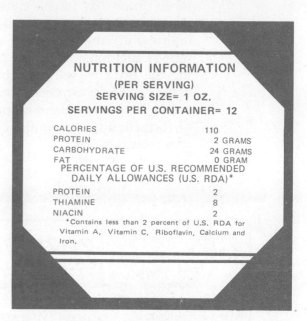

Minimum Information That Must Appear on a Nutrition Label

NUTRITION INFORMATION
(PER SERVING)
SERVING SIZE= 1 OZ.
SERVINGS PER CONTAINER= 12

CALORIES	110
PROTEIN	2 GRAMS
CARBOHYDRATE	24 GRAMS
FAT	0 GRAM

PERCENTAGE OF U.S. RECOMMENDED
DAILY ALLOWANCES (U.S. RDA)*

PROTEIN	2
THIAMINE	8
NIACIN	2

*Contains less than 2 percent of U.S. RDA for Vitamin A, Vitamin C, Riboflavin, Calcium and Iron.

A Label May Include Optional Listings for Cholesterol, Fats, and Sodium

NUTRITION INFORMATION
(PER SERVING)
SERVING SIZE= 8OZ.
SERVINGS PER CONTAINER= 1

CALORIES	560	FAT (PERCENT OF	
PROTEIN	23 G	CALORIES, 53%)	33 G
CARBOHYDRATE	43 G	POLYUNSAT-	
		URATED	2 G
		SATURATED	9 G
		CHOLESTEROL*	
		(20 MG/100 G)	40 MG
		SODIUM	
		(365 MG/100 G)	830 MG

PERCENTAGE OF U.S. RECOMMENDED
DAILY ALLOWANCES (U.S. RDA)

PROTEIN	35	RIBOFLAVIN	15
VITAMIN A	35	NIACIN	25
VITAMIN C		CALCIUM	2
(ASCORBIC ACID)	10	IRON	25
THIAMINE			
(VITAMIN B1)	15		

*Information on fat and cholesterol content is provided for individuals who, on the advice of a physician, are modifying their total dietary intake of fat and cholesterol

the labels. Such information must include size and number of servings in the container; number of calories and grams of protein, carbohydrates, and fat in each serving; and the amount (or absence) of seven required vitamins (vitamins A and C, thiamine, riboflavin, niacin, calcium, and iron) per serving. Auto manufacturers must list for all new cars the Environmental Protection Agency's (EPA) average miles per gallon rating for both city and highway driving. For room air conditioners, the energy efficiency ratio (EER) must be on the label. This ratio (determined by dividing the Btu's by watts) enables the consumer to compare various brands of room air conditioners in order to make the best buy in saving both energy and money. More and more requirements will be forthcoming to help the consumer. Be on the lookout for these new requirements.

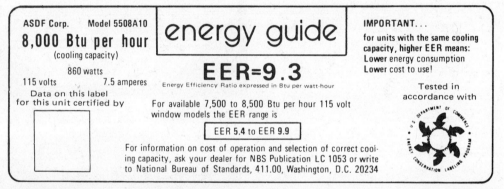

EER for this imaginary model is 9.3 (largest figure). This model has cooling capacity of 8,000 Btu's per hour (upper left). Since room air conditioners are classified by their Btu range, this model can be compared with other 115-volt models that offer 7,500 to 8,500 Btu's per hour (2 lines below EER). EERs for all 115-volt models in this class range from 5.4 to 9.9 (figures in box); thus, this model has high efficiency rating. The range for each class is different.

How to Read Commerce Dept. Efficiency Tag

Trade Names and Terms. There are many trade names and terms used in the labeling of various products. Most of these names and terms are not meant to be deceptive or misleading. However, they are confusing unless a person knows what they mean and knows something about the difference in quality. For instance, stainless steel is a general term used to identify a steel

Labels provide important descriptive information.

In 1964 we introduced this consumer guide to buying clothes made of 100% wool.

PURE WOOL ®

The sewn-in Woolmark.

It's been a best-seller from the start. Millions and millions of Americans have seen it and believed in it in suits, coats, dresses, trousers, jackets and lots of other places. It was their assurance of a 100% pure wool product that had been tested by The Wool Bureau for fiber content, color-fastness and more. And inspected for quality of workmanship. It still is.

Source: *The Cincinnati Enquirer,* April 23, 1976.

alloy that will not tarnish as easily as ordinary steel, but there are many qualities of stainless steel.

Let us consider a few other common examples. Wool cloth may be made from all virgin wool, reprocessed wool, reused wool, or a mixture of these with some other fibers. Parchment paper and parchment lamp shades are very seldom made of sheepskin; they are usually made of paper. Chinaware usually does not come from China; the word designates a type of clay from which the pottery is made. The product may or may not be better than a similar product made in China. Silverware is not sterling silver but usually plated ware. Sterling silver is solid silver.

How to Read the Label. The buyer should read labels carefully to obtain information with regard to (a) the weight or the volume, (b) the grade or the quality, and (c) an analysis or a description of the contents. The labels of some private agencies have been discussed previously.

Until uniform grade standards are established and used for a particular product, it is impossible to rely upon the existing grade designations without knowing what those grades mean. Much of the terminology in use means one thing to the seller but a different thing to the buyer. If buyers take a designation at its face value, they are sometimes misled into believing the goods to be of a grade higher than they actually are. Furthermore, the terminology is made confusing by the wide range in its use. In other words, buyers and sellers do not speak the same language. When this situation exists, grade designations are of very little value.

For instance, one would suppose that the "first" grade of butter is the best grade, but as a matter of fact it is the third grade when compared with government standards. To get the best grade of butter, one has to buy the "AA" grade. Similar confusing grades are used for other products.

The partial label shown below illustrates the type of information that a consumer may find on a good label. Consumers should learn to use such helpful labels. To do so may encourage other producers and distributors to use equally informative labels.

GRADE A LARGE SWEET PEAS

An Example of Specifications and Information on a Food Label

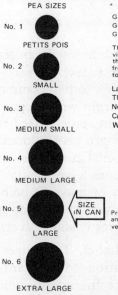

REGULATION
PEA SIZES

No. 1

PETITS POIS

No. 2

SMALL

No. 3

MEDIUM SMALL

No. 4

MEDIUM LARGE

No. 5 — SIZE IN CAN

LARGE

No. 6

EXTRA LARGE

Comparative grading as defined by Agricultural Marketing Service, U.S. Department of Agriculture

GRADE A..........Country Club Quality........Scores 90/100 points
GRADE B....................................Scores 75/89 points
GRADE C....................................Scores 60/74 points

These are Grade A Large Sweet Peas (No.5) packed just a few hours off the vine. Because Country Club Grade A Peas are rushed from vine to can, they retain their excellent flavor, tenderness and color. The peas in this can are from a lot that has been sampled and tested by accepted methods, and found to be Grade A quality.

Large Sweet Peas, No. 5 Sieve, Sweet variety.
This is a No. 2 can.
Net Contents—1 Lb. 4 Oz. Peas and Liquid.
Can contains about 2¼ cups drained peas, ¾ cup liquid
Will yield five to six average servings.

CREAMED DRIED BEEF AND PEAS ON TOAST

1 cup Country Club Grade A Large Sweet Peas, drained
¼ cup Kroger Butter
¼ cup Country Club Flour
1 cup Country Club Evaporated Milk diluted with equal quantity liquid drained from peas
½ pound dried beef, chopped
Dash Sudan Pepper

Prepare white sauce from butter, flour and liquid. Pour hot water over beef and drain immediately. Add beef and peas to sauce, stirring carefully to prevent mashing peas. Serve hot on toasted Clock Bread. Yield: 5 to 6 servings.

Many products, including food products, sold in stores today do not carry information in regard to standards or grades; but many labels, particularly on foods, do contain certain helpful information. This information can be relied on to be generally truthful and accurate.

The contents indicated on labels are also important, since the size of the container is frequently misleading. Deceptive containers are now illegal if the products are sold in interstate commerce. In examining a label, one should look for the following information:

1. Specific descriptive statements.
2. Facts regarding quality.
3. Facts regarding quantity.
4. Grades or other similar designations.
5. Certificate or other mark of approval or guarantee.
6. Instructions for proper use and care.
7. Warnings.

Generic Labeling

A number of supermarkets stock their shelves with nonbrand labeled items such as canned goods, detergents and cleansers, and paper products. Nonbranded labeling is also called *generic labeling*. These labels are easily identified by their plain white wrappers, single-color printing, and lack of a company name. Often these products are not uniformly graded. For example, a can of sweet peas may contain several sizes, not just one uniform size. However, information pertaining to nutrition will appear on the label. Since the manufacturer, canner, and assembler do not have to worry about grading, selecting, and maintaining a public image, they can sell these generic products much cheaper. It is not uncommon to save as much as 20% on many grocery items that carry the generic label.

Cash and Credit Buying

Buying on the installment plan may allow you to have what you want earlier than if you pay cash, but installment buying costs more than cash buying. If you can save and wait to pay cash, you can get more for your money.

FACTS EVERYONE SHOULD KNOW ABOUT BUYING

1. Buying is a matter of making many kinds of choices.

2. Determine your needs and shop to fill those needs rather than to satisfy impulses.

3. Buying should be based on a spending plan.

4. Some advertising is misleading, some is helpful and informative, and some is meaningless.

5. Advertising should be studied carefully as a guide in buying.

6. Some standards are measures of size, weight, and distance; others are used to measure quality.

7. Informative labels give information about standards, grade, content, and other characteristics of goods.

8. Consumers should learn what standards and grades mean.

REVIEW QUESTIONS

Section A

1. What is the difference between wants and needs?
2. What is impulse buying? Identify some items that one might buy on impulse.
3. What should be the relationship between a spending plan and buying?
4. What are some of the factors that determine quality in a product?
5. For what types of products are service, repairs, and maintenance very important?
6. As a season progresses, why do merchants gradually reduce the prices of their seasonal merchandise?
7. What are some examples of merchandise that may be sold at high prices or at low prices, depending on the time of the year?
8. Is quantity buying always a good practice? Explain.
9. What are some examples of true bargain sales?
10. How should you determine whether you should buy where trading stamps are given?
11. What is a discount house?
12. What two important points should one consider when buying merchandise from a discount house?

Section B

13. What are some examples of how advertising is of general value to you?
14. What suggestions do you offer as a guide in helping you to analyze advertisements?
15. Are brand names of any value in buying merchandise?
16. What is a standard?
17. What is a grade as applied to a product?
18. What type of information should one expect to obtain from a good informative label?

19. How is it possible to get more for your money by saving until you can pay cash rather than buying earlier on the installment plan?
20. What is generic labeling?

DISCUSSION QUESTIONS

Section A

1. In making a choice between one product and another of the same kind, could you turn a need into a want simply by making the wrong choice? Give an example.
2. How can a considerable amount of money be spent and possibly wasted by a family on the purchase of impulse items?
3. How is it possible for the highest priced item to be the best bargain? Give an example.
4. How can you save money by quantity buying if you have the money or the credit to do so?
5. What do you think of the practice of buying at discount houses?

Section B

6. Describe a recent advertisement you saw that you feel was informative. What are your reasons?
7. Describe a recent advertisement you saw that you feel was deceptive and not informative. What are your reasons?
8. Assume that you went into a strange grocery store for the purpose of buying peas and found on the shelf two brands of peas, one of which was well known to you and the other not known. What procedure would you follow in buying? Why?
9. From the viewpoint of the buyer, what are some of the advantages and disadvantages of brands or trade names?
10. What are some grades and descriptions of products you have seen that have meant nothing to you?
11. What are some of the arguments for and against informative or descriptive labeling without fixed standards for grades?

APPLICATION PROBLEMS

Section A

1. For your birthday your parents have agreed to buy you a hand electronic calculator for your school work. You have been looking at various models and have narrowed your choice to two. One has an 8-digit answer display; operates on 2 pen light batteries; adds, subtracts, multiplies, divides; and has a constant (repeat) key as well as a memory recall button. This model sells for $29.95. The other model can do all the same arithmetic functions as the first model. In addition, it has a 10-digit answer display, can operate on either batteries or household current, and can extract square roots and square numbers automatically. This model sells for $69.95. Which of the two models would you recommend that your parents buy for you? Justify your recommendation.
2. Leslie Cardona, a high school student, has signed up 12 customers during the summer months to keep their lawns mowed and trimmed at an average of $5 a lawn. Each lawn will need to be mowed at least 12 times before school starts in September. The old lawn mower, a $40, 18-inch rotary, 2½ h.p. engine, is only two years old but is already causing consid-

erable trouble. Leslie is trying to decide between buying another power mower similar to the old one or a $100, 20-inch rotary, self-propelled, 3½ h.p. engine mower with a grass catcher attachment. Which would be a better buy for Leslie? Why?

3. Make a record of the number of items of an impulse nature you buy for one week. Keep an account of the nature of each impulse item as well as the cost of each. Without identifying any student with a particular list, compile all lists and make a bulletin board display of the variety of impulse items bought by the class, the total money spent on each item, and the grand total spent by the class members for one week. Prepare some statements or conclusions the class can draw from this information and add these statements to your display.

Section B

4. Bring to class examples of advertising that appeal to your emotions and examples of advertising that appeal to your common sense and needs. Some examples may include both types of appeals, for example toothpaste that includes brighteners (emotion) and fluoride (common sense and need). Discuss these examples in class.

5. Check 3 different brands of room air conditioners that operate on 115 volts of household current to determine which brand has the highest energy efficiency rating (EER). The higher the EER rating, the greater are the savings in energy usage and cost of operation. If the manufacturers have failed to list the EER rating, then calculate the rating by dividing the Btu's per hour by the watts used to operate the air conditioner.

COMMUNITY PROJECTS

Section A

1. From your school library or city library, check one year's edition (January through December) of *Changing Times* or a consumer magazine to see which foods for each month are considered the best buys for those months. Prepare a poster with two columns. In one column list the foods considered best buys for each month, and in the second column list reasons why you feel the magazine editors listed these particular foods.

2. Compare price and service agreements for two identical products (for example, a television set and a portable tape player) sold at a discount house and at a regular appliance store. Determine which place of business offers the better buy. Give your reasons.

3. Compare prices of a number of identical products at a store that gives trading stamps versus a store that does not. Group your products into two lists. One list would be for products that cost no more with stamps than without stamps. The stamps would be a true premium for products on this list. The second list would be for those products where the consumer is paying for the stamps. Indicate for each item on this second list how much the consumer is paying for the stamps. (Remember, if the product costs even one cent more on the dollar, the consumer is paying the cash value of the stamps.)

Section B

4. Prepare a bulletin board display using labels from foods and clothing in which you point out the important information consumers need to know about the products. The display should be constructed in two parts, one

display showing good labels that give the consumer considerable information, the other showing poor labels that provide the consumer with insufficient information.

5. Check a local supermarket that stocks nonbranded grocery items. Select 10 or 12 items (canned goods, detergents and cleansers, and paper products) and make a 3-way price comparison (generic label, supermarket's own brand, a national brand) on these products. Be careful that your price comparisons are based on the same quantity of the product (you may have to resort to unit pricing). Set up your findings for bulletin board display similar to the example below.

Product	Nonbrand Price	Supermarket's Brand Price	National Brand Price
Green Beans (16 oz — 454 g)	28¢	33¢	35¢

Summary

Total savings — Nonbrand over Supermarket's Brand _____%

Total savings — Nonbrand over National Brand _____%

Total savings — Supermarket's Brand over National Brand _____%

18 Understanding and Using Credit

PURPOSE OF THE CHAPTER

Credit is used by business and industry in the production and distribution of goods and services. Credit is used by consumers in buying the goods and services provided by business firms. The American family uses many forms of credit primarily to improve its level of living. The development of a variety of good sources of credit, combined with the improved judgment of consumers, has led to the current widespread use of consumer credit. The purpose of this chapter is to help you understand credit, its importance to you, and how to use it most wisely.

After studying this chapter, you will be able to:

1. Explain how credit may help to shape a family's growth and financial security.
2. Identify the common forms of consumer credit.
3. Explain what qualifies one to use credit.
4. State the economic problems of the use of credit.

A. ESSENTIALS OF CREDIT

The United States has been called a credit economy because the use of credit is so widespread. If we are to have a sound economy, we must understand credit and use it wisely.

Importance of Credit

Credit is a vital force in our economy. It is of economic and social importance to every family and business organization. Credit was first used in business transactions to make barter (the exchange of goods for goods) more flexible. Credit was used before the existence of money. The custom of charging interest began early, and the cost of credit is something that has been reckoned with in all of recorded history.

In Chapter 14 we learned that *credit* means an advance (or loan) of money with which to buy goods and services. Credit can also mean an advance of goods and services in exchange for a promise to pay at a later date. The use of credit by consumers is similar to its use by government units and by private businesses. Whenever an immediate need for cash, goods, or services is met through the proper use of credit, the economy of the nation is strengthened and the level of living is raised. The immediate need is actually met because of the faith one person has in the honesty and responsibility of another — faith that the debt will be repaid at maturity or that each installment payment on the debt will be paid as it becomes due.

Credit first became important in the United States when people needed cash to help them meet financial emergencies for which they were unprepared. More recently, its importance has increased as people have used the installment plan as a means of adjusting the high and low points that develop in their spending patterns. This is illustrated in the purchase of an automobile with a rather high price tag which is paid over a period of many months in small payments.

Similarly, the installment plan is used in the purchase of insurance when an individual pays monthly, semiannual, or annual premiums throughout a lifetime. This lets the person have a large amount of protection from the very beginning of the life of the

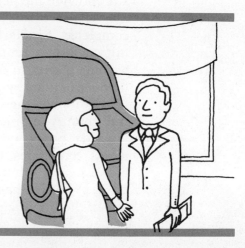

By spreading the payment of costly purchases over many months, credit can adjust the high and low points in spending.

policy. Insurance premiums are based on the past experience of large groups who have shared risks. Thus, it is possible to determine accurately the amount of the installment payments or premiums that an individual must pay to maintain proper financial protection.

Since the late 1940s, the widespread use of long-term credit by families in buying homes has been very important to the national economy. Throughout this nation, concern is felt whenever consumer resistance to the use of credit tends to slow down the buying of automobiles, homes, and other major items.

Short-Term Consumer Credit

In general, *consumer credit* is debt that is incurred by a consumer for a home, goods, or services for personal and family use. For certain purposes, however, consumer credit is made up of debts for goods and services for personal and family use having a maturity of less than five years. The Federal Reserve Board classifies debts such as these as *short-term credit* and *intermediate-term credit*. A debt on an owner-occupied home that is financed by a long-term loan backed by a real estate mortgage is not always considered to be consumer credit. Debt incurred for repair or modernization of an owner-occupied home usually matures within one to five years and, therefore, is classified as consumer credit.

It is interesting to note that many consumer transactions that involve cash rather than credit actually are forms of "credit-in-reverse." For example, when one travels on a bus, the ticket is bought prior to beginning the ride. The bus company must thereafter provide the person with transportation, and considerable time may elapse before the trip and the credit transactions are finally completed. Similarly, when consumers pay in advance for school tuition, house rent, vacation tours, and layaway purchases, they become parties in the use of reverse forms of credit. This is credit that is extended by the purchaser rather than the seller.

Obviously, the large credit needs of salary and wage earners in this country are met through the use of many forms of credit. Retail merchants, commercial and industrial banks, consumer finance companies, sales finance companies, credit unions, pawnbrokers, and others help consumers use the different forms of credit. With its many aspects and in its many forms, credit is truly one of the important tools of money management used by consumers.

Installment Debt. Debts on which payments are to be made at periodic intervals are known as *installment debts* or *installment credit*. Such consumer debts may arise from purchases of goods and services for personal and family use or from obtaining loans for the payment of such purchases. Much installment credit involves arrangements between consumers and retail merchants for purchases of automobiles and other consumer goods. A smaller part of total installment credit consists of cash loans from commercial banks, credit unions, sales finance companies, and consumer finance companies. The money borrowed is used to buy goods, to meet emergencies, and to consolidate debts.

CONSUMER INSTALLMENT DEBT
IN THE UNITED STATES
May, 1979
(Millions of Dollars)

Automobile debt	$109,161
Mobile home debt	16,453
Revolving debt:	
Commercial banks	25,052
Retailers	17,898
Gasoline companies	3,537
All other	115,494
Total installment debt	$287,595

Source: *Federal Reserve Bulletin* (July, 1979).

Every installment contract sets forth the specific terms of the purchase. Included in the terms are: (1) the amount of the down payment, (2) dates and amounts of future payments, (3) finance charges, and (4) the protection to the seller in case payments are not made as scheduled. Under the Uniform Commercial Code the seller is protected beyond the general right to sue the buyer for the purchase price by a security agreement. A *security agreement* is a written statement signed by the buyer indicating that the seller has rights to repossession as well as rights to sue for the purchase price. This signed agreement must also include a general description of the article being sold. Thus, most installment sales are called *secured credit sales* because of this written, signed security agreement. In a secured credit sale the possession and risk of loss pass to the buyer. However, the seller has a security interest in the article until it has been paid for in full. A copy of a retail installment contract and security agreement is shown on page 340.

Contract # *1402*

Seller's Name: *HOWARD'S HOUSEHOLD APPLIANCES*

INDIANAPOLIS, INDIANA

RETAIL INSTALLMENT CONTRACT AND SECURITY AGREEMENT

The undersigned (herein called Purchaser, whether one or more) purchases from *HOWARD'S APPLIANCES* (seller) and grants to *HIM* a security interest in, subject to the terms and conditions hereof, the following described property.

PURCHASER'S NAME *MR. ROBERT M. WEAVER*

PURCHASER'S ADDRESS *7234 N. COLLEGE AVE.*

CITY *INDIANAPOLIS* STATE *IN.*

ZIP *46224*

QUANTITY	DESCRIPTION	AMOUNT	
1	GAS COMBINATION	295	00
	CLOTHES WASHER		
	AND DRYER		

Description of Trade-in:

Sales Tax	5	90
Total	300	90

1. CASH PRICE — $*295 00*
2. LESS: CASH DOWN PAYMENT $ *30.00*
3. TRADE-IN _____
4. TOTAL DOWN PAYMENT *30.00* $ *30.00*
5. UNPAID BALANCE OF CASH PRICE — $*265.00*
6. OTHER CHARGES:
   SALES TAX $ *5.90*
   CREDIT LIFE INSURANCE *2.00*
7. AMOUNT FINANCED — $*272.90*
8. FINANCE CHARGE — $ *49.12*
9. TOTAL OF PAYMENTS — $*322.02*
10. DEFERRED PAYMENT PRICE (1 + 6 + 8) — $*352.02*
11. ANNUAL PERCENTAGE RATE *18* %

Insurance Agreement

The purchase of insurance coverage is voluntary and not required for credit. (Type of ins.) insurance coverage is at a cost of $ *2.00* for the term of credit.

I desire insurance coverage

Signed *Robert Weaver* Date *1/8/80*

I do not desire insurance coverage

Signed _____ Date _____

Purchaser hereby agrees to pay to *HOWARD'S HOUSEHOLD APPLIANCES* at their offices shown above the "TOTAL OF PAYMENTS" shown above in *12* monthly installments of $*26.83* (final payment to be $*26.89*) the first installment being payable *FEB. 8* 19 *80*, and all subsequent installments on the same day of each consecutive month until paid in full. The finance charge applies from *1/8/80*

Signed *Robert M. Weaver*

Notice to Buyer: You are entitled to a copy of the contract you sign. You have the right to pay in advance the unpaid balance of this contract and obtain a partial refund of the finance charge based on the "Actuarial Method." [Any other method of computation may be so identified, for example, "Rule of 78's," "Sum of the Digits," etc.]

Retail Installment Contract and Security Agreement

Noninstallment Debt. Debts for which the full payment is to be made in a single payment at a stated maturity date are known as *noninstallment debts* or *noninstallment credit*. A single-payment cash loan may be made to a consumer by a commercial bank, pawnbroker, savings and loan association, or private lender for any one of many good reasons. About one third of all noninstallment credit is in the form of single-payment loans. Also, noninstallment credit is used by consumers whenever they arrange to make a single payment for goods charged at a retail store; for gas, electric, or telephone service; or for a hospital, medical, or other similar debt. Less than 20% of all consumer credit is in the form of noninstallment debt. Over 80% is in the form of installment debt.

B. CHARGE ACCOUNTS

More and more charge accounts and service accounts are being used by consumers. Billions of dollars of credit each year are used in this manner.

The Charge Account

Many stores and business firms sell merchandise through a *charge account* or *open account*. This means that at the time of the sale the title to the merchandise passes to the purchaser. The store accepts the customer's promise to pay for it later, usually within 30 days. The customer is required to sign the sales slip as proof that the merchandise has been received.

A *service account* is similar to a charge account except that the charges made to it are for services rendered, such as legal or medical service.

The privilege of charging purchases may be withdrawn by a business firm at any time the customer fails to pay the amount owed. A brief summary of the advantages of a charge account to a customer appears at the top of the next page.

A charge account may be a disadvantage for persons who have a tendency to spend beyond their income or ability to pay.

Credit Terms

No down payment is required for purchases through a charge or open account. The time allowed between the date of purchase on a charge account and the date the payment is due is the length

---

ADVANTAGES OF CHARGE ACCOUNT TO CUSTOMERS

1. A charge account represents a very convenient and simple way to buy.

2. Payment for purchases may be delayed until a future stated time.

3. A record of purchases is made automatically.

4. Money is not needed at the time of purchase; therefore, the danger of loss while shopping is minimized.

5. Charge accounts make it easy to order merchandise by mail or telephone.

6. Salespeople and owners may learn to know a charge customer, which may result in better service.

7. The privilege of charging purchases adds to one's prestige.

8. Payment for several purchases may be made at one time.

---

of the *credit term*. The usual credit term for charge accounts is 30 days; however, it may be for a different period of time. A charge account usually carries no service charge. The customer is expected to pay the full amount that was charged at the end of each credit term. In most stores, if this part of the bargain is not fulfilled, a service charge is made on the past-due balance and added on at the next billing. In most states the charge is 1½% for each 30 days that the debt is past due. Thus, when a consumer postpones payment of a debt, the cost of that credit is at the rate of 18% a year.

Under a plan known as *cycle billing*, the balance owed by a certain customer falls due regularly on a certain day of the month regardless of the date of the last purchase. This means that a bill for a purchase made late in a customer's credit month becomes due in much less than 30 days. Some stores use cycle billing because it spreads the work of preparing monthly statements over an entire month, since certain groups of customers are billed each day during the month.

Types of Charge Accounts

Many types of charge accounts are available to the consumer. They operate on the same general principles but differ in details. Some of the most common types of charge accounts are discussed on the next page.

Regular Charge Account. Under the *regular charge account* plan, many retailers provide customers who have been approved for credit with 30-day, interest-free charge accounts. The customers are expected to pay their accounts in full on receipt of their bills or within a stated number of days from the billing date. Large retailers often provide regular charge account customers with an identifying charge plate for convenience in making charge purchases. Such a plate may be the store's own plate, which can be used only at that store. Or it may be a plate, such as "Charga-Plate" or "Shopper's Plate," that can be used in several participating stores.

Revolving Charge Account. The *revolving charge account* is in common use in some cities. Under this plan, payment for purchases may be extended to 4, 5, or 6 months. The consumer and the store representative determine at the time the account is opened the maximum amount that may be owed to the store at any one time. To illustrate the revolving charge account, let us assume that the maximum amount that may be owed is set at $300 and that the store will allow the consumer a maximum of 6 months to pay for purchases. Equal monthly payments of $50 ($300 ÷ 6 months) are to be made whenever there is an unpaid balance in the account at the end of a month. New purchases to be charged to the account may be made at any time so long as the total amount owed by the consumer does not go over the maximum of $300. Usually a service charge of 1½% of the unpaid balance is charged each month for this type of account, amounting to 18% a year.

Budget Charge Account. A *budget charge account* is a system of credit under which regular purchases can be made. Payments must be made in monthly installments based on the size of the account balance (examples: $10 monthly on a $40 account balance; $20 monthly on an $80 account balance). Interest is charged on the monthly balance.

Divided Charge Account. One charge account plan permits a consumer to charge a large item such as a refrigerator or a living room suite and then pay one third of the cost in each of the succeeding 3 months. This plan is known as a *divided charge account*. Often no service charge is added for the final 2 months.

Credit-Bank Plan. Also called instant credit, this is a type of charge account in which the bank issues a credit card (such as Master Charge and VISA) which the customer can use at participating businesses. The business firms send all bills to the bank, which in turn sends the customer one bill for total monthly purchases. Some bank credit cards can be used to obtain instant loans up to a limited amount at the bank or at one of its automatic bank teller facilities.

In many instances life insurance premiums may be paid in the same way. The policyholder authorizes the insurance company to send a draft to the bank at regular intervals (usually monthly) for payment. The policyholder also authorizes the bank to pay these drafts when received. When paid, the canceled draft is returned to the policyholder so that the amount can be deducted from the checkbook balance. The policyholder enjoys an economic advantage in such a plan as the insurance company charges a slightly lower premium for authorized payments of this kind.

Credit Cards

A *credit card* is issued by some business firms, such as banks, oil companies, restaurants, hotels, airlines, railroads, and telephone companies. The card identifies a customer when he or she is traveling. This lets the customer charge purchases of goods and services even though the customer is not known in the city where the purchase is made. There is no charge for most of these credit cards. The credit card companies bill their customers monthly, and the customers are expected to pay the entire amount upon receipt of the statement or within 25 days of the billing date. If for some reason the full amount cannot be paid, the company will add on a service charge of 1% to 1½%. This charge must be paid along with the unpaid balance at the next monthly billing date. Two of the best-known, all-purpose credit cards controlled by banks are Master Charge and VISA (BankAmericard).

Other organizations issue the more general-use type of credit card. For example, the American Express Company issues a credit card that permits a person carrying this card to charge meals, hotel rooms, flowers, gifts, auto rentals, and other services. The bills are sent to the American Express, which sends a monthly bill for all purchases to the person holding the credit card. For combining the charges, collecting from the consumer, sending payments to the sellers, and absorbing losses from the few nonpayers, the American Express takes a discount from the business organizations. The card-holding consumer pays an annual fee of $20. A similar plan is operated by the Diner's Club and by Standard Oil with its Torch Club card.

Credit cards are convenient substitutes for cash.

Cost of Charge Accounts

Selling on credit adds extra cost to every sale. The principal extra costs result from: (a) the clerical work necessary for recording sales and collecting accounts, (b) loss of interest on the money that is invested in accounts receivable from customers, (c) losses due to bad debts, and (d) the greater tendency of charge customers to return goods for exchange.

Merchants who sell on open account may be classified as follows: (1) those who have uniform prices for credit sales and for cash sales; (2) those who charge more for credit sales than for cash sales.

Some stores set their sales prices high enough to cover the cost of charge accounts; others use a two-price system, one for cash sales and one for sales on account. Let us assume that a television set is priced at $159.95 cash or $164.95 if charged, payable in 30 days. The actual cost of charging the purchase to the customer's account is $5. This means that the customer is paying $5 for the use of $159.95 for 30 days. This is an annual rate of interest of 37½%.

Stores that fail to investigate a customer's ability to pay before charging sales to the account are apt to have high losses from failure to collect debts. One may well expect to find high prices in stores that recklessly advertise generous credit terms to everyone. Stores that have sound credit policies have practically no losses from bad debts. We need not assume, therefore, that a merchant who sells on credit must necessarily sell at higher prices than a merchant who sells for cash. If selling on credit increases sales, the total overhead cost of each sale may actually be decreased. On the other hand, the costs of selling on credit are reported by some stores to be as much as 6% to 8% higher than the costs of selling for cash. Also, stores that regularly sell on credit often provide delivery services and other conveniences. These services, combined with possible higher costs due to charge accounts, may cause the store to sell at higher prices than a cash-and-carry store.

C. USING CREDIT

At one time or another almost everyone needs to use credit. Thus, it is important that we can get credit when it is needed.

Establishing a Credit Standing

Our *credit standing* or *credit worthiness* is an indication of our ability to secure goods, services, and money in return for a promise to pay. It represents our ability to incur debts because some lender trusts us. A favorable credit standing does not come automatically. It comes as the result of slow growth. It must be nurtured, fostered, strengthened, and improved. It is an asset of tremendous value to those who develop it over a long period of years. It can be destroyed easily; it is sensitive to abuse; and it usually continues only as long as it is justified. A favorable credit standing over a period of time is enjoyed only by persons who deserve it and who protect it.

A common formula for determining the credit of a person or a business consists of the "three C's" — character, capacity, and capital.

Character. *Character* is revealed in one's conduct, attitudes, and achievements. It does not necessarily have any relation to one's wealth. It represents the sum total of the principles for which one stands. One's reputation is the result of how other people evaluate one's character traits. We are not able to borrow money or buy goods and services with the promise to pay later if others judge our character to be questionable.

Capacity. *Capacity* is merely another term for earning power. It represents one's ability to earn and to pay obligations when they become due. An individual may have an honorable character and perfectly good intentions of paying an obligation; but without the ability or capacity to pay, the person cannot pay satisfactorily. It is often more difficult to judge character than it is to judge capacity. Capacity, or earning power, can be measured reasonably accurately, but character is an intangible quality.

Capital. The third measuring standard, *capital*, applies only to people who have property (land, home, cars, or anything else of value). Naturally our net worth or capital affects our ability to pay debts when they become due and, consequently, affects our credit standing. People with a temporary lack of earning power but with a substantial net worth may still have a favorable credit standing; that is, others will be willing to make loans to them or to sell to them based on their promises to pay.

Capacity and capital without character will affect our credit standing adversely, making it impossible to borrow money or buy goods and services on time.

Establishing a Line of Credit

Credit standing or credit worthiness refers to the chances or the probability that one will pay a debt when it becomes due. We have just learned that it depends on the trust or confidence others have in our intention to pay. *Line of credit* means the maximum amount a lender or creditor will permit a customer to owe at any one time.

Every responsible family should establish its line of credit with a good retail store or retail credit association regardless of whether it is used extensively or not. By so doing you also will take your first step in establishing your line of credit with a bank.

To establish your credit standing and your line of credit, the usual procedure is to go to your favorite store and discuss the matter frankly with the credit manager or the owner. The credit manager will request information of a personal nature about your character, capacity, and capital. Such information should be provided accurately and completely. The credit manager must have such information as a basis for determining how much credit to extend to you.

The illustration on page 348 shows a typical application for credit for department store customers. In some cases the forms are more complicated, but in general they require the same information.

ROYER'S SPORTING GOODS

PLEASE PRINT ALL INFORMATION

Account Number	Please circle number of cards desired. ① 2	☒ SINGLE ☐ MARRIED ☐ WIDOWED ☐ SEPARATED ☐ DIVORCED	Limit	Date Appr.
			Taken by	Approver
			No. Cards	Promo No. / St. No.

| Name | First Lisa | Initial J. | Last Thomas | Age: 26 | Spouse Name: | Tel. No. 335-2131 |

| Address | 1313 Hatch Street #203 | How Long 5yrs. | Name–Address–Phone of Landlord or Mortgage Co. | Morrison Realty Freeport, Ohio |

| City Freeport | State Ohio | Zip 46310 |

| Own Home | Renting— Furnished | Renting— Unfurnished ✓ | Boarding | Live With Parents | Monthly Rent or Mortgage Pymt. $140.00 |

| Former Address if At Present Less Than 3 Yrs. | | City | State | Zip | How Long |

| Employer McKay and Nelson | Address: 101 East Avenue | Tel. No. 335-2131 | How Long 3yrs. |

| Position Legal Secretary | Soc. Sec. 155-31-0126 | Timecard or Badge No. | Salary Wk/Mo $145.00 |

| Former Employer if Less Than 3 Yrs. With Present Employer | | Position: | How Long |

| Spouse Employer | Address | Salary Wk/Mo | Position: | How Long |

| Banking | Bank First National Bank | Checking Acct. No. 261 | Relative Mark Thomas | Relationship Brother |
| | Bank " | Savings Acct. No. 311 | | |

| Credit References | Company Rutgers Dept. Store | Acct No. 6188 | Bal due: $35 | Address 615 Michigan Street |
| | Company Boston Dept. Store | Acct No. 5175 | Bal due: $22 | City Freeport, Ohio | Tel. No. 335-0831 |

I, THE UNDERSIGNED APPLICANT, HEREBY CERTIFY TO ROYER'S SPORTING GOODS THAT INFORMATION FURNISHED BY ME TO ROYER'S SPORTING GOODS IN CONNECTION WITH THIS APPLICATION IS TRUE AND CORRECT, AND AUTHORIZE ROYER'S SPORTING GOODS OR ASSIGNEE TO MAKE SUCH CREDIT INQUIRIES AS MAY BE NECESSARY TO PROCESS THIS APPLICATION. FURTHER, UNDERSIGNED ACKNOWLEDGES RECEIPT OF ROYER'S SPORTING GOODS CHARGE AGREEMENT AND JOINTLY AND SEVERALLY AGREES TO THE TERMS AND CONDITIONS THEREOF.

Applicant's Signature: *Lisa J. Thomas* Date: 9-7-80   Spouse's Signature: _____ Date: _____

An Application for Credit

Credit-Rating Agencies

In general there are two types of credit agencies: (1) agencies that provide credit rating information on businesses and (2) agencies that provide credit ratings on individuals.

Banks sometimes give confidential credit information on individuals and businesses. It is therefore important to maintain satisfactory relations with a bank if a good credit rating is desired.

Private credit agencies collect information and issue confidential reports for the benefit of their subscribers who are retailers. Each subscriber contributes information about customers to the agency. Additional information is gathered from local newspapers, notices of change in address, death notices, and court records. Such information is valuable to retailers in protecting them from loss on accounts. If one of their customers moves, they will want to know of the change in address. If a customer dies, they will want to be sure that claims are presented. If someone is taking court action against one of their customers, they will want to protect their own claims.

The Associated Credit Bureaus of America has more than 3,000 credit bureau members serving over 600,000 business firms. Any of these local credit bureaus can develop a report on any individual in North America and in many foreign countries within a short period of time. Through the interchange of information, the credit records of an estimated 100 million consumers are already compiled and are readily available to all members of the Associated Credit Bureaus of America. The services of this nationwide credit reporting system are an advantage to you if you have safeguarded your credit. You can move from one community to another and your credit record will follow you or it can be checked on very easily. However, a bad credit reputation also will follow you wherever you go.

Dun and Bradstreet, Incorporated, issues a book of credit ratings on commercial houses and manufacturers. The service, which is available on a subscription basis, covers the entire United States. In addition, a subscriber can obtain a special report on any business person or professional person in any part of the country. The reliability of this agency has been established through many years of effective service.

In 1971 the Fair Credit Reporting Act prevented credit agencies from giving out wrong credit information about consumers. An individual who has been denied credit, employment, or insurance because of a bad credit agency report may demand to know the source of that report. The individual then has the right, upon request, to know everything (except medical information) on file at the credit agency. The individual may have wrong information and information that cannot be proven removed from the file.

Responsibility for Debts

Responsibility for the payment of one's debts is one of our oldest moral and ethical principles. In addition to this principle, laws have been enacted specifying a person's legal responsibility for debts. Furthermore, one's relationship to creditors in case of failure to pay has also been fixed by law.

Parents generally are legally responsible for debts incurred by their children when permission has been given to the children to make purchases and to charge them to the parents' account. For instance, if it has been customary for a child to use a charge account of the parents, the parents are responsible for the debts.

Creditor's Remedies. If a person does not or cannot pay a debt, the creditor has several legal courses open. The account can be turned over to a lawyer or a collection agency for collection. The merchandise may be repossessed. Or suit may be brought in court against the debtor to enforce payment of the debt. In some instances, a person's salary may be garnisheed or attached.

Garnishment. If a debtor refuses to pay a debt, the creditor may succeed in having a court order issued against the debtor. This court order would require the employer of the debtor to pay part of the debtor's wages to the creditor until the debt has been paid. This procedure is called *garnishment* or *garnisheeing* of wages. Some states do not permit garnishment. Those states that do must abide by the federal Consumer Credit Protection Act of 1968. This act states that the most that can be taken from a debtor's weekly take-home pay is the lesser of: (1) 25% of take-home pay or (2) the difference between a debtor's take-home pay and $87 (30 times the current federal minimum wage of $2.90 per hour). An illustration of the amount that can be garnisheed is given below.

Weekly Take-Home Pay	Amount That Could Be Garnisheed Under	
	(1)	(2)
$150	$150 × 25% = $37.50*	$150 − $87 = $63
$110	$110 × 25% = $27.50	$110 − $87 = $23*

*The amounts that can legally be garnisheed.

Attachment. If you owe a debt and refuse to pay or cannot pay as agreed, you may be sued in court to force you to pay it. A common procedure in such a case is to ask the court for an attachment on some of your property until the case is settled. An *attachment* is simply a legal process whereby the property attached comes under the control of the court until the case is settled. Property on which an attachment order has been placed may not be sold and may not be moved except by court approval. The court can order the property sold to pay the debt.

Debtor's Remedies. When a person is unable to pay a debt, that person has a number of courses open. It may be possible to borrow money to pay the current debt. It may be possible to make an arrangement with the creditor to pay off the debt in small installments over a period of time. Or, the debt may be discharged by a statute of limitations or by a bankruptcy proceeding.

Arrangement. This is usually the most desirable plan for both the debtor and the creditor. In most cases debtors want to pay their debts and creditors want to be paid without having to take legal action against the debtors. Therefore, creditors are usually quite willing to make an arrangement for the debtor to make small regular payments over a long period of time until the debt has been paid. Usually, as a part of this arrangement, the debtor cannot make additional credit purchases from the creditor until the original debt has been paid.

Statutes of Limitations. The *statutes of limitations* in most states set a time limit after which a creditor cannot enforce a legal claim. For instance, in one state if an account is not collected within 5 years, the creditor cannot sue for the amount. If the debtor, however, makes a payment or a promise to pay during the 5 years or at any time thereafter, the account is revived or reinstated.

Bankruptcy. If one is unable to pay debts when they become due, one is said to be *insolvent*. If the debts are greater than the total fair value of one's assets, a federal court may declare the person to be *bankrupt*. Recognizing the impossibility of paying one's debts, a person may ask the court to declare him or her bankrupt. This process is known as *voluntary bankruptcy*.

Any one of a person's creditors who holds a past-due debt against the person may also petition or ask the court to declare that person bankrupt. This process is known as *involuntary bankruptcy*.

The circumstances under which one may petition for voluntary bankruptcy are regulated by law. If the court declares a person to be bankrupt, a *trustee* is appointed as an agent of the court. The trustee then takes charge of the bankrupt's affairs, sells the property, and pays off the debts on a proportional basis among the creditors. The latest federal bankruptcy laws, under certain circumstances, provide that a debtor may alter or modify his or her relation with creditors. This may be done by extending the time for payment or rearranging the payment plan. If such a request seems possible and is granted, the debtor may be able to pay the debts in due time.

Bankruptcy discharges all of a debtor's former debts and enables that person to start to acquire property again. Property acquired after bankruptcy proceedings have been completed is not subject to claims for prior debts. The great advantage of bankruptcy to creditors is that they all fare proportionately to their claims in the net proceeds resulting from the sale of the bankrupt's property. No one creditor gets an unfair preference over others.

Bankruptcy should not be looked upon by a debtor as an easy way out of paying one's debts. When bankruptcy has been filed against a person, that person may have to operate strictly on a cash basis for a number of years. This means, in most instances, one might be denied the use of charge accounts, credit cards, and loans for automobiles, homes, and other consumer goods. One may even be denied admission to a hospital unless one can prove that one has the cash (or insurance) to pay the hospital bill. After declaring bankruptcy, a person cannot declare bankruptcy a second time until 6 years have elapsed.

Consumer Credit Laws

Since 1975, some laws regarding credit have been passed that are important for consumers. Some of these new laws will be discussed briefly.

Nondiscrimination. Under the Equal Opportunity Act, sex discrimination is banned in the granting of credit. In the past women were often denied credit by stores, lending institutions, and credit-card companies. This practice is now illegal. Women applying for credit must be judged the same as men. If women have steady incomes and can qualify in other respects as good credit risks, they are equally entitled to credit.

Billing Errors. Under the Fair Credit Billing Act, consumers can preserve their credit ratings while settling disputes with stores and credit-card companies. If you think there is an error on your bill or some charge you don't understand, you must notify the creditor in writing within 60 days after the bill was mailed to you. The creditor must respond to your inquiry within 30 days and must resolve the problem within 90 days. During this time the creditor cannot report you as delinquent to any credit agency for your failure to pay the portion of your bill that is under dispute.

Cash Discounts. Since stores pay credit-card companies from 5% to 7% to collect charges from credit-card users, many cash customers feel they are entitled to cash discounts on their purchases. In the past most credit-card companies would not permit stores who honored their cards to offer cash discounts to cash customers. Now stores have the right to offer cash discounts up to 5% if they wish. However, there is no law stating that cash discounts must be given.

Economic Problems of Credit

The use of credit tends to increase purchases and to stimulate business. Government officials, bankers, business people, and many others constantly watch the figures that are collected to show the amount and the nature of debt that is owed by individuals. If consumer debt increases too fast and is not being paid off, this situation indicates that buyers on credit are not able to pay their debts. Such a condition would, therefore, be an indication that we might be entering a period of bad business conditions.

The delicate economic problem is to keep purchases and payments in balance. When one cannot pay one's debts, the business that sold to the person may suffer a loss. Therefore, when great numbers of people buy more on credit than they can repay, we experience an overexpansion of consumer credit. The result may be that many businesses lose money because they cannot collect for goods sold on credit. You will recall that in Chapter 10 you learned how we are all affected by bad business conditions that arise when great numbers of people cannot pay their debts.

FACTS EVERYONE SHOULD UNDERSTAND ABOUT CREDIT

1. Consumer credit is debt that is incurred for a home, goods, or services for personal and family use.

2. In its many forms, credit is a useful tool if one does not use it unnecessarily and gets it at low cost.

3. Because it is convenient and often is a means of adjusting high and low points in spending, credit is used by people at all income levels.

4. Each credit transaction remains incomplete until such time as all legal responsibilities and repayment obligations of the debt are met.

5. A good credit rating must be earned and maintained if one wants to get credit when it is needed and to get it at a reasonable cost.

6. If it becomes impossible for one to pay one's debts, prompt action should be taken to notify creditors and to establish an adjusted payment schedule that can be met.

7. When credit is used as a substitute for good money management, there is usually a tendency to overuse it.

8. When overuse of credit forces a person to declare bankruptcy, there is a weakening of the economic and social structure.

REVIEW QUESTIONS

Section A

1. What two meanings does "credit" have?
2. When should credit be used by the consumer?
3. What is involved in using consumer credit to adjust the high and low points in personal spending?
4. What is the principal item purchased by installment credit?

Section B

5. From the point of view of the customer, what are some of the advantages of a charge account?
6. What is cycle billing? Why have some stores adopted it?
7. How does a revolving charge account work in a retail store?
8. What extra costs are incurred by business in making charge sales?

Section C

9. What are the "three C's" for determining credit? Explain each.
10. What are some of the agencies through which credit information can be obtained?
11. What is meant by the garnishment of wages?
12. What is meant by an attachment?
13. What is the purpose of the statutes of limitations?
14. What relief may an individual debtor obtain under the bankruptcy laws?
15. Why are governmental officials, bankers, and business people sometimes concerned about the amount of debt owed by individuals?

DISCUSSION QUESTIONS

Section A

1. What are some examples (other than buying a car or modernizing a home) that illustrate the high and low points that develop in a family's spending pattern where credit could be useful in adjusting this pattern?
2. What are some of the kinds of goods and services that consumers most frequently buy on credit? What are the advantages and the disadvantages of buying them on credit?

Section B

3. Most people appreciate the advantages of using credit cards but are unaware of the disadvantages and dangers. What are some disadvantages and dangers of using credit cards?
4. What is your point of view toward the use of charge accounts?

Section C

5. (a) Can you open a charge account in the name of your parents?
   (b) Can you use a charge account already opened by your parents?
6. How may the use of credit affect the individual consumer, the community, and jobs in industry?
7. How can a good credit reputation at your present place of residence help you if you move to another city?
8. Why is it that many retailers seem to be more considerate of credit customers than of cash customers?
9. Millions of people now buy on credit terms. How does this affect the prices we pay for important durable goods?
10. Nancy Wong has been away from her job without pay for 6 weeks because of illness. She is now behind in the payment of her bills. She owes $75 to a department store, $30 to an oil company, and $150 to her doctor. How should Nancy handle this situation?

APPLICATION PROBLEMS

Section A

1. Using the table on consumer installment debt in the United States on page 339, find answers to the following:
   (a) What percentage of total consumer installment debt is represented by automobile loans?
   (b) What percentage of total consumer installment debt is represented by commercial bank revolving credit?

Section B

2. Assume that under cycle billing your billing date is the 25th of each month and that you have 25 days from the billing date to pay the entire bill without incurring a finance charge. Also assume that on April 28 you made a charge purchase of $50.
   (a) By what date must you pay the $50 charge without incurring a finance charge?
   (b) How many days of "free" credit did you receive with this $50 charge purchase?
   (c) Assume you had borrowed $50 from a bank at 6% for the same number of "free" days of credit you received. What would you have paid in interest charges?

3. Luis Camargo buys clothes for $100 on a revolving credit plan. The store requires him to make payments of $20 a month. It charges 1½% on the unpaid balance at the beginning of each month, and it calculates this credit charge before deducting each payment. To determine the cost of this revolving credit, prepare a table using the following headings. The first month's calculation is given as an example. The fifth and final payment will be the amount of the beginning balance plus the finance charge.

Payment No.	Balance at Beginning of Month	Finance Charge @ 1½%	Balance Plus Finance Charge	Amount of Monthly Payment	New Balance
1	$100.00	$1.50	$101.50	$20.00	$81.50
2					

   (a) What is the total amount of the finance charge?
   (b) What is the total amount of the monthly payments?

Section C

4. Under the new federal garnishment regulations, what legal amount could be taken from the weekly pay of a young person earning $100 take-home pay?

COMMUNITY PROJECTS

Section A

1. From local merchants, your local credit bureau, or your state credit association, obtain information with regard to (a) the percentage of merchandise sold on credit in your community or state, (b) the average amount of credit losses, (c) the reasons for the credit losses, and (d) policies with regard to uniformity in granting credit.

Section B

2. Assume that you lost your or your parents' Master Charge or VISA credit card. Inquire of an employee of a local bank that issues either of these cards to find out to what extent you are responsible for charges made to the card by the finder.

Section C

3. Obtain credit application forms from several local merchants. Study these various forms to see how similar and how different they are. Then match the items of information requested on the forms with the three C's of credit worthiness.

4. Make a survey in your community of stores honoring credit cards to see how many of them will give a cash discount to cash customers. Report your findings to the class.

Planning Insurance Protection

PURPOSE OF THE CHAPTER

Every day individuals and businesses face the risk of economic loss resulting from illness, death, and accidents. A home or a factory can be destroyed by fire or damaged by a severe storm. An automobile or a commercial airplane may be totally destroyed in an accident. A family may be without income if the primary wage earner has a disabling illness or dies. Few individuals or businesses can absorb such economic losses by themselves. In this chapter you will learn how people share the risks of economic losses.

After studying this chapter, you will be able to:

1. Define important insurance terms.
2. Identify some of the hazards involved in home ownership and how the owner can protect the family against these hazards.
3. Identify some of the hazards involved in automobile ownership and how an owner can be protected against these hazards.
4. Identify different types of life insurance and describe major characteristics of each.
5. Explain how health insurance can assist in family financial planning.
6. State why federal and state social insurance programs are needed.
7. Identify factors that should be considered in planning an insurance program.

A. NEED FOR INSURANCE

In our free enterprise economy individuals have the right to own property. To lose that property through fire, accident, or theft would be a severe economic blow to the owner. Much of the property people or businesses possess (homes, automobiles, farm equipment, factories, inventories) is not fully paid for. Thus, if that property is destroyed by some accidental means or if the owner dies before fully paying for the property, the balance owed still must be paid before the property can be replaced. This puts even more economic burden on the property owner. Most of us simply could not replace such property.

Also, in a free enterprise economy the work ethic is popular. This means that individuals and families rely on their own individual productive talents for financial support. Thus, if the primary wage earner dies, the survivors lose this financial support and suffer a severe economic loss.

Sharing Losses

The big question is what can individuals, families, and businesses do to reduce the economic burden resulting from loss of life and property? One way would be for groups of individuals, families, and businesses to band together and agree to share equally in any loss suffered by any member of the group. Problems would arise, however. For instance, how much would each member pay? Who would hold the funds? How should the funds be invested? What would happen if losses were greater than the balance in the fund? How would the funds be used if no losses occurred in a given period? An additional problem would arise from such an arrangement. Suppose that all of the families and businesses were from one community and that a fire, tornado, or flood destroyed the entire community. Under such conditions, it is obvious that the funds would not be adequate to pay for all of the losses.

Insurance Companies in a Free Enterprise Economy

To handle all the problems listed above (and many more), enterprising people have organized insurance companies. These insurance companies receive small payments from large numbers of families and businesses in many different communities. They invest part of these funds and pay for losses sustained by the members. The amount of the small payment required of each member, for example, is based on the experience of the insurance company. Assume that Midland Insurance Company carries fire insurance on 100,000 homes, that each home has an average value of $60,000, and that each homeowner pays an average of $200 a year for fire insurance. The company would collect $20,000,000 a year from the owners of the property with which to pay its operating expenses and losses due to fires. Most property owners can afford to pay $200 a year, but they cannot afford a $60,000 fire loss. In a sense, the 100,000 homeowners are pooling or sharing their risks, and the insurance company is the agent that handles the financial matters.

It may seem strange at first that an insurance company can assume the risk of paying all losses and yet charge each policyholder only a small fee. Often the total yearly fee for property insurance is as low as $1/10$ of 1% of the possible loss. The reason insurance companies can follow this practice is that they know from experience what losses can be expected. They can, therefore, keep in a reserve fund enough money to pay each loss as it occurs. It is true that unusual events, such as an exceptionally large fire, may cause unplanned losses; but over a long period of time, losses can be predicted fairly well. The reserve fund of an insurance company is used as a protection against unusual losses.

Insurance Contracts and Terms

To understand an insurance contract, one must be familiar with definitions of certain insurance terms and with the concept of insurable interest.

Definitions. An insurance agreement is a form of contract. An insurance contract is called a *policy*. The amount paid for insurance is called a *premium*. The person who buys an insurance policy is known as the *policyholder, insured*, or *assured*. The party from whom the insured buys the insurance and who agrees to pay the loss is called the *insurer* or *underwriter*. *Risk* is the possibility of loss. *Face value* is the amount of insurance stated in the contract; *cash value* is the actual market value of the property destroyed. Cash value may be greater or less than the face value of the contract; however, no amount greater than the face value will be paid for any loss. In life insurance, a *beneficiary* is the person named in the insurance policy to receive the insurance benefits upon the death of the insured.

Insurable Interest. The purpose of property and liability insurance is the protection of the financial interest of the person who buys the insurance. The policyholder must have an insurable interest in the property. A person is said to have an *insurable interest in property* if there is reason to expect that the person will receive a financial benefit from the property. A person also is said to have an insurable interest in property if that person will suffer a loss from damage to or destruction of the property. For instance, both the owner of a home and the company that holds a mortgage on the home have an insurable interest. If the property is not insured and is later destroyed, the owner will lose the money invested in it. Also, the company that owns the mortgage may lose the money that is due it on the mortgage.

In the case of property, the insurable interest ordinarily must exist at the time of the loss; otherwise, the contract is not enforceable. For example, you might carry some insurance on property that you rent and occupy. If you move out of the property without canceling the insurance, you could not collect for a fire loss should the building burn after you move.

Life insurance may be bought only by persons having an insurable interest. Everyone has an insurable interest in his or her own life. Parents have an insurable interest in each other and in their children. One need not be a relative of a person in order to insure that person's life. A person may have an insurable interest in another if the person would be deprived of some benefit by the death of the other. For instance, a creditor in some cases may insure the life of a debtor. A business organization may insure the life of one

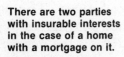

There are two parties with insurable interests in the case of a home with a mortgage on it.

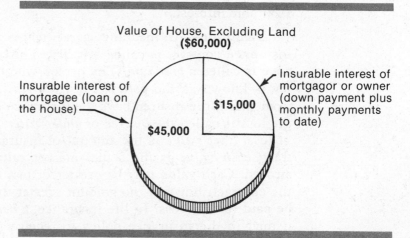

Value of House, Excluding Land
($60,000)

Insurable interest of mortgagee (loan on the house) — $45,000

$15,000

Insurable interest of mortgagor or owner (down payment plus monthly payments to date)

of its key employees. Close kinship is often, but not always, enough to claim an insurable interest.

State Regulation of Insurance Companies

The operations of insurance companies within a particular state are regulated by the state, usually through a department of insurance and/or an insurance commission. One of the important functions of the insurance commissioner is to make sure that the insurance companies keep enough reserves to pay all claims as they are filed by policyholders.

State regulation also protects insurance buyers from fraud. Most states require reports from insurance companies, as well as inspection of the securities, accounting records, and business methods of the companies. In most states, insurance companies are regulated as to the ways in which they can invest the money collected from policyholders. These investments are usually confined to high-grade bonds of federal, state, and city governments and of utilities, as well as to high-grade real-estate mortgages and mortgage bonds. Although special bureaus provide information for setting fire and casualty rates, the state governments have the right to regulate these rates.

B. PROPERTY AND LIABILITY INSURANCE

Family life has become complicated, particularly as it relates to home ownership and automobile ownership. Family investment in a home built up over a period of years may be lost in a matter of minutes by a fire, tornado, or flood. Family funds may be completely wiped out by a judgment resulting from a lawsuit involving an automobile accident. Businesses in the United States also face financial risk and need to insure property (buildings, equipment, inventories) and to protect themselves from legal liability. However, in this chapter we will deal only with insurance needs of the individual and the family.

Insurance for the Home

The homeowner must consider the possible loss of the home, its contents, and other personal property. The homeowner must also consider possible losses arising from lawsuits that result from personal injury to guests. While each of these risks can be insured against separately, insurance companies have developed insurance policies that insure against groups of perils (dangers which lead to economic loss). These are called *homeowners policies*. Homeowners policies are also referred to as "all-risk" policies and are less costly than insuring each peril separately.

An example of a homeowners policy covering all risks would have the following coverages and limits:

Coverage A — Dwelling building, $60,000 (as an example).

Coverage B — Appurtenant (attached or accompanying) private structures, 10% of Coverage A.

Coverage C — Personal property, 50% of Coverage A.

Coverage D — Additional living expense, 20% of Coverage A.

Coverage E — Comprehensive personal liability, $100,000 per occurrence.

Coverage F — Medical payments, $5,000 per person.

Coverage G — Physical damage to property, $500 per occurrence. (This coverage provides payment of losses to property of another caused by the insured regardless of legal liability).

Buildings and Personal Property. Under a homeowners policy, the house or dwelling is covered. Guest houses, sheds, garages, and other structures used in connection with and belonging to the home are known as *appurtenant private structures*. They usually are covered up to 10% of the amount of coverage carried on the house.

Personal property is covered along with the house. *Personal property* includes household contents and other personal belongings used, owned, worn, or carried by the family. The protection applies both at home and away from home. Pets are not included as personal property. Automobiles and the property of roomers or boarders are not covered.

The chart on page 363 shows the three basic policy coverages (standard, broad, and comprehensive) that may be purchased to protect against certain perils to the house and appurtenant private structures.

Comprehensive Personal Liability. Coverage under a comprehensive personal liability policy protects the homeowner against claims arising from bodily injury to others or damage to the property of others. No claim is paid by the insurance company under this provision unless it has been established that the insured is legally liable. A guest in the home might fall down a basement stairway, break a leg, and then file suit for damages. Under this

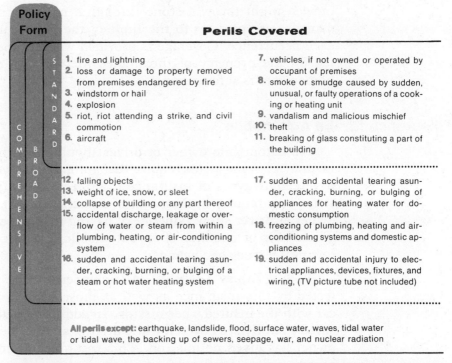

Homeowners Policy—Property Insurance
Summary of Coverage—Standard, Broad, and Comprehensive Forms

Policy Form	Perils Covered
STANDARD	1. fire and lightning 2. loss or damage to property removed from premises endangered by fire 3. windstorm or hail 4. explosion 5. riot, riot attending a strike, and civil commotion 6. aircraft 7. vehicles, if not owned or operated by occupant of premises 8. smoke or smudge caused by sudden, unusual, or faulty operations of a cooking or heating unit 9. vandalism and malicious mischief 10. theft 11. breaking of glass constituting a part of the building
BROAD	12. falling objects 13. weight of ice, snow, or sleet 14. collapse of building or any part thereof 15. accidental discharge, leakage or overflow of water or steam from within a plumbing, heating, or air-conditioning system 16. sudden and accidental tearing asunder, cracking, burning, or bulging of a steam or hot water heating system 17. sudden and accidental tearing asunder, cracking, burning, or bulging of appliances for heating water for domestic consumption 18. freezing of plumbing, heating and air-conditioning systems and domestic appliances 19. sudden and accidental injury to electrical appliances, devices, fixtures, and wiring, (TV picture tube not included)
COMPREHENSIVE	**All perils except:** earthquake, landslide, flood, surface water, waves, tidal water or tidal wave, the backing up of sewers, seepage, war, and nuclear radiation

Source: *A Family Guide to Property and Liability Insurance,* Insurance Information Institute.

provision, the insurance company would represent the homeowner in court. The company would pay the cost of defending the homeowner and would pay the damages, if any, up to the limits of the policy. Usually, the basic coverage of this provision is $100,000 for each occurrence.

Medical Payments. A medical payments provision protects the homeowner from accidental injury claims of others arising from actions of the homeowner, family members, or family pets either on or off the homeowner's property. The insurance company pays the claims of the injured party, regardless of who is at fault. The claim would include the cost of medical and surgical services incurred within one year of the accident. The amount of coverage for each person usually is $5,000. This coverage, however, does not apply to members of the homeowner's family or the homeowner.

Physical Damage to Property of Others. A clause providing coverage for physical damage to the property of others protects the homeowner and the family when any member of the family damages someone's property. For example, the homeowner's lawn mower might throw a stone through a neighbor's window. Such damages are paid up to the limit of the policy, usually $500 for each occurrence. Coverage is provided whether the act is committed on the property of the homeowner or off and whether the homeowner is at fault or not.

Insurance for the Automobile

No automobile owner or driver should be without automobile insurance. Some states require that automobile owners and drivers have certain types of insurance to protect others from loss. Other states may require in the event of an accident that the automobile owner or driver show evidence of having insurance or post a bond. The owner or operator of an automobile should consider the following six types of coverages.

Bodily Injury Liability. All members of the family are protected by this insurance as well as those who drive the insured's car with the insured's permission. In addition, members of the insured's family are covered while driving another person's car if the owner has given permission. This insurance protects the insured against claims or suits of people injured or killed by the insured's car. State financial responsibility laws indicate the minimum amount of this coverage that must be carried. The minimum amount of coverage issued is $5,000 for one person or $10,000 in total for more than one person who is injured in any one accident. Some automobile owners carry as much as $100,000 for one person or $300,000 in total for more than one person who is injured.

Property Damage Liability. All members of the family and all those driving the family car with permission are covered by this policy provision. And members of the family are covered even while driving someone else's car as long as they have permission from the owner. The insured is covered whenever the insured's car damages the property of others. It does not cover damage to the insured's automobile, however. Property damage liability is usually available in amounts ranging from $5,000 to $100,000.

Both bodily injury and property damage coverage are indeed vital for the car owner. The perils that face the car owner are too great to risk without adequate insurance coverage. In purchasing

The owner or driver of a wrecked car may need insurance for bodily injury, property damage, medical payments, and collision.

this coverage, the car owner should remember that large amounts of coverage cost relatively less than smaller amounts. For example, if coverage of 25/50/5 ($25,000 bodily injury for one person, $50,000 bodily injury for more than one person, and $5,000 property damage) costs $100 a year, 50/100/10 might cost only $111. Thus, the insured may double the coverage with an increase of only 11% in premium costs.

Medical Payments Coverage. This coverage is similar to that discussed under the homeowners policy. However, this coverage applies only to the operation of an automobile, and it covers all members of the family and any guests while riding in the insured car. The insurance company agrees to pay all reasonable medical expenses incurred within one year of the date of the accident. The coverage includes all necessary medical, surgical, X-ray, and dental services, up to the limits set in the policy. It may also include ambulance services, hospital services, nursing services, and funeral services. The insurance company pays regardless of who was at fault. The limits of coverage for each individual may range from $500 to $5,000.

Medical payments coverage is very important for families with children and for families who transport other children as in a school car pool.

Comprehensive Physical Damage Insurance. This insurance coverage protects the insured against possible loss if the car is damaged or stolen. However, damage due to collision is not covered. Causes of damage covered include fire, lightning, flood, and windstorm. Glass breakage is covered under this insurance. Since this type of insurance is relatively inexpensive, most car owners include it in their coverage. The cost of replacing one windshield very likely would be greater than total premium payments on comprehensive insurance for two or three years.

Collision Insurance. Collision insurance coverage protects against loss arising from damage to the insured's own car as the result of collision. This is the most expensive insurance coverage among those discussed, mainly because of the many minor accidents that require costly body and paint work. The car owner can reduce the cost of this type of insurance by buying a deductible policy, usually either $50 or $100 deductible. In the event of damage, the insurance company would pay only the amount of the loss in excess of $50 or $100. Since a new car represents a large investment, the car owner should carry collision insurance on it. As the car gets older and its value decreases, the owner should weigh the cost of this insurance coverage against the potential loss. For example, there would be little reason to carry $100 deductible collision insurance on a car valued at $250.

Costs for collision insurance vary widely from one geographic area to another. They also vary within an area according to driver classification. Unmarried male drivers under 25 pay the highest rate. The person who finances the purchase of a car will be required to buy collision insurance as well as other coverages.

Protection Against Uninsured Motorists. This insurance coverage is designed to protect the family against risk due to injury by hit-and-run drivers and uninsured drivers. It covers the insured as

---

FACTS EVERYONE SHOULD KNOW ABOUT PROPERTY AND LIABILITY INSURANCE

1. Property and liability insurance is possible through small payments collected from many people to pay unexpected losses that may occur to any one of the policyholders.

2. Property and liability insurance rates are determined primarily from past experience.

3. The homeowners policy is the most economical way of insuring the homeowner against the perils of home ownership.

4. It is vital for the family to carry adequate automobile insurance.

5. The family should buy its property and liability insurance from a company it knows to be reputable and fair or from an agent in whom the family has complete confidence.

though the uninsured driver had been insured or as though the hit-and-run driver had been identified. The insured cannot collect from the insurance company unless the uninsured motorist was legally liable. The coverage is limited to the amount of liability required under the financial responsibility laws of the various states. The cost of this coverage is very low.

C. LIFE INSURANCE

Life insurance serves several purposes. First, it may provide a cash reserve or a monthly income in case of the death of a member of a family, especially the death of the primary wage earner. Second, life insurance may provide funds for future use, such as financing a college education, meeting financial emergencies, or providing either income or a cash reserve for use in retirement years. And finally, many people make regular premium payments on life insurance as a means of saving. Thus, life insurance has many uses whether the primary wage earner lives or dies.

What Is Life Insurance?

Life insurance is a voluntary financial plan whereby an individual makes periodic payments to an insurance company. The company in turn repays the individual or the beneficiary at a stated future time or upon the occurrence of certain events such as death or disability.

Life insurance is a cooperative plan through which people pay the same rates under similar conditions. Most general forms of life insurance require a physical examination to determine the condition of health. This is done so that the cost of insurance and the protection to all members of the insured group will be fair. Many persons with poor health or in extradangerous occupations can obtain insurance but at higher rates than normal.

Life insurance premium rates are based on the experience of the insurance company and on expected claims. Accurate estimates of expected claims are made from *mortality tables*. These tables show the percentage of a certain age group that will die from all causes each year. Many life insurance policies call for payment of the same premium each year. This is known as *level-premium* insurance because it equalizes yearly or monthly payments even though the probability of death increases as the age of the insured increases. If it were not for level-premium insurance, the premium costs would increase each year.

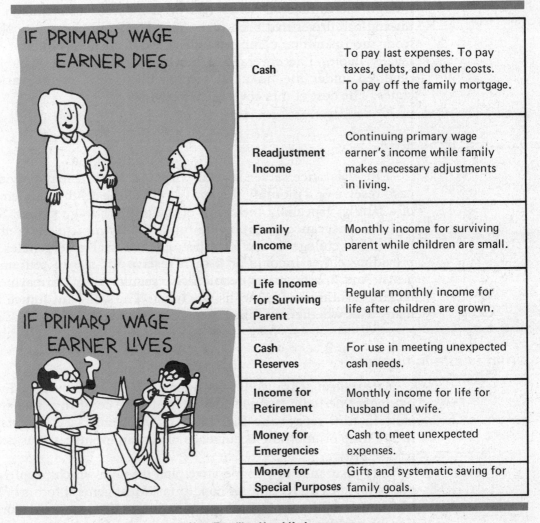

IF PRIMARY WAGE EARNER DIES		
Cash	To pay last expenses. To pay taxes, debts, and other costs. To pay off the family mortgage.	
Readjustment Income	Continuing primary wage earner's income while family makes necessary adjustments in living.	
Family Income	Monthly income for surviving parent while children are small.	
Life Income for Surviving Parent	Regular monthly income for life after children are grown.	
Cash Reserves	For use in meeting unexpected cash needs.	
Income for Retirement	Monthly income for life for husband and wife.	
Money for Emergencies	Cash to meet unexpected expenses.	
Money for Special Purposes	Gifts and systematic saving for family goals.	

How Families Use Life Insurance

Many states require insurance companies to keep on hand a cash balance known as a *legal reserve*. This reserve is to make certain that funds will be available to pay the insured or the beneficiary when the policy comes due. In some ways this reserve is like the reserves that member banks must keep on deposit in a Federal Reserve bank (Chapter 15). Much of the premium payment not needed to pay operating expenses is invested by the insurance company. The income earned on this investment helps to lower the cost of life insurance protection.

If a person wants to cancel life insurance, that person's share of the reserve funds is called the *cash value*. The cash value of a policy increases until the policy matures (comes due). The policy matures either as an endowment or at the end of the span of life on which the rates were based. The cash value is also the basis for a policy loan if the policyholder needs to borrow money.

Types of Life Insurance

There are many types of life insurance contracts or policies. The basic types of ordinary life insurance are: term, straight life, limited-payment life, endowment, and annuity.

Term Insurance. *Term insurance* provides protection for a stated period of time. It is often used to cover a special need. For example, a person who has a debt that is to be paid in 10 years can buy a 10-year term policy for the amount of the debt. If the person dies before paying the debt, the insurance will pay the debt. Consumer-credit insurance or credit life insurance is one form of term insurance.

Term insurance is often referred to as "pure insurance" because it provides protection only. It does not have a cash value or a loan value. One of the major advantages of term insurance is its low cost for a young person compared with that of other types. Term insurance makes it possible for a young person to buy more insurance coverage at the time protection is needed but when income is too low to buy permanent protection.

The most common periods covered by term insurance are 5 years and 10 years, but it may cover any period of years. Some term insurance can be exchanged for other types of insurance contracts that provide permanent protection and cash values.

Straight Life Insurance. The basic life insurance policy that provides protection over a long period of years is called *straight life insurance.*

If one has dependents and wishes to provide for their protection in the event of the insured's death, the straight life plan is ideal. The premium rate is lower than that for any other type of permanent insurance. The policyholder has a loan value or a cash value in the policy. The insured person pays premiums for life or to age 100, at which time the face value of the policy is paid.

Most policyholders of straight life contracts do not pay premiums all the way to the end of the mortality table (which may be age 96 or 100). A very few do. Many people stop paying premiums and take a reduced paid-up policy, which at age 65 amounts to from 60 to 70% of the face value.

Before one invests in life insurance, it is wise to consider all types of contracts and policies.

Limited-Payment Life Insurance. A *limited-payment life insurance* contract is the same as a straight life contract except that premiums are paid for a limited time. Payments may be for 10, 20, or 30 years instead of for life. Since premiums are paid only for a limited time, the rates are higher than for straight life insurance. When these premiums have been paid, the insurance policy is said to be fully paid. However, the face amount of a limited-payment policy will be paid only in the event of death. For example, a 10-year limited-payment policy for $10,000 will be fully paid after 10 years, but the insurance company will pay the $10,000 only when death occurs.

Endowment Insurance. An insurance company that issues an *endowment policy* pays a definite sum of money (face value of the policy) to the insured at a stated time. In the event of the insured's death before that stated time, the company pays the beneficiary. An endowment policy costs more than a limited-payment policy for an equal number of years. The face amount of an endowment policy, however, is available as cash at the time of death or at the end of the stated period.

An endowment policy is a good way not only to save a definite amount for a future need but also to have protection while saving. However, the amount of insurance that can be bought is less than with other types of permanent insurance. One could buy over 4 times as much straight life insurance as a 20-year endowment for the same cost. Long-term endowments, maturing at age 60 or later, are quite desirable. When one nears retirement age, often reduced earning power occurs. The endowment policy would provide income at face value at a time when extra money would be helpful.

Annuity Contracts. An *annuity* is a sum of money payable yearly. Many people buy an annuity by giving an insurance company a certain sum of money as a single premium or in regular payments. In return for this sum of money, the insurance company agrees to pay a stated monthly or yearly income for a definite number of years or for life. Some contracts guarantee a minimum number of payments. Any guaranteed payments not made before death will be paid to the beneficiary.

There are many types of annuity contracts. However, the main feature of an annuity is guaranteed income starting at a certain age. Therefore, through an annuity one may, during one's earning years, provide for an income after retirement.

Group Insurance. Group insurance is usually used to protect the workers of a single employer or group (such as a union). Under this plan many employees can be insured through one policy and without medical examination. The cost is based on the losses indicated by the ages, environment, occupation, and general health of the members. The rates are usually low. Employers usually pay part or all of the premiums.

There are two types of group insurance: one is *group term insurance* that does not build up any cash value; the other is *group permanent life insurance* that does build up a cash value.

When an employee covered under a group term policy leaves

FACTS EVERYONE SHOULD KNOW ABOUT LIFE INSURANCE

1. A life insurance policy is a contract.

2. Nearly all life insurance premiums are paid at a constant rate.

3. Term insurance is the least expensive form of life insurance, but it does not build up a cash value.

4. Straight life insurance is the least expensive form of permanent insurance.

5. Endowment insurance builds the greatest cash values.

6. Group insurance generally does not require a physical examination.

the employer, the protection usually stops. When an employee covered under a group permanent policy leaves the employer, the former employee (1) may get a paid-up policy equal to the amount of premiums paid or (2) may exchange the group policy for a regular policy at the same face value.

D. HEALTH INSURANCE

The main purpose of health insurance is to protect the family against financial problems that might arise from illness or an accident to any member of the family. Health insurance may provide for one or all of the following coverages.

Hospital Expense Insurance

This insurance coverage provides benefits equal to all or part of the cost of a hospital room and board. A provision of the policy usually limits the number of days covered by the policy. Other benefits may be provided for, such as medications, X-ray services, and operating room services. Hospital expense insurance is the most widely used form of health insurance.

Surgical Expense Insurance

Surgical expense insurance provides for payment of surgical costs according to a schedule of fees payable for each type of operation. The schedule of fees is based on the nature of the operation. For example, the surgeon's fee for a tonsillectomy may be $200; for an appendectomy, $500. Surgical expense insurance is the second most widely used form of health insurance.

General Medical Expense Insurance

This type of insurance pays part of the costs for doctor's calls at the hospital or home and for visits by the patient to the doctor's office. Benefits may also provide for diagnostic X-ray and laboratory expenses.

Major Medical Expense Insurance

This type of insurance is meant to cover the major portion of the costs incurred as the result of major illness or serious acci-

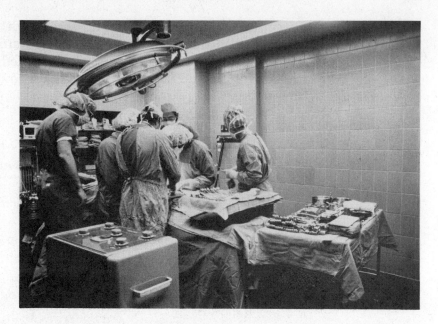

The basic purpose of major medical expense insurance is to cover the major portion of costs incurred as the result of major illness or a serious accident.

dent. Major illness and serious accidents may result in expenses amounting to $10,000, $20,000, or even more.

Major medical insurance is designed to begin where hospital, surgical, and general medical insurance leave off. For this reason, most major medical policies have a *deductible clause*. Thus, the insured person may have to pay the first $100 of any cost not covered by the basic policies. Also, the insured may be required to pay 20 to 25% of any amount above the first $100. This feature is known as *coinsurance*. It helps to keep down the costs of the insurance by discouraging the insured from incurring charges for unnecessary services during an illness and recuperation.

Dental Care Insurance

Dental care insurance is a growing type of coverage to help with dental costs. This insurance helps pay for normal dental care, such as regular checkups, fillings, and cleaning, as well as for more complicated dental work.

Loss-of-Income Insurance

A prolonged illness or serious accident may cause you to lose your income. Loss-of-income insurance is designed to replace all or part of that lost income. Premiums are based on the amount of income that is to be replaced and the length of time for which payments will be made. Usually, there is a waiting period of some days or weeks before benefits are payable. Whether a family should carry loss-of-income insurance depends on the sick leave provisions of the wage earner's job, workmen's compensation provisions, and other factors.

FACTS EVERYONE SHOULD KNOW ABOUT HEALTH INSURANCE

1. Health insurance protects a family or an individual against financial loss due to accident or illness.

2. The most common types of health insurance are hospital expense, surgical expense, and general medical expense.

3. Many businesses provide hospital and surgical insurance coverage for their employees. This group insurance is paid for fully or in part by the employer.

4. Major medical insurance insures against the major portion of the cost of major illness or accident.

5. The family should insure against only the most serious losses. Minor medical expenses should be taken care of as part of the regular family financial plan.

E. SOCIAL INSURANCE

Legislation to protect and aid those who cannot help themselves is often called *social legislation*. Some of the first social legislation provided for compensation of workers for loss due to accidents and illness. These laws, which now are common in all states, are known as *workmen's compensation laws*. Next, the concern for old people who had no wealth or income led to state old-age pension laws. From these beginnings social legislation has been increased to include a wide range of benefits for larger and larger numbers of people.

In 1935 the United States government started a *social security system* to help protect its citizens from economic insecurity. The social security system is insurance that provides a base on which individuals may build protection for themselves and for their dependents. The cost is paid by both the worker and the employer. Since 1935, the details of the social security legislation have been changed a number of times.

Social insurance programs do not provide complete economic security. For this reason, most families buy private insurance protection to add to the social insurance provided by government.

Federal Social Security Act[1]

The federal Social Security Act involves two phases: (1) benefits for old age, death, the needy aged, dependent children, and the blind and (2) benefits for unemployment. The first phase of this program is administered directly by the federal government from taxes collected by the federal government. The second phase is handled primarily through state agencies with federal assistance.

Coverage. Almost all kinds of employment and self-employment today are covered by social security. In fact, 9 out of 10 workers in the United States are covered by social security. For some self-employed workers, coverage under social security is voluntary. For employees in occupations covered by social security, social security protection is compulsory.

Old-Age and Survivor's Insurance. Monthly payments may be made to a retired worker and to the worker's family. Family would include:

1. Unmarried children under 18 (or 22 if full-time students).
2. Unmarried children 18 or over who were disabled before age 22 and who are still disabled.
3. Wife or husband 62 or over.
4. Wife under 62 if caring for worker's child under 18.

Upon the death of a worker covered by the Social Security Act, two types of payments may be made to eligible survivors: (1) a single lump-sum death benefit of $255 and (2) monthly benefit payments to the surviving family. In this case family includes:

1. Unmarried children under 18 (or 22 if full-time students).
2. Unmarried children 18 or over who were disabled before age 22 and who are still disabled.
3. Widow or widower 60 or older.

---

[1]Since the first federal Social Security Act was passed in 1935, the laws have been changed several times and will be changed again. Major changes were made in 1967, 1971, 1972, 1973, and again in 1978. Therefore, any published information cannot be assumed to be up to date and accurate for more than a short time. However, the principles of providing social security will probably not be changed. For up-to-date information on coverage, tax rates, and benefits, you should consult your local social security office.

4. Widow, widower, or surviving divorced mother if caring for worker's child under 18.
5. Widow or widower 50 or older who becomes disabled not later than 7 years after worker's death, or within 7 years after mother's or father's benefits end.
6. Dependent parents 62 or older.

Examples of Benefits. Social security benefits are based on the average yearly earnings of the insured worker during the time of employment. Major changes in the federal social security program were made in the 1970s and will be made in the future. It is therefore impossible to say exactly what benefits a person may expect upon retirement. However, the table below shows examples of monthly social security retirement payments effective in July, 1979.

EXAMPLES OF MONTHLY SOCIAL SECURITY RETIREMENT PAYMENTS
FOR WORKERS WHO REACH 62 BEFORE 1979

| Benefits can be paid to a: | Average yearly earnings after 1950 covered by social security | | | | | | |
	$923 or less	$3,000	$4,000	$5,000	$6,000	$8,000	$10,000*
Retired worker at 65	121.80	251.80	296.20	343.50	388.20	482.60	534.70
Retired worker at 62	97.50	201.50	237.00	274.80	310.60	386.10	427.80
Wife or husband at 65	60.90	125.90	148.10	171.80	194.10	241.30	267.40
Wife or husband at 62	45.70	94.50	111.10	128.90	145.60	181.00	200.60
Wife under 65 and one child in her care	61.00	133.20	210.00	290.40	324.00	362.00	401.00
Maximum family payment	182.70	384.90	506.20	633.80	712.10	844.50	935.70

*Maximum earnings covered by social security were lower in past years and must be included in figuring your average earnings. This average determines your payment amount. Because of this, the amount shown in the last column generally won't be payable until future years. The maximum retirement benefit generally payable to a worker who is 65 in 1979 is $503.40.

Disability Insurance. Disability insurance gives workers protection against loss of earnings due to disability. Under the present law, a disabled worker may qualify for disability benefits regardless of age. If a worker has worked long enough under social security and if the disability is severe enough to meet the legal definition, benefits may be drawn. The disability benefit paid to a qualified disabled worker is equal to the retirement benefit at age 65 or later.

Dependents of a disabled worker are entitled to the same benefits they would have received had the worker retired at age 65 or later.

Hospital and Medical Insurance for the Aged. In 1965 a major addition to the social security benefit program was made. This addition was a provision for hospital and medical care for the aged. The popular term given to this program is *Medicare*. Medicare, the program for hospital and medical care for people 65 and over, has two parts:

1. Hospital insurance (automatic coverage).
2. Medical insurance (voluntary coverage).

Hospital insurance is financed through a separate social security payroll tax. Hospital insurance covers: (1) inpatient hospital care, (2) inpatient care in a skilled nursing facility, and (3) home health care. There is a limit on the number of days covered in a hospital or nursing facility and on the number of home health visits. Hospital insurance is on a deductible basis, as the patient must pay the first $92 of hospital costs, and then pay a part of the cost for each day beyond 60 days.

Medical insurance is financed by a monthly premium (presently $8.70 but subject to change) paid by the person covered; the federal government supplies an equal amount out of general revenues. Medical insurance covers physicians' services, home health services, and numerous other medical and health services in and out of medical institutions. There is an annual deductible of $60; then the plan covers 80% of the patient's bill above the deductible.

Unemployment Insurance. Under the Social Security Act, each state has set up its own law providing for an unemployment insurance system. This plan is operated in cooperation with the federal government. In most cases the tax is levied directly on the employer. In a few states the employee also is required to pay a tax for disability or unemployment contributions.

The federal and state unemployment insurance that is operated under the social security laws applies to workers in factories, offices, stores, mines, shops, mills, and other places of business and industry. However, these laws do not cover farmers, domestic help, federal employees, professional workers, and some other groups.

Unemployed persons are entitled to compensation if they have been employed in occupations covered by the law for a certain length of time prior to unemployment.

Other Social Security Programs. The previous discussion on social security dealt with the benefits that are paid as a result of deductions from wages and on the basis of previous earnings. Under the Social Security Act, however, the federal government has made provisions for assistance to other needy groups. In general, the plan provides for funds to be furnished for: (a) needy aged, (b) needy dependent children, (c) needy blind, (d) maternal welfare of infants and mothers, (e) crippled children, (f) child welfare, (g) vocational rehabilitation, and (h) public health. If a state has a plan satisfactory to the federal government, that state may obtain from the federal government a contribution up to 50% of the state expenditures.

The federal government also shares with state governments the cost of providing health benefits to low-income families. This form of medical aid to medically needy families is known as *Medicaid*. A medically needy family is defined as one whose income provides for basic necessities but not for adequate medical care or large medical bills.

Workmen's Compensation

As was mentioned in the first part of this section, workmen's compensation, sponsored by all states, is another form of social security. The laws providing protection against accidents and sickness differ from state to state. You should become familiar with the plan in operation in your state. These laws have no connection with the federal Social Security Act.

Workmen's compensation provides protection against injury arising out of employment and sometimes against diseases due to the nature of the work. The worker is not covered for an injury that occurs away from the normal place of employment. Under most of these laws, the employee receives compensation for an accident whether the employer or the employee is at fault. Exceptions to this law are cases of intoxication or recklessness in ignoring danger.

All states have workmen's compensation laws. In some states employers are required to pay into a fund for the protection of the workers. In other states these payments are optional. If the employer is not insured, an employee can sue for compensation as a result of an accident and can receive compensation. If intoxicated on the job or reckless in ignoring danger when injured, the worker cannot sue the employer.

The laws of all states provide that all medical and hospital bills will be paid regardless of the amount.

If injured, the worker will also receive compensation each week while disabled. In most states this compensation will be paid for life if the worker is permanently disabled.

In the case of death of the worker resulting from an injury at work, the spouse and children will receive weekly compensation.

FACTS EVERYONE SHOULD KNOW ABOUT
SOCIAL SECURITY INSURANCE

1. Most workers are covered by old-age and unemployment insurance.

2. Old-age benefits are generally determined by the average yearly income during the time of employment.

3. The amount of income earned by a retired worker may affect the amount of old-age benefits collected.

4. Wives, widows, widowers, children, parents, and survivors of insured workers are entitled to certain benefits under old-age insurance.

5. Social security does not replace the need for life insurance and other retirement income.

6. Workmen's compensation is a form of social security.

F. DEVELOPING AN INSURANCE PROGRAM

Every individual and family should consider an insurance program at the time major property is acquired (automobile, home, valuable gems, furs, and art objects) and at the time of marriage. The program should change as conditions warrant, such as acquiring more property and rearing children. Three major problems are involved in insurance planning: (1) what kind of financial protection through insurance the individual or family needs, (2) how much life and health insurance the individual or family needs, and (3) how much insurance the individual or family can afford.

Property, Liability, and Health Insurance

As was mentioned earlier in the chapter, most of us could not afford to absorb the loss of property severely damaged or totally destroyed by accident. Neither could we afford heavy law suits filed against us if through accident or negligence our property resulted in death or injury to others. With present medical and hospitalization costs, few of us could afford total health care without some form of insurance. Thus, in planning a property, liability, and health insurance program, the following should be considered:

1. Value of property owned and replacement cost of that property.
2. Risk potential of that property in bringing harm to others.
3. Availability of other sources of income should the primary wage earner be hospitalized or disabled for several months.
4. Present and future costs of medical (doctors, surgeons, and specialists) and convalescent care (hospitals, nursing homes, and convalescent centers).
5. Availability of medical and hospitalization insurance as a part of one's employment fringe benefits.

Since an insurance program is a unique package for each individual and family, it would be impossible to illustrate a "typical" program. However, to assist you in individual planning, consider the following examples.

The Johnson Family. Doug Johnson, age 21, and his wife, Suzie, also 21, have a 1-year-old daughter. The Johnsons own a $6,000 automobile and a home valued at $40,000. Doug is the primary wage earner grossing $12,000 a year. With the help of an insurance agent, the Johnsons have planned the following property, liability, and health program:

Type of Coverage	Annual Premium
Automobile insurance (including liability and medical coverage)	$ 350
Homeowners policy (comprehensive form, including liability coverage)	300
Hospital expense and major medical (premium shared by employer) — the Johnsons' share	240
Loss of income insurance	125
Total annual premiums	$1,015

Elaine Posthuma. Elaine Posthuma, single, age 22, earns an annual salary of $9,500. She owns an automobile valued at $5,500. Elaine rents a 3-room unfurnished apartment and has personal property valued at $5,000. She has planned the following property, liability, and health insurance program:

Type of Insurance	Annual Premium
Automobile insurance (including liability and medical coverage)	$200
Personal property and liability insurance coverage	100
Dental care insurance (premium shared by employer)	60
Hospital expense & major medical (premium shared by employer) — Elaine's share	190
Total annual premiums	$550

Life Insurance

As is true with property, liability, and health insurance, a life insurance program will be unique with each individual and family. Usually, the life insurance needs for an individual are quite different from the needs of a family. However, a single person caring for a parent or a divorced parent caring for a child may have needs similar to that of a family.

In planning a life insurance program for an individual, coverage should be provided for:

1. Final expenses in case of death, such as medical care (costs not covered by medical and hospital insurance), funeral costs, and taxes. This coverage would prevent one's parents or family from having to absorb these expenses.
2. Mortgage payments and other debts (such as automobile payments, credit card charges, and personal loans). This coverage would protect the value of the equity (ownership) of one's personal property so as to provide an estate to be willed to one's parents, other members of one's family, or to a favored organization.
3. Retirement needs.

In planning a life insurance program for a family, coverage should be provided for the following additional needs:

4. Survivor's living expenses. Insurance for this purpose should be arranged so that payments are made monthly for a certain period of years or for an indefinite period of years.

5. Special needs, such as a fund of cash for the period of readjustment so the family can operate until it makes necessary changes in living style, a fund for emergencies and major illness, and a fund for education of children.

Let us look at how the Jackson family planned their life insurance program. The Jackson family consists of James Jackson, age 31; his wife, Nancy, age 28; and three children, ages 7, 4, and 1. James earns $10,000 a year (take-home pay after taxes).

Mr. and Mrs. Jackson have planned an insurance program that they believe provides the best financial protection they can afford. Beginning at their marriage, the Jacksons have at intervals increased their insurance to provide family income during the years their children were too young to earn their living. They also have planned for an expense fund, an emergency fund, and a means of income for Mrs. Jackson after the children have reached a wage-earning age. The policies purchased are shown in the following table.

Policy	Age at Purchase	Amount and Type		Annual Premium
A	22	$ 1,000	Straight life	$ 14.85
B	23	1,000	Straight life	15.25
C	25	3,000	Straight life	48.30
D	27	5,000	Group life	36.00
E	29	5,000	Ten-year term	40.00
		$15,000	Total	$154.40

The chart at the top of page 383 shows the monthly income available to the family in the event of Mr. Jackson's death. The total monthly income available is made up of insurance income and social security payments. Mrs. Jackson would receive a monthly income of $676.80 until the 7-year-old child became 18. She would also continue to receive the same monthly income until the 4-year-old child became 18. At that time the monthly income would be reduced to $558.40. Mrs. Jackson would receive this reduced amount until the 1-year-old child became 18, at which time the social security payments would stop.

Under the Jacksons' insurance program, it is planned to leave $9,000 of the insurance (Policies B, C, and E) with the insurance companies. These companies will pay Mrs. Jackson $19 each month for the first 17 years after Mr. Jackson's death. In addition, Mrs. Jackson will receive $24 each month from $4,000 of the

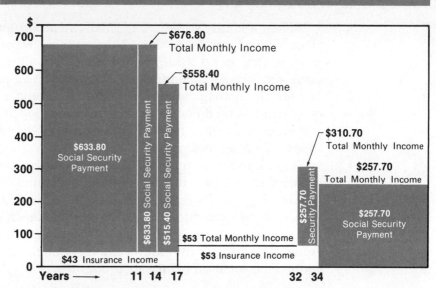

Social security payments are based on 1978 rate tables and assume that Mr. Jackson earned an average of $5,000 a year for 6 years prior to his death.
Plus: $1,000 expense fund from Policy A; $1,000 emergency fund from Policy D; $255 death benefits from social security.

group life Policy D. The remainder of the group life policy, $1,000, will be set aside in a savings account as an emergency fund.

When the youngest child is 18 and Mrs. Jackson is 45, the $9,000 (Policies B, C, and E) will be paid out to Mrs. Jackson for the next 17 years at the rate of $53 a month. At age 60, Mrs. Jackson can again draw social security payments, which will then amount to $257.70 a month. At age 62, all life insurance benefits will have been used up, but social security payments will continue for Mrs. Jackson at $257.70 each month. Under 1978 laws, Mrs. Jackson could earn $250 a month and still draw full social security benefits.

At the time of Mr. Jackson's death, Mrs. Jackson will need cash for various purposes. The Jacksons' insurance program is so planned that Mrs. Jackson will receive $1,000 from Policy A, which will be used for funeral and other expenses. From the group life Policy D, $1,000 will be set aside as an emergency fund in a savings account. This emergency fund may need to be used for living expenses until the monthly insurance and social security checks start. Mrs. Jackson will also receive a lump-sum payment of $255 from social security for funeral expenses.

Relationship of Life Insurance Expenditures and Personal Income

When a family's income is small, some insurance is needed to protect the dependents should the primary wage earner die. The amount that is set aside for insurance should be planned in the same way other expenditures are planned. As a person's salary increases, the amount spent for insurance should also increase. The only people who do not need life insurance for protection purposes are those who have investments that provide enough income to support their dependents.

The amount of insurance that should be bought is a special problem in the case of each individual. It must be determined by considering the income, the necessary expenditures, the amount of a cash savings fund, and the care of dependents. There are, however, reasonable percentages that have proved to be a good guide. The table below shows the recommended percentage of income to be spent on insurance premiums.

GUIDE TO A REASONABLE OUTLAY FOR LIFE INSURANCE

Annual Income	Percentage (Including Social Security)	Annual Outlay (Including Social Security)
$ 6,000	8– 9	$ 480 to $ 540
7,000	9–10	630 to 700
8,000	10–11	800 to 880
9,000	11–12	990 to 1,030
10,000	12–13	1,200 to 1,300
12,000	13–14	1,560 to 1,680

Obviously, the percentage expended in any particular case will depend on (a) one's level of living, (b) one's sense of responsibility, (c) the cost of living, (d) the number of dependents, and (e) the type of insurance that is bought.

Of course, a person without family responsibilities may not feel the need for much insurance. Such a person may prefer to invest the money in other ways.

G. ECONOMIC IMPACT OF INSURANCE

Billions of dollars of property are destroyed each year through fire, storms, floods, explosions, and accidents. The vast majority of individuals and businesses suffering such losses would not have savings large enough to replace these losses. Thus, many individuals would be without homes, clothing, or transportation, and many businesses would no longer be able to manufacture and sell goods. Large debts (on homes, furniture and appliances, automobiles, business buildings, and inventories) could not be repaid, and creditors would also experience a loss. With little or no savings available to replace destroyed property and fewer creditors with money to lend, economic activity would suffer greatly.

However, with an insurance system operating, there is money available to replace destroyed property. Debts would continue to be repaid on schedule so creditors would not suffer. Many workers would be needed to rebuild the homes and factories and to manufacture furniture, appliances, clothing, and automobiles. The economy as a whole would continue to operate to replace the property destroyed.

By collecting small sums of money from many policyholders, insurance companies have enough money to replace economic losses. In addition, insurance companies have large sums of money remaining that they can invest. This money is loaned for building homes, factories, churches, offices, and schools. Some of the money is also invested in municipal bonds, government bonds, and corporation stocks. Thus, by paying small insurance premiums, individuals not only save money (through life insurance) and protect themselves against unexpected losses (through property, liability, and health insurance) but also help fulfill the economic needs of the entire nation.

REVIEW QUESTIONS

Section A

1. How can an insurance company protect a person against possible large losses?
2. How do "face value" and "cash value" differ?
3. What is the relationship among the following terms: assured, insured, policyholder?
4. What is meant by the term "insurable interest"?
5. How are insurance companies regulated? Why?

Section B

6. What is the outstanding feature of a homeowners policy?
7. What are the names of each of the three forms of homeowners policies? Which gives the greatest protection? The least protection?
8. What is meant by liability insurance?
9. What are the types of insurance coverage for loss and for liability that are available to owners and drivers of automobiles?
10. How does property damage insurance protect the owner of an automobile insurance policy?
11. What insurance is necessary to protect the driver and the driver's family against losses due to injury to the driver or the family as a result of an automobile accident?

Section C   12. What is the major advantage of term insurance?
                     13. What is the major advantage of level-premium insurance?
                     14. How do policyholders use endowment insurance policies in their life in-
                         surance programs?
                     15. What is an annuity?
                     16. Why do all types of ordinary life insurance with the exception of term
                         insurance include an element of savings?

Section D   17. What is the primary purpose of health insurance?
                     18. Why do most major medical insurance policies include a deductible
                         clause?

Section E   19. Why was the federal social security plan developed?
                     20. Does social security provide complete economic security?
                     21. Who is eligible to receive monthly social security payments for a retired
                         worker?
                     22. At what age can the widow of an insured worker receive social security
                         benefits if she has no children?
                     23. What is the purpose of workmen's compensation?
                     24. What do workmen's compensation laws provide regarding medical and
                         hospital bills?

Section F   25. In planning a property, liability, and health insurance program, what
                         should be considered?
                     26. In planning a life insurance program, what are some of the specific needs
                         of survivors that should be taken into consideration?

DISCUSSION QUESTIONS

Section A   1. Are the following statements contradictory? Why or why not?
                        (a) Total losses for a given period of time in a given state due to fire
                            can be predicted with reasonable accuracy.
                        (b) The locations and amounts of individual losses due to fire for a
                            given period of time in a given state cannot be predicted with any
                            degree of accuracy.

Section B   2. Over a lifetime the amount of premiums on household insurance would
                        amount to several hundred dollars. Why is it not advisable for a home-
                        owner to save the money paid in insurance premiums for the purpose of
                        replacing or repairing the house if it should be damaged by fire?
                     3. What are some illustrations of the kinds of liability claims to which a
                        homeowner might be subject?
                     4. Of all the available types of automobile insurance coverage, which type(s)
                        do you feel is (are) absolutely necessary?

Section C   5. A widowed mother with limited funds is financing most of the college
                        education for her son, although he is paying part of the cost from his own
                        part-time work. Should she buy a life insurance policy on his life? If so,
                        what kind? Should he buy a policy? Why?
                     6. Mr. Brown has no dependents but he wants to purchase a home ten years
                        from now. What type of insurance would allow him to build up the largest
                        cash value and yet provide an estate for his heirs in the event of his
                        death?

7. Explain the difference in the uses of the term "cash value" when referring to property insurance and life insurance.

Section D   8. Should the head of the family carry more than one health insurance policy?

9. Should all families carry loss-of-income insurance?

Section E   10. How do the provisions for old-age benefits under social security eliminate certain economic risks?

11. Why do you think that widows under 60 years of age are not entitled to benefits under social security if they have no children under 18?

12. Under workmen's compensation, can you collect benefits if you slip on the ice at home and break an arm? Why?

13. If a worker gets lead poisoning from materials that he handles and becomes ill, do you think he can obtain benefits under workmen's compensation? Explain your answer.

Section F   14. What should be the relationship of one's life insurance program and the benefits one may be entitled to under social security?

Section G   15. In what ways does the insurance industry affect the national economy?

APPLICATION PROBLEMS

Section A   1. Make a list of the types of insurance coverages a family of 4 (both parents working) might wish to purchase.

Section B   2. Using the chart below, indicate to which party or parties each of the homeowners policy coverages apply.

LIABILITY INSURANCE COVERAGE

		Applies to	
Type of Insurance Coverage	Policyholder	Policyholder's Family	Other Persons
HOMEOWNERS POLICY COVERAGE:			
Comprehensive personal liability	yes no	yes no	yes no
Medical payments	yes no	yes no	yes no
Physical damage to property of others	yes no	yes no	yes no

3. A $100 deductible collision insurance policy on an automobile has cost Mr. Hulbert an average of $75 a year for five years. At the end of the fifth year he had a wreck costing $650 to repair the car.
   (a) How much has he saved or lost by carrying the insurance as compared with assuming his own risk and paying all his own damages?
   (b) If he would save by carrying his own insurance, is it wise for him to do so?

4. Prepare charts showing (a) the number of automobile accidents in the U.S. for the last ten years and (b) the total dollar value of losses resulting from auto accidents for the same years. What are the trends?

Section C

5. The following charts show life insurance rates issued by a certain company for two types of policies. The rates shown are for $1,000 of protection.

Age	10-Year term		Straight life	
	Annual	Monthly	Annual	Monthly
20	$4.90	$.44	$13.44	$1.19
25	5.17	.46	15.41	1.37
30	5.37	.48	17.88	1.58

(a) What will be the annual premium for a $15,000 10-year term policy issued to a 20-year-old woman? Assume she elects to pay the premium annually.

(b) What will be the annual cost for a $10,000 straight life policy issued to a man who is 30 years old? Assume he elects to pay the premium monthly.

(c) A 25-year-old woman is trying to decide whether to pay for her 10-year term policy monthly or annually. (1) On a $10,000 policy, how much will she save each year if she pays the premium annually? (2) How much would she save over the 10-year period? (Assume that it costs 10 cents for every check written and 15 cents postage for every premium payment mailed.)

6. The following chart shows the premium rates charged on a straight life policy by a certain company for $1,000 of protection for a person aged 20:

	Straight Life			
Age	Annually	Semiannually	Quarterly	Monthly
20	$13.44	$6.86	$3.50	$1.19

(a) How much money does a 20-year-old person save by paying the insurance premium annually rather than monthly? quarterly? semiannually?

(b) What percent savings does an annual premium payment represent over 12 monthly payments? 4 quarterly payments? 2 semiannual payments?

(c) If one considers that it costs a minimum of 10 cents for every check written and 15 cents postage for every check mailed, what would one annual premium payment represent in total cash savings over 12 monthly payments? What percent savings does this represent?

Section D

7. Mr. Martinez was involved in a serious automobile accident that resulted in his suffering several broken bones and requiring a delicate abdominal operation. Mr. Martinez was in the hospital 30 days and his total medical expenses were: hospital room, $1,950; surgical fees, $1,500; doctor's visits, $50; medication and dressings, $1,200. Mr. Martinez's hospital insurance coverage pays $55 a day up to 30 days for any one accident. His surgical insurance covered $850 of his expenses. His general medical coverage paid $40 for the doctor's visits and $900 for medication and

dressings. He also had $100 deductible major medical with a 20% coinsurance clause for amounts above the first $100. How much of the total medical expenses did Mr. Martinez have to pay?

Section E

8. Assume that Don Attebury earns $8,000 a year and that his income is taxed at 6.13% for social security.
   (a) How much social security tax is deducted from Don's wages each year?
   (b) What is the total amount of social security tax Don's employer must send to the federal government each year on Don's wages?

9. Ivan Reznik is fully insured for social security retirement payments. His family consists of a wife and a daughter. His average annual earnings computed under the Act are $8,000. According to the table of benefits on page 376, how much monthly income will Ivan and his family receive if:
   (a) He retires at age 62, at which time his wife is 55 and his daughter is 17?
   (b) He retires at age 65, at which time his wife is 62 and his daughter is 21?
   (c) He retires at age 65, at which time his wife is 62 and his daughter is 21 and a full-time college student?

Section F

10. Steve Ingmire has just graduated from high school and has married his childhood sweetheart. He feels he should start planning an insurance program. He has a full-time job that pays $160 a week, out of which his employer deducts 6.13% for social security taxes. Steve owns an automobile valued at $3,000. He and his wife have just rented a 3-room unfurnished apartment, which they have furnished with credit purchases amounting to $2,000. He has no medical or hospitalization insurance. What types of insurance coverage would you recommend for the Ingmires?

COMMUNITY PROJECTS

Section A

1. Write to the insurance commissioner of your state (your city or county library can give you the correct name and address) to find out what state regulations are imposed on "mail-order" insurance companies. Report your findings to the class.

Section B

2. From a local insurance agent, collect information regarding unusual or unexpected insurance claims involving personal liability in connection with homes, pets, and places of business. In addition find out the approximate cost of liability insurance for a homeowners policy. What conclusions can you draw from this investigation?

3. Consult the *Reader's Guide* for articles on no-fault insurance. From these articles prepare a bulletin board display presenting "Arguments For No-Fault Insurance" on one side and "Arguments Against No-Fault Insurance" on the other side.

Section C

4. From a local life insurance agent find out: (a) the procedure for borrowing on one's life insurance policy, (b) how much can be borrowed, and (c) the advantages and disadvantages of borrowing on a life insurance policy.

5. Obtain a life insurance policy at home or from an insurance agent. Study it carefully as to the nonforfeiture value, the cash-surrender value, restrictions on flying, and any other special provisions that are new to you. Make a list of the facts you learn from the examination of this policy and write a report on them.

Section D

6. Check with a member of your family whose wage contract includes health insurance coverage. Report in class on the benefits of this insurance. Are the premiums paid wholly by the employer or jointly by the employer and the employee?

7. Check with an official in your school to learn of the features of the health and accident policy covering each student in your school. Report to the class what the coverages are and how much the insurance costs for each student. You might also report on the total number of claims filed by students in your school for the past year.

Section E

8. Visit your local social security office. Obtain an assortment of materials about the social security program and in particular about Medicare. Using the resource materials you obtained and the information given you by people in the local office, prepare a written report in which you describe: (a) the highlights of Medicare, (b) the need for supplemental health insurance, and (c) free benefits for needy aged people.

9. Interview a person working in your local social security office to find out exactly who is not covered under social security. Try to get reasons for these workers not being covered. Present your findings to the class.

Section F

10. Consult an insurance agent and ask what types and amounts of life insurance he or she would recommend for a typical high school graduate earning $100 a week (and covered under social security), married and no children, paying $125 a month for rent and $55 a month for car payments (for 12 more months). Then ask the agent what he or she would recommend if all conditions above were the same except there is one small child of 6 months.

Planning Housing Needs

PURPOSE OF THE CHAPTER

Every individual or family must have housing. Many choices are open: buy a house, an apartment, or a mobile home; rent a house or an apartment; or build a house. The two big problems are to decide on one of the many choices and to find a way to pay for the housing. The purpose of this chapter is to study those things people must think about in making choices related to housing.

After studying this chapter, you will be able to:

1. List the advantages and disadvantages of owning a home.
2. List the advantages and disadvantages of renting a home.
3. List places where money can be borrowed to pay for a home.
4. Identify the important points that should be included in a lease.
5. Identify the rights and duties of both the landlord and the tenant.
6. State the legal steps in buying real property.

A. HOUSING PROBLEMS

Providing housing is one of the most important economic problems faced by an individual or a family. In many cases housing is one of the most costly purchases made by an individual or a family. In addition, comfort and satisfaction that comes from housing is also very significant. Thus, it is most important that wise choices about housing be made.

Owning vs. Renting

Individuals and families should consider buying a house if (1) they can pay for the house out of savings or by monthly payments out of current wages, (2) they expect to continue to live in the same area, and (3) they will get more pleasure and satisfaction from owning than from renting. Home ownership involves responsibilities for financing, repairing, and improving the physical condition and appearance of the house. Such responsibilities might help an individual or a family to have a sense of pride in the home. All the costs of owning a home should be carefully figured and should then be included in the spending plan of the individual or family.

ADVANTAGES OF HOME OWNERSHIP

1. Home ownership gives a sense of security, and it usually assures a home in old age.

2. Home ownership forces the setting up of a plan of savings. Payments beyond the costs of maintenance and ownership are a form of savings.

3. Home ownership improves the credit rating of the individual or the family if payments are made when they are due.

4. Home ownership is a source of enjoyment, satisfaction, and pride.

5. Interest paid as a part of mortgage payments is tax deductible.

DISADVANTAGES OF HOME OWNERSHIP

1. The owner's equity or investment in the house is not readily available for use in making other purchases.

2. The homeowner must assume responsibility for financing, maintenance and care, and improvements; renters pay their rent and leave the other responsibilities to the landlord.

3. Home ownership makes moving from one community or city to another difficult.

4. In some locations property values may not appreciate, making it difficult to build equity to keep pace with inflation or to sell the home in a short period of time.

Even though owning a home may appear desirable, it may be economically unwise to buy or to build a house. For instance, if

Although it involves many responsibilities, home ownership is a source of enjoyment, satisfaction, and pride.

Jefferson-Pilot Corporation, Greensboro, NC

one expects to move soon to another town, if property values are falling, if not enough money is available to make the down payment, or if there is any chance that payments on the home cannot be made, buying a home would be unwise. In this case, renting or leasing a home or an apartment may be the proper step to take.

Generally speaking, renting and leasing mean the same thing. However, some people think of renting as using property without a written agreement and of leasing as using property with a written agreement. The term "renting," however, can be properly applied to the use of property both with and without a written agreement.

A tenant may use property under an agreement covering (1) a definite period, (2) an indefinite period, or (3) an indefinite period with both parties having the right to end the agreement when they wish. Any of these agreements may be written or oral, but the last two are more likely to be oral agreements.

ADVANTAGES OF RENTING

1. The yearly cash outlay for renting is usually less than for buying a dwelling of comparable size.

2. No sizable down payment is required for renting.

3. The tenant has no responsibility for maintenance and upkeep of the property other than taking reasonable care of the property and making minor repairs.

4. The tenant has freedom to move with no worry as to whether the property can be sold at a suitable price, as in the case of home ownership.

DISADVANTAGES OF RENTING

1. No portion of monthly rental payments is building up equity or ownership (thus savings).

2. The tenant has no freedom to make major alterations in the living structure or grounds where the dwelling is located.

3. Property taxes are passed on to the renter as part of the rental payments.

4. No portion of the monthly rental payments is tax deductible.

5. Without a written lease, the tenant may be given a 30-day notice to vacate the premises at any time by the owner.

Paying for the Home

All authorities in home management, financing, and home building insist that no family should buy a home until a very careful spending plan has been worked out. After shopping for a desirable location for a home that will take care of the individual or family for several years, a spending plan should then be prepared that includes the down payment, all carrying and operating charges, and the monthly payments. Ways of figuring these estimates will be discussed in greater detail later in this chapter.

Buying for Cash. If you buy a house for cash, you should not invest so much that there are no funds left in case of an emergency. For instance, if you use all your cash to purchase a house, you may not have any reserve cash in case of a serious illness or some other emergency.

A person who buys a house with borrowed money makes a

serious mistake if it is beyond that person's capacity to pay the interest charge and to repay the loan. If the loan is too great, one may become discouraged because of the need to lower the level of living, which may deprive an individual or a family of certain essentials such as adequate health protection. One may even lose the house through foreclosure proceedings.

In buying a house, many young people gamble to the extent of assuming that their earnings will increase. They therefore take on a greater debt than they should. If future earnings do not become greater, or if they become less, discouragement and inability to repay the loan may result.

Cost of Home and Annual Income. The amount that a person should spend for the interest and principal on a home loan is always a question. Builders, realtors, and lenders of money estimate that between 20 and 25% of the assured income of a family may safely be spent in financing a home. This should include interest, amount of principal, taxes, and insurance (but not the down payment).

If a family that has been renting a house decides to buy it, they may be faced with greater expenses than those required in renting. If it has not been possible for them to save money while renting, it will probably not be possible to finance the purchase of a home. Some people do, however, take on such a purchase because they are then forced to follow some definite plan of saving.

Down Payment. There are many ways of financing the purchase of a home, but usually a person must pay part of the original price in cash. The lender, of course, states the amount of down payment considered necessary as partial protection for the loan. Plans developed by the Department of Housing and Urban Development (HUD) and the Federal Housing Administration (FHA) permit minimum down payments of as low as 3%. Many lenders, however, require that a person who buys a home on installments should make a cash down payment of at least 20% of the purchase price.

Monthly Payments. Most loans on houses today are made on the basis of monthly payments. Three critical factors that an individual or a family must consider in purchasing a home are: (1) the amount of the monthly payments; (2) the conditions of payment, such as paying off the loan before it is due or missing some monthly payments because of emergencies; and (3) whether the monthly payment is to include the cost of the insurance and the taxes.

Initial Occupancy Cost. When moving into a new house or into one recently bought, there are many expenses that do not recur until much later if at all. Examples of such expenses are curtains, draperies, floor coverings, and, in some instances, shrubbery and the establishment of a lawn. Although an individual or a family may be able to make the down payment and the required monthly payments, the resources may not be enough to meet all first-year costs.

Low-Cost Government Housing

Wherever a need exists, the federal government tries to provide low-cost rental homes and apartments for low-income families and for the aged. Also, low-interest mortgage loans are made available to low-income and moderate-income families for the purchase of homes.

Rental Housing. In some cases the federal government builds public housing projects to rent to low-income families and the aged. The government also contracts with private owners to provide similar public housing. It is also possible to rent individual dwellings that are not a part of a public housing project. The rent charged for such housing is based on the yearly income of the family. Such rents can be as low as $30 a month for a modern, furnished or unfurnished home or apartment. In some federal housing projects the rental payments include most utilities. In all federal housing projects, central laundry and entertainment facilities are provided to renters at no extra cost.

Home Buying. Both low-income and moderate-income families can qualify for low-cost mortgage loans for the purchase of a home. To qualify, a family can earn no more than 80% of the median family income in its geographic area. If the median family income is $20,000 a year, a family would qualify for such a mortgage loan if its annual income were no greater than $16,000. The family would have to make a down payment of at least 3% of the value of the home and pay no less than 20% of adjusted gross income toward monthly house payments. At present these low-cost mortgage loans are being offered by the government for as low as 3% interest compared to 10½% to 12% most lenders are charging.

Buying a Mobile Home

In recent years there has been a growing interest in mobile homes among home buyers of all ages. It is estimated that 1 of every 4 families moving into single-family housing in the 1970s moved into a mobile home. Mobile homes provide moderately priced living quarters for people who need only a limited amount of space. Mobile homes can be financed almost as easily as conventional homes.

Mobile homes are usually bought completely furnished. The average price of a new, low-cost mobile home completely furnished is $10,000, while the average price of a new, low-cost conventional home unfurnished is $40,000. However, the mobile home owner must provide land on which to park the mobile home or must rent space in a mobile home park and pay monthly rental fees (from $20 to $150). There are many attractive mobile home parks in convenient locations. These parks provide a foundation, water and electrical connections, central laundry facilities, and sometimes recreational facilities.

Some advantages of mobile homes over conventional homes are: (1) they can be moved to other locations if their owners are transferred, (2) upkeep costs are lower, and (3) there is less housekeeping required.

Some disadvantages of mobile homes are: (1) zoning laws are rather strict as to where mobile homes can be located, (2) living space is small, (3) there is little yard space, and (4) they provide rather poor protection against fires and tornadoes because of their lightweight construction.

Many people rent mobile homes in established mobile home parks. This is especially true in recreational and retirement areas or in other places where temporary housing is required. The cost of renting a mobile home is frequently lower than the cost of renting a conventional apartment or house.

Choosing housing is a family decision.

B. FINANCING YOUR HOUSING

Few people can buy a home without borrowing. Most people borrow about 80% of the cost of their homes. In early 1979 consumer credit amounted to $1.12 trillion. Of this amount $725.9 billion (or two thirds) was for mortgage debt. In the next few pages you will learn what a mortgage is and where to borrow money for a home.

Mortgages

A *real estate mortgage* is a contract between the borrower and the lender for purposes of buying property. It states the conditions under which the money is lent and must be repaid. It serves as security for the loan and grants certain privileges to the lender if the loan is not repaid according to agreement.

Partial-Payment Mortgage. Most mortgages on homes provide for monthly payments of a part of the principal and the accumulated interest. This is sometimes called a *partial-payment mortgage*. Payments are arranged so that at the end of the term specified in the mortgage the entire loan will be repaid. There are several different types of this mortgage.

Insured Mortgage. An *insured mortgage* is one in which the lender is insured against loss by a government agency.

Package Deals. Some mortgage contracts are called *package deals*. The payments not only include interest and principal, but also include insurance on the building, taxes, life insurance on the borrower, and sometimes household appliances, such as a stove, refrigerator, and dishwasher.

Open-End Mortgage. Another type of mortgage is called an *open-end mortgage*. This type of mortgage permits a borrower, after having made substantial repayments on the loan, to borrow additional sums under the same mortgage contract without arranging for an additional loan. This extra money may be needed from time to time for making repairs.

Appraisals

When one applies for a loan from any lending agency, it is necessary to fill out an application. The lender will then insist on having experts make an *appraisal*, which is an examination of the property and the setting of its value. This is done to determine its value and condition. The appraisal is important to the lender and to the borrower because it should help to find any defects and should help to determine a fair value of the property. In many cases, the borrower is required to pay for the appraisal fee.

Sources of Loans

There are many sources from which money can be borrowed to finance the purchase of a home. Generally, these include savings and loan associations, banks, credit unions, mortgage companies, and private investors. There are other special types of lenders in some cities.

Savings and Loan Associations. Savings and loan associations are usually liberal in their lending. They extend loans for reasonably long periods, usually 10 to 20 years. They often appraise property at a value equal to the full market price. First-mortgage loans are sometimes made on property up to 70 to 90% of the valuation. The ease in getting a loan depends largely on local and general business conditions and on the availability of funds.

Banks. The size of the loan that a bank can make is generally limited by state law (or federal regulations in the case of national banks) to a certain percentage of the value of the property. State laws do not, however, limit banks with respect to making liberal or conservative appraisals. Thus, a liberal bank in a state that limits loans to 50% of the property value might lend more than a conservative bank in a state that limits loans to 60% of the property value.

Banks commonly extend loans for 15–20 years, but some banks extend loans for only short periods, such as 3, 5, or 10 years. Short-term loans can usually be renewed, but a charge may be made for that privilege. Unless good care has been taken of the property, it is difficult to renew the loan.

Credit Unions. Federally chartered credit unions are now authorized to offer real estate loans up to 30 years. The amount that may be loaned is 80% of the assessed value of the property up to $65,000.

Mortgage Companies. In many large communities, mortgage companies are an important factor in home financing. There are two classes of these companies. One class lends on first, or senior, mortgages; and the other lends on second, or junior, mortgages. There is a great lack of uniformity in the policies and the methods of these companies. They are usually not placed under the legal restrictions that are applied to savings and loan associations, banks, trust companies, and insurance companies. On a first mortgage they usually do not lend over 50% of the valuation of the property. When a greater amount is lent, an extra fee may be charged.

Private Lenders. Private lenders, who are unorganized, are free to operate as they please so long as they keep within the bounds of state laws on lending. They usually follow the methods of the lending institutions in their communities. They are frequently willing to lend a higher percentage of the property value than are financial institutions, especially when it is possible for them to get a slightly higher rate of interest. Private lenders often include one's relatives or the seller of the property.

The person who borrows from a lending institution can usually depend on being able to renew the mortgage if payments have been made promptly. When one borrows from an individual, however, there is nothing but personal assurance that the loan can be renewed. Such unforeseen circumstances as the death of the lender may cause a situation in which the borrower would immediately have to pay back the loan to the estate.

Land Contracts

A common form of financing used by home buyers who can make a down payment of only 5 to 15% involves a land contract. This plan is popular in the central part of the United States. A *land contract* is an agreement between the buyer and the seller of the property, under the terms of which the buyer usually makes a small down payment and agrees to pay the full purchase price in monthly installments. The seller does not give the buyer legal ownership of the property, but agrees to transfer the title to the buyer when a stated percentage of the purchase price has been paid. When the title is transferred, the buyer either takes care of the unpaid balance or obtains a loan from someone else to pay the balance due the original seller.

This type of agreement enables an individual who does not have enough savings for a large down payment to occupy the property and make payments like those on a mortgage. When the payments are equal to a required down payment or some other agreed upon amount, the title is transferred to the buyer, who then mortgages the property for the unpaid balance. A land contract has the effect of leasing with the right to buy.

Payments and Rates

The final decision in choosing an agency to finance buying or building a home should be based on the reputation of the agency and the economy with which the home can be financed.

The method of calculating the interest charges and the expenses involved in obtaining the loan should be studied carefully.

Interest Charges. Different types of financial institutions have very different plans of charging interest. Some loan companies calculate interest annually; others calculate it semiannually or quarterly. Loans may be obtained for 10, 15, 20, or 25 years. Of course, each borrower will have to arrange a loan to fit his or her own spending plan. The faster the borrower repays a loan, however, the less interest will be paid.

Extra Charges. When loans are obtained, special care should be used to detect any extra charges. Premiums, commissions, and points on loans result in higher interest rates for the borrowers. *Points* are a charge made by the lender to get around the low interest ceiling permitted on government-insured mortgages. Each point is 1% of the mortgage loan. For example, if a buyer with a Veterans Administration mortgage needs $15,000, each point will be $150 ($15,000 × .01). Assume that the lender asks for 5 points, or $750, to grant the loan and that the buyer accepts the terms. The buyer will receive only $14,250 but will pay interest on the full $15,000.

Settlement Costs. *Settlement costs*, often called *closing costs*, are additional charges incurred in obtaining a loan. In some states a tax is charged. In practically every state there is a fee for having the deed recorded. The cost of having the title examined is usually from $75 to $150. The cost of an appraisal should not exceed $25 to $50. Some lenders require title insurance, which is also charged to the borrower. Usually, these settlement costs are borne by the person who obtains the loan, but occasionally they are paid by the company granting the loan.

Under 1976 legislation, lenders are required to give borrowers a government booklet explaining settlements. Lenders must also provide "good faith" estimates of settlement costs at the time of the loan application and a complete settlement sheet at the closing. The lender must let the borrower examine the settlement statement one day before closing.

Real Estate Loan Protective Insurance. Term life insurance or mortgage redemption insurance is good protection for a family that is financing the purchase of a home. If the borrower should die before the loan has been repaid, the insurance will pay the balance of the loan for the family. Some mortgage agreements include or require such protective insurance.

Government-Secured Real Estate Loans

In order to promote home ownership, the federal government has encouraged both the purchase and the building of houses by insuring loans on houses on which the prospective owners make small down payments. Under certain conditions, one program insures a lending institution against loss if an owner is unable to pay and the other guarantees the payments on houses.

FHA-Insured Loans. The Federal Housing Administration (FHA), established under the National Housing Act of 1934, is now under the jurisdiction of the Department of Housing and Urban Development (HUD). The FHA provides federal insurance on loans that are obtained through an approved lending agency, such as a bank. If the FHA approves the loan, the money can be borrowed from the regular lending agency. The lending agency is protected because the FHA insures the loan, thus guaranteeing its payment. Money may be borrowed for repairing or improving a home, buying or building a new home, buying an existing home, buying a mobile home, or buying a multiple-family dwelling. (An apartment building would be an example of a multiple-family dwelling.)

From the viewpoint of an individual seeking a loan, an FHA-insured loan is usually no better than many other types of loans. However, a qualified person who can make only a small down payment can sometimes obtain an FHA-insured loan when it may not be possible to get some other kind of loan. FHA regulations will not permit a loan to be made if it requires monthly payments exceeding a certain amount of the take-home pay of the principal wage earner of the family.

Any regular lending agency, such as a savings and loan association, bank, credit union, mortgage company, or private investor, can help an individual apply for an FHA-insured loan. A contractor, an architect, or a real estate agent can also help a home buyer to apply for an FHA-insured loan. If a loan is desired for repairing or improving a home, assistance can be obtained through a contractor or a dealer in building supplies.

A loan obtained under FHA may be repaid over periods of 10, 15, 20, 25, or 30 years, or in a lump sum at any time. The minimum down payment required on the purchase of a new home is less than that required for buying an old home. Down payments (as low as 3%) under FHA are usually lower than under other plans of borrowing.

A charge is added to the interest rate to cover mortgage insurance. This charge is based on the decreasing balance of the loan. The interest rates permitted on FHA-insured loans are regulated by law, and these rates change from time to time as the law is changed. However, FHA-insured loan rates may be lower than those ordinarily charged for real estate loans because FHA-insured loans are insured by the federal government.

VA-Insured Loans. For persons with service in the Armed Forces during World War II and the Korean and Vietnam conflicts, special loan privileges are granted by the Veterans Administration (VA). These privileges are similar to those obtainable under FHA-insured loans. The loan must be obtained through a regular lending agency. It is then guaranteed by the federal government. This privilege helps veterans to obtain real estate and borrow money for business or agricultural purposes on very favorable terms.

VA (also called GI) loans are insured by the Veterans Administration in about the same way that FHA loans are insured. If a veteran fails to repay the loan, the Veterans Administration has a claim against the borrower and has the privilege of deducting this amount from any pension, insurance dividend, or other compensation due the borrower.

Interest rates on VA-insured loans are generally lower than those on other real estate loans. However, these rates are changed from time to time through changes in the federal law. In addition to the interest rate, the borrower on a VA-insured loan must also pay a small monthly charge for insurance. A down payment is urged and recommended, but the VA loan law permits the Veterans Administration to guarantee loans with no down payment if the lender is willing to make the loan for the full amount of the purchase price. A VA-insured loan is not permitted if the monthly payments exceed a certain amount of the take-home pay of the principal wage earner in the family.

C. LEGAL ASPECTS OF RENTING A HOME

Renting or leasing involves the legal rights, duties, and responsibilities of the landlord and the tenant. It is desirable and necessary that both should fully understand the relationship that exists between them.

If you are the owner of a house or an apartment building and, by agreement, allow the property to be occupied and controlled by another, you are a *landlord*. The one who occupies the property is the *tenant*.

The agreement between the landlord and the tenant is known as a *lease*. The landlord is the *lessor* and the tenant is the *lessee*. The lease may be oral or written, the form depending on the laws of each state. A written lease is desirable in many cases because it clearly defines the rights of the landlord and the tenant. The lease may specifically state the rights of each party, but some other legal rights may not be mentioned in the lease. A typical lease is shown below.

A Lease

Agreement of Lease

THAT   John E. Hansen and Evelyn M. Hansen, husband and wife,
HEREBY LEASE TO   Charles L. Burroughs

the premises situate in the City   *of* Miami   *in the County of*
Dade   *and State of* Florida   *described as follows:*

Building to be used as a single-family dwelling located at 232 Collins Avenue, Miami, Florida

with the appurtenances thereto, for the term of ten (10) years   *commencing*
June 1,   *19-- at a rental of* Two hundred fifty (250)

dollars per month   *. payable* monthly.

SAID LESSEE AGREE S *to pay said rent, unless said premises shall be destroyed or rendered untenantable by fire or other unavoidable accident; to not commit or suffer waste; to not use said premises for any unlawful purpose; to not assign this lease, or underlet said premises, or any part thereof, or permit the sale of* his *interest herein by legal process, without the written consent of said lessor* S; *to not use said premises or any part thereof in violation of any law relating to intoxicating liquors; and at the expiration of this lease, to surrender said premises in as good condition as they now are, or may be put by said lessor* S, *reasonable wear and unavoidable casualties, condemnation or appropriation excepted. Upon nonpayment of any of said rent for* thirty *days, after it shall become due, and without demand made therefor; or if said lessee or any assignee of this lease shall make an assignment for the benefit of his creditors; or if proceedings in bankruptcy shall be instituted by or against lessee or any assignee; or if a receiver or trustee be appointed for the property of the lessee or any assignee; or if this lease by operation of law pass to any person or persons; or if said lessee or any assignee shall fail to keep any of the other covenants of this lease, it shall be lawful for said lessor* s, their *heirs or assigns, into said premises to reenter, and the same to have again, repossess and enjoy, as in* their *first and former estate; and thereupon this lease and everything herein contained on the said lessor* s 'behalf *to be done and performed, shall cease, determine, and be utterly void*

SAID LESSOR S AGREE   *(said lessee having performed* his   *obligations under this lease) that said lessee shall quietly hold and occupy said premises during said term without any hindrance or molestation by said lessor* s, their   *heir or any person lawfully claiming under them.*

Signed this first   *day of* May   *A. D. 19--*

IN THE PRESENCE OF:

Louis K. Whitfield   *John E. Hansen*
Robert K. Crowell   *Evelyn M. Hansen*
                                       Charles L. Burroughs

The tenant has the right to the peaceful use of the property. The landlord has no right to enter the property to show it to a prospective buyer.

Rights and Duties of the Tenant

The tenant of a piece of property is entitled to peaceful possession of the property. If deprived of that, the tenant may sue for damages. The tenant is also entitled to use the property for any purpose for which it is suitable, unless certain uses (such as subleasing) are forbidden by the agreement. The property may not be used for unlawful purposes.

The tenant must pay the rent when it is due. Leases usually require payment of rent in advance; but in the absence of an agreement to that effect, rent is not due until the end of each month. A "clean-up and breakage" or "security" deposit is often required. The amount of this deposit should be refunded at the end of the leasing period if the property is left as clean and sound as when it was first occupied, less ordinary wear and tear.

The tenant must take reasonable care of the leased property. The tenant is usually responsible for minor repairs, such as replacing a broken window, but not for structural improvements. The tenant should notify the landlord when major repairs become necessary. In some states, the tenant may use up to a month's rent to make necessary repairs if the landlord does not do so after reasonable notice.

The tenant should carefully inspect the property to be rented or leased. In the absence of any agreement with the landlord, the tenant accepts the property with the risk of defects, except those that are hidden, being present. In most states, the tenant is liable for injuries to guests resulting from defects that should have been known and repaired.

Unless there are specific laws or agreements to the contrary, the tenant is responsible for injuries arising from defective conditions of the property.

If the lease is for a definite period of time, the tenant is not required to give notice when vacating the property. The lease may be ended, however, before the expiration of the period if an agreement is reached with the landlord. If the lease is for an indefinite period of time, the tenant must notify the landlord of any intention to give up the lease. The form and the time of notice are regulated by the customs or the laws of the community or state.

Bedford, Virginia, June 1, 19--

Mr. Robert Burdan
   I hereby give you notice that I will quit and deliver possession, July 1, 19--, of the premises at No. 417 Reading Road, in the city of Bedford, Virginia, which I now hold as tenant under you.

Shirley Korth

A Tenant's Notice of Intention to Terminate a Lease

If you, the tenant, do not believe the landlord is living up to agreements of the lease, you can check on your rights in your state at no cost. The state attorney general's office is one source to check on your rights. A local tenants' group is also a good source of information. Your city or county consumer protection agency or the legal aid society can tell you if a tenants' group exists.

Rights and Duties of the Landlord

A landlord does not have the right to enter the premises of a tenant except to do what is necessary to protect the property. The landlord must not interfere with the tenant's right of possession. If the tenant moves from the property, however, the landlord may take possession.

At the expiration of the lease, the landlord is entitled to take possession of the property. If the tenant refuses to give up possession, the landlord may bring legal proceedings against the tenant.

The landlord is entitled to receive the rent as specified in the lease. In most states, through legal proceedings, the landlord may have the court seize personal property of the tenant and have it sold to pay the rent that is due. Unless the lease specifies otherwise, taxes and assessments must be paid by the landlord.

In some states, the landlord is under no obligation to make repairs or to pay for improvements on the property unless such an agreement has been made with the tenant. In most states, however, the landlord is required to keep the house in livable condition.

When the landlord retains control over a part of the property — as in the case of a landlord who leases part of a building to a tenant — the landlord is liable for certain injuries caused by the defective condition of that part of the property. For instance, Mr. Adams owns a two-story building. He lives on the first floor and retains control over the porch and the yard, but he rents the second floor to Ms. Brown. If Ms. Brown or a member of her family is injured as a result of the defective condition of the porch or the sidewalk, Mr. Adams is liable for the injuries. The landlord also is usually liable for injuries to any friend or guest of the tenant who may have been injured because of defects in the property that the landlord controls.

When a tenant occupies property for an indefinite period of time, the landlord may obtain possession of it by giving notice. The form and the time of the notice are regulated by local customs or laws.

Cincinnati, Ohio, April 30, 19--

Mr. J. Michael Kuharic

I hereby notify you to surrender possession of the premises at 5942 Ridge Avenue, Cincinnati, Ohio, on or before June 1, 19--. Your lease of the said premises expires on June 1, and I shall take possession of the property on that date.

Terry Enlow

A Landlord's Notice Requesting a Tenant to Vacate Property

Improvements and Fixtures

Unless there is an agreement to the contrary, improvements that are attached to the property become a part of the property and thus belong to the owner. For instance, if the tenant builds a shed or a garage on the lot belonging to the landlord, the tenant cannot tear it down or take it away without permission. If a tenant installs shelves or cupboards in a rented house, the tenant normally cannot take them away when moving. A tenant may get a written agreement from the landlord to remove certain improvements when the tenant vacates the property. For example, a tenant may get written permission to fence in the backyard and to remove the fence when moving. The landlord would probably require the tenant to fill in the holes caused by the removal of the fence posts and to resod these areas.

FACTS EVERYONE SHOULD KNOW ABOUT THE LEGAL ASPECTS OF RENTING A HOME

---

1. Renting and leasing are legally the same and agreements may be written or oral.

2. A tenant has a right to peaceful and uninterrupted possession of the property.

3. A tenant is generally obligated to make normal repairs, but not structural improvements.

D. LEGAL ASPECTS OF BUYING A HOME

Legal ownership of real estate is one of the important privileges and rights of free people. Every civilized country has laws to protect those privileges and rights. The laws are concerned with the public record and title of ownership, the transfer of title from one person to another, and the regulations about payment. The services of a lawyer should always be obtained when real estate is being bought or sold.

Title to Real Estate

The *title* to real estate is the proof of ownership of the property. If a person has a clear title to a piece of real estate, there are no other claims against that property. To make certain that a title is clear, an investigation to prove the true ownership of the property is necessary. The investigation is done by tracing the history and the legality of the previous transfers of the title. Usually a loan on a piece of property cannot be obtained until the lender is certain that the title is clear. The charge for examining the title is usually added to the loan or is paid as a special charge.

Deed

A *deed* is written evidence of the ownership of a piece of real property and serves as a means of conveying the title from one person to another. The one who transfers the title to the property to another is called the *grantor* of the deed, and the one to whom the title is transferred is called the *grantee* of the deed. There are two main types of deeds: (1) the warranty deed and (2) the quit-claim deed.

A Warranty Deed

Know All Men by These Presents

That Brett Mason

of Clermont *County, Ohio,*

in consideration of Five thousand dollars ($5,000)

to him *in hand paid by* James Grammer

whose address is 402 Gaskins Road, Cincinnati, Ohio, *does* hereby **Grant, Bargain, Sell and Convey**

to the said James Grammer,

his heirs

and assigns forever, the following described **Real Estate,**
Lot sixteen (16), block three (3),
Royal Oak Subdivision

and all the **Estate, Right, Title and Interest** *of the said grantor* in and to said premises; **To have and to hold** *the same, with all the privileges and appurtenances thereunto belonging, to said grantee* , his *heirs and assigns forever. And the said* Brett Mason

does hereby **Covenant and Warrant** *that the title so conveyed is* **Clear, Free and Uncumbered,** *and that* he *will* **Defend** *the same against all lawful claims of all persons whomsoever.*

In Witness Whereof, *the said grantor* has *hereunto set* his *hand* , *this* third *day of* August , *19 -- .*

Signed and acknowledged in presence of us:

Dianne Potter   Brett Mason

John Zift

State of Ohio, Hamilton   **County, ss.**

On this third *day of* August , *19 -- , before me, a Notary Public in and for said County, personally came* Brett Mason

the grantor in the foregoing deed, and *acknowledged the signing thereof to be* his *voluntary act and deed.*

Witness *my official signature and seal on the day last above mentioned.*

Marilyn Chase

A Warranty Deed

A *warranty deed* not only conveys the interest of the grantor to the grantee, but also involves statements that certain facts relating to the title are true. A warranty deed is illustrated on page 409. The warranty deed is more commonly used than the quitclaim deed.

A *quitclaim deed* merely gives up the interest that the grantor may have in the property. The grantee assumes the risk that the title may not be good. In some communities a quitclaim deed is used instead of a warranty deed.

Consider this example: Ms. Ward desires to transfer real estate to Mr. Bush. She grants a warranty deed as evidence of the transfer of the title. In investigating the title, Mr. Bush discovers that a former owner, Mrs. Carter, at one time had a claim against the property. Mr. Bush is not quite sure that the claim has been settled fully. To protect the rights that are granted to him in the warranty deed, Mr. Bush therefore gets Mrs. Carter to grant a quitclaim deed relinquishing any rights that the latter may have had in the property.

The important parts in a deed are the description of the property, signature, seal, witnesses, acknowledgment, delivery, and acceptance. The laws in different states vary in some respects. To assure a clear title, the person granting the deed should become familiar with local laws. For instance, the laws in various states differ with regard to ownership of property by husband and wife. Some states require the signatures of both, whereas others require only one signature. In some states witnesses must sign in the presence of one another, whereas in others they must sign only in the presence of an authorized public officer. Because of the many technicalities, the average person should obtain legal advice in granting a deed or in taking title to real estate.

Rights and Duties of the Mortgagor and the Mortgagee

Any person who owns an interest in land, buildings, or even crops raised on land may mortgage that interest. The person who owns the land and borrows the money through a mortgage is called the *mortgagor*. The person who lends the money and holds the mortgage as evidence of the claim is called the *mortgagee*.

In the eyes of the law, the mortgagor is the legal owner of the property. The property is merely pledged as security for the payment of a debt, and the mortgage is the written contract acknowledging the debt. A mortgage on real estate includes equipment that has become so permanently attached to the real estate that it is considered a part of it. If a piece of land is mortgaged, and a house is later built on the land, the house will be included in the mortgage.

The mortgagor is under duty not to destroy or damage the property. The mortgagee must not interfere with the occupancy of the property except through agreement with the mortgagor or through legal procedure. If a mortgagee sells a mortgage to a third person, the mortgagor must be given notice of transfer.

When the debt is paid, the mortgage is automatically canceled. It is wise, however, for the mortgagor to obtain the mortgage, the mortgage note, and a statement acknowledging the payment of the debt. The notice acknowledging the payment of the debt should be recorded in the proper place of registration, usually the county or parish courthouse.

E. ECONOMICS OF BUYING REAL ESTATE

Prices of real estate rise and fall depending on economic conditions. If economic conditions are stable, real estate values in terms of dollars will remain about the same, but the property will lose some value because of depreciation.

If the income of a family continues as expected and if the payments have been arranged to fit the spending plan, there probably will be no serious problems. If the family income decreases, however, it may become difficult to make payments on the home. The home may also decrease in dollar value because most property decreases in value when business conditions become bad.

During times of rising prices and rising wages, not only is it easier to repay a loan, but the property may also actually increase in dollar value. Thus, it will be worth more than when it was bought. Some economists believe that as the population increases and land available for building homes decreases, real estate will continue to be a good investment even when economic conditions are poor.

The economy of the United States is affected greatly by the building, buying, and financing of homes. In 1978 about 2.1 million new housing units were started. The building of these homes required large amounts of building supplies and equipment, which in turn meant jobs for many people.

But the construction of new homes is only a part of the total economic significance of home building and home owning. Many home builders and owners borrow money to finance the building or buying of a home. These loans on homes provide a good place for people to invest surplus money safely and profitably. The total amount of mortgage debt outstanding on residential property is more than $725.9 billion. The interest on these debts provides a good source of income for investors.

FACTS EVERYONE SHOULD KNOW ABOUT RENTING, BUYING, AND FINANCING A HOME

1. Some people should rent, but others should own a home.

2. There are important factors to check in renting a home.

3. The location is important whether buying or renting a home.

4. A budget will determine whether you can afford to buy a home.

5. A new home is not always the best buy.

6. No more than 20% to 25% of after-tax income should be spent on housing (mortgage payments, property taxes, insurance, utilities, maintenance).

7. A mortgage is a contract between the borrower and the lender.

8. An appraisal is necessary and desirable.

9. The extra charges should be studied in obtaining any loan.

10. HUD and VA insure certain types of loans obtained through regular lenders.

REVIEW QUESTIONS

Section A

1. What are some of the disadvantages of owning a home?
2. What are some of the factors or conditions that will help to determine when a family should buy a home?
3. What are some of the advantages of renting a home?
4. On what basis would a family qualify for a low-cost government loan?
5. What are the advantages of mobile home ownership over conventional home ownership?

Section B

6. What is a real estate mortgage?
7. What is an open-end mortgage?
8. What is meant by an appraisal?
9. Why is it possible sometimes to obtain a loan from a private individual when it is not possible to obtain a loan from a financial institution?
10. What are the principal features of a land contract?
11. How is life insurance sometimes used in connection with borrowing to buy a home so that the family will be protected if the insured parent dies?
12. Who can assist a person in obtaining a HUD loan?
13. Since the FHA and the VA do not lend money to purchase a home, how do they help the prospective home buyer?

Section C
14. What is a real estate lease?
15. In a renting or leasing arrangement, who is the lessor and who is the lessee?
16. Does a lease have to be in writing?
17. Who is liable for damages if an invited guest of the tenant is injured on the property?
18. If a tenant occupies property under an agreement covering an indefinite period of time, may a landlord take immediate possession of the property after giving the tenant a written notice?
19. May a landlord enter the premises of a tenant at any time the landlord wishes?
20. Under what circumstances must the landlord make repairs and improvements?

Section D
21. What is a deed?
22. Who is the grantor and who is the grantee of a deed?
23. (a) What are the two general types of deeds?
    (b) In what ways do they differ?
24. Who is a mortgagor and who is a mortgagee?
25. If the mortgagor fails to pay the claim against the mortgaged property, what right has the mortgagee?
26. After the mortgage on real estate has been foreclosed, is there any means by which the mortgagor may recover the property?

Section E
27. How is the economy affected by the building, buying, and financing of homes?

DISCUSSION QUESTIONS

Section A
1. Under what circumstances would a person be justified in making a down payment of only 5 or 10% of the purchase price of a home?
2. Why might it not be a good idea to take all your savings in order to make a sizable down payment of 20% or more on a home?
3. Why would some people prefer to buy a mobile home rather than a house and lot?

Section B
4. For what reason would a lender want the monthly payments on a home loan to include insurance premiums on the home and property taxes in addition to the amount to reduce the principal and interest?
5. Assuming that you have all sources of loans available to you, from what source do you think you could obtain the greatest loan in proportion to the value of the property? Give your reasons.
6. Which do you consider the safer type of mortgage from the viewpoint of the borrower: (a) a mortgage that extends for a short term of 3 or 4 years, or (b) one that extends for a long term of 10 to 15 years? Why?
7. Can you see any advantage in the package mortgage? Explain your answer.
8. Why do savings and loan associations lend more than twice as much money on home mortgage loans as do commercial banks?

Section C
9. Ms. Wells rents a home in a residential neighborhood from Mr. Hunt, the landlord. Ms. Wells decides to open a beauty shop in a spare room in the house and operate a lawful business. May she do so?

10. Mr. Jones rented a house from Mrs. Scott. Mr. White was injured on a broken step while visiting Mr. Jones. Who is responsible for the injury?

11. Under what conditions may a TV and FM antenna installed by a tenant be removed when the tenant moves?

Section D

12. Why must agreements about the buying and selling of real estate be in writing?

13. Mr. Orlando made a contract with Majestic Home Builders to construct a house and arranged to borrow money from the First National Bank to pay for it. Before the bank will make the final payment to the builder, it has insisted on proof that the plumber, carpenter, and all other workers and suppliers have been paid. Why has the bank asked for such proof?

Section E

14. Although a house gradually gets older and therefore gradually wears out, why does a house sometimes increase in dollar value? Does it ever decrease in dollar value faster than the ordinary wearing out? Why?

APPLICATION PROBLEMS

Section A

1. Mr. and Mrs. Jackson have $3,000 in a savings account which has been earning 5% interest, calculated annually. They buy an $18,000 home, using the $3,000 as down payment. They succeed in obtaining a mortgage of $15,000 at 9½% interest.

   Considering the loss of the interest on their savings as a part of the cost, figure the total interest cost during the first year if the interest on the loans is computed annually.

Section B

2. All of one's savings should not be used for a down payment on a home. Some money needs to be held back for settlement costs, moving expenses, and emergencies. However, the size of the down payment greatly affects the amount of interest one pays. The following U.S. Department of Agriculture table shows the effect of size of down payment on cost of a $20,000 loan:

Down Payment	Monthly Payment (Principal and Interest)			Total Interest (8%)		
	20 Years	25 Years	30 Years	20 Years	25 Years	30 Years
$ 0	$167	$154	$147	$20,110	$26,280	$32,780
500	163	151	143	19,610	25,630	31,960
1,000	159	147	139	19,110	24,970	31,140
2,000	151	139	132	18,100	23,650	29,500
3,000	142	131	125	17,090	22,340	27,860
4,000	134	124	117	16,090	21,030	26,220
5,000	126	116	110	15,080	19,710	24,580

(a) How much interest is saved on a 20-year mortgage loan if you increase your down payment from $500 to $2,000?

(b) How much interest is saved if you take out a mortgage loan for 25 years instead of 30 years with a $1,000 down payment?

    (c) How much interest is saved if you take out a mortgage loan for 20 years with a down payment of $500 instead of a mortgage loan for 25 years with a down payment of $1,000?

    (d) What conclusions can you draw from the answers to the above questions?

3. Assume that the monthly payment on a 20-year mortgage loan at 9½% interest is $9.33 for each $1,000 borrowed.

    (a) Calculate the monthly payment on a $20,000, 20-year mortgage at 9½% interest.

    (b) Calculate the total payments made over the 20-year period.

    (c) How much interest was paid in the 20 years this mortgage ran?

Section C

4. Mr. Hall rents the second floor of his home to Mr. and Mrs. Paul Perrino. The second floor has its own outside stairs and porch entranceway. A guest visiting the Perrinos falls and sustains an injury on a broken step of the stairway leading to the apartment. Who is responsible for the injury to the guest?

5. Jane Wong rented a house from Olaf Olsen under a written lease extending for one year. Six months before the expiration of the lease, Mr. Olsen decided that he wanted to remodel the house to get it ready for sale. Miss Wong objected, but Mr. Olsen brought workmen to the house and insisted on entering in order to begin the work. Who is right in this argument?

Section D

6. Six months ago, Mr. Krug bought from Mr. LeMoyne a lot valued at $3,200. Mr. LeMoyne delivered a quitclaim deed to the property. In reading tax-notice information in the local newspaper, Mr. Krug was surprised to learn a few days ago of an unpaid tax lien on the property for property taxes not paid over the past 3 years. Mr. Krug must pay $157 in taxes to retain undisputed ownership of the lot. Does he have any recourse to Mr. LeMoyne for this unexpected cost?

COMMUNITY PROJECTS

Section A

1. Prepare a report on the availability of low-cost government housing for low-income families in your community or in a nearby community. Answer the following questions:

    (a) What types of government housing are provided?

    (b) How many families are being provided such housing?

    (c) What is the maximum annual income families can have and yet qualify for such housing?

    (d) What are the minimum and maximum monthly rental fees being paid and how do these fees compare with private rental property in your community?

    (e) How long is the waiting list of families wanting such housing?

    (f) Do any groups from your school sponsor projects (service and/or entertainment) for the aged who are living in such housing?

Section B

2. Study the advertisements of real estate for sale in your local newspaper or in the newspaper from a nearby larger city. Make a list of the prices asked for houses so that you can compare those prices for houses of different sizes, in different locations, and so forth. Note information in the advertisements about the possibilities of VA, FHA, and conventional types of financing. Make a report of your findings to the class.

3. Visit the office of the register of deeds at your county courthouse. Obtain information about the procedure in your community for recording deeds and mortgages. Describe the procedure to be followed and the fees that are charged.

Section C

4. Visit the office of an apartment building or an apartment development in your community. Find out whether a written lease is used when a new tenant moves into one of the apartments. Also find out the answers to the following questions: What is the length of the tenancy period? Who must make repairs to the property? Is the rent paid in advance? Is a deposit of a certain amount of money required before the tenant can take possession? Is there a particular manner in which payment must be made? What other conditions and agreements are stated in the lease?

Section D

5. Check the legal notices in a local newspaper (or consult a lawyer or an officer of a bank or savings and loan association) to learn of legal actions being taken in connection with rental and mortgaged property. Discuss these cases in class with respect to: rights and responsibilities of lessees, lessors, mortgagees, and mortgagors; financial hardships that result to the parties; and how such hardships could have been avoided.

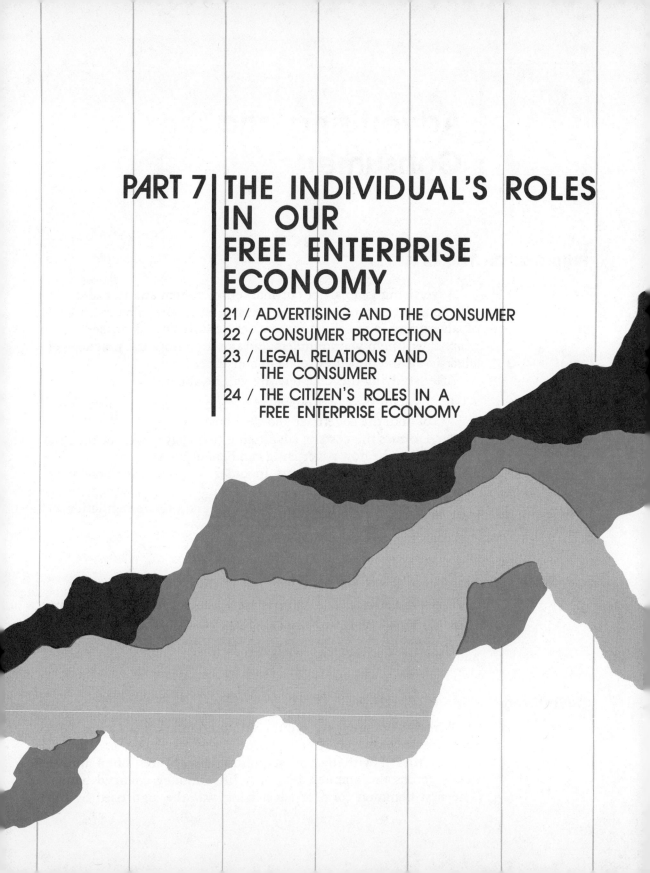

PART 7 | THE INDIVIDUAL'S ROLES IN OUR FREE ENTERPRISE ECONOMY

Advertising and the Consumer

PURPOSE OF THE CHAPTER

Advertising is a part of our marketing system and is, therefore, an important part of our free enterprise economy. The main goal of advertising is to sell goods and services for the advertiser. This chapter will help you to understand the functions and practices of advertising and how they relate to consumer interests.

After studying this chapter, you will be able to:

1. Explain the functions of advertising from the point of view of both the advertiser and the consumer.
2. Discuss the costs of advertising (who pays and how much).
3. Describe how advertising can benefit consumers.
4. Analyze advertisements in order to make wise consumer choices.
5. Discuss the types of government and private regulation of advertising.

A. FUNCTIONS OF ADVERTISING

From the advertiser's point of view, the purpose of advertising is to sell goods and services. From the consumer's point of view, the purpose of advertising is to obtain information about goods and services that are available for sale.

Advertising and Mass Marketing

When our country was young, production and marketing were very simple. Most consumers produced the goods they consumed, or they traded with nearby acquaintances. Stores often traded goods across the counter, and very little money changed hands. The first common form of advertising was the sign used by the

Foster and Kleiser Outdoor Advertising (A Metromedia Company)

It is important to the seller for advertising to establish a trade name, slogan, or product image.

doctor, the merchant, the blacksmith, the wigmaker, or other professional people. In those days mass production was not known, so there was no need for mass marketing.

Now we have mass production with producers and consumers widely separated. A complicated system of transportation and communication is needed to help producers reach the consumer and to tell the consumer in distant places what the producer has to sell. Under our present economic system, advertising is essential. Advertising helps both consumers and producers. It also creates jobs, both directly in advertising occupations and indirectly by stimulating demand for many products.

In our economy, mass production makes mass marketing necessary. Stated another way, mass marketing makes mass production possible. Mass marketing would be impossible without advertising. Mass production, in turn, has made it possible for us to buy many goods at a greatly reduced price. For instance, in the early 1920s when income was much lower than it is today, only a few thousand people could afford radio sets, which cost $100 to $500. In the 1970s, however, when income was much higher, 99.8% of all homes in the United States had one or more radios. In some cases these radios cost as little as $5 to $10. Mass production has made these radios available; mass marketing has brought them to the people at greatly reduced prices.

Of course, in the controlled economies, advertising is not as useful because producers are told what and how much to produce. Consumers can buy only those goods placed at their disposal. Few kinds of goods are available from which to make a selection.

Specific Functions of Advertising

The final purpose of all advertising is to sell goods and services. Manufacturers, wholesalers, and retailers seek to achieve this objective through the several functions of advertising, which are listed below. Many functions of advertising are beneficial to consumers as well as to producers and distributors.

MAJOR FUNCTIONS OF ADVERTISING FROM THE STANDPOINT OF THE SELLER

---

1. Stimulate consumer demand by obtaining:
   a. Wider acceptance and greater use of products not yet universally used, such as microwave ovens.
   b. Greater use of products already widely used, such as potatoes or citrus fruits.
   c. Wider acceptance of a commodity by consumers who have not used it.

2. Educate prospective consumers regarding:
   a. The personal benefits and satisfactions to be derived from using a particular product.
   b. Various uses of a product.
   c. Merits of a particular brand or make.

3. Inform consumers about new products, developments in present products, and changes in fashions and customs.

4. Maintain contact with consumers who, without advertising, may never know a product is available.

5. Stress exclusive features and important advantages of a product.

6. Build consumer preference for a particular brand of product, thus making it possible to price the product above competitive brands.

7. Develop large-scale distribution, thus making possible low-cost mass production.

8. Establish a trade name, slogan, or product image.

9. Create goodwill and develop consumer respect for the firm.

10. Obtain a list of prospective customers in order to prepare the way for sales representatives.

11. Obtain a larger share of the available business.

12. Promote the use of one class of product, such as margarine as opposed to butter.

Cost of Advertising

Advertising costs are reflected in the selling price of a product or service. Therefore, the consumer ultimately pays for advertising. It may seem unreasonable to spend $40,000 for a full-page advertisement in one issue of a national magazine or $250,000 for one television program. But, these advertising media reach hundreds of thousands and even millions of people; hence the advertising cost per unit of product sold is very small. Consumers should be interested in knowing how much of the dollar cost of their purchases represents advertising cost.

Expenditures for Advertising. More than $38 billion a year is spent for advertising. This amount is about 3% of the total value of all goods and services produced in the United States (the GNP). About 55% of the total expenditure is for national advertising and about 45% is for local advertising. Of the $38 billion spent for advertising in 1977, newspapers accounted for the greatest percentage, followed by television, and then direct mail, radio, magazines, business and farm publications, and outdoor media, in that order.

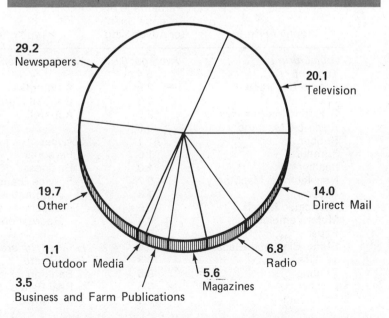

Percentage of Advertising Expenditures by Medium, 1977

29.2 Newspapers

20.1 Television

14.0 Direct Mail

6.8 Radio

5.6 Magazines

3.5 Business and Farm Publications

1.1 Outdoor Media

19.7 Other

Source: Adapted from *Statistical Abstract of the United States*, 1978.

For every $100 spent for goods and
services in the United States, an
average of 80 cents is for advertising.

Advertising Cost Per Dollar of Sales. An analysis of advertising expenditures indicates that on the average manufacturers, wholesalers, and retailers spend almost 1 cent per dollar of sales. In the table below, the largest expenditure by type of industry in manufacturing was 5.4 cents per dollar by tobacco manufacturers.

ADVERTISING EXPENDITURES AS A PERCENTAGE OF REVENUE

Type of Firm	Percentage of Revenue Spent for Advertising	Type of Firm	Percentage of Revenue Spent for Advertising
Manufacturing	*Average: 0.9*	*Wholesaling and Retailing*	*Average: 0.9*
Tobacco	5.4	Food	0.8
Food & Beverages	2.9	Automotive	0.5
Chemicals	1.6	General Merchandise	2.6
Scientific Instruments	2.0	Apparel	2.1
Electrical Machinery	0.9		
Rubber	1.1	*Services*	*Average: 1.3*
Furniture	1.6	Personal	3.9
Leather	1.0	Business	1.2
Nonelectrical Machinery	0.7	Service Stations and	
Apparel	1.3	Automotive Repair	0.8
Fabricated Metals	0.6	Amusement and	
Motor Vehicles	0.8	Recreation	2.2
Paper	0.5		
Stone, Clay, and Glass	0.5	*Finance, Insurance, and*	
Textiles	0.3	*Real Estate*	*Average: 0.7*
Printing	0.5	Banking	0.8
Lumber	0.5	Real Estate	2.6
Petroleum	0.1	Insurance	0.3

Sources: Adapted from *Statistical Abstract of the United States*, 1978, p. 857, and Schonfeld & Associates Inc., "Estimates of Average Advertising to Sales and Advertising to Gross Profit Margin by Industry — 1977," *Advertising Age* (September 18, 1978), p. 56.

Advertising and Its Benefits to Consumers

Advertising has a tremendous influence on the development of our standard of living by improving our diet, health, living conditions, comforts, and conveniences. This lifting of our standards has been brought about through constructive education and by increasing our wants for things that now seem necessary although at one time they may have seemed unnecessary. It may be true that advertising has caused us to want things that we really do not need; but, after all, we should be free to decide what we need. Consumers need to be informed so that they may make intelligent decisions.

Educational Value of Advertising. The history of food consumption is a good illustration of the educational influence of advertising on our diet and general health. For example, authorities on diet long have advocated the use of orange juice, tomato juice, fresh vegetables, and fresh fruits in our everyday diet. Very little progress was made in establishing these foods as a part of our basic diet until producers began to use advertising as a means of educating the people as to the desirability of the daily use of these foods.

The story of popularizing desirable foods is somewhat parallel to the story of popularizing the telephone, sanitary plumbing, ventilation, lighting, refrigeration, radio, television, and many types of labor-saving devices that are now considered essential in the home. We can live without these conveniences, but our level of living would decrease greatly.

Advertising may have educational value.

Product Information. Another benefit of advertising is that it acquaints consumers with the uses of certain products, particularly new ones. In many instances, consumers must become familiar with the uses of a product before they are willing to buy. A typical example of such a product is a portable room air purifier. People need to know that it is used to remove pollen and dust to which some are allergic, to remove unpleasant odors, and to introduce oxygen.

Economic Benefits. No less important than the educational benefits of advertising are the economic benefits. As stated earlier in the chapter, advertising stimulates large-scale marketing, which in turn provides an outlet for the products of mass-production methods. Thus, many products are available to consumers at reasonable prices that, without advertising, would not be available at all or only at prohibitive prices. Many of the products we enjoy we could not have if it were not for advertising to stimulate a demand for them, thus lowering the cost of production.

Social and Cultural Goals. Finally, because advertising arouses mass desire and penetrates so deeply into American life, it has a powerful influence on the health, social, and cultural goals of the people. For example, as our wants increase we may demand better food, better housing, better education, better recreation, better health, and a better environment.

Advertising and Its Critics

Although large-scale marketing and, therefore, mass production would not be possible without advertising, there are critics who believe that advertising is both unnecessary and wasteful.

The fact that critics argue against advertising does not necessarily make their arguments valid. It is easy for us to look at a disadvantage or an undesirable outcome of advertising without considering the advantages and the benefits.

The critics of advertising seem to fall into two camps: (1) those who criticize advertising itself and (2) those who criticize certain advertising techniques. The first group opposes all advertising and feels that advertising expenses are wasteful. The second group is not opposed to advertising, but it feels that much of today's advertising can and needs to be improved. These critics are concerned with educating consumers to demand more informative advertising. They believe that advertisers must accept high moral, social, and ethical standards. Most individual advertisers and advertising associations actively support and laud the activities of these constructive critics.

Whether advertising is an economic plus or a cost to society is not an important question in the everyday operation of business affairs. Obviously, a business must let potential customers know what products are available.

SOME MAJOR VIEWS OF ADVERTISING

Critics state that advertising:

1. Promotes brand switching rather than increasing total demand and is an economic waste.

2. Increases the prices of goods.

3. Promotes wasteful obsolescence.

4. Appeals too much to emotions rather than to reason.

5. Controls the press.

6. Is often in poor taste, filled with half-truths, or outrightly deceptive.

7. Creates undesirable wants.

Supporters of advertising answer that advertising:

1. Increases total demand.

2. Often makes lower prices possible.

3. Enhances economic and individual freedom by allowing consumers the right of "uneconomical" obsolescence.

4. Frees the presses from political control.

5. Can and should be improved.

6. Expands markets for new and better products.

Critics and supporters alike need to recall that advertising has not caused our economic system; advertising has resulted from it.

The argument that advertising should be presented in good taste does seem to have merit. A problem arises, however, when one tries to define good taste. What a person considers to be good taste is strictly an individual matter. Usually a person's judgment on this issue rests with whether or not the person agrees with the action the advertiser is suggesting. For example, some persons would applaud advertisements that appeal to thrift, economy, honesty, and similar goals but reject advertising that appeals to fear, envy, style, and other similar appeals. There is no completely satisfactory way to resolve the issue of good taste.

Probably the only way an advertiser could avoid the accusation of poor taste would be to give a strictly factual description of the product or service and make no suggestion as to why the potential consumer would be interested in buying it. Even an advertisement that is considered to be in poor taste by some persons does contain information for the buyers, even if it is no more than telling them that the advertiser uses poor taste. Alert buyers should be their own judges of how an advertisement helps or fails to help them in their buying decisions.

B. USE OF ADVERTISING

Advertising is everywhere — on TV and radio, in newspapers and magazines, on billboards and walls, in stores and in our mail. Every day we are exposed to all kinds of advertising. We cannot escape it, so we should put it to the best possible use.

Kinds of Advertising

The advertising with which we are chiefly concerned is directed toward the ultimate consumer, that is, the person who buys for personal or household use, not for a business or a profession. Advertising addressed to or intended for the ultimate consumer is known as *consumer advertising*.

Advertising may be classified also as to "approach," that is, as to its intention. If the advertising is intended to stress the benefits of a certain class or type of product rather than particular brands of that product, it is known as *primary advertising*. An example of this type is the dairy industry stimulating the demand for cheese through advertising.

Another classification of advertising as to approach or intention is known as *selective advertising*, which attempts to persuade consumers generally to buy one brand rather than another. This is the kind of advertising to which consumers are most frequently exposed.

The primary approach in advertising focuses attention on a type or a class of product, rather than on a particular brand.

Types of Advertising Appeals

To market goods and services successfully, the advertiser needs to understand the motives that influence human behavior. These motives are often referred to as *advertising appeals*.

Advertising is often classified in terms of rational appeals and emotional appeals. *Rational appeals* are those that supposedly center on logic by providing basic facts and information. *Emotional appeals* are those that involve the emotions and excite people to buy even if the decision to buy is not a logical one. In many advertisements, the two appeals overlap.

Psychologists today no longer make a precise distinction between rational and emotional behavior. More typically, psychologists take the approach that a person performs that behavior which is either most desirable or least threatening. This approach to human behavior is more refined than attempting to decide what behavior is rational and what is emotional. Consequently, advertisers tend to stress those appeals that would be most desirable to the potential consumer if the consumer were to purchase a particular good or service.

Deceptive Advertising

Every buyer must recognize the fact that, although the majority of advertisers are honest, some are unscrupulous. Deceptive advertising hurts both consumers and businesses. Consumers are cheated, and businesses lose repeat customers.

Some unscrupulous advertisers use deceptive advertising appeals, claims, and schemes in spite of all efforts to stop them. Ad-

vertisers who use deceptive practices usually find them so successful that they can make big profits before any action can be taken to
force them to stop. Because deceptive advertising practices appear
repeatedly, consumers should know how to recognize them and be
on guard against them. Some of the types of deceptive advertising
found most frequently are discussed below.

One type of deceptive advertising is called *bait and switch*. A
product is advertised at a cut-rate price, but no mention is made
that the seller has only a few such items on sale at that price.
Consequently, when customers enter the store, they are told that
the item is out of stock and then an attempt is made to switch the
customers to a higher-priced item. The ad is merely "bait" to lure
the customers into the store for a "switch" to another item.

Fictitious pricing and *misrepresentation* are other forms of deceptive advertising. Examples are: overstating the "manufacturer's
suggested price" to convince the buyer that the advertised price is
a special bargain; advertising "50% off the regular price" when
the seller has never sold the goods before; and making false or
exaggerated claims about the quality and performance of a product.

Another type of deceptive advertising is the sending of *unordered products* through the mail followed by a letter demanding
payment. Consumers should be aware that they are under no obligation to make payment for unordered products sent through the
mail, nor are they under any obligation to return the merchandise.

Some *contests* sponsored by advertisers might also be viewed as
deceptive advertising. Often the prize given is extremely small and
is simply intended to allow the advertiser a chance to make a sales
pitch.

Consumer Analysis of Advertising

As consumers, we are exposed daily to literally hundreds of
advertising messages — in newspapers and magazines, on billboards and show cards, and by radio and television. Without
doubt, these advertisements develop in us desires for products and
services that otherwise we would not want. This, in many respects, is good for us, for it acquaints us with commodities and
services that may make living more pleasant. It is important, however, that as consumers we not only understand the motives,
methods, and practices of advertisers but also that we know how to
use advertising wisely in satisfying our wants. In order to use advertising wisely, we must be able to analyze it. In Chapter 17, we

discussed how advertising may be used in buying wisely. Here we shall merely summarize some general guides for consumers to use in analyzing advertisements.

**GUIDES FOR CONSUMERS IN
ANALYZING ADVERTISEMENTS**

---

1. Study advertisements continually to learn about new products and services, improvements, and developments. Learn to recognize trademarks, brand names, and both the manufacturers and retailers of the commodities you want. Use advertisements as a source of information.

2. Discover the kind of appeal used in an advertisement — emotional or reason-why. This knowledge will help you in using the advertisements wisely in making consumer choices.

3. Look for statements indicating the quality of the product advertised. If the advertisement is not adequate, seek more information from the manufacturer or retailer.

4. Do not be influenced by absurd and meaningless statements and implications in advertisements. Many of them are not complimentary to your intelligence if you permit them to influence you.

5. Evaluate with great care testimonials used in advertisements; ordinarily an advertising testimonial is of little value to you.

6. Search for informative statements that explain the essential features of a product — specifications, standards, and performance.

7. Develop a pattern to follow in analyzing advertisements. You will be a more efficient consumer and a wiser consumer if you form good habits for analyzing advertisements.

C. REGULATION OF ADVERTISING

Well-established business concerns recognize the fact that honesty is the basis for permanent success. Of the thousands of advertisements that are printed and broadcast over the air annually, only a very small percentage are dishonest or misleading. In a recent year the Federal Trade Commission examined more than a half million advertisements and made complaints to the advertisers in only 72 cases. The best safeguard of advertising integrity is the sense of responsibility that advertisers have.

Types of Regulation

There are two effective types of regulation of advertising. One type is government regulation through federal and state laws. The second type of regulation of advertising is standards self-imposed by the advertisers. These standards are adopted by individual business firms; by advertisers' associations; and often by businesses providing advertising media, such as newspapers, magazines, radio, and television. The publishers of magazines and newspapers recognize the fact that dishonest advertising reacts unfavorably against their publications as well as against the products advertised.

Government Regulation

The major responsibility for government regulation of advertising rests with the Federal Trade Commission (FTC). It is the responsibility of this Commission not only to see that advertisers follow accepted standards for integrity and reliability but also to take action against most kinds of deceptive claims in all advertising media.

As indicated previously, the FTC has tended to make very few complaints to advertisers after examining large numbers of advertisements. However, in 1969, Ralph Nader, a consumer advocate, and his associates issued a report criticizing the FTC. Since that time the agency has taken a more active role in regulating deceptive and false advertising. The FTC is often unable to enforce regulations because a large number of cases involve lengthy and costly court battles. Sometimes there are long periods until a court acts on the complaint of the FTC. Recently, however, the FTC has ruled that advertisers who are found guilty of deceptive or false advertising must correct the situation through "corrective" advertising. Under the corrective advertising policy, an advertiser found guilty of false or deceptive advertising must run a corrective advertisement and indicate that the previous advertising might have been misleading.

The FTC also now requires that all advertisers make available to consumers the data on which all claims for products or services are based. The consumer must be aware, however, that the FTC is able to examine only some of the more flagrant complaints since the amount of advertising is enormous compared to the number of people on the staff of the FTC.

In addition to the regulation imposed by the FTC, most states have laws that regulate deceptive and false advertising. Many of the state laws tend to be weak and ineffective because they require proof that the advertiser intended to deceive. Also, in most cases the state laws deal only with deceptive information and do not deal with advertising that is simply in bad taste. However, there is evidence that state laws regulating advertising are being strengthened and will be improved in the years to come. Recently a few states have adopted the Unfair Trade Practices and Consumer Protection Law developed by the FTC, which appears to have the potential to protect consumers if enforced. Under this particular law, the state attorney general has the power to control deceptive and false advertising at the state level.

There are additional laws, discussed in Chapter 22, that protect the consumer regarding certain products and practices.

Self-Imposed Regulation

For many years business groups and professional organizations have imposed self-restriction on the advertising industry. As early as 1911 a magazine called *Printer's Ink* published what it entitled "A Model Statute" for advertisers to follow to present fair and unbiased advertising. This model statute proposed by *Printer's Ink* became the basis for many of the state laws that control advertising.

In 1971 the National Advertising Review Board, the American Advertising Agencies, and the Association of National Advertisers joined forces with the Council of Better Business Bureaus to establish a procedure to focus on complaints about advertising. The complaints are examined by the National Advertising Review Board. The Board consists of representatives of advertisers, advertising agencies, and the general public. At the present time the Board has primarily been examining defective claims. However, the Board plans to expand its activities to consider advertisements that are simply in bad taste. The first step in controlling and regulating advertising by business itself will be to use persuasion against the advertisers directly. When this does not work, the Board plans to refer all deceptive advertisements to the FTC and other governmental regulatory agencies that would be appropriate.

Many radio and television stations as well as individual newspapers and magazines screen the advertising they carry for any misleading claims and try to eliminate advertisements that are in bad taste. As might be expected, the criteria or standards used vary greatly from one business group to another. Also, trade publications frequently speak out against advertising considered to be deceptive or in bad taste. For example, a major advertising publication, *Advertising Age*, often criticizes advertisements and practices it considers to be misleading or in poor taste.

It is not surprising that many individual businesses are directing more attention to weeding out any deceptive advertising or advertising that is in poor taste. In recent years, advertising of this nature has been criticized severely. Many businesses realize that advertising that is deceptive or in poor taste has a tendency to damage the image of the business involved. Consequently, self-imposed restrictions of advertising by business groups are becoming more common.

FACTS ABOUT ADVERTISING EVERYBODY SHOULD KNOW

1. The objective of advertising is to sell goods and services by stimulating demand and influencing consumer choices.

2. Advertising is essential to distribution. It stimulates mass production, which in turn means many more products are made available at costs consumers can afford.

3. Advertising costs consumers from a fraction of 1 cent to over 5 cents per dollar paid for goods. The cost of advertising paid by consumers is offset in part or wholly by the benefits consumers receive either directly or indirectly.

4. There is disagreement among economists and consumers as to the value of advertising to consumers. The criticisms of advertising are focused primarily on its usefulness in relationship to its cost.

5. Advertising provides valuable consumer benefits, some of which are educational or cultural and others economic in nature.

6. Various kinds of advertising are intended to serve specific purposes, such as informing and educating consumers about certain products; promoting sales for an entire industry, such as citrus fruits; and persuading consumers to select and buy a particular product.

7. An analysis of the motives, methods, and contents of advertisements should provide the basis for wise consumer decisions.

8. Advertising is controlled by (a) state and federal legislation and (b) self-imposed standards of advertisers and advertising associations. For the most part, the integrity of advertisers is commendable, and advertising in general maintains high standards.

REVIEW QUESTIONS

Section A

1. What is the purpose of advertising (a) from the advertiser's point of view and (b) from the consumer's point of view?
2. Why is advertising essential in a market economy?
3. How does advertising stimulate low-cost mass production?
4. What are the major functions of advertising from the standpoint of the seller?
5. Who ultimately pays for advertising?
6. Approximately how much is spent each year for advertising?
7. What manufacturing industry spends the most per dollar of sales for advertising?
8. What are the major benefits of advertising for consumers?
9. What are some examples of the educational value of advertising?
10. What are some examples of the economic value of advertising?
11. What are the major criticisms of advertising?

Section B

12. What is meant by "consumer advertising"?
13. How does selective advertising differ from primary advertising?
14. What are "advertising appeals"?
15. What are some common types of deceptive advertising?
16. What are some guides that consumers should use in analyzing advertisements?

Section C

17. What are the two types of regulation of advertising?
18. What government agency has the major responsibility for regulation of advertising?
19. Under the corrective advertising policy of the Federal Trade Commission, what must an advertiser who is found guilty of deceptive or false advertising do?
20. What are some of the principal sources of self-imposed regulation of advertising?

DISCUSSION QUESTIONS

Section A

1. Is advertising necessary for mass production and mass consumption? Explain.
2. Why is advertising little used in completely state-controlled countries, such as in a country under communistic rule?
3. In what ways does advertising stimulate consumer demand?
4. Assume that you buy a new suit costing $69.95 of which $1.50 is advertising cost. Explain how you have benefited by that $1.50 cost.
5. How has advertising affected our diets?
6. What would happen to consumption if all consumer advertising were limited to a factual statement of the characteristics of the product?
7. Of what social value is advertising?
8. How may advertising promote unwise choice making?
9. Are the major criticisms of advertising justifiable? Discuss, from the standpoint of the possible effect upon you and other members of the class, each of the seven criticisms listed on page 425.

Section B   10. What kind of advertising appeals do you think advertisers should stress?

11. To what extent do you think that advertisements are misleading or dishonest?

12. Why should consumers analyze advertisements?

Section C   13. How does dishonest or distasteful advertising react unfavorably against magazines and newspapers as well as against the products advertised?

14. Why do many of the state laws regulating advertising tend to be weak and ineffective?

15. What are some steps that you think can be taken by consumers to regulate advertisements that are in bad taste?

APPLICATION PROBLEMS

Section A   1. Select from a popular magazine an advertisement that educates the consumer. Paste this advertisement on a sheet of paper. Below it, explain just how the advertisement is educational.

2. Frequently a large manufacturer will combine its advertising with that of one or more local distributors of the product. Bring a sample of this type of advertising in for class discussion. Why might this type of advertising be of benefit to both the large manufacturer and the local businesses that participate in the advertisement?

Section B   3. In magazines or newspapers in your home, find advertisements that contain appeals to (a) health, (b) beauty, and (c) economy. Paste these on a sheet of paper. Opposite each one, write a brief notation indicating the type of appeal and whether the appeal is of benefit to the consumer.

4. (a) From five magazines or newspapers make a list of all the high-sounding titles and terms used in advertising products. This list should include meaningless, but attractive, slogans and terms.

(b) After listing these terms, analyze their truthfulness, their intent, and their usefulness from the point of view of the buyer.

Section C   5. From a magazine or newspaper in your home, obtain an example of advertising that you consider to be false or in poor taste. Paste this advertisement on a sheet of paper. Below it, write a brief statement of why you feel it is false or in poor taste.

6. In a recent issue of a newspaper or magazine, find either (a) an article in which the Federal Trade Commission has issued a warning to or ruled against an advertiser or (b) an article in which Ralph Nader or some other consumer advocate has brought suit against a business firm for false or misleading advertising. Report to the class a summary of the contents of the article you select.

COMMUNITY PROJECTS

Section A   1. Read a daily newspaper for one week; clip the advertisements of the "special bargains" that appear. What kind of aid would be available to help you determine whether or not each of these "specials" is an outstanding bargain? Analyze one or two of the offers to determine the factors that one would need to consider before purchasing the product.

2. Invite a representative from one of your local daily or weekly newspapers to discuss with the class the policies of the paper regarding (a) acceptance of advertising and (b) publication of articles relative to product information of value to consumers.

Section B

3. On a large cardboard or on a bulletin board prepare a display of advertisements properly captioned and labeled to illustrate each of the following contrasting features: (a) emotional and rational appeal; (b) business and consumer advertisements; and (c) primary and selective advertising.

   Prepare another display of properly captioned and labeled advertisements to illustrate each of the following characteristics: (a) quality emphasis; (b) essential features emphasis, such as specifications, standards, and performance; (c) absurd and meaningless statements; and (d) information of an educational nature.

Section C

4. If your community has a better business bureau, interview the business manager to find out exactly what functions it performs in regard to maintaining the ethics of local advertising. Report your findings to the class.

5. Assume that you buy a product sold in interstate commerce on the basis of an advertisement in a national magazine and find that the article does not conform to the quality or the description in the advertisement. What means of protection have you against this deceptive advertising?

Consumer Protection

PURPOSE OF THE CHAPTER

If consumers are to be wise buyers and get the most from their income, they need information and protection. While many private and government sources supplied information and protection in the past, the rise of the consumer movement in recent years has accelerated the demand for more and better aid for consumers. In this chapter you will learn about the activities of some of the agencies, laws, and services available to help consumers.

After studying this chapter, you will be able to:

1. Explain the need for consumer protection.
2. Explain what is meant by the "consumer bill of rights."
3. List and explain government sources of consumer protection.
4. List and explain private sources of consumer protection.

A. NEED FOR CONSUMER PROTECTION

As the United States grew into a highly industrialized nation and its cities became larger, consumer problems of many kinds appeared. Poverty, poor housing conditions, unsafe working conditions, adulterated food, and fraudulent trade practices made more protection necessary. Throughout the years, laws protecting consumers have been passed. Beginning in the 1960s, an even more urgent need for consumer protection appeared when it became apparent that our natural resources were not unlimited and that pollution was threatening our very lives.

The Consumer Movement

The *consumer movement* refers to a greater consumer awareness of problems as well as a drive to achieve greater consumer protection. The consumer movement in the United States has come in three waves:

1. In the early 1900s, when there was a rapid growth of cities and industrialization.
2. In the 1930s, when the Depression created great social problems and the need for wise use of limited income.
3. In the 1960s and 1970s, when consumers became aware that their survival was threatened by irresponsible use of limited natural resources, by unsafe and unhealthy products, and by pollution of water, land, and air.

The need for additional consumer protection became more and more evident. New regulation by government, by businesses themselves, and by private agencies became essential in order to improve the quality of life for all.

Consumer Bill of Rights

President John F. Kennedy, in his 1962 State of the Union Address, proposed a consumer bill of rights that included:

1. *The right to safety* — protection against the marketing of goods that are dangerous to life or health.
2. *The right to choose* — assurance of access to a variety of products and services at competitive prices.
3. *The right to be informed* — protection against fraudulent, deceitful, or grossly misleading practices and assurance of being given the facts necessary for an informed choice.
4. *The right to be heard* — assurance of representation in forming government policy and of fair, prompt treatment in enforcement of the laws.

During the current consumer movement, a number of consumer protection laws have been passed that closely follow the consumer bill of rights. Among these are the Fair Packaging and Labeling Act in 1965, the National Traffic and Motor Vehicle Safety Act in 1966, the Federal Cigarette Labeling and Advertising Act in 1967, the Truth-in-Food Labeling Act in 1972, the Consumer Product Safety Act in 1972, the Equal Credit Opportunity Act and the Fair Credit Billing Act in 1975, and the Fair

Debt Collection Bill in 1977. Other consumer legislation is pending.

In 1964, the first special presidential advisor for consumer affairs was appointed. For the first time there was a person at the highest level of government to represent the consumer. Later this office was transferred to the Department of Health, Education, and Welfare, where its current responsibility is to advise the President on matters of consumer interest and to coordinate all federal activities in the consumer field. Other government consumer agencies have since been established, which will be discussed later in this chapter.

The consumer movement, not only in the United States but throughout the world, is growing in impact and in importance. Consumers, singly and in groups, are speaking out and being heard. As a result, the rights of consumers are being recognized, protected, and expanded.

B. GOVERNMENT SOURCES OF CONSUMER PROTECTION

Government agencies concerned with consumer interests exist at federal, state, and local levels. They provide standards for products and services, information about them, and protection from questionable and unethical practices on the part of sellers.

Federal Consumer Agencies

Over 50 different federal agencies provide direct or indirect services and protection to consumers — and the number is growing. The following are some of the most important:

Department of Agriculture. The primary functions of the United States Department of Agriculture involve research and experimentation dealing with scientific production of farm products, farm management, and the agricultural education of people in rural areas. Of particular value to consumers are the services provided by:

1. The *Agricultural Marketing Service*, which inspects food for wholesomeness and grades it for quality.
2. The *Consumer Marketing Service*, which regulates, improves, and protects the nation's food-marketing system.
3. The *Food and Nutrition Service*, which provides information on nutrition and food programs such as the food stamp program, special milk programs, and the school food services.

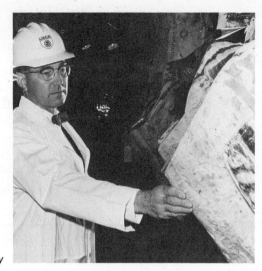

The Agricultural Marketing Service grades meats for quality and inspects for wholesomeness.

Swift & Company

Civil Aeronautics Board (CAB). The Civil Aeronautics Board regulates rates and fares for air transportation and promotes safety in civil aviation.

Department of Commerce. The primary purpose of the United States Department of Commerce is to serve business; however, in serving business, the Department also serves consumer interests. The following agencies are particularly important to consumers:

1. The *National Bureau of Standards*, which sets measurement standards, product standards, and safety standards.

One of the many research projects conducted by the National Bureau of Standards involves developing test methods to measure the energy use of major home appliances.

National Bureau of Standards

2. The *National Business Council for Consumer Affairs*, which encourages business firms to meet their responsibilities to consumers.

Consumer Product Safety Commission (CPSC). This agency, created in 1972, has vast powers to ensure product safety. It sets safety standards for all common household and recreational products (but not food, drugs, cosmetics, and motor vehicles). It has the power to regulate the production and the sale of potentially hazardous products. It can ban dangerous products from the market, and it can require manufacturers and retailers to repair, replace, or make refunds on unsafe products.

THE TOP TEN IN THE HAZARD PARADE

1. Bicycles and bicycle equipment (including add-on features).

2. Stairs (including folding steps), steps, ramps, landings.

3. Football, related equipment and apparel.

4. Baseball, related equipment and apparel.

5. Swings, slides, seesaws, and playground equipment.

6. Power lawnmowers and unspecified lawnmowers.

7. Skates, skateboards, and scooters.

8. Swimming, swimming pools, and related equipment.

9. Nonglass tables and unspecified tables.

10. Beds (including springs, frames, bunk beds, and unspecified beds).

Source: Office of Consumer Affairs, *Consumer News*, Vol. 8, No. 12 (June 15, 1978).
Rankings: Based on information collected in 1977.

Environmental Protection Agency (EPA). This agency is concerned with developing programs to protect and improve the quality of our environment.

Federal Trade Commission (FTC). The basic objective of the Federal Trade Commission, which was established in 1915, is the maintenance of free competitive business. The purpose of the Commission is to prevent injury by monopoly or by unfair or deceptive trade practices. The FTC has the major responsibility for regulating deceptive and false advertising, as discussed in Chapter 21.

Government Printing Office (GPO). The Government Printing Office provides over 25,000 government publications. Publications of interest to consumers are listed in the free pamphlet *Consumer Information*, which can be acquired from the Consumer Information Center in Pueblo, Colorado.

Department of Health, Education, and Welfare. All of the programs in the field of health, education, and welfare administered by this Department are vitally important to all of us. Of greatest importance to consumers are:

1. The *Food and Drug Administration (FDA)*, whose primary purpose is to develop and enforce food, drug, and cosmetic standards. Its activities are directed mainly toward promoting purity, standard strength, and truthful and informative labeling of essential commodities. The laws enforced by the Administration are among the most important of all federal laws for the protection of consumers.

2. The *Office of Consumer Affairs (OCA)*, which analyzes and coordinates all federal government activities in the area of consumer protection. It is the center of the government's effort to help consumers. It constitutes the staff of the Special Assistant to the President for Consumer Affairs.

A Food and Drug inspector uses a hollow tube to take cocoa bean samples in the storage area of a chocolate manufacturer. The beans will be checked against legal standards set by law "to promote honesty and fair dealing in the interest of consumers."

Food and Drug Administration

State and Local Consumer Agencies

State and local governments provide information, services, inspections, and other forms of protection for consumers. Many states have passed laws and cities have passed ordinances to protect the health, safety, and rights of citizens. Common among these are regulations pertaining to sanitation, food handling, weights and measures, quality standards, safety, advertising, and trade practices.

ILLUSTRATIVE SUBJECTS OF STATE LAWS FOR CONSUMER AID AND PROTECTION

Many states have consumer laws and are considering additional ones on subjects such as:

1. Consumer loans and credit, savings and investments.

2. Solicitations for contributions to foundations and associations purporting to make significant contributions to society.

3. Wholesomeness, sanitation, and quality standards of foods both for consumption at home and in public eating places.

4. Health and personal welfare through licensing of medical personnel, licensing and inspection of private and public hospitals and nursing homes, use of drugs, and licensing and control of funeral homes and cemeteries.

5. Standards for and regulation of the sale of household goods, such as bedding, upholstery, and fabrics.

6. Sanitation — water supply, sewage disposal, etc.

7. Real estate zoning and restrictions.

8. Insurance — life, liability, and casualty.

9. Private and public education.

10. Recreation — movies, pools and beaches, travel, motels, etc.

11. Standards — weights and measures, quality grades.

12. Personal care — licensing and control of barber and beauty shops.

The laws for consumer protection vary so widely among the states that it is possible to give here only illustrations of the subjects covered by the laws.

In response to consumer demands, a growing number of state and local governments are providing consumer protection in the form of laws, agencies, and consumer advocates to investigate complaints. City and county health, welfare, fire, and police departments may assist with consumer problems. Local newspapers often give information as to where consumers can get help.

FACTS EVERYONE SHOULD KNOW ABOUT CONSUMER AIDS AND PROTECTION PROVIDED BY GOVERNMENT AGENCIES

---

1. Informative and protective services for consumers are provided by three levels of government agencies — local, state, and federal.

2. Through the federal government, business and consumer statistics, weather reports, and other information are made available to consumers, producers, and distributors.

3. Several agencies of the federal government conduct extensive research to discover new truths and procedures that will assist consumers.

4. The federal government promotes free and fair competition among business firms and among individuals, thus assuring better products and reasonable prices.

5. The consuming public receives governmental protection from false and deceptive advertising.

6. Enforcement of standards and regulations insuring purity, potency, and truthful and informative labeling of drugs and cosmetics protects consumers.

C. PRIVATE SOURCES OF CONSUMER PROTECTION

Consumers can help themselves make good choices and avoid being influenced by misleading labeling, deceptive advertising, or questionable business practices. The wise consumer seeks information about the product or service being considered and then uses that information as a basis for a buying decision. The information obtained serves as a guide in choosing the right product or service. There are a number of private sources that provide information, standards, and protection for the consumer. Some of the most important are discussed in this section.

The consumer needs to be able to determine enough about the product to be protected from unethical practice and poor choice.

Consumer-Sponsored Services

Information about consumer products is sometimes difficult, if not impossible, for an individual to obtain. In some cases, the consumer does not have access to the information. In other instances, obtaining the needed information requires investigation and tests that the individual cannot do. Because of this difficulty, agencies and organizations have been established whose primary purposes are to obtain and distribute product information to consumers.

Consumers Federation of America (CFA). The CFA is a federation of national, state, and local consumer organizations with a membership of 30 million persons. It is dedicated to consumer action through education and legislation.

Consumers' Research, Inc. (CR). Consumers' Research, Inc. is a nonprofit corporation with extensive laboratory and testing facilities. The organization tests and rates the efficiency of consumer products through scientific testing methods and provides consulting service on technical problems of consumers, government agencies, and others. To guide buyers, Consumers' Research publishes tests and ratings of products in its monthly magazine, *Consumers' Research Magazine*, and in annual reports.

Consumers Union of the United States, Inc. (CU). Consumers Union is a nonprofit corporation with the world's largest laboratory and testing facilities for consumers. The organization tests products, provides information about them to consumers, and acts as an advocate for consumer protection. To guide buyers, Consumers Union publishes tests and ratings of products in its monthly magazine, *Consumer Reports*, and in annual reports.

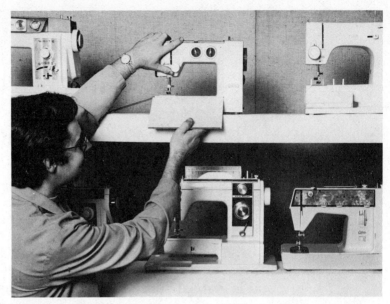

Sewing machines are tested at Consumers' Research to determine quality and value in performance so that ratings may be developed for the guidance of buyers.

Courtesy of Consumers' Research, Inc., publishers of Consumers' Research Magazine, *Washington, N.J.*

Seals of Approval

There are many businesses, periodicals, stores, associations of businesses, and independent testing and certifying agencies that provide information for the guidance and protection of consumers. In many cases, the products that are tested as to safety, quality, use, content, strength, or other characteristics may carry a seal of approval or in some cases a guarantee as advertised. Among the most well known are:

Good Housekeeping. "If product or performance defective, Good Housekeeping guarantees replacement or refund to consumer." This is the legend contained within the Good Housekeeping Consumers' Guaranty Seal. This seal is available for use with properly qualified consumer goods. To qualify for its use, a company must submit samples of its product for evaluation by the Good Housekeeping Institute. They must submit their advertising copy for Good Housekeeping review. When Good Housekeeping is satisfied that the product is a good one and that the claims in advertisements to appear in *Good Housekeeping* magazine are truthful, it may license the company to reproduce this seal in acceptable advertising appearing in other media. The company may also reproduce the seal on labels, on package inserts, etc. Complaints directed to Good Housekeeping, under the terms of this guarantee, receive prompt and effective handling.

Parents' Magazine. The *Parents' Magazine* Guaranteed Seal is granted only to products and services that are advertised in *Parents' Magazine* and that *Parents' Magazine* believes are suitable for families with children. When an advertiser applies for permission to use the seal, the Consumer Service Bureau considers the request. If in its judgment it believes such action merited, the seal is granted. This, subject to verification, guarantees refund or replacement to the consumer if such product or performance is found to be defective.

Underwriters' Laboratory, Inc. Underwriters' Laboratory tests products from more than 13,000 manufacturers all over the world. The Underwriters' Laboratory marker is not a guarantee; it signifies, however, that the item has been tested for fire, casualty, and electrical safety and has been judged to be safe for normal use.

Professional Associations

Some of the associations of professional people have as an objective the welfare of consumers. In some instances the activities to achieve this objective are legislative in nature; in other cases, informational and educational materials are prepared and distributed. Some of the influential professional associations are:

American Dental Association. The function of the Council on Dental Therapeutics, which was established by the American Dental Association, is to protect and inform the public about dental products. Most of the products studied by the Council are used or prescribed directly by the dentist in the treatment of diseases of the mouth. Upon investigation, a product may be accepted by the Council, which means that it meets certain standards with respect both to its composition and to the manner in which the product is advertised. A seal of acceptance may be used by the manufacturer of a product if it has been accepted by the Council.

American Home Economics Association. For over 60 years the American Home Economics Association has been one of the most effective influences in the United States in promoting the education, welfare, and protection of consumers. This association helps to improve the quality of individual and family life through research, cooperative programs, education, and public information. Through the Consumer Interests Committee, the American Home Economics Association makes available a series of buying guides that are valuable to consumers.

American Medical Association. One aspect of the program of the American Medical Association of particular value to consumers is the improvement of the quality of medical products. The responsibility for testing medical products and apparatus is assigned to special committees and councils. The Association makes useful information available to medical societies and the public through a monthly periodical known as *Today's Health*.

Better Business Bureaus

Better business bureaus handle more consumer contacts than all other agencies combined. There are almost 150 independent local better business bureaus, which are joined together in a national organization called the *Council of Better Business Bureaus*.

The better business bureaus were originally organized to improve advertising by the elimination of misleading advertising and unethical promotional schemes. The activities have expanded now

FUNCTIONS OF BETTER BUSINESS BUREAUS

1. Elimination of causes of customer complaints against business by —
   a. Preventing unfair treatment.
   b. Promoting fair advertising and selling practices.
   c. Promoting informative advertising.

2. Cooperation with educators and business to provide students with sound knowledge of the functions of our economic system.

3. Provision for adult education in matters pertaining to management of personal business affairs and understanding of the American economy.

to include investigations of unfair competition among distributors and unfair treatment of consumers.

Consumers can protect themselves from unfair business practices and from fraudulent schemes by consulting the local better business bureau. Consumers who have become the victims of unfair practices should report such incidents to the bureau so that other citizens may be protected. Many local better business bureaus publish booklets providing information for consumers.

FACTS THAT EVERYONE SHOULD KNOW ABOUT CONSUMER PROTECTION BY PRIVATE AGENCIES

1. Several consumer-sponsored organizations provide informative and protective services, such as testing and rating widely used consumer goods and publishing newsletters and pamphlets on issues of interest to consumers.

2. Consumers derive benefits from activities of professional organizations in the sponsorship of legislation, preparation of informative materials, and encouragement of informative labeling and advertising.

3. Many large retail stores and mail-order houses do research and testing of consumer goods. The results usually are made available to buyers through labels on the merchandise and special consumer reports.

4. Some trade associations have set up institutes for testing consumer items and for establishing standards to assure acceptable quality. Seals of approval and seals of acceptance are issued by a few trade associations for products meeting specified minimum standards.

5. Some firms and business associations that provide services, such as dry cleaning, laundering, and lending money, assist consumers through the publication of consumer information.

how to complain successfully

To speed up complaint processing and to achieve satisfactory solutions require especially courtesy and knowledge and sometimes courage and patience. Reporting unsatisfactory service and poor merchandise not only helps you, the consumer, but assists a company to identify and correct mistakes. Here's a few helpful hints:

★ Read and follow instructions carefully as to using, washing, servicing, oiling and general care which may eliminate the need for a product return.

★ Obtain a receipt for items left for repair or for a refund later by mail.

★ Return merchandise personally to the store and department where purchased if at all possible.

★ Assemble receipts, copy of cancelled check used in payment, hang tags, warranty and care labels before returning everything purchased in original package if available.

★ Make store returns NOT at rush hours, closing or lunch times and when you don't get to see the person who could be able to do the most for you, speak to a person higher in authority.

★ Think through why you're dissatisfied so you can present clearly and well your reason for complaint or return.

★ Find through the public library the proper company name, department involved, address and zip code before writing a company or returning by mail.

★ Save time by writing a legible, businesslike letter, keeping your own carbon copy.

★ Provide brand name, model number, size and color which will help identify the problem product.

★ Try to explain specifically what is wrong; send your letter with the package if small and insure it; with certified mail you can obtain a return receipt so you'll know it was received; include your name, address, zip code and telephone numbers on your correspondence.

★ Send a second letter if you don't hear from the company. Most firms try to acknowledge customer service correspondence within two to three weeks. If there's no word, refer the matter to your Better Business Bureau.

WHERE TO COMPLAIN ABOUT ALMOST ANYTHING

Got a gripe about something you've bought? An overcharge, for example? Or a failure to get delivery of an order? Or an out-and-out gyp? You're not alone. Latest figures from the Council of Better Business Bureaus say 6,400,000 inquiries or complaints were filed with its branches last year.

If you have a complaint, you'll save time by knowing in advance where to turn, assuming you cannot get satisfaction from the store or manufacturer involved. The list below (based on a compilation in *Consumer Views*, published by the First National City Bank of New York) will help you. As you will note, many agencies handle the same types of complaints, and it's up to you to decide where you want to go. Often, a good place to start is the office of your mayor, city manager, or county executive. It may be able to locate the right agency for you, and it can be useful in complaints relating to violation of health and housing regulations and weights and measures.

	complaints handled
city & county consumer protection agencies	Fraud, sales deception, false advertising, other shopping complaints.
state attorney general	As above, plus complaints concerned with possible criminal gyps and frauds. Also, violation of state credit regulations.
local Food & Drug Administration office (check phone book under "U.S. Government")	Adulterated food, drugs, cosmetics. Mislabeling of same.
regional offices of Federal Trade Commission. Get addresses from FTC, Washington, D.C. 20580	Deceptive business practices, misleading or fraudulent ads involving interstate companies. Illegal credit practices. Misleading fabric care and content labeling.
National Highway Traffic Safety Administration, Office of Public Affairs and Consumer Services, 400 Seventh St., S.W., Washington, D.C. 20590	*complaints handled* Safety problems with cars, tires, motorcycles, children's car seats.
Consumer Advocate, U.S. Postal Service, 475 L'Enfant Plaza West, S.W., Washington, D.C. 20260	Postal service gripes, such as rude clerks, long service lines, lost or damaged packages.
Office of Consumer Affairs, Civil Aeronautics Board, 1825 Connecticut Ave., N.W., Washington, D.C. 20428	Problems involving air travel and shipments (domestic and international).
Office of Consumer Affairs, Dept. of Health, Education, and Welfare, 330 Independence Ave., S.W., Washington, D.C. 20201	Any type of problem, which will either be handled directly or referred to the proper agency.
Consumer Product Safety Commission, Washington, D.C. 20207	Unsafe products, including household appliances, housewares, dangerous packaging, garden tools, textile items, toys, etc. 24-hour hot line available for serious complaints: continental U.S., except Md., 800 638-2666; Md., 800 492-2937.
Council of Better Business Bureaus, 1150 Seventeenth St., N.W., Washington, D.C. 20036	Misleading business practices, fraudulent ads of national companies, other types of deception. Also, national fund-raising gyps.
your local Better Business Bureau	Same as above, but involving local business complaints.
Major Appliance Consumer Action Panel, 20 N. Wacker Dr., Chicago, Ill. 60606	Problems with major appliances and repairs if dealer or manufacturer is not responsive.

Source: *Changing Times, The Kiplinger Magazine* (August, 1974).

REVIEW QUESTIONS

Section A

1. As the United States grew more industrialized and cities became larger, why did new consumer problems appear?
2. What is the consumer movement and how did it develop in the United States?
3. What is the consumer bill of rights?

Section B

4. What are the functions of the government agencies that are related to consumer interests?
5. What is the main function of the Department of Agriculture as it relates to the consumer?
6. What are the main functions of the Civil Aeronautics Board?
7. What are some of the major agencies under the Department of Commerce that provide services to the consumer?
8. What is the purpose of the Consumer Product Safety Commission?
9. What is the primary purpose of the Environmental Protection Agency?
10. What is the purpose of the Federal Trade Commission?
11. How does the Government Printing Office assist the consumer?
12. In what way does the Department of Health, Education, and Welfare assist the consumer?
13. How do state and local consumer agencies assist the consumer?

Section C

14. What is the Consumers Federation of America?
15. What is the purpose of Consumers' Research, Inc.?
16. What is the Consumers Union of the United States, Inc.?
17. What are some of the more common seals of approval designed for the protection of consumer interests?
18. What are some of the more important professional associations designed to protect the consumer?
19. What is the primary function of better business bureaus?

DISCUSSION QUESTIONS

Section A

1. Why has the need for consumer protection grown over time in the United States and throughout the world?
2. How has the consumer movement changed through the years?
3. What impact did the consumer bill of rights have on consumer legislation?

Section B

4. How do the grading and inspection services of the Department of Agriculture aid the consumer?
5. In what way does the standardization program of the National Bureau of Standards help you as a buyer?
6. Why is it necessary to have state laws — in addition to federal laws — that control deceptive and fraudulent advertising?

Section C

7. Some manufacturers oppose such organizations as Consumers' Research, Inc. and Consumers Union, Inc. whereas others approve them. How do you account for the differences in attitude?
8. Why do you think that some manufacturers organize an association and

use a seal indicating that products of the members of that association meet certain requirements?

9. Some people assert that the scientific laboratories maintained by publishers of periodicals are operated for the benefit of manufacturers and therefore render little service to buyers. Do you think this assertion is true? Why?

10. Suppose a door-to-door salesman calls on you. You would like to obtain information as to his reliability and that of his company. From what source might you be able to obtain help or advice?

APPLICATION PROBLEMS

Section A

1. Research the Consumer Protection Act of 1974, a major controversial piece of legislation that was not passed by Congress. (a) What are the arguments for and against the Act? (b) Several large well-known manufacturers and retailers came out for the Act and some came out against it. What influence did they have? (c) What is your opinion of why the Act was not passed?

Section B

2. Prepare a brief report about the Federal Trade Commission, covering its main purposes and the principal laws that it administers.

3. Prepare a report on the provisions of the Fair Debt Collection Bill of 1977.

4. Make a list of several different articles, such as cigarettes, medicine, cosmetics, packaged foods, and so forth. Indicate what type of information is given on each package. What conclusions can you draw about the completeness of the information given? What additional information do you think would be desirable?

Section C

5. Prepare a complete list of the products that are advertised in a current issue of some popular magazine. Opposite the name of each product indicate whether there is any seal, label, certified test, or testimonial used to indicate the standard of quality of the product. Indicate the specific proof that is given.

6. Make a list of food products and medicines that you find bearing seals or labels of approval. Indicate the particular seal or label for each product. If you find any seal or label with which you are not acquainted, inquire about the conditions under which it is awarded.

7. Analyze a recent copy of *Consumers' Research Magazine* and one of *Consumer Reports*. What special contributions do these publications make to the consumer? Prepare a one-page paper on the nature of the contents of these publications and their value to consumers.

COMMUNITY PROJECTS

Section A

1. Prepare a report indicating how the need for consumer protection has directly affected your community.

2. It has been stated that the Consumer Movement of the Seventies was similar to, yet distinctly different from, the Consumer Movement of the Thirties. Prepare a list of the similarities and the differences. For source material use the library, and also interview business people and consumers who are familiar with both areas.

Section B

3. Through library research, prepare a list of recent federal consumer legislation designed to protect the consumer. Describe the major characteristic of each piece of legislation either in writing or orally to the class.
4. Prepare a list of laws and regulations in your state that in some way protect consumers. Examples to help start the list are: laws governing small loans and credit, sanitation laws, and laws for the licensing and control of barbers.
5. Most states have some form of consumer fraud or protection agency functioning for the most part in the Office of the Attorney General. While the exact makeup of such bodies and the functions assigned to them vary from state to state, generally they are empowered to protect the consumer through mediation, education, legislation, and litigation. To determine the situation in your own state, check with the Office of the Attorney General. Make a report to the class.

Section C

6. Prepare a list of local sources of consumer protection and help in settling grievances, indicating what each source handles.
7. Assume that you bought a wristwatch at a local store. After one week, the watch stopped running. You returned the watch to the store and received another in exchange. The second watch does not keep accurate time, even after being taken back for regulation three times. It also stops running when you are not wearing it. What course of action should you take to handle your complaint?

Legal Relations and the Consumer

PURPOSE OF THE CHAPTER

Many of our economic problems involve dealings with other people, and many of these dealings involve legal relations. There are laws that guide and protect us in our everyday dealings. This chapter discusses some common legal problems of consumers.

After studying this chapter, you will be able to:

1. List the essential elements of a contract.
2. Explain when a minor can be held responsible for debts.
3. Explain when a contract must be in writing.
4. Discuss remedies for breach of contract.
5. Explain why you need legal advice.

A. CONTRACTS

Laws are not exactly the same in all states. However, under the Uniform Commercial Code (law), which has been adopted by all of the states except Louisiana, the laws relating to sales contracts are essentially the same. The discussions in this chapter follow the Code.

What Is a Contract?

A *contract* is an agreement between two or more competent parties that creates an obligation enforceable by law. If one of the parties does not carry out his or her part of the agreement, the other party may resort to court action.

When you buy goods on account in a store, you make a contract with the store to pay the cost of the merchandise. If you leave

RUBBER HEELS

By accepting the shoes, the shoe repairer promises that they will be repaired. The customer promises that payment will be made.

shoes in a repair shop to be repaired, a contract is made on the part of the repairer to repair the shoes and on your part to pay the prescribed charges. When you rent a house, you enter into a contract to pay the rent and the owner is obligated to let you have possession of the property. Many other situations that involve contracts exist in everyday life. Buying life insurance, buying fire insurance, shipping merchandise, or accepting a job offer all involve contracts.

The basis of a contract is an agreement between the parties. But not all agreements are contracts because some agreements do not have all the essentials of contracts. For example, Anne Compton agrees to go camping with Ginny Dunn; but if Dunn changes her mind and decides not to go, she is not breaking a contract. On the other hand, if Compton and Dunn make arrangements to go on a camping trip together and arrange for a professional guide to provide them with equipment, food, and lodging, they have entered into a contract with the guide. They are both responsible to

ELEMENTS OF A CONTRACT
1. There must be offer and acceptance.
2. The parties must be competent.
3. The purpose or subject of the agreement must be legal.
4. There must be a consideration.
5. The agreement must be in proper legal form.

the guide for carrying out the contract or for settling it in some satisfactory manner if they change their minds. It is also quite possible that a court would decide that there was a contract if both or either had made certain preparations and spent any money for mutual benefit.

Element No. 1: Offer and Acceptance (Mutual Assent)

In every contract there is an *offer* and an *acceptance*. For example, one person offers a one-acre tract of land for sale at a price of $2,500. Another person accepts the offer, therefore promising to pay the price asked. There was *mutual assent* between the two parties: one made the offer, the other accepted the offer.

Under the principles of law, it is not considered that there is mutual assent unless both parties have freely, intentionally, and apparently assented to the same thing.

Offer. The essential characteristics of an offer are: (a) the proposal must be definite; (b) the proposal must be made with the intention that the *offeror* (person making the offer) be bound by it; and (c) the proposal must be communicated by words or actions to the *offeree* (the one to whom it is made).

If you were to offer to work for an employer for "all that you are worth," the offer would be too indefinite to be the basis of an enforceable agreement. If an offer is made in obvious or apparent jest, or in disgust or anger, it is not a real offer. If someone in jest says that he or she would give a thousand dollars to see the expression on a friend's face when opening a comic birthday greeting, the offer is not real. Or, if the motor in your new automobile will not start, it would not be a real offer if in disgust you say, "I would take $5 for it."

Most advertisements are not offers. They merely invite the prospective customer to buy or to make an offer to buy. If you walk into a store and find goods on display with a price marked on them, you might think the goods are offered for sale at that price; but the law holds that price tags on merchandise merely indicate a willingness to consider an offer made by a buyer on those terms.

Acceptance. An offer for the purchase of goods may be accepted in any way that is reasonable. For example, the seller may ship the goods or may promise to do so promptly.

As in the case of an offer, the acceptance must be indicated by some word or act. For instance, you cannot be bound against your will by an offeror who states in his offer, "If I do not hear from you by ten o'clock, October 10, I shall consider that you have accepted this offer." The acceptance must also be made by the party to whom the offer was made. If someone has made an offer to you and you tell a friend about it, the person who made the offer does not have to recognize an acceptance by your friend. The acceptance may be in the form of a definite promise that completes the mutual agreement, or it may be made in the form of some act.

For example, Mrs. Burton bought a stove, had it sent out to her home, and used it for two weeks. When the store asked for payment, she insisted on returning the stove although she had no complaint as to its performance. She insisted that she had never accepted it because she had not paid for it. Courts would undoubtedly hold that there was an offer and an acceptance. On the other hand, if she had ordered it sent out on approval, an acceptance would not have been indicated until she had signified her approval or had kept the stove an unreasonable length of time without expressing dissatisfaction or a willingness to return it.

A definite and reasonable expression of acceptance is legal and binding if it is within a reasonable time. It may also include additional conditions not in the original offer.

As a general rule, when offers are made by letter with the acceptance to be made by mail, the offer is considered to be accepted when the acceptance is deposited in the mail. Likewise, if the acceptance is to be made by telegram, the agreement is considered to be completed when the message is given to the telegraph company.

ACCEPTANCE IS INDICATED BY:

1. Specific indication that the buyer accepts the goods.

2. Use of the goods (unless the goods were not ordered).

3. Keeping the goods for an unreasonable length of time.

Terminating an Offer. An offer can be terminated in many ways. It may be terminated at a definite time stated in the offer. If no definite time is stated, the offer will be terminated in a reasonable amount of time, which often has to be determined by the court if a dispute arises. Definite refusal of the offer or a *counteroffer* (a new offer by the person to whom the original offer was made) will terminate the original offer. Unless it is specified that an offer must be accepted just as made, it may be accepted and at the same time propose new or additional terms without being considered a rejection if the offeror assents to the changes. The withdrawal or revocation of the offer before it is accepted is a clear termination. Other unusual circumstances that terminate offers are death or insanity of the offeror.

Ordinarily, if an offer is made for a specified length of time, it may still be revoked before the expiration of that time if proper notice is given of the withdrawal. However, if a general offer is made to the public, such as a reward published in a newspaper, it is in effect until it is withdrawn in the same way that it was offered.

Keeping an Offer Open. Offers are sometimes kept open for specified periods of time by a special contract that is known as an *option*. If the offeror receives cash or something of value as an inducement to keep an offer open for a certain specified time, the offer cannot be withdrawn for the period of time covered by the option. This is an important type of offer that is used in large transactions. For example, a person considering buying a home or a company considering buying a new factory would want time to consider the matter with the assurance that if a decision were made to buy the property, the original price quotation would be accepted.

Options are useful in many types of negotiations leading to a sale. It is important, however, that an option be in writing and signed by the person granting it. An offer in writing by a merchant to sell goods and to keep the offer open for a reasonable time (not over 3 months) cannot be revoked and does not require a consideration.

Element No. 2: Competent Parties

The question of competence of parties determines who is legally qualified to make contracts. Anyone who is not otherwise prevented by law from making enforceable agreements may make a contract. Intoxicated persons and insane persons are not competent to contract. The reason for voiding the contracts entered into by these persons is obvious: they are not considered capable of exercising their own judgment. In certain states there are special laws applying to contracts that may be made by convicts, foreigners, or married women, but there is a wide variation in these laws.

In recent years, at both national and state levels, the rights of women have been broadened considerably through new nondiscrimination acts. Until recently, many women, particularly divorced women and widows, had difficulty getting credit because of discrimination. The rights of women and many minority groups are now protected much more clearly under new credit protection legislation.

In many cases, *minors* (those who are not of legal age) are not competent to contract and may not be required by law to carry out agreements. There are, however, some exceptions to this rule, such as contracting for necessaries. When a minor makes an agreement with an adult, the adult is required to fulfill the contract if it is legal; but if the minor chooses to *rescind* (cancel) the contract, he or she can, in most cases, escape responsibility. When minors reach the minimum age at which they may make a contract, they are said to have attained the *age of majority*.

AGE OF MAJORITY (BECOMING OF AGE)
(Minimum legal age to make a contract)

Until recently any person, male or female, under 21 years of age was considered to be a minor under common law. Minority ended on the day before the 21st birthday. In recent years, however, the 21 years of age has been reduced to 18 years in two thirds of the states and to 19 years in a few states. The "day before the birthday" rule is generally still followed. Some states provide for the termination of minority upon marriage, and some states specify that the minority of girls shall terminate sooner than that of boys.

Usually, contracts made by a minor are *voidable* (that is, they may be broken) by the minor. He or she may break them while still a minor or within a reasonable time after coming of age. If a minor reaffirms the agreement after coming of age, it becomes a binding contract. The voidability of a contract applies generally whether it has been fully performed or only partially performed.

For example, the Ridge Hardware Store accepted a properly signed order for a bicycle for $60 from Amy Hansen, age 12. When the bicycle arrived from the factory, the price had risen and the dealer insisted on getting $75 for the bicycle or canceling the contract. The dealer argued that the original agreement was not binding because Amy Hansen was a minor and was, therefore, incompetent to contract. This agreement, however, is binding on the dealer; but Amy, because she is a minor, could cancel the contract if she wished.

Although minors may void contracts to buy, they are held responsible when they contract for necessaries (food and clothes).

JCPenney Co., Inc.

A minor who acquires reasonable necessaries is obligated to pay the reasonable value of the purchases. A merchant who furnishes such things as jewelry, tobacco, or sporting equipment to an ordinary minor usually cannot collect payment. But one who furnishes necessary clothes or food can collect if the amounts charged are reasonable and the goods are needed and are actually delivered. On the other hand, if all these necessaries of life are provided by the parents, any contract made by the child to obtain them is voidable. A contract by a poor child to buy expensive clothing would be voidable also.

Because contracts made by minors for some things are voidable, some merchants ask the parents of the minor to *countersign* the contract, thus confirming it. An increasing practice is for department stores to open charge accounts for minors, permitting the minors to buy on account in a manner similar to adults. Many times, the store asks the parents of the minors to countersign the agreement between the store and the minors.

For example, Howard Martin, age 20, signed a contract for the purchase of an automobile. The dealer asked his age, and he assured the dealer that he was 21 on his last birthday. When the dealer notified him that the car was ready, Howard refused to accept it, asserting that he misrepresented his age at the time of making the contract and therefore could not be held responsible.

In some states minors are held responsible for agreements if they deliberately misrepresent their age. But if a child, age 12, were to misrepresent his or her age, the dealer might find it difficult to hold the child responsible because of the obvious young age. The reason for this principle of law is that a minor who misrepresents age places the other party in an unfair position, particularly if the minor is close to the age of majority. However, it is assumed that if a much younger child misrepresents his or her age, the other party would enter into the agreement knowing that the person is a minor.

SOME OTHER EXAMPLES IN REGARD TO COMPETENT PERSONS

1. A person who cannot read is bound by a contract if it has been read to him or her and is understood by him or her before signing.

2. A person who cannot read or write but who signs a contract with an "X" or other symbol is bound by the contract if it has been read to him or her and is understood by him or her.

3. Generally, a person who has made a contract while a minor may repudiate or affirm the contract when coming of age, but failure to repudiate it generally makes the contract binding.

Element No. 3: Legal Purpose

The purpose for which a contract is made must not be contrary to law or to the interests of society. In other words, the subject of the bargain must be legal. This is referred to as *legal bargain*. In fact, in most cases, when the purpose of the contract is not legal, there is not even a contract. Neither party can be held under the agreement.

Examples of illegal bargains are those involving agreements to steal or to accept stolen goods. Anyone buying stolen goods does not get a valid title to the goods. The goods must be returned to the rightful owner if ownership can be proved. All agreements to wager or gamble are illegal except in the cases of certain states in which betting on horse and dog racing has been legalized. For instance, if you make a bet with somebody, you have not made a legal contract. However, in a state where betting on horse races is legal, your placing of a bet is a legal contract.

In all states there are so-called *usury laws* that establish the highest contract rate of interest that may be charged. If a contract is made and interest is charged at a higher rate than that stated by law, the contract is an illegal one. Exceptions to these laws are the small loan regulations that permit licensed small loan organizations to charge higher rates.

It is illegal to enter into any contract to obstruct justice, such as an agreement to give false testimony or to avoid giving testimony.

Generally, when a certain type of business or professional person is subject to licensing, any contract made with one who is unlicensed may be void. For instance, in most cities electricians and plumbers are licensed. If you make an agreement with an unlicensed electrician or plumber, the agreement may not be a legal contract.

In almost all cases, agreements that unreasonably restrain trade are void. Examples of such agreements that are void are those involving control of prices, limiting production, creating a monopoly, creating an artifical scarcity, or causing unreasonable injury to competitors.

Element No. 4: Consideration

A contract usually is an agreement whereby one person agrees to do something and another person agrees to do something else in return. What either party agrees to do in return for that which was promised by the other is known as *consideration*. For example, an automobile dealer and you may enter into a contract for you to buy an automobile in which you promise to pay for it and the dealer promises to transfer ownership of it to you in return. Every legal contract must have consideration.

For example, Ann Humphrey, a wealthy member of Summit Hills Country Club, offered to give her old set of golf clubs to a caddy at the end of the golf season. She changed her mind and did not give them to the caddy. The caddy insisted that a contract had been made. Miss Humphrey insisted that there was no consideration on the part of the caddy in the nature of goods, money, services, or promises. If the caddy can prove that the clubs were promised in return for caddy service or any other favor to Miss Humphrey, there probably is a contract. In the absence of such proof, there is no contract; it is simply in the nature of a promise to make a gift. A gift without a consideration is not regarded as a contract.

Ordinarily, the promise made in an agreement is not enforceable unless something of value is received for the promise. The value may consist of goods, money, services, refraining from doing something that one has a right to do, or giving up a privilege. A common example of a consideration is the down payment made to a merchant when an agreement has been reached for the delivery of a piece of furniture. When one takes a job, the employer promises to pay for the services and the employee promises to perform the duties required in the job. A landlord may pay a tenant a certain sum of money to give up the lease and vacate the property. The amount paid by the landlord is the consideration for the giving up of a legal right on the part of the tenant if the lease has not expired.

In a sale of goods, a change agreeable to both parties can be made in the contract without additional consideration being required.

Element No. 5: Proper Legal Form

To qualify as legal contracts, certain agreements must be made in the form specified by law. Most contracts, however, are informal and very simple. Every day you enter into informal contracts. It may be as simple as placing on your tray in the school cafeteria the food you have selected from the variety that was offered and accepting the offer by paying the amount the cashier requests. Other contracts, such as the purchase of real estate, must be formal.

Oral and Written Contracts. Generally, there are two main types of contracts: (1) *oral* and (2) *written*. Ordinarily, oral evidence of a sale is sufficient when the price is less than $500. If the requirements are not met, the oral agreement to sell goods is legal but is voidable by either party. However, it may be carried out by mutual agreement. If it is evident that the parties reached an agreement, the contract is binding, even if some elements are missing, such as the date, the exact method of fulfilling the contract, or a price to be set later.

A great many contracts do not have to be in writing because the offer, acceptance, payment, and delivery of goods often occur within a short space of a few seconds or a few minutes. Contracts for medical and dental services need not be in writing regardless of the amount involved. Contracts for labor and materials generally need not be in writing.

A contract should be written instead of oral when there is any chance for misunderstanding or disagreement between the parties

THE ESSENTIALS OF A WRITTEN CONTRACT ARE:

1. The date and the place of the agreement.

2. The names and the identification of the parties entering into the agreement.

3. A statement of the agreement covered by the contract.

4. A statement of the money, the services, or the goods given in consideration of the agreement.

5. The signatures of *both* parties or the signatures of legal agents.

6. In the case of some contracts, witnesses are required. In such cases the witnesses must sign in accordance with the provisions of the law.

THIS AGREEMENT is made on May 10, 1980, between James A. Wiley, 3144 Beechwood Drive, Columbus, Ohio, the party of the first part, and Diana L. Segal, 5967 Rosetree Lane, Columbus, Ohio, the party of the second part.

The party of the first part agrees to install 4 aluminum triple-track storm windows in the home of the party of the second part at 5967 Rosetree Lane, Columbus, Ohio, by June 10, 1980, in accordance with the specifications attached hereto. In consideration of which the party of the second part agrees to pay the party of the first part $385.75 upon the satisfactory completion of the work.

James A. Wiley

Diana L. Segal

A Contract

or when a written contract is required by law. For example, Ms. Peggy Waltham bought a house from the Eastside Realty Company for $30,000 on an oral agreement. This is not an enforceable contract because the law requires agreements of this type to be in writing.

THESE CONTRACTS MUST BE IN WRITING

1. An agreement to be responsible for the debt, default, or obligation of another person.

2. An agreement that is not to be executed or performed within a period of one year after it is made.

3. An agreement to buy or sell real estate, including land, buildings, minerals, or trees.

4. An agreement to sell goods in excess of $500. (Exceptions are when there has been a part payment or part of the goods have been delivered.)

5. An installment contract.

The contract signed by both parties constitutes evidence of their agreement when a written contract is required by law.

Virginia National Bank

FOR YOUR PROTECTION

---

1. Read the entire contract *before* you sign.

2. Ask for an explanation of parts you do not understand.

3. Make sure the contract states all conditions and promises as you understand them.

4. Do not accept your copy without the signature of the other party on the contract.

5. Keep your copy of the contract in a safe place.

A *bill of sale* is a written contract with which many consumers are acquainted. It is required in most states for the transfer of ownership of such items as automobiles or refrigerators. Even in states where a bill of sale is not required for these items, it is often desirable to obtain one because it provides evidence of ownership. In states where the bill of sale is used, it is usually necessary to register the bill of sale with the proper county authority so that the ownership of the property can be established.

Express and Implied Contracts. Contracts may be classified in another way. They are said to be either express or implied. An *express contract* is one that arises out of an agreement expressed by oral or written words. If you agree orally to buy a stereo at a specified price and the dealer agrees to sell it to you at that price, you have made an express contract that is legally binding. An *implied contract* is one that is made through an agreement implied by the acts or the conduct of the parties involved. If you pick up an article in a store and hand the required amount of money to the clerk, who wraps the article and hands it to you, you have made an implied contract.

Defective Agreements

An agreement may not be enforceable because it is found to be defective. Misrepresentation, use of undue influence, concealment of vital facts, or use of threats or force in obtaining agreement may make an agreement *defective*.

Agreements that are not enforceable may be classified as void or voidable. When an agreement is *void*, it has no legal force or effect. In other words, neither party can enforce the agreement. A *voidable contract* is one that may be broken (rescinded or voided) by one or both of the parties. Such an agreement becomes an enforceable agreement if the party or parties having the option to reject the agreement choose not to do so.

Ordinarily, a mistake made by one party, such as quoting the wrong price, does not make the contract void or voidable. Mistakes that make a contract void include mutual mistakes as to the existence of the subject matter or a mistake as to the identity of the parties. For instance, a man agreed to sell a certain dog at a definite price, but later it was found that the dog had died before the agreement was made. The agreement was void because of a mistake as to the existence of the subject matter.

EXAMPLES OF VOIDABLE AGREEMENTS

1. If there is fraud in the form of misrepresentation or concealment of vital facts.

2. If a person makes an agreement as a result of a threat or the use of violence.

3. If there has been undue and unfair influence and pressure to the extent that one person has not reached the agreement through the free exercise of his or her own judgment.

B. CARRYING OUT A CONTRACT

Never sign a blank contract or one with part of the figures or conditions left to be filled in. If someone hurries you or suggests that you sign the contract with the rest of the information to be filled in later, your suspicion should be aroused.

Do not sign a contract with the understanding that supplementary agreements will be made later. Be sure that all agreements are in the contract. In the absence of substantial proof with regard to oral agreements or supplementary written agreements, only the agreements stipulated in the contract are enforceable.

Warranties

The promises a seller makes before or after the sale that an article will operate in a specific way or that it has a certain specific quality are statements on which the buyer has a legal right to rely. These promises or representations are called *warranties*. There are two types of warranties: (1) express and (2) implied.

An *express warranty* is an assurance of quality or a promise of performance by the seller. It may be oral or written, and it usually is given before or at the time of sale. An express warranty may be a general statement, such as "This rebuilt television set is as good as new"; or it may be limited to some particular fact about the goods, such as "This set will get Channel 19 without an outdoor antenna."

An *implied warranty* is an obligation imposed by law. In many cases, the law requires sellers to provide certain minimum standards of quality and performance even if no actual promises are made at the time of sale. The buyer has a right to expect that the article purchased will serve the purpose for which it is sold, although there is no definite statement in regard to it. For example, if you buy an air conditioner, you have a right to expect that it will operate. If it does not operate, you have a legal recourse. If you go into a restaurant and order food, there is an implied warranty that the food is fit to eat. If you become poisoned, the restaurant owner is liable. If it can be proved that the manufacturer or processor of the food was responsible because of improper processing or handling of the food, that party may also be held liable for any resulting damages.

"Trade puffs" or "trade talk" are not warranties and should not be relied upon by the buyer. A *trade puff* is a general claim, such as "This is the best merchandise you can buy," "This is the most popular item on the market," or "This suit is very becoming to you."

The Magnuson-Moss Warranty and Federal Trade Commission Improvement Act of 1975 helps to make warranties less deceptive. The Act rules as deceptive any written warranty that could mislead reasonable consumers through false or fraudulent statements, promises, descriptions, excessive hedging, or omission of relevant information.

For products selling for more than $5, the warranty must include (1) the names and addresses of the warrantors, (2) exactly what is covered and for what, (3) a step-by-step description of the consumer's procedure in getting the warranty honored, (4) legal remedies available to the consumer, and (5) the duration of the warranty.

For products selling for more than $10, the warranty must state whether it is a "full" or "limited" warranty. A warranty is "full" if there are no limitations on rights under implied warranty. A "limited" warranty must state what the limitations are, such as tires on a new automobile.

A Warranty

> **GUARANTEE**
>
> Upon receipt of the guarantee registration card packed with this appliance, your Suntrol Automatic Toaster is guaranteed for one (1) year against electrical and mechanical defects in material and workmanship, which will be repaired or parts replaced free of charge during this period. The guarantee does not cover damage caused by misuse, negligence, or use on current or voltage other than that stamped on the appliance. This guarantee is in lieu of any other warranty either expressed or implied. If service is required, send the appliance prepaid to the nearest Suntrol Appliance Service Company branch or authorized service station. Please include a letter explaining the nature of your difficulty.
>
> This warranty gives you specific legal rights, and you may also have other rights which vary from state to state.

Remedies for Breach of Warranty

In the case of misrepresentation or if goods do not fulfill the reasonable expectations of a warranty, there has been a *breach of warranty*. Several different remedies are available in case of a breach of warranty. The following general recourses are open to the buyer:

1. To keep the goods and to deduct the amount of the damages from the price of the goods.
2. To keep the goods and to bring an action against the seller for damages.
3. To refuse to accept the goods and to bring an action against the seller to recover damages.
4. To rescind (break, void, or refuse) the contract and to refuse to receive the goods or, if the goods have been accepted, to return them and to recover the price paid.

Passing the Title

When a cash sale is made, the title passes immediately. This means that the seller ceases to own the goods and the buyer becomes the owner. When a sale on credit is made, the title also passes immediately; the buyer merely has an agreement as to the time when he or she will pay for the goods. Ordinarily, COD (cash on delivery) sales result in a transfer of the title at the time the goods are shipped; the seller merely does not give possession until the charge is paid.

When one buys something on approval, the title does not pass to the buyer until the article has been approved and an acknowledgment of its acceptance has either been given or implied. The buyer has the right to return all the goods or any whole units. For example, the buyer could use one can out of a case of 12 and return the rest.

In the case of installment sales in which the conditional contract is used, the seller has a right to reclaim the goods if payments are not made regularly. The buyer may, in that case, lose what has already been paid and may even have to pay something extra for not fulfilling the provisions of the contract. When the provisions of the contract are fulfilled, the title then passes to the buyer.

In a sale subject to return, the title passes at the time of the sale; but if the goods are returned, the title reverts to the seller.

Remedies of Seller When Buyer Fails to Perform

If the buyer of merchandise fails to perform the buyer's part of the contract, the seller may select any of the following remedies:

1. The seller may sue for payment if the title has passed. When the buyer refuses or neglects to pay, the seller may sue for the price of the goods.
2. The seller may sue for damages if the title has not passed. When the buyer wrongfully refuses or neglects to accept and pay for the goods, the seller may sue for damages. The amount of damages will usually be the difference between the contract price and the market price.
3. The seller may rescind the contract. When the buyer repudiates the contract, cannot perform it, or fails to perform it, the seller is allowed, under most laws, to rescind the contract.

When a buyer does not fulfill his or her part of an installment sales contract, the seller may reclaim the item.

Remedies of Buyer When Seller Fails to Perform

If the seller of merchandise fails to perform the seller's part of the contract, the buyer has the choice of one of the following remedies:

1. The buyer may obtain possession of the goods if the title has passed and payment has been made. When the seller wrongfully refuses or neglects to deliver the goods, the buyer may sue for the possession of the goods, for the recovery of the value that has been paid, or for damages.

2. The buyer may sue for damages if the title has not passed. If the seller wrongfully refuses or neglects to deliver the goods, the buyer is entitled to damages for nondelivery. The amount of the damages is ordinarily the difference between the contract price and the market price at the time and the place of delivery. The amount may also include any other damages for loss resulting from the failure to fulfill the contract.

3. The buyer may insist upon the fulfillment of the contract. The buyer has the right to sue for specific performance if damages will not be adequate compensation or if they cannot be computed. When the buyer sues for specific performance and wins the case, the seller is ordered by the court to carry out the original contract.

4. The buyer may cancel the contract and refuse to accept the goods. If the seller has broken or in any way failed to carry out the seller's part of the contract, the buyer may refuse to accept delivery of the goods or may return them if delivered. If damages have resulted, the buyer may also sue for damages.

The buyer need not accept delivery
if the seller violates the contract.

Sales Made at Consumer's Home

In order to give consumers some protection from the evils of high-pressure salesmanship at their homes, the Federal Trade Commission has issued a regulation giving a consumer 3 days to set aside a signed contract for a home purchase of goods or services of $25 or more. The seller is required to give the buyer a contract stating the buyer's right to rescind. This remedy gives the buyer a chance to think things over after the salesperson has gone and to decide whether the purchase is wanted after all. It is a reasonably good remedy for the consumer against "hit-and-run" salespeople, provided the consumer knows the remedy is available and has not paid in full.

Unordered Merchandise

Some firms and organizations make a practice of sending unordered merchandise in the hope that persons receiving it will pay

When you have repair work done, make sure you are dealing with a reliable repairer and have a written contract so that you will know exactly what you are getting and the terms.

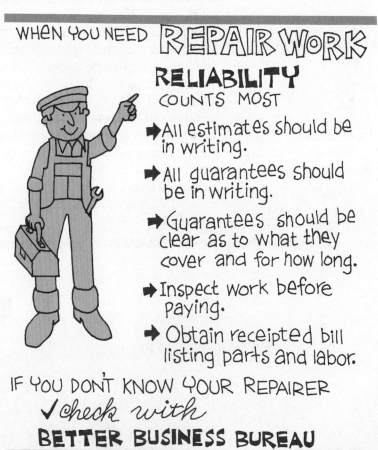

for it. You do not have to pay for or return unordered merchandise received in the mail. You may use it or dispose of it in any way you wish. The fact that you do not return the goods does not mean that you have accepted them. The U.S. Postal Service states: "Any unsolicited or unordered merchandise may be treated as a gift by the recipient, who has the right to retain, use, or dispose of it in any manner without any obligation whatsoever to the sender."

A practical solution to the problem of receiving unordered merchandise is to mark the package "return to sender" and place it in the mail unopened without any additional postage.

Goods Entrusted to Others

Let us say that you entrust your automobile to a garage or a parking lot for safekeeping. The garage or parking lot is responsible for its safekeeping. This is especially true if you are given a ticket that is a receipt for your car and if you are required to leave the keys in the car so that it can be moved. However, if you regularly place your own car in a lot and take the keys with you, the operator of the parking lot is generally not liable.

If you rent or borrow an article, such as a lawn mower, you are responsible for taking reasonable care of it to prevent damage or theft. Likewise, if you take a lawn mower to be repaired and it is damaged in the process of being repaired, the repairer is liable because such a person is expected to exercise reasonable care and skill. The repairer is assumed to have the skill to do the job.

Generally, people who accept the property of others are responsible for it. On the other hand, if neighbors bring you some jewelry and ask you to keep it while they are away on a vacation, you are not responsible for its loss or theft if you exercise reasonable care over it.

Consulting a Lawyer

In this world of specialization it is sound practice to go to a doctor when one is ill. Likewise, it is sound business procedure to obtain competent legal advice on important problems. Some of the problems on which an individual should consult a lawyer are the writing of an important contract, the writing of a will, protecting or gaining one's rights, and obtaining protection against lawsuits. In selecting a lawyer, one should be careful to avoid the so-called shyster who is often too eager to take a case or who solicits a case. It is a practice among reputable lawyers to wait for the client to request legal counsel. Only lawyers who are members of the local or state bar association should be considered. Select your lawyer with the same care that you would use to select your physician or dentist.

If you ask a lawyer a question, the answer will be given to you in the form of an *opinion*. Most lawyers will never state an answer definitely because the answer depends on many circumstances. What appears to be true may not be so when all the facts are known. For example, two judges in different courts, giving decisions on what may appear to be identical sets of circumstances, may give completely opposite decisions. Sometimes these decisions are reversed by higher courts.

Although many things in law appear to be definite, it must be borne in mind that any statement in the field of law cannot be completely definite without knowledge of all the circumstances. Therefore, the statements in this chapter are general statements of law and represent additional reasons why in many cases you should consult a lawyer.

COMMON LEGAL QUESTIONS

Here are some common legal questions.

THE ANSWER TO EACH OF THESE QUESTIONS IS "NO":

1. Is a contract binding if it is entered into under pressure or a threat?

2. Is a contract binding if it involves breaking the law?

3. Is an agreement of a boy 14 years of age to buy a bicycle binding?

4. Is it necessary to sign a written order for the purchase of a suit of clothes in order for the contract to be binding?

5. Are you obligated to return or pay for merchandise sent to you that has not been ordered?

THE ANSWER TO EACH OF THESE QUESTIONS IS "YES":

1. Is a contract binding if it is signed without being read?

2. Is a contract binding if you sign it just to get rid of a persistent salesperson?

3. Is a contract binding if you misunderstand part of it?

4. Is an installment sale agreement a contract?

5. Must a contract to purchase real estate be in writing?

People without money can get legal aid.

Legal Aid Societies

Under the belief that getting justice should not depend on one's ability to pay fees and hire a lawyer, organizations that are generally called *legal aid societies* or *legal aid organizations* have been formed throughout the country. These organizations are found principally in the larger cities. Sponsored by lawyers, they provide an organized method of handling cases for persons who cannot afford to obtain legal assistance.

LEGAL INFORMATION AND PRINCIPLES THAT EVERYONE NEEDS TO UNDERSTAND

1. A contract involves five elements: (a) offer and acceptance, (b) competency of the parties, (c) legal purpose, (d) a consideration, and (e) required legal form.

2. Some contracts must be in writing.

3. Some contracts are expressed or implied.

4. Some contracts are voidable.

5. There are specific remedies if a warranty is broken.

6. The seller has a choice of remedies if the buyer fails to perform.

7. The buyer has a choice of remedies if the seller fails to perform.

8. Generally, when property is entrusted to another party, that party is responsible for reasonable care in safekeeping.

9. Consult a lawyer for legal advice; do not attempt to serve as your own lawyer.

REVIEW QUESTIONS

Section A

1. What is a contract?
2. What are some of the situations in everyday life that involve contracts?
3. What are some examples of agreements that are not contracts?
4. What is meant by mutual assent?
5. What are the three essential characteristics of an offer?
6. What evidence may there be that a buyer has accepted the goods offered?
7. How and when can an offer be terminated?
8. What is an option?
9. (a) What is meant by "age of majority"?
   (b) Why is an adult dealer in merchandise held to a contract made with someone who has not reached the age of majority?
10. Under what conditions may a minor be held to a contract?
11. For what kinds of bargains are contracts not legal?
12. What is meant by a consideration?
13. Why is the promise of a gift by a competent person not enforceable as a contract?
14. Under what conditions may a contract for a sale be oral?
15. What is a bill of sale?
16. How does an express contract differ from an implied contract?
17. Under what circumstances is a contract voidable?

Section B

18. Why should you never sign a blank contract or a contract containing blank spaces?
19. What is an express warranty?
20. In case of a breach of warranty, what possible recourses are open to the buyer?
21. What remedies does a seller have when the buyer of merchandise fails to perform the buyer's part of the contract?
22. What remedies does a buyer have when the seller of merchandise fails to perform the seller's part of the contract?
23. When a sale of goods or services amounting to $25 or over is made at the consumer's home, why is the buyer given 3 days to set aside the contract?
24. What obligation does a person who receives unordered merchandise in the mail have?
25. (a) What responsibility do you have for property you have rented or borrowed?
    (b) What responsibility do you have for property entrusted to you by a neighbor for safekeeping?
26. When should a person consult a lawyer?
27. How should you select a lawyer and what factors should you consider in selecting one?
28. Why does a lawyer give advice in terms of an "opinion"?

DISCUSSION QUESTIONS

Section A

1. Why is or is not each of the following an offer: (a) an advertisement, (b) an application letter, (c) goods on display with the price marked?

2. Assume that Brown offers a car for sale at $2,000 and Jones submits a written reply stating, "I accept your offer with the understanding that the snow tires will be included." Is the offer terminated?

3. When making a contract, what facts should you know about competence of the other party in order to assure the enforceability of the contract?

4. What would be the effect on business (a) if all contracts had to be in writing? (b) if implied contracts were prohibited?

5. Jean Martin insists that she will not fulfill a contract because she did not know all the terms of the contract when she signed it. Her reason for not having read the contract carefully is that she finds it difficult to read fine print. She admits, however, that the signature is genuine. Is there anything she can do to avoid fulfilling the contract?

Section B

6. You are given a sales demonstration in a store. During the demonstration the salesperson tells you many ways in which the product is better than some other product. Later you find what you have been told is not true.
   (a) Do the statements constitute fraud?
   (b) Have you any legal basis for returning the merchandise and demanding your money?

7. Several days after you purchased a raincoat, you had occasion to use it. At that time it was found that the buttons had been omitted and that in stitching, certain seams had been missed. What recourse do you have?

8. Why is it possible for two different judges to give essentially opposite rulings in apparently similar or identical cases?

APPLICATION PROBLEMS

Section A

1. Jim Wade, age 14, bought an electric road racing kit from the Ace Model Toy Shop and asked the proprietor to bill his father (whom the proprietor knew) for the $25 cost of the kit. Upon receipt of the bill two weeks later, Jim's father refused payment and returned the racing kit. The proprietor claimed that since Jim had played with the model racing kit, the proprietor could not resell it as new and that Jim's father should at least pay the difference between what the kit cost new and what it would bring used. Does the proprietor have a legal claim against Jim's father or Jim?

2. Mueller agreed to sell his outboard motorboat and 75 h.p. motor to his neighbor, Barnes, for $495. Barnes said he would need a few weeks to get the money but that he would pay Mueller $75 down and the balance in five weeks at which time he, Barnes, would take possession and title to the motor and boat. Three weeks later Mueller was offered $700 for the boat and motor by Vandercook. Mueller tried to get Barnes to take back the $75, claiming that there was no legal contract since the agreement was not in writing. Can Barnes hold Mueller to the original agreement?

3. On March 1, Ms. Warren, proprietor of Warren's House of Cameras, sold a camera to Mr. Reedy for $100. The following day Mr. Reedy came storming into Warren's House of Cameras, slammed down a newspaper advertisement, dated February 28, which advertised for only $85 a camera like the one Reedy had purchased, and demanded a refund of $15. Ms. Warren claimed that the contract entered into between Mr. Reedy and herself was legal and that Mr. Reedy was not entitled to the refund of $15. Does Reedy have a legal claim against Warren?

Section B

4. Dennis Kato arranged for the Ace Building Company to build a house for him. He did some of the work himself and went to a furnace company and selected a furnace, which the heating company said would heat satisfactorily. After the house was completed, Mr. Kato could not get his furnace to heat the house to a warm enough temperature to suit him in cold weather. Was there any warranty, and does Mr. Kato have any claim against the contractor or against the heating company?

5. Both Perez and Kobick live in New York State. Perez owned a hunting lodge in Colorado. On July 15, Kobick entered into a written agreement to purchase the lodge for $50,000, possession to be given on the date of the contract. Perez accepted Kobick's check for $50,000 and transferred the title to Kobick. On July 16, Perez was notified that the lodge had been destroyed by fire on July 14. Discuss Perez' rights and obligations in this case. Discuss Kobick's rights and obligations.

COMMUNITY PROJECTS

Section A

1. Obtain copies of five written contracts. Probably some of these may be obtained from members of your family; others may be obtained from friends and business people. Your class officers may have entered into a contract with a dance band for a school dance. Examine each of the five contracts to identify: (a) each of the five elements of a contract and (b) each of the six parts of a written contract. Prepare a report in which you list your findings.

2. Give examples of three different kinds of contracts that you, a member of your family, or a friend made within the last week and show how all five essential elements of a contract were present in each. For each contract, explain when and how the offer was made; how it was accepted; and if it could have been accepted in any other way. For each contract, indicate when each offer would have been terminated if it had not been accepted.

Section B

3. Court cases involving contracts are reported in local newspapers. Search the papers to locate three cases involving contracts. Try to discover from the newspaper reports the real question of controversy in each case. Then, analyze the case in light of each of the five elements of a contract and also in light of the six parts of a written contract. Which, if any, of the essential elements of the various contracts were involved in each case? What, if any, parts of the written contract were involved in each case?

4. Many communities — particularly larger cities — have legal aid societies or legal aid organizations. Check to see if such an organization or other form of free legal help is available in your community. If you cannot find the agency listed in the telephone directory or do not know of its existence, call a government agency such as the city prosecutor's office, the municipal court, the police department, or the mayor's office. If an organization such as a legal aid society or a legal aid organization or other form of free legal help exists in your community, prepare a report for the class indicating the services that are available through that organization.

24 The Citizen's Roles in our Free Enterprise Economy

PURPOSE OF THE CHAPTER

"Free enterprise is the commercial expression of individual freedom. Without free enterprise, individual freedom would die."[1] In order to preserve individual freedom, every citizen must help to make the free enterprise system work.

In a free enterprise economy, citizens are free to vote in the marketplace to decide what, when, and how much to buy and how much they are willing to spend for a good or service. These votes largely determine what and how much of a good or service will be produced and what price can be charged. In a democratic society, citizens have other rights and freedoms. Two of these rights and freedoms will be discussed in this chapter. First is the freedom to choose the kind of work we wish to pursue. Second is the freedom to vote for government leaders whom we feel will best represent us when considering and acting on society's concerns.

After studying this chapter, you should be able to:

1. Explain the three economic roles citizens play in the United States.
2. Identify the 15 career clusters.
3. List several sources where you can acquire career information.
4. Describe the importance of all citizens exercising their voting rights.
5. Describe ways citizens can act alone to bring about a cleaner, safer environment and to conserve natural resources.

---

[1]Margaret Thatcher, Prime Minister of Great Britain.

A. ECONOMIC ROLES OF CITIZENS

Citizens in the United States play three important economic roles. First, they are workers who produce goods and services. Second, they are consumers who use goods and services. Third, they are collective decision makers.

Citizens as Workers

Individuals serve as workers, for which they earn or receive income. Most of this income is used to buy goods and services. Some of this income is put to work through savings and investments in order to produce more goods and services.

Not all citizens are workers. The very young, retired persons, the mentally disabled, and people with total physical disabilities are not expected to be workers. That means that the rest of us must produce not only for ourselves but for the nonproducers also. Of the 219 million citizens in the United States in 1979, 101.8 million were considered eligible to be workers. However, only 96.3 million were actually employed. The rest (5.6 million) were unemployed for a number of reasons. One reason for unemployment is that some individuals do not have the knowledge and skills required to fill certain available jobs. Some of the unemployed are full-time students who do not have the time to hold a full- or part-time job. Other reasons for unemployment are strikes, temporary layoffs, and poor economic conditions.

Citizens serve as workers when producing goods and services to earn income.

Pennyslvania Power and Light Company

Citizens serve as consumers when buying goods and services.

Citizens as Consumers

The reason most people work is to earn an income with which to buy goods and services that they cannot provide for themselves. Consumers have many decisions to make when spending income. First, there are the basic necessities (food, clothing, shelter, health care) that must be purchased. Second, after providing for the necessities, any income remaining (called *discretionary funds*) can be spent (or saved) to satisfy additional wants. There are many decisions to be made both in providing for our necessities and in using our discretionary funds. You were introduced to many of these decisions in Part 6 (Chapters 16–20) of this text.

Citizens as Collective Decision Makers

There are some things we want as citizens that we cannot provide for ourselves. To satisfy these wants we must join with many of our citizen-neighbors and collectively try to fulfill our wants. In a democratic society we do this by electing public officials to carry out our wishes. Of course, we have to pay these government officials and we have to pay for the goods and services they decide to buy. We do this through our system of taxation (see Chapter 12).

Obviously, all 219 million citizens won't want the same kinds or the same amounts of the goods and services we might like to have individually. Opportunity cost will be at work again (see

By voting to elect public officials, citizens serve as collective decision makers.

Chapter 1). If, however, we have chosen our public officials wisely, they should make decisions that will be in the best interest of most of the citizens.

AN INDIVIDUAL PLAYS THREE BASIC ROLES
1. As a worker or receiver of income.
2. As a consumer or user of income.
3. As a citizen joining with other individuals in collective decision making.

B. CAREER OPPORTUNITIES

In the United States there are over 35,500 different job opportunities or careers that one may pursue. In a democracy you have the right to pursue whichever career appeals to you.

The Job Market

The U.S. Department of Labor estimates there will be a 19% increase in employment between 1976 and 1985. This means that 17 million new jobs must be made available during this 10-year period, or an average of 1.7 million new jobs each year. In addition to these 17 million new job openings there will be 29 million job openings resulting from retirement, illness, and death.

Job Categories. Jobs are divided into four broad categories: white-collar, blue-collar, service, and farm occupations. *White-collar workers* are salaried employees whose duties do not require the wearing of work clothes, such as scientists, business executives, office workers, and teachers. *Blue-collar workers* are wage earners whose duties call for the wearing of work clothes, such as laborers, truck drivers, machinists, carpenters, and electricians. *Service workers* are those engaged in service jobs, such as barbers and beauticians, police officers, chefs, service station attendants, telephone operators, and retail trade salespersons. *Farm workers* are those who work to cultivate land or crops or to raise livestock, such as farmers, ranchers, and farm laborers including migrant workers.

The following chart shows how these four categories of workers made up the work force in the past and how they are expected to be divided in the future. Note that by 1985 white-collar

The shift toward white-collar occupations will continue through 1985.

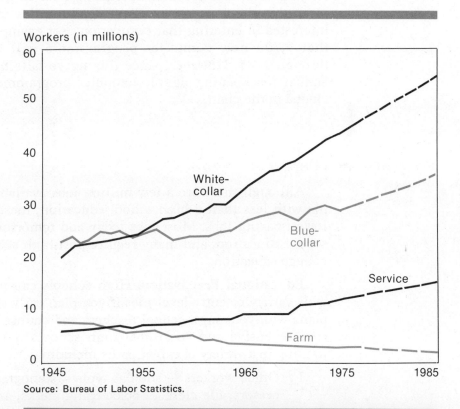

Workers (in millions)

Source: Bureau of Labor Statistics.

workers are expected to make up over half the work force in the United States; blue-collar workers and service workers, nearly one quarter; and farm workers less than 2%. The number of farm workers has been steadily declining for half a century.

Career Clusters. The U.S. Department of Labor has grouped the over 35,500 job titles into 15 career clusters. These clusters are: agriculture; natural resources and environment; industrial production; office; service; education; sales; construction; transportation; scientific and technical; mechanics and repairers; health; social scientists; social service; and art, design, and communications.

The job outlook chart on page 485 considers only 13 of these clusters and 72 job titles. These clusters and job titles were selected on the basis of representing the best job markets through 1985. A specific job title had to employ at least 10,000 new employees each year to be included. From the chart you can see that 295,000 new openings exist each year for secretaries and stenographers.

Just because a job title does not appear in the chart does not mean that there are no excellent opportunities for those who are interested in entering that occupation. For example, it is expected that 9,700 new computer programmers will be hired yearly through 1985. However, since this figure falls below the 10,000 annual job opening figure, computer programmers were not included in the chart.

Preparing for a Career

Although there are a few million jobs available today for people with less than a high school education, these are usually the lowest-paying jobs. Most jobs today and tomorrow require a high school education, and many require post-high school technical or college education.

Educational Preparation. High schools can prepare you for a wide variety of entry-level jobs if you plan early and discuss these plans with your high school teachers and counselors. Most of our comprehensive and vocational high schools offer education and training in a variety of career paths including:

1. Office workers — such as typists, stenographers, word processors, file clerks, bookkeeping clerks, and keypunch operators.

JOB OUTLOOK 1976–1985
Average Annual Openings in Best Job Markets

Occupation	Jobs Available	Occupation	Jobs Available
Industrial Production & Related Occupations	367,360	Sales Occupations	298,400
All-round machinists	20,000	Service station attendants	14,800
Machine tool operators	22,000	Manufacturers sales workers	17,600
Assemblers	70,000	Real estate agents/brokers	45,500
Blue-collar worker supervisors	79,000	Retail trade salespersons	155,000
Inspectors (manufacturing)	52,000	Wholesale trade salespersons	41,000
Power truck operators	14,600	Construction Occupations	260,900
Waste water treatment operators	10,400	Carpenters	67,000
Welders	33,800	Construction laborers	40,000
Office Occupations	970,650	Electricians (construction)	13,700
Bookkeeping workers	95,000	Operating engineers	41,000
Cashiers	92,000	Painters	27,000
File clerks	16,500	Plumbers/pipefitters	30,000
Receptionists	38,000	Transportation Occupations	130,200
Secretaries/stenographers	295,000	Local truckdrivers	73,000
Shipping/Receiving clerks	23,000	Long distance truckdrivers	15,400
Statistical clerks	21,000	Scientific & Technical Occupations	183,420
Stock clerks	25,000	Engineers	56,500
Typists	63,000	Electrical engineers	12,800
Bank clerks	36,000	Industrial engineers	10,500
Bank officers/managers	28,000	Life scientists	12,000
Bank tellers	21,000	Engineering/science technicians	29,000
Insurance underwriters/agents	27,500	Mechanics and Repairers	155,150
Accountants	51,500	Air-conditioning/heating mechanics	17,400
Lawyers	23,400	Auto mechanics	32,000
Personnel/labor relations workers	23,000	Industrial machinery repairers	30,000
Purchasing agents	13,800	Maintenance electricians	15,900
Service Occupations	624,800	Health Occupations	392,700
Building custodians	160,000	Dental assistants	13,500
Bartenders	17,800	Physicians	21,800
Cooks/chefs	79,000	Emergency medical technicians	37,000
Dining room attendants/dishwashers	22,400	Medical laboratory workers	20,000
Food counter workers	33,000	Registered nurses	83,000
Waiters/waitresses	71,000	Practical nurses	53,000
Cosmetologists	30,000	Nursing aides/orderlies	83,000
Private household workers	53,000	Health service administrators	16,000
Guards	63,000	Social Scientists	14,900
Police officers	32,500	Social Service Occupations	92,700
Telephone operators	11,600	Homemaker/home health aides	37,000
Education and Related Occupations	145,300	Social workers	25,000
Kindergarten/elementary teachers	70,000	Art, Design, and Communications-Related Occupations	31,800
Secondary school teachers	13,000		
College/university teachers	17,000	Total Annual Job Openings (1976–1985)	3,668,280
Teacher aides	29,000		

Source: *Occupational Outlook Quarterly* (Spring, 1978), pp. 6–33.

2. Sales workers — such as salespersons, inventory clerks, and service station attendants.
3. Service workers — such as barbers, beauticians, cooks, and food counter workers.
4. Mechanics and repairers — such as auto mechanics, motorcycle mechanics, appliance repairers, and factory machine operators.
5. Construction workers — such as carpenters, painters, and construction laborers.

Post-high school programs (technical institutes, private schools, and junior and community colleges) offer education and training of a more specialized nature than do high schools. These institutions provide training for careers in areas such as computer programming, data processing, and electronics, as well as training for semiprofessional positions as legal and medical secretaries, dental and medical technicians, and practical nurses.

Colleges and universities provide education and training for all the professional careers requiring from 4 to 8 years of study. These institutions provide training for professions in areas such as medicine, dentistry, registered nursing, law, education, business management, engineering, and architecture.

Career Information. A very good source of information for over 800 occupations is the *Occupational Outlook Handbook*, published for the U.S. Department of Labor. Information pertaining to (1) nature of the work, (2) places of employment, (3) training, education, and other qualifications needed, (4) employment outlook, (5) earnings and working conditions, and (6) sources of additional information are given for each of the occupations described in the *Handbook*.

High school teachers and counselors can provide you with helpful information regarding a number of careers. Counselors have collected much information about careers and educational institutions that they will be happy to discuss with you.

Libraries are yet another valuable source for career information. Librarians in school, city, and county libraries can be very helpful in directing you to some excellent career pamphlets published by private publishing firms.

Do not overlook the opportunity to get first-hand information from people working in various occupations. They can describe for you the nature of their work, the desirable and undesirable aspects of their occupations, and the opportunities for advancement in their fields of work.

STEPS IN PLANNING YOUR CAREER

1. Select an occupation that sounds interesting to you.

2. Read information about that occupation.

3. Talk with parents, teachers, counselors, and a person in that occupation to get more information and to get answers to your questions.

4. Match the qualifications needed for that occupation with your own talents, interests, and long-range goals.

5. Determine the availability (location and cost) of educational training opportunities to prepare you for the occupation.

6. With the help of your teachers and counselors, select those courses in high school that would be helpful in reaching your career goal.

C. CITIZENSHIP RESPONSIBILITIES

Earlier in this chapter you learned that one of your roles in a democratic society was to act as a collective decision maker. This is a major responsibility for citizens, since we must decide together on a number of issues at the city, state, and national level. For example, do we want to build a new school, hire more fire fighters, or build a new recreational facility in our community? Do we want more state police, better roads, or free state parks in our state? Do we want more federal aid given to welfare, a national health program, or a stronger national defense system for our nation? These and many other decisions must be made collectively through elected public officials. Being good citizens also demands that we do some things individually for our own welfare as well as for the good of society.

Citizens as Collective Decision Makers

One of the most important rights and responsibilities in a democratic society is to elect into public office those officials who will act best for us in collective decision making. If we don't exercise this right, then we really should not complain about the decisions that are made. Voting alone, however, isn't the whole responsibility. Since public officials are in office from 2 to 6 years each term, we need to advise them from time to time regarding our feelings about certain issues. We need to inform them as to how we wish them to vote on various issues.

Voting Record by Age Group. Since 1970 all citizens 18 years old and over have been given the right to vote.[2] Young men and women between the ages of 18 and 20, however, did not exercise their citizenship rights and responsibilities very remarkably in either the 1972 or the 1976 presidential elections. As you can see from the table below, the 18–20 age group had the worst voting record of all age groups in these two elections.

The 18–20 age group had only a 48.3% voting record in the 1972 presidential election. In the 1976 election this dropped to 38%. A dismal record indeed. Compare this with the 70.8% and 68.7% record of the 45–64 age group for these same two elections.

VOTING RECORD
By Age Group
1972 and 1976 Presidential Elections

Age Group	1972				1976			
	No. of Voters*	No. Voting*	% Voting	% Not Voting	No. of Voters*	No. Voting*	% Voting	% Not Voting
18–20	11.0	5.3	48.3	51.7	12.1	4.6	38.0	62.0
21–24	13.6	6.9	50.7	49.3	14.8	6.8	45.6	54.4
25–34	26.9	16.1	59.7	40.3	31.5	17.5	55.4	44.6
35–44	22.2	14.7	66.3	33.7	22.8	14.4	63.3	36.7
45–64	42.3	30.0	70.8	29.2	43.3	29.8	68.7	31.3
65–over	20.1	12.7	63.5	36.5	22.0	13.7	62.2	37.8

*In millions.

Source: *Statistical Abstract of the United States*, 1978, p. 520.

Voting Record by Educational Level. Another interesting aspect of the voting record is the effect that years of education have. As you can see from the table on page 489, the voting record (percentage) improves greatly as the years of education increase. One conclusion to draw from this is that the more education people have, the more responsible they are in trying to shape the political climate of our country.

A strange thing happens to voters when they go to the polls: They don't exercise their rights to vote for all offices. For example, in the 1976 election, 54.3% of the 150 million eligible voters voted for the presidential candidate of their choice. However, only 49.6% of these same voters voted for their congressional representatives (house members and senators).

---

[2] In Georgia, 18-year-olds have been eligible to vote since 1944; in Kentucky, since 1946. Nineteen-year-olds in Alaska and 20-year-olds in Hawaii have been eligible to vote since 1960.

VOTING RECORD
By Years of Education Completed
1976 Presidential Election

Education Completed	No. of Voters*	No. Voting*	% Voting	% not Voting
8 years or less	24.9	11.0	44.1	55.9
9–11 years	22.2	10.5	47.2	52.8
12 years	55.7	33.1	59.4	40.6
More than 12 years	43.7	32.2	73.5	26.5

*In millions.

Source: *Statistical Abstract of the United States*, 1978, p. 520.

Citizens as Individual Decision Makers

As was mentioned in the introduction to this section, there are some things individuals can do alone that will benefit both themselves and society in general. The more things individuals can do alone to benefit society, the less legislation and collective decision making will be required. The more we depend on legislation and collective decision making to solve our problems, the more it will cost each of us in taxes and higher prices.

Conservation. Acting alone and without legislation, an individual can help to conserve limited natural resources. Each of us can voluntarily cut back on energy usage. We can walk more and ride less. We can lower heating temperatures in the winter and raise cooling temperatures in the summer. We can make more use of car pools and lower our driving speeds. We can open our houses and cars in summer rather than use air conditioners.

By recycling glass, metal containers, newspapers, and magazines, we can conserve scarce resources. By using common sense, we can prevent most forest fires, which destroy millions of board feet of lumber each year in our country.

Volunteer Service. Acting alone and as concerned citizens, there are many things we can do to bring about a cleaner, safer environment by volunteering our services. For example, we can dispose of trash in designated containers rather than using our streets, highways, and parks. We can organize volunteer groups to clean up parks and other recreational areas. These types of volunteer services can save us many tax dollars.

We can organize neighborhood watch programs. This type of volunteer service can protect our lives and property by discouraging crime and detecting fire early enough so that fire fighters can

A concerned citizen can help to clean up the environment by disposing of litter.

save property. Through neighborhood watch programs we can eliminate the need to hire additional police protection, which costs us in higher taxes.

Millions of political campaign dollars can be saved by volunteering our services in helping to elect those candidates we want to represent us in collective decision making. The dollars we save through our volunteer service can be spent for other useful goods and services (opportunity cost, remember).

FACTS EVERYONE SHOULD KNOW ABOUT THE ROLES OF CITIZENS IN A FREE ENTERPRISE ECONOMY

1. Citizens in a free enterprise economy play three economic roles: consumer, producer, and collective decision maker.

2. There are over 100 million people employed in over 35,500 different jobs in the U.S. annually.

3. U.S. citizens have the right to study, select, and pursue the career of their choice in light of their interests and talents.

4. As collective decision makers we elect public officials to represent our views and desires on issues and policies of a public nature.

5. As individual citizens, we can conserve natural resources and provide a clean, safe environment by acting responsibly.

6. It takes individual effort to make the free enterprise system work. Every citizen must help by acting responsible as a worker, as a consumer, and as a collective decision maker.

REVIEW QUESTIONS

Section A

1. What are the three economic roles citizens play in a free enterprise economy?
2. Why do people work?
3. What are some reasons why citizens may be unemployed?
4. What is meant by discretionary funds?
5. There are some wants citizens cannot satisfy by themselves. How may such wants be satisfied?

Section B

6. How many job openings does the Department of Labor predict each year between 1976 and 1985?
7. What are the four broad job categories?
8. What job cluster is predicted to have the greatest number of job openings each year between 1976 and 1985?
9. What specific job title is predicted to have the greatest number of job openings each year between 1976 and 1985?
10. Where may a high school student find information about careers?

Section C

11. What are some decisions that must be made collectively at the local (community) level?
12. What age group had the best voting record in both the 1972 and 1976 elections?
13. Of the 86.8 million citizens who voted in the 1976 presidential election, how many (and what percent) had 12 or more years of education?
14. What are some things individuals can do alone to benefit themselves and society without using costly collective decision-making action?

DISCUSSION QUESTIONS

Section A

1. Can we expect all citizens to be productive workers? Explain.
2. How does opportunity cost play a role in collective decision making?
3. Could people in our prisons be considered productive citizens?

Section B

4. Why is it expected that by 1985 most jobs will be in the white-collar category?
5. By 1985 most jobs in the United States will require a college education. Do you agree with this statement? Why?
6. Why is it important to explore career opportunities while still in high school?

Section C

7. What explanations could be given for the poor voting record of 18–20 year olds?
8. What may account for those voters with 12 or more years of education having the best voting record?
9. Why is conservation a wise economic activity whether exercised voluntarily by individuals or collectively decided on by our representatives?

APPLICATION PROBLEMS

Section A

1. Most employment statistics released by the U.S. Department of Labor are reported as "adjusted for seasonal employment." Seasonal employment

is represented by jobs that cannot be performed 52 weeks a year. Make a list of jobs that you feel fall into this category.

2. Make a list of goods and services that individuals in your community want but are unable to provide for themselves except through collective decision making.

Section B

3. Jot down two or three specific jobs you think you would like to perform as your career goal. Select one of these and investigate the nature and requirements of that job, the employment outlook for that job, the desirable and undesirable features of that job, and how closely your interests and abilities match that job.

4. From the line graph on page 483 prepare a pie chart showing the distribution of the four categories of workers for 1985.

Section C

5. Find out what is required of you to register as an eligible voter in your city, state, and nation.

6. Inquire of your parents, teachers, and friends of efforts known to them where individuals or small groups in your community have practiced conservation, environmental improvement activities, and volunteer service measures for the good of the individual and society. Make a list of these activities to post on the bulletin board.

COMMUNITY PROJECTS

Section A

1. From your local Employment Security Division office find out how many citizens are employed in your city or county. Compare the number employed with the total population of your city or county. How do your local employment figures compare with the national employment figures?

2. Prepare a list of offices up for election in your city (state and/or nation) for the next election (1980, 1982, or 1984). What are the requirements of the candidates running for these offices?

Section B

3. From your local Employment Security Division office find out what the current employment needs (by specific job titles or career clusters) are for your city or county. Prepare a pie chart or bar graph to display these figures.

4. From a current issue of the *Occupational Outlook Handbook* (or the *Occupational Outlook Quarterly*), find the number of openings expected yearly in two or three jobs in which you are interested. Do not select those jobs that are listed in the table on page 485.

Section C

5. Campaign speeches made by those running for public office are usually filled with promises to provide certain services to the electorate. Analyze speeches made by opposing candidates to see opportunity cost in action. You might display your finds as follows:

Candidate A	Candidate B
1. Will increase spending for national defense to ensure a stronger nation.	1. Will cut defense spending and increase welfare and social security payments.

Glossary

A

absolute advantage: a nation's production advantage when it can produce a product more efficiently than another nation can

acceptance: an agreement to another person's offer which is part of a contract

ad valorem **tariff:** a tariff on a commodity which is a percentage of the value of the commodity

advertising appeals: the motives that influence human behavior

agency shop: a business where all employees in the bargaining unit pay dues to the union, but do not have to join it

age of majority: the minimum legal age at which a person can make a contract

aggregate income: the combined or total income earned in the country

aggregate production: the combined or total production of all goods by all people and all business firms in the country

aggregate supply of goods: the total supply of goods for the country

annuity: a life insurance policy in which, beginning at a stipulated age, the amount of the policy is paid back to the insured in regular payments with interest

appraisal: an examination of property and setting of its value

apprentice: a young beginner in a craft who works for his room and board while learning about the trade

appurtenant private structures: all structures used in connection with and belonging to a home

arbitration: a process for settling labor disputes whereby the dispute is submitted to a third person or group of persons agreed upon by both sides

arbitrator: a third person who is agreed upon by both sides to settle a labor dispute

arrangement: an agreement between a debtor and creditor whereby the debtor makes small regular payments over a long period of time until the debt has been paid

assembling: accumulating or gathering goods from various sources

assets: all valuable items owned by a family or individual

assured: the person who buys an insurance policy

attachment: a legal process in which some of the property of a debtor comes under control of the court until the debt is paid

automation: a continous operation in production, such as the assembly line, through the use of automatic equipment

B

backing: an item of real value available to exchange for money in case one doesn't want to buy goods and services

bait and switch: a type of deceptive advertising in which the seller advertises a product at a cut-rate price in order to lure customers into the store and persuade them to switch to another item

balance of payments: the difference between total payments to other nations and total receipts from foreign nations

balance of trade: the balance between a nation's exports and its imports of goods

bankruptcy: the legal status, declared by a federal court, of a person whose debts are greater than the total fair value of the person's assets

base period: the period of time whose production or prices are used for comparing current prices or current production

beneficiary: the person named in an insurance policy to receive the insurance benefits upon the death of the insured

bill of sale: a written contract which provides evidence of ownership

blue-collar worker: a wage earner whose duties call for the wearing of work clothes

bond: a written promise to pay a specified amount plus interest at a certain time

boycott: a mass effort to withdraw and to influence others to withdraw from business relations with an employer

brand name: a trade name placed on a product to encourage people to keep buying that particular product

breach of warranty: violation of a warranty due to misrepresentation or failure of the goods to fulfill the reasonable expectations of the warranty

budget: a guide for spending and saving one's income

budget charge account: a charge account in which interest is charged and payments must be made in monthly installments based on the size of the account balance

business: any organized activity conducted by either a person or an organization that in any way helps to satisfy the wants and needs of people for economic goods and services

business agent: a full-time employee of a local union who acts as its general business manager

business cycle: alternating periods of expansion and contraction in production, employment, income, and other economic activities

business organization: an organization that produces and makes available the economic goods and services we want and need

buyer's market: the condition that exists when the supply is great and the demand is low

buying: activities pertaining to 1: agreement on prices and terms of purchase, date of shipment or delivery, and transfer of title; 2: careful determination of needs; 3: selection of sources of supply, that is, from whom to purchase; and 4: determination of the quality and suitability of the goods

buying power of money: the quantity of goods that a given amount of money will buy

C

capacity: one's ability to earn and to pay obligations when they become due

capital 1: any buildings, equipment, or other physical property (other than raw materials) used in a business; **2:** a person's net worth

capital consumption allowances: the amount of depreciation and obsolescence of capital goods which is subtracted from the GNP to get the net national product

capital goods: goods which are used by manufacturers, farmers, transportation companies, and others who produce consumer goods or who produce goods for other producers

cash: any ready money that a person or business firm actually has, including money deposited in a checking account

cash value 1: the actual market value of insured property destroyed; **2:** a person's share of the reserve funds of a cancelled life insurance policy

channel of distribution: the route taken by goods as they move through various middlemen from the producer to the consumer

character: one's conduct, attitudes, and achievements

charge account: an arrangement between an individual and a store or business firm whereby the individual receives merchandise at the time of the sale in return for a promise to pay later

charter: a license, issued by the state in which a corporation is organized, which authorizes the formation and operation of the corporation

checkbook money: checks drawn on money deposited in checking accounts in commercial banks

civilian labor force: the portion of the total labor force which includes self-employed persons but does not include students while in school, unpaid family workers, those in the armed services, retired persons, or those not able to work

closed shop: a business in which the employer is not allowed to employ non-union workers

closing costs: additional charges incurred in obtaining a loan

coins: money made of metal

coinsurance: a provision in which a person agrees with his insurance company to pay a percentage of his medical expenses

collateral: bonds, notes, or other negotiable paper which are used by a borrower to guarantee the payment of a loan when it is due

collective bargaining: the bargaining between employers and representatives of organized groups of workers for wages and working conditions

command economy: an economy in which the basic economic decisions are made by a central authority that consists of either a person or a group

commercial credit: credit used by businesses to cover the cost of producing and marketing goods

communication: the exchanging of information with others

comparative advantage: a nation's production advantage when it has an efficiency advantage or a cost advantage between two products

competition: the effort of many firms or individuals acting independently to attract a customer

compound interest: interest which is paid on accumulated interest as well as on the original deposit

conciliation: the procedure of having a government agent (mediator) meet with labor and management to help reach an agreement to end a dispute

consideration: what either party in a contract agrees to do in return for that which was promised by the other

consumer: any person, business firm, or governmental unit that chooses goods and services, spends money for them, and uses them primarily to satisfy its own wants

consumer advertising: advertising addressed to or intended for the ultimate consumer

consumer credit: debt that is incurred by a consumer for a home, goods, or services for personal and family use

consumer good: a material object which is used or consumed by the final user

consumer movement: an increasing consumer awareness of problems as well as a drive to achieve greater consumer protection

Consumer Price Index: a monthly index of the average change in prices of a fixed group of goods and services

consumer prices: the cost in dollars of nondurable goods used by consumers

consumer service: a service which is used or consumed by the final user

consumption: the act of using goods and

services to satisfy our wants

contract: an agreement between two or more competent parties that creates an obligation enforceable by law

cooling-off period: a delay before a strike which is sometimes required by the federal government

cooperative: a business that is owned by its members, who are also its customers

corporation: a business that has the legal right to act as one person but that may be owned by a number of people

counteroffer: a new offer by the person to whom an original offer was made

countersign: to add one's signature to that of another on a contract in order to confirm the contract

craft guild: a guild made up of handicraft workers

craft union: a union whose members usually work in a single occupation or in closely related occupations

credit: an advance or loan of money with which to buy goods and services or an advance of goods and services in exchange for a promise to pay at a later date

credit-bank plan: a type of charge account in which the bank issues a credit card that the customer can use at participating businesses; all bills are sent to the bank, which in turn bills the customer once a month

credit card: a card issued by some business firms to a customer which identifies the customer when he or she is traveling and allows the customer to charge purchases of goods and services even in cities where the customer is not known

credit standing: an indication of one's ability to secure goods, services, and money in return for a promise to pay

credit term: the time allowed between the date of purchase on a charge account and the date the payment is due

credit union: a cooperative association operating both as a savings and as a lending instution for the benefit of its members

credit worthiness: an indication of one's ability to secure goods, services, and money in return for a promise to pay

cross picketing: picketing by rival unions claiming to represent a majority of workers in a struck plant

currency: paper (or folding) money

customs duty: a tax levied on exports or imports, usually the latter

cycle billing: a billing system for charge account customers in which the balance owed by a certain customer falls due regularly on a certain day of the month regardless of the date of the last purchase

D

daily cash record: a form on which to record actual receipts of income and actual expenditures on a daily basis

deductible clause: a clause in most major medical insurance policies which states that the insured person has to pay the first $100 of any cost not covered by the basic hospital, surgical, and general medical insurance policies

deed: written evidence of the ownership of a piece of real property

defective agreement: an agreement which is not enforceable because of a defect such as misrepresentation or concealment of vital facts

deficit budget: a budget in which the government expects to spend more than it expects to receive

deflation: a decrease in the amount of available money or credit which results in a noticeable rise in the purchasing power of the dollar

depression: a phase of the business cycle during which economic activity drops to its lowest level in the cycle

descriptive labeling: labeling which is more

informative than that required by government standards

devaluing the dollar: increasing the price of gold in terms of dollars

directed economy: an economy in which the basic economic decisions are made by a central authority that consists of either a person or a group

direct marketing: any process by which the producer sells to the consumer directly or through a representative

direct strike: a strike that is aimed against the employer and does not involve a third party

direct tax: a tax that is levied directly on a particular group of persons or businesses and that is not passed on to others

discount houses: stores which try to sell goods at prices lower than those of any other store

discounting: the process by member banks of "selling" securities they own and their customer's promissory notes to the Federal Reserve bank at a discount from the face value in order to receive borrowed funds

discretionary funds: any income remaining after one has provided for the basic necessities

disguised unemployment: the condition which exists when a person is working at a job that does not take advantage of his or her skills and training

dislocation: movement of farm workers to city areas due to underemployment

disposable personal income: the amount of income that people have left after all local, state, and federal income tax payments have been deducted from personal income

divided charge account: a charge account which permits a customer to charge a large item and then pay one third of the cost in each of the succeeding three months

division of labor: assigning an employee to perform one particular task rather than to perform all tasks pertaining to an operation

durable goods: long-lasting items such as automobiles, household appliances, and furniture

E

economic efficiency: the practice of making the best use of limited resources

economic freedom: an individual's freedom to make economic choices

economic good: any material object useful to people in satisfying wants or needs and scarce enough so that people are willing to pay for it

economic growth: the improvement in the level of living

economic institution: a rule, custom, or law pertaining to the ownership and use of property, the use of money, the role of competition, and the role of profits

economic justice: equality in the distribution of wealth

economic rent: that portion of income which is due solely to the land without buildings and other improvements

economics: a study of the process by which people make and spend their incomes

economic security: the condition in which every person maintains a certain minimum level of living

economic service: a personal service which satisfies a want or need and has monetary value

economic stability: the practice of smoothing out the ups and downs of business activities to eliminate unemployment, inflation and deflation

economic value: the estimate of worth or usefulness that individuals and businesses place on goods and services based on their ability to satisfy wants and needs

economic wants: any goods that can be valued in terms of money

economizing: the process of making choices when buying goods and services in order to get the most satisfaction possible

economy: the place in which income making and spending decisions are made

effective demand: a condition in which a person is willing and able to buy

elastic demand: a demand for a commodity which is affected considerably by a change in the price of the commodity

emotional appeals: advertising appeals that involve the emotions and excite people to buy even if the decision to buy is not a logical one

employment status and wages: the number of persons employed and unemployed and the average hourly, weekly, and monthly wages of employees

endowment policy: a type of life insurance policy which pays a definite sum of money (face value of the policy) to the insured at a stated time

essential want: a want that must be satisfied for a person to live

estate tax: a tax calculated on the entire amount of the net estate before the property passes on to the heirs, regardless of the beneficiaries' interests

excess reserve: a deposit into the Federal Reserve bank which is made by a member bank and is in addition to the deposit required by the Federal Reserve Board

excise tax: any tax that is levied on commodities, facilities, privileges, or occupations within a country

expenditure: an amount of money spent for a good or service

exports: the goods we sell to other countries

express contract: a contract that arises out of an agreement expressed by oral or written words

express warranty: an oral or written assurance of quality or a promise of performance by the seller given before or at the time of sale

F

face value: the amount of insurance stated in the contract

factors of production: the resources which are needed in order to produce goods: land, labor, capital (tools and machinery), and management

farm worker: a person who works to cultivate land or crops or to raise livestock

favorable balance of trade: the situation in which the value of a nation's exports exceeds the value of its imports

featherbedding: the employment of more workers than are needed to perform the work

Federal Reserve note: our main type of currency, which serves as credit money and is accepted in all business channels

Federal Reserve System: a nationwide banking system set up by the federal government to control the nation's supply of money and credit

fictitious pricing: deceptive advertising such as overstating the "manufacturer's suggested price" to convince the buyer that the advertised price is a special bargain

final good: a product or a service as it is when sold to its final purchaser

financing: the process of providing the money that is invested in the goods while they are moving from the producer to the consumer

fiscal policy: government decisions affecting spending and taxation

fixed payment: a payment which must be made and which is often a constant amount

foreign trade: the buying, selling, and exchanging of goods and services by individuals and business firms between nations

free enterprise economy: an economy in which each person is "free" to go into whatever business he or she chooses

free reserve: a deposit into the Federal Reserve bank which is made by a member bank and is in addition to the deposit required by the Federal Reserve Board

full employment: full or maximum use of all productive resources, including labor

G

garnishment: a legal procedure by which a creditor may require the employer of a debtor to pay part of the debtor's wages to the creditor until the debt has been paid

general strike: a strike that involves the workers in all industries in a city, region, or other large area

generic labeling: labeling which is characterized by plain white wrapping, single-color printing, and lack of a company name

gift tax: a tax levied by the federal government on a gift from one person to another

government credit: credit used by the government in order to fund projects for public use

grade: a term applied to standards of quality when more than one quality of a particular food is defined

grading: the process of separating the supply of a commodity into classes according to established standards

grantee: one to whom the title to property is transferred

grantor: one who transfers the title to property to another

grievance procedure: a procedure for handling complaints and disputes originated by workers or unions which is often part of the union contract between the employer and the union

gross national product (GNP): the dollar value of all goods and services produced in an economy in a given period, usually a year

group permanent life insurance: life insurance which protects the workers of a single employer or group and builds up a cash value

group term insurance: a type of life insurance which protects the workers of a single employer or group and does not build up any cash value

guild: an association of people with similar skills

H

hedging against inflation: dividing one's savings among different investment options

hidden tax: a tax which most people are not aware they are paying

home mortgage: a loan that is backed by real estate

homeowners policy: an insurance policy that insures against groups of perils which may befall a person's home, the contents of the home, and other personal property

I

implied contract: a contract that is made through an agreement implied by the acts or the conduct of the parties involved

implied warranty: an obligation imposed by law

imports: the goods and services we buy from other countries

impulse items: inexpensive little luxury items that a customer buys on the spur of the moment without thinking

income: the reward for an individual's share in producing tangible goods, in rendering services, and in lending funds and the use of tangible property to others

index number: a percentage figure to measure an economic activity factor such as industrial production, consumer prices, and wholesale prices

indirect tax: a tax that is levied on a group of persons or businesses but that is passed on indirectly to others

industrial production: the quantity of durable and nondurable products manufactured and of minerals mined

industrial union: a union composed of all classes of workers in one industry

industry-wide strike: a strike that is carried out for the purpose of achieving or maintaining a system of collective bargaining on some issue in a given industry

inelastic demand: a demand for a commodity which is not affected much by a change in the price of the commodity

inflation: the situation which occurs when total demand for goods and services is greater than the supply available at a given time; this results in a shortage of goods and an increase in prices

inheritance tax: a tax levied on a dead person's estate which is either taken out of each share of the will or taken out of the part of the estate remaining after specific bequests have been distributed

injunction: an order from a court commanding an individual or a group to do or to refrain from doing an act or acts

insolvency: inability to pay one's debts when they become due

installment credit: debt on which payments are to be made at periodic intervals

installment debt: debt on which payments are to be made at periodic intervals

institution: a social arrangement that influences how we think and behave

insurable interest in property: a financial interest in insured property

insured: the person who buys an insurance policy

insured mortgage: a mortgage in which the lender is insured against loss by a government agency

insurer: the party from whom the insured buys the insurance and who agrees to pay the loss

intangible want: a desire for something which cannot be touched or felt, such as love, respect, etc.

interest: the amount paid for the use of borrowed funds

interest rate: the price that one must pay in order to obtain the use of money

intermediate-term credit: a debt having a maturity of one to ten years

international trade: the buying, selling, and exchanging of goods and services by individuals and business firms between nations

investment funds: savings available to buy an interest in business

involuntary bankruptcy: bankruptcy declared by the court upon petition or request from a person's creditors

J

journeyman: a craftsman employed by a master on a day-wage basis

jurisdictional strike: a strike that arises out of a dispute between rival unions

L

label: a written statement attached to an article or a product describing its main characteristics

labor 1: all forms of human effort, physical and mental, that provide value to finished products or services; **2:** the kind of work that is commonly performed by members of organized labor unions

labor force: all those who are willing and able to work and who are employed or are seeking employment

labor movement: the organization and activities of labor unions

land: all natural resources, such as land, minerals, water, and oil

land contract: an agreement between the buyer and the seller of property, such that the buyer usually makes a small down payment and agrees to pay the full purchase price in monthly installments

landlord: the owner of a house or an apartment building which is by agreement occupied and controlled by another

law of diminishing returns: the rule which states that, after a certain point, adding additional amounts of one factor of production (land, labor, or capital) results in smaller returns per added factor

lease: the agreement between a landlord and a tenant

legal aid society (organization): a society which provides an organized method of handling legal cases for persons who cannot afford to obtain legal assistance

legal bargain: a contract whose purpose is not contrary to law or to the interests of society

legal reserve: a cash balance which many states require insurance companies to keep on hand

legal tender: any kind of money (coin or currency) that by law must be acceptable in paying debts and taxes

lessee (tenant): one that occupies property under a lease

lessor (landlord): one that leases property to another

level of living: the quality and quantity of the goods and services we are able to buy

level-premium insurance: a type of insurance that calls for payment of the same premium each year

liabilities: debts owed by a family or individual

limited-payment life insurance: life insurance that provides protection over a long period of years although premiums are paid for a limited time

line of credit: the maximum amount a lender or creditor will permit a customer to owe at any one time

liquid liability: a financial obligation on which payment may be requested at any time

loanable funds: savings available for loans to business

lockout: a temporary stopping of the operation of a business by an employer in an attempt to win a dispute with employees

M

management: the person who takes the risk of investing and borrowing money to put all factors to work in an attempt to earn a profit

manpower: the combined ability or capacity of labor and management to produce goods and services

manpower resources: the combined ability or capacity of labor and management to produce goods and services

market economy: an economy in which each person is "free" to go into whatever business he or she chooses

market information: news about markets which is needed by wholesalers and retailers

marketing: the process that carries out business activities that direct the flow of goods and services from producer to consumer or user

marketing channel: the route taken by goods as they move through various middlemen from the producer to the consumer

marketing institutions: places where the marketing functions are performed

mass picketing: the parading or assembling of a considerable number of strikers before the workplace in order to emphasize the strike or to provide a display of strength in opposition to workers who refuse to recognize the strike

mass production: making one or a few products in large quantity rather than making a smaller quantity of many products

master: an older craftsman in whose home the work of a guild used to be performed

maturity: the due date of a note

mediation: the procedure of having a government agent (mediator) meet with labor and management to help reach an agreement to end a dispute

mediator: a government agent who meets with labor and management to help settle a dispute

Medicaid: a federal program which provides health benefits to low-income families

Medicare: a federal program of hospital and medical care for people 65 and over

merchandising: the process of actually filling demand for products

merchant guild: a guild composed of shopkeepers and retailers

middleman: any person or business concern that performs one or more of the eight marketing functions

minor: a person who is not of legal age

misrepresentation: deceptive advertising such as making false or exaggerated claims about the quality and performance of a product

monetary policy: a plan to promote economic growth and to maintain a stable economy through control of the supply of money and bank credit

money: anything that is generally accepted in exchange for goods and services or in payment of debts

monopolist: the only supplier of a good or service

monopoly: the only supplier of a good or service

moonlighting: the practice of holding two jobs at a time

mortality tables: tables showing the percentage of a certain age group that will die from all causes each year

mortgagee: a person who lends money to a property owner and holds a mortgage as evidence of the claim

mortgagor: a person who owns land and borrows money through a mortgage

mutual assent: the arrangement in which one person makes an offer and another person accepts the offer

N

national debt: the amount of money that the federal government has borrowed from individuals and business firms

national income: the amount of annual earnings derived from the production of goods and services

national income accounting: the system and process used by the government for recording statistical information about the total economic activity of all people, business firms, and government

national output: the money value of the goods and services produced in a year

natural resources: materials supplied by nature, then utilized by people

net exports: the difference in dollars between our total exports and our total imports

net national product: the result obtained after subtracting the capital consumption allowances from the gross national product

net profit: the income remaining after paying all expenses that require money to satisfy

nondurable goods: items that are consumed quickly, such as food, clothing, and gasoline for our automobiles

nonessential want: a want that may be satisfied for pleasure or comfort

noninstallment credit: credit for which the full payment is to be made in a single payment at a stated maturity date

noninstallment debt: a debt for which the full payment is to be made in a single payment at a stated maturity date

nonprice competition: the practice of offering incentives other than low price, such as higher quality and latest styles, in order to attract consumers

O

offer: one person's proposal to another which is part of a contract

offeree: a person to whom an offer is made

offeror: a person who makes an offer

open account: an arrangement between an individual and a store or business firm whereby the individual receives merchandise at the time of the sale in return for a promise to pay later

open-end mortgage: a type of mortgage in which a borrower is permitted to borrow additional sums under the same mortgage contract after having made substantial repayments on the loan

open shop: a business where the employer is free to hire employees without reference to union membership

opinion: a lawyer's belief about a case after

examination of all the facts

opportunity cost: the value of the economic want which one gives up when deciding to choose another economic want

option: a special contract which keeps an offer open for a specified period of time

P

package deal: a mortgage whose payments include not only interest and principal, but also insurance on the building, taxes, life insurance on the borrower, and sometimes household appliances

parity: an established minimum market price below which subsidy payments are made to the farmer

partial-payment mortgage: a mortgage whose monthly payments are arranged so that at the end of the term specified in the mortgage the entire loan will be repaid

partnership: a business formed, owned, and managed by two or more persons

personal income: the annual income received by persons from all sources

personal property: household contents and other personal belongings used, owned, worn, or carried by the family

picketing: the practice of stationing one or more persons near the entrance of a place of employment which is affected by a strike

policy: an insurance contract

policyholder: the person who buys an insurance policy

preferential shop: a business in which the employer is required to give special consideration to union members in hiring, layoffs, or promotions

premium: the amount paid for insurance

price: the exchange value of goods or services stated in terms of money

price ceiling: the maximum price allowed for a commodity

price competition: the practice of offering goods and services at lower prices than the competitors in order to take business away from the competitors

price index: a measure which compares the average of the prices of a group of goods and services in one period with the average of the prices of the same goods or services in another period

price-wage spiral: a continuous process in which an increase in prices brings about an increase in wages, thereby causing a subsequent price increase, and so on

primary advertising: advertising which is intended to stress the benefits of a certain class or type of product rather than particular brands of that product

primary boycott: a boycott in which the workers agree not to patronize a firm because of their own complaint against the management

primary want: a want that must be satisfied for a person to live

private property: the portion of a person's income which he or she keeps, regardless of whether it is kept in money, invested in bonds, or held in the form of material assets

producer goods: goods used by manufacturers, farmers, transportation companies, and others who produce consumer goods or who produce goods for other producers

Producer Price Index: an index which measures the average change in prices of farm products, processed foods and feeds, and industrial commodities

profit: the portion of a business owner's income remaining after all expenses have been paid and all claims of those contributing to production have been met

promissory note: a written agreement to repay borrowed money at a specified future date

property tax: a tax levied on real estate or any personal property that has value and that can be bought and sold

prosperity: a phase of the business cycle during which all economic activity is at a relatively high level

public property: public buildings, public

schools, and other facilities that can be provided by local, state, or federal governments, but that would be impractical or impossible to provide through private ownership

pump priming: government spending, made possible by borrowing, to stimulate business

pure profit: the income remaining after all expenses have been deducted

Q

quitclaim deed: a deed which gives up the interest that the grantor may have in the property

R

rational appeals: advertising appeals that supposedly center on logic by providing basic facts and information

real cost: the value of the economic want which one gives up when deciding to choose another economic want

real estate mortgage: a contract between the borrower and the lender for the purpose of buying property

real wages: the amount of goods and services your wages will buy

recession: a phase of the business cycle during which there is a marked decline in the level of economic activity

recovery: a phase of the business cycle during which the level of economic activity begins to increase

regular charge account: a 30-day, interest-free charge account

rent: the contract price received from a tenant for the temporary use of land including buildings and other improvements

required reserve: a deposit into the Federal Reserve bank which is made by a member bank and is equal to a fixed percentage of the member bank's own deposits

rescind: cancel

resources: the factors of production: labor, land (natural resources), capital, management (entrepreneur), and government

restriction of output: the withholding of a reasonable amount of effort on the part of workers

revolving charge account: a charge account which stipulates a maximum amount that may be owed at one time and a maximum time for payment (4, 5, or 6 months)

right to be heard: assurance of representation in forming government policy and of fair, prompt treatment in enforcement of the laws

right to be informed: protection against fraudulent, deceitful, or grossly misleading practices and assurance of being given the facts necessary for an informed choice

right to choose: assurance of access to a variety of products and services at competitive prices

right to safety: protection against the marketing of goods that are dangerous to life or health

risk: a predictable and insurable chance of loss

S

sales and inventories figures: figures which show the dollar value of goods sold to consumers and of inventories of merchandise that business has on hand

sales tax: a tax on sales

saving: setting aside a part of one's income regularly

scarcity: the condition in which a person or a nation is not able to have all the goods and services wanted

secondary boycott: an action by a labor union whereby the union (not involved in the dispute) forbids its members to work for or to have any dealing with a concern whose employees are on strike

secondary picketing: picketing against a second employer who may be doing business with the employer against whom the employees are striking

secondary want: a want that may be satisfied for pleasure or comfort

secured credit sales: installment sales

security agreement: a written statement signed by the buyer in an installment sale indicating that the seller has rights to repossession as well as rights to sue for the purchase price

selective advertising: advertising which attempts to persuade consumers generally to buy one brand rather than another

self-controlled market: a market in which decisions on the basic economic questions of how to satisfy consumers' economic needs stem from the operation of the free enterprise system

self-regulated market: a market in which decisions on the basic economic questions of how to satisfy consumers' economic needs stem from the operation of the free enterprise system

seller's market: the condition that exists when the demand is high and the supply is low

selling: the activities of creating and stimulating demand; finding buyers; determining terms of sale, prices, and delivery dates; and providing for a method of payment and transfer of title

service account: an arrangement between an individual and a service organization whereby the individual is able to charge services and pay later

service workers: workers who are engaged in service jobs, such as barbers, beauticians, police officers, etc.

settlement costs: additional charges incurred in obtaining a loan for a house

shifting the tax burden: the process of increasing the cost of a product to include a tax

shop steward: a person elected by a department in a unionized establishment to handle grievances of members with the employer

short-term credit: a debt having a maturity of less than one year

slowdown: a form of strike that occurs when employees stay on the job but agree among themselves to restrict the amount of work they perform

social accounting: the system and process used by the government for recording statistical information about the total economic activity of all people, business firms, and government

social institution: a social arrangement such as marriage, the family, the school, and the church

social legislation: legislation to protect and aid those who cannot help themselves

social security system: a federal insurance system that provides a base on which individuals may build protection from economic insecurity for themselves and their dependents

social security taxes: payroll and self-employment taxes collected by the federal government to provide partial financial support for the social security insurance program

sole proprietorship: a business that is owned by one person

specialization: assigning an employee to perform one particular task rather than to perform all tasks pertaining to an operation

specific tariff: a tariff on a commodity which is a given payment on a unit of the commodity, as per bushel or per ton

speculation: the practice of purchasing a commodity months in advance, even before it is produced, in the belief that the price will increase and that it can be sold later at a profit

spending plan: a guide for spending and saving one's income

stagflation: a combination of stagnation (decline or economic slump) and inflation (rapidly rising prices)

stamp tax: a tax that is collected through the use of revenue stamps

standard: a measure of quantity, weight, or extent, and sometimes of quality

standardizing: the process of preparing a definition or description of the various qualities of a commodity

standard of identity: a definition of a quality pertaining to a particular grade of food

standard of living: a goal or guide people have in satisfying their needs and wants

statement of assets and liabilities: a statement which lists how much a family or individual owns, how much is owed, and the net worth of the family or individual

statute of limitations: a statute assigning a certain time after which a creditor cannot enforce a legal claim

stockholder: a person who has a share in the ownership of a corporation

straight life insurance: the basic life insurance policy that provides protection over a long period of years

strike: a temporary stoppage of work by a group of employees for the purpose of compelling an employer to agree to their demands

strikebreaker: a person hired by an employer to replace a striking employee

subsidize: to aid financially with public funds

subsidy: a government grant to a private person or company

substitution: the practice of buying a commodity to replace one whose price has increased

supply: the quantity of goods offered for sale at a given time and price

surplus budget: a budget in which the government expects to spend less than it expects to receive in income

sympathetic strike: a strike that does not arise from a grievance against the employer; its purpose is to assist other employees in a dispute with their employer

T

take-home pay: the amount of pay available after the employer has withheld deductions for taxes and other purposes

tangible want: a desire for a physical necessity such as clothing, food, or shelter

tariff: a tax levied on exports or imports, usually the latter

tax: a compulsory contribution of money made to a government to provide for services for the common good

taxation: the device or plan that a federal, state, or local government has for raising funds to pay the expenses and costs of providing protection and services for the people

tax system: all of the fund-raising devices and plans of a government

technology: the invention of machines and discovery of new processes in industry which enable workers to produce more per day and often with less effort

tenant: one who occupies a house or apartment building which is owned by another

term insurance: a type of life insurance which provides protection for a stated period of time

time deposit: a deposit which is made for a specified period of time, at the end of which time the deposit plus interest may be withdrawn

title: the proof of ownership of property

total labor force: all persons, including military personnel, who are willing and able to work and who are employed or are seeking employment

trade channel: the route taken by goods as they move through various middlemen from the producer to the consumer

trademark: a symbol or word placed on a product to identify the origin or ownership of the product and to encourage people to keep buying the product

trade puff: a general claim which should not be relied upon by the buyer of merchandise

trade union: a union whose members usually work in a single occupation or in closely related occupations

traditional economy: a nonindustrialized economy in which economic life is determined by such things as habit, custom, and religious traditions

transfer payment: income received by individuals, from government, business, or other individuals, for which no goods or services were currently exchanged or rendered

transportation: the physical movement of goods from one place to another

trustee: a person appointed as an agent of the court to take charge of a bankrupt person's affairs, sell the property, and pay off the debts on a proportional basis among the creditors

type of representation: the status of a business concerning just which of its employees are to be represented by the union

type of shop: the status of a business in regard to its contractual freedom to employ nonunion workers

U

uncertainty: doubt concerning the occurrence of possible events for which one could not make an estimate based on experience

underemployment: the condition which exists when a person is working at a job that does not take full advantage of his or her skills and training

underwriter: the party from whom the insured buys the insurance and who agrees to pay the loss

unemployed labor force: those persons who are willing and able to work but who are unable to find jobs

unfavorable balance of trade: the situation in which a nation has imported more than it has exported

union: an organization of workers formed for the purpose of bargaining with employers for better wages and working conditions

union picket: a person stationed near the entrance of a place of employment by a labor organization during a dispute with the employer

union security: acceptance and recognition of a union by the employer

union shop: a business in which any nonunion worker who is employed is required to become a member of the union at the end of a specified probationary period

unit pricing: calculating prices of products per unit of weight in order to compare the prices of two products

usury laws: laws which establish the highest contract rate of interest that may be charged

utility: the ability of goods and services to satisfy human wants

V

variable payment: a payment which is smaller in amount than a fixed payment and more subject to change

voidable contract: a contract that may be broken by one or both of the parties

voluntary bankruptcy: bankruptcy declared by the court upon a request from the impoverished person

W

wage-price spiral: a continuous process in which an increase in prices brings about an increase in wages, thereby causing a subsequent price increase, and so on

wages: income earned by those who perform either mental or physical labor

warranty: a promise made by a seller before or after a sale that an article will operate in a specific way or that it has a certain specific quality

warranty deed: a deed which not only conveys the interest of the grantor to the grantee, but also involves statements that certain facts relating to the title are true

wealth: the total money value of the tangible goods owned at a given time

white-collar workers: salaried employees whose duties do not require the wearing of work clothes

wholesale prices: the dollar cost to producers and distributors of farm products, processed foods, and industrial commodities

wildcat strike: a strike which occurs when the members of a local union quit work without authorization from their national union

work force: all employed persons

working capital: money for day-to-day business expenses such as wages and material costs

workmen's compensation laws: laws providing for compensation of workers for loss due to accidents and illness

Index